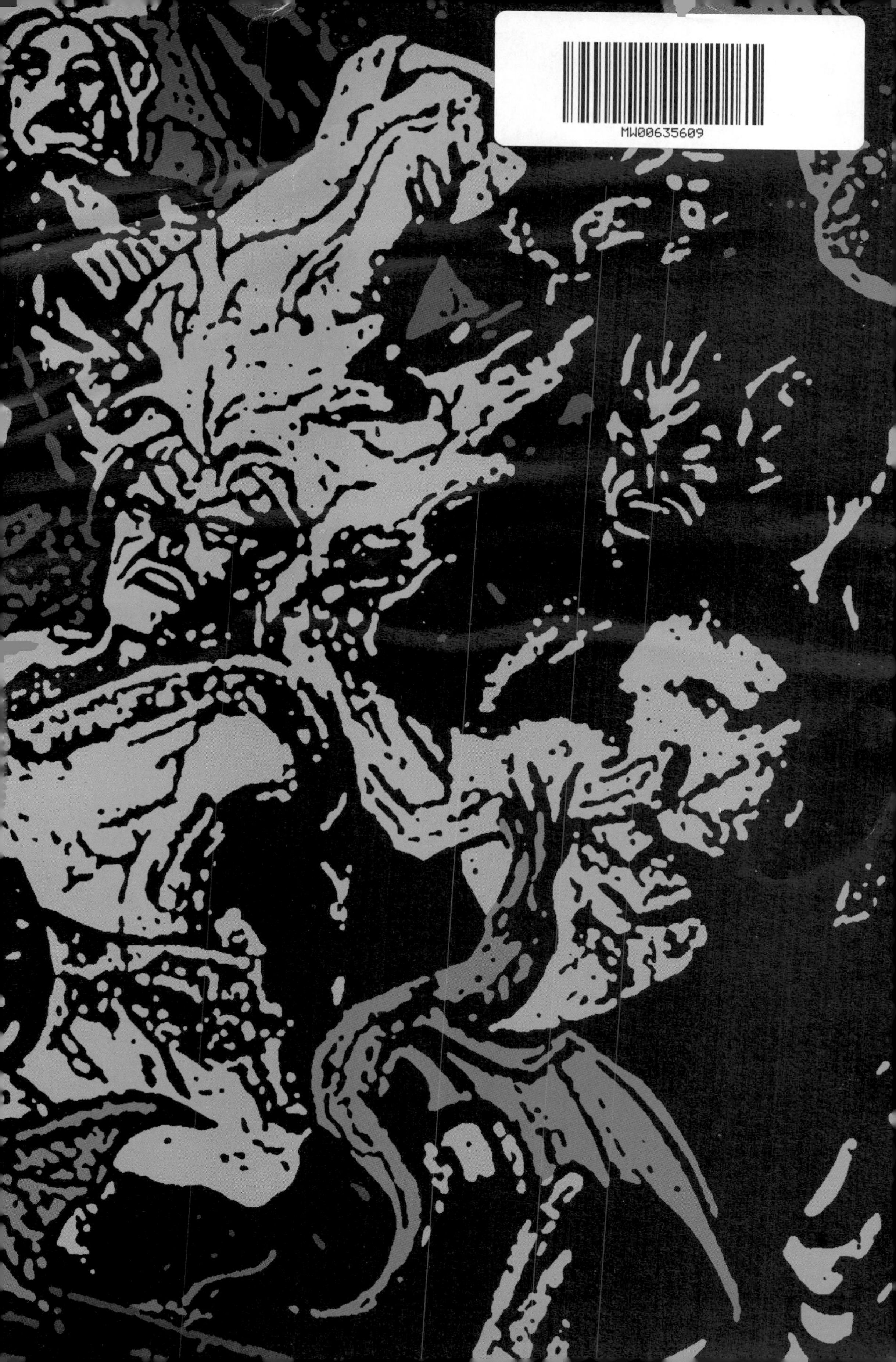

NOCTURNALS®

Black Planet

WRITTEN & ILLUSTRATED BY
DAN BRERETON

LETTERED BY
BILL OAKLEY & LOIS BUHALIS

FOREWORD BY
KEN SANZEL

PIN-UP ART BY
MIKE ALLRED
GENE COLAN
BRUCE TIMM
JILL THOMPSON
DAVID WILLIAMS

LOGO DESIGN BY
NANCY OGAMI

COLLECTION EDITED BY
JAMIE S. RICH
WITH SHANNON T. STEWART

COLLECTION DESIGN BY
STEVEN BIRCH AT SERVO

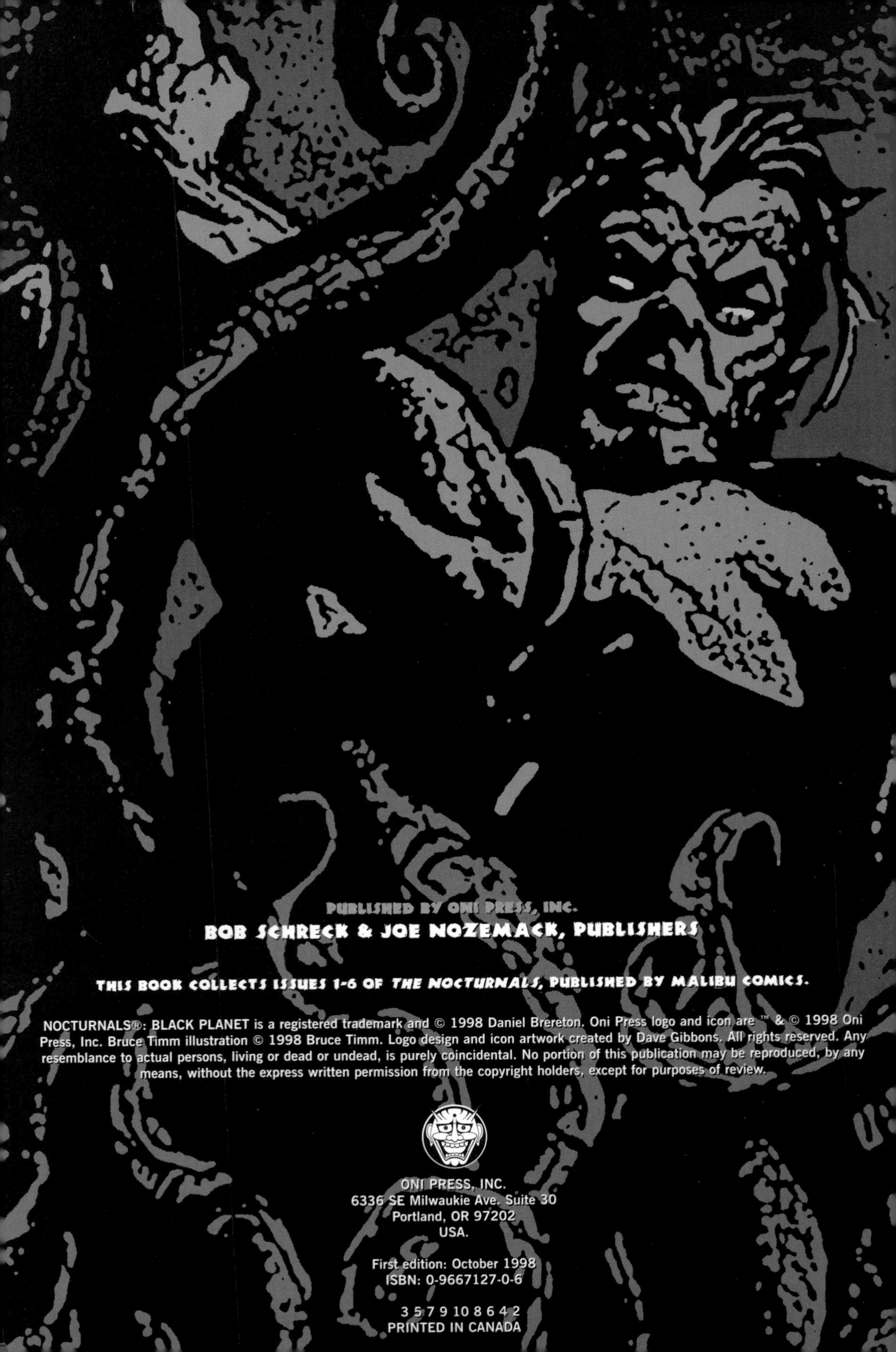

PUBLISHED BY ONI PRESS, INC.
BOB SCHRECK & JOE NOZEMACK, PUBLISHERS

THIS BOOK COLLECTS ISSUES 1-6 OF *THE NOCTURNALS*, PUBLISHED BY MALIBU COMICS.

ONI PRESS, INC.
6336 SE Milwaukie Ave. Suite 30
Portland, OR 97202
USA.

First edition: October 1998
ISBN: 0-9667127-0-6

3 5 7 9 10 8 6 4 2
PRINTED IN CANADA

THE NOCTURNALS

FOREWORD BY KEN SANZEL
Writer/Director of *Scarred City*, Writer of *The Replacement Killers*

You don't know how lucky you are to be reading this book.

Most of those comics and graphic novels and collections you've read lately didn't really do it for you, did they? You picked them up for one reason or another, and by the time you were done, you wondered why you even bothered.

Why did you buy this book? Was it because you liked the cover? Did you flip through the pages? Was it the gunplay, the cool-looking characters, a page you just happened to read? Something in a review you read, something you heard, something that one guy at the comics store whose taste comes close to yours told you?

It doesn't really matter. The fact that you're reading this introduction means that you intend to spend a little time absorbing Dan Brereton's artistic sensibility, which makes you lucky.

The Nocturnals is the kind of book that shouldn't work. Fusing '50s "B" science fiction, pulp violence, Lovecraftian creatures, and a dash of Sergio Leone into one saga is just begging for disaster. In the hands of a first-time writer, the smart money has to figure that the end result is going to be completely unintelligible.

But **The Nocturnals** does work, and it works in a truly inventive way.

Maybe that's because Brereton's enthusiastic story about — well, about pretty much *everything* — doesn't so much fuse these elements as encourage them toward collision. The result is something that defies an easy pigeonhole, and more's the thanks for that.

Dan's sensibility is dark without being hopeless, violent without being lurid. And it celebrates the above mentioned genres without parroting them. Hell, it probably celebrates one or two genres that I missed; the story is too true to itself to give away all of Dan's influences.

But that's not why you're lucky to be reading this book. **The Nocturnals** is the kind of comic that IS, almost by definition, doomed to failure; too intelligent for the splash-panel-and-big-tits crowd, too unapologetically cool for the "cerebral" comics reader, and not crass enough for the rest of the mainstream (whoever they really are, anyway). It's amazing that anyone bought the six-issue miniseries from which this book is collected when it first came out in 1994-95.

In fact, I don't know how many people *did* buy the miniseries. Launched as part of Malibu Comics' creator-owned *Bravura* imprint, **The Nocturnals** fought for rack space during one of the comics industry's bigger boom periods, a time in which companies seemed to emerge almost as frequently as #1 issues.

And, just as the miniseries came to a close, opening the door to a thousand other stories, **The Nocturnals** was trampled under the foot of industry politics. The whys and wherefores would only call attention to people who are best left under the rocks they crawled out from under in the first place.

Those of us who happened upon **The Nocturnals** didn't forget about it. We wondered when the hell someone was going to have the good sense to give it a second life.

And here it is. Why tell you what the book is about? You'll read it soon enough, and Dan Brereton does a better job telling this story in a hundred-someodd pages than I can telling it in two.

I'll say that his artwork — all painted — is angular and intense, hard-nosed but not alienating. His dialogue is sharp, frequently ingenious, but never pretentious or affected (you know which books I'm taking an oblique swipe at; you just don't want to admit it because they were all you had until this book came along). His plot twists without confounding — although I have to say that it's a better read in one sitting than serialized over six months.

So, **Oni Press** has given you another chance to discover something worth discovering. In an industry that has discarded almost everything interesting from its ranks, that's a pretty cool thing. Almost as cool as the book you're lucky enough to be reading.

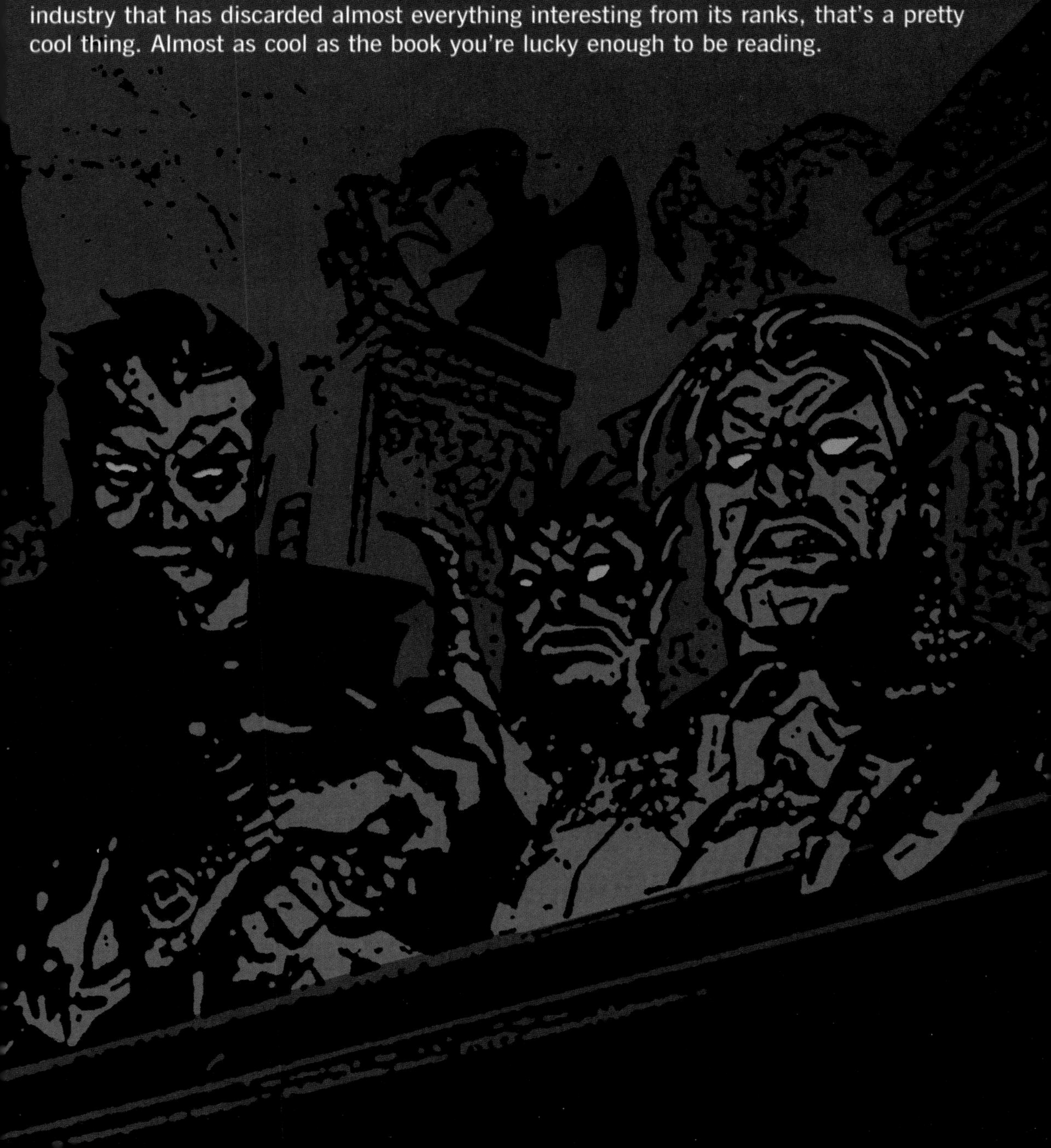

PROLOGUE.

THE DAYTIME WORLD NEVER TAKES THE TIME TO PONDER WHAT'S GOING ON WHILE IT SLEEPS.

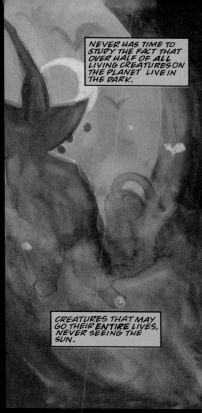

NEVER HAS TIME TO STUDY THE FACT THAT OVER HALF OF ALL LIVING CREATURES ON THE PLANET LIVE IN THE DARK.

CREATURES THAT MAY GO THEIR ENTIRE LIVES, NEVER SEEING THE SUN.

WHILE THE REST OF THE WORLD DREAMS...

...THE NOCTURNALS RULE THE NIGHT.

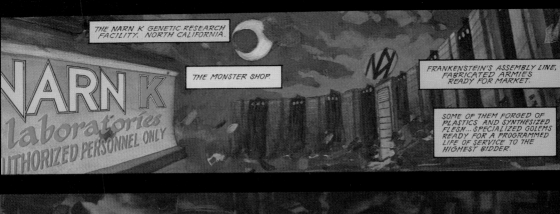

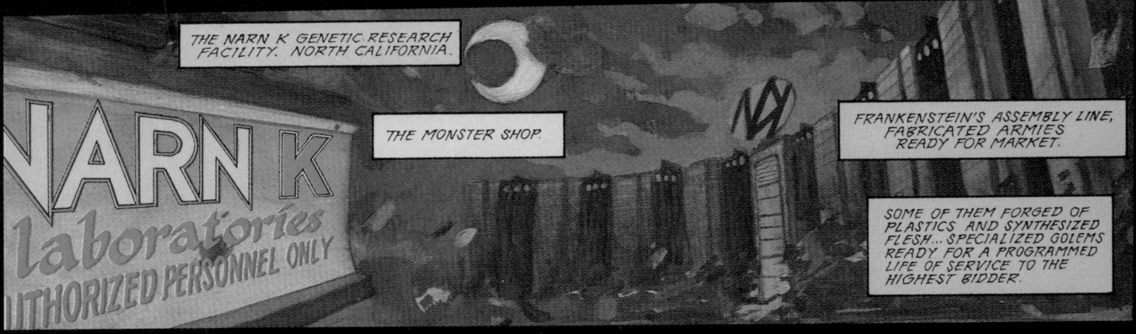
THE NARN K GENETIC RESEARCH FACILITY. NORTH CALIFORNIA.
THE MONSTER SHOP.
FRANKENSTEIN'S ASSEMBLY LINE, FABRICATED ARMIES READY FOR MARKET.
SOME OF THEM FORGED OF PLASTICS AND SYNTHESIZED FLESH... SPECIALIZED GOLEMS READY FOR A PROGRAMMED LIFE OF SERVICE TO THE HIGHEST BIDDER.
NARN K
laboratories
UTHORIZED PERSONNEL ONLY

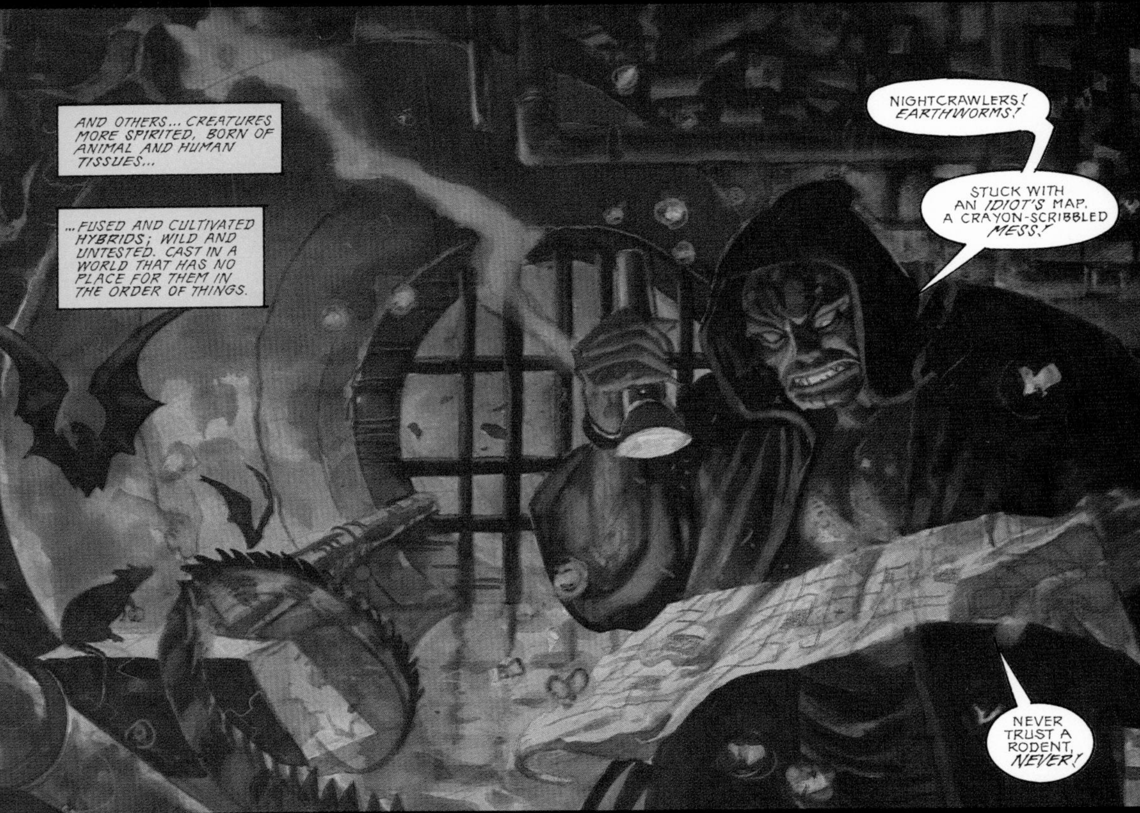
AND OTHERS... CREATURES MORE SPIRITED, BORN OF ANIMAL AND HUMAN TISSUES...
...FUSED AND CULTIVATED HYBRIDS; WILD AND UNTESTED. CAST IN A WORLD THAT HAS NO PLACE FOR THEM IN THE ORDER OF THINGS.
NIGHTCRAWLERS! EARTHWORMS!
STUCK WITH AN IDIOT'S MAP. A CRAYON-SCRIBBLED MESS!
NEVER TRUST A RODENT, NEVER!

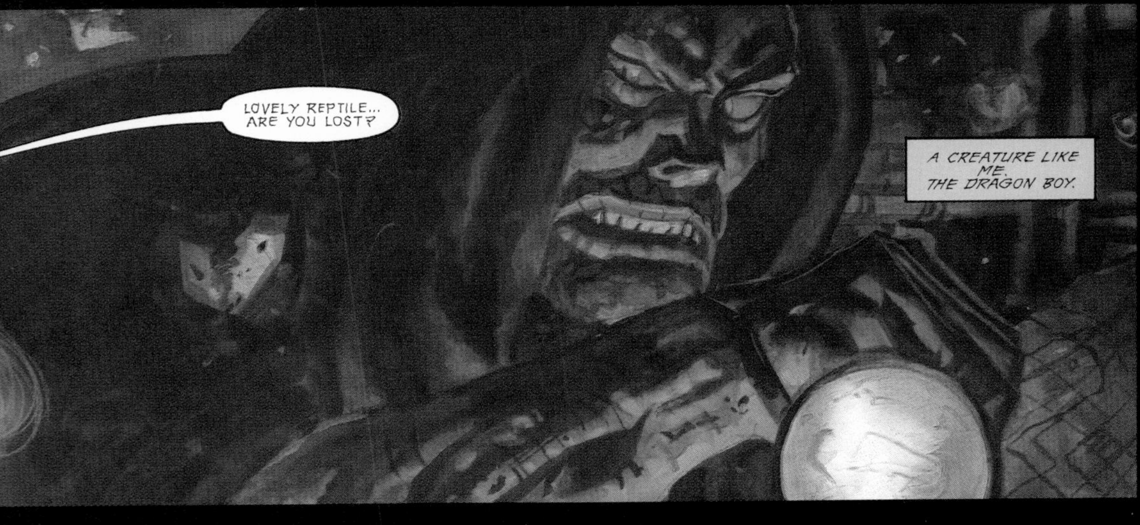
LOVELY REPTILE... ARE YOU LOST?
A CREATURE LIKE ME. THE DRAGON BOY.

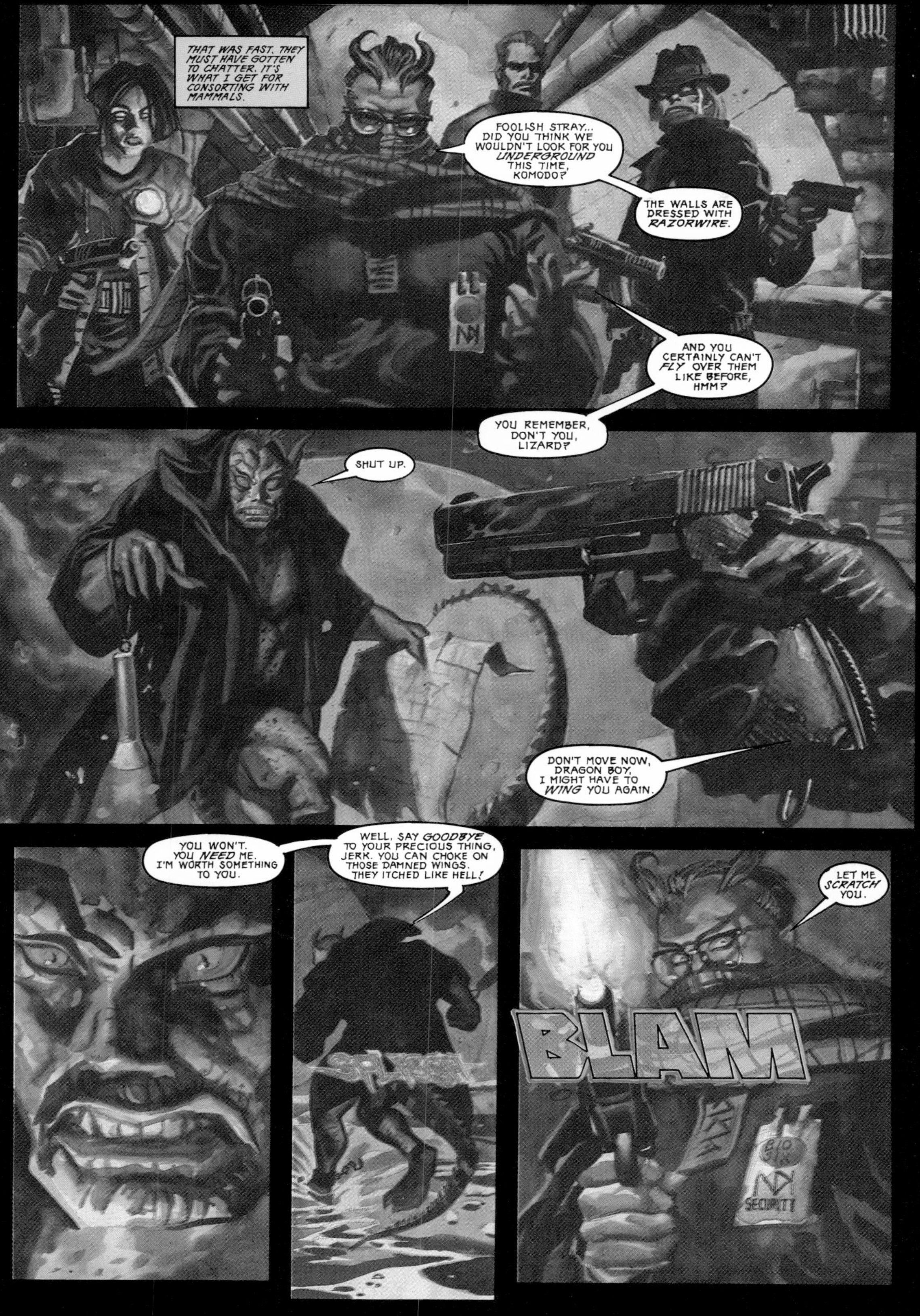
THAT WAS FAST. THEY MUST HAVE GOTTEN TO CHATTER. IT'S WHAT I GET FOR CONSORTING WITH MAMMALS.
FOOLISH STRAY... DID YOU THINK WE WOULDN'T LOOK FOR YOU UNDERGROUND THIS TIME, KOMODO?
THE WALLS ARE DRESSED WITH RAZORWIRE.
AND YOU CERTAINLY CAN'T FLY OVER THEM LIKE BEFORE, HMM?
YOU REMEMBER, DON'T YOU, LIZARD?
SHUT UP.
DON'T MOVE NOW, DRAGON BOY, I MIGHT HAVE TO WING YOU AGAIN.
YOU WON'T. YOU NEED ME. I'M WORTH SOMETHING TO YOU.
WELL, SAY GOODBYE TO YOUR PRECIOUS THING, JERK. YOU CAN CHOKE ON THOSE DAMNED WINGS. THEY ITCHED LIKE HELL!
SPLASH
LET ME SCRATCH YOU.
BLAM
BIO SIX
SECURITY

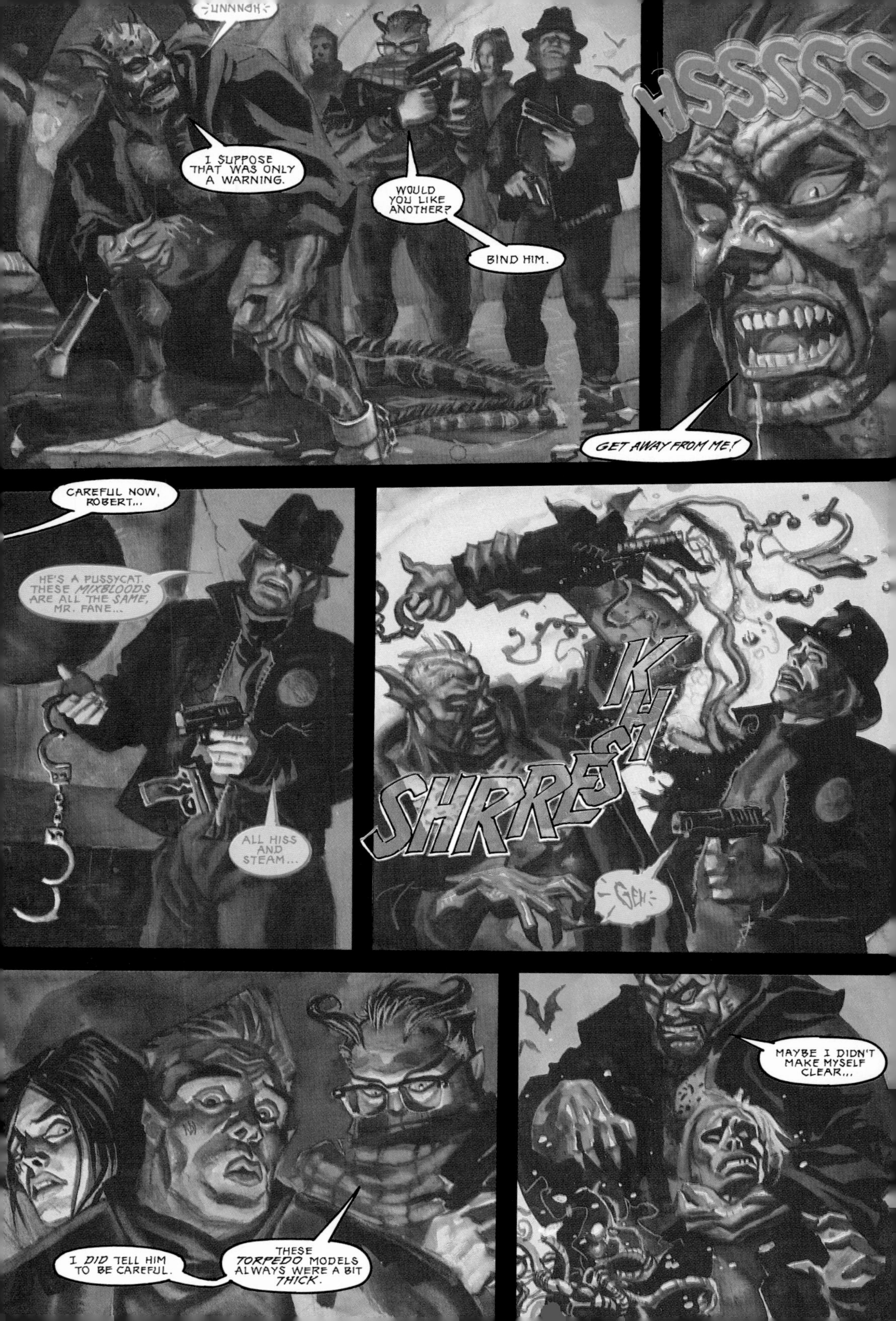
-UNNNGH-
I SUPPOSE THAT WAS ONLY A WARNING.
WOULD YOU LIKE ANOTHER?
BIND HIM.
HSSSSS
GET AWAY FROM ME!
CAREFUL NOW, ROBERT...
HE'S A PUSSYCAT. THESE MIXBLOODS ARE ALL THE SAME, MR. FANE...
ALL HISS AND STEAM...
KKH
SHRRESH
-GEH-
I DID TELL HIM TO BE CAREFUL.
THESE TORPEDO MODELS ALWAYS WERE A BIT THICK.
MAYBE I DIDN'T MAKE MYSELF CLEAR...

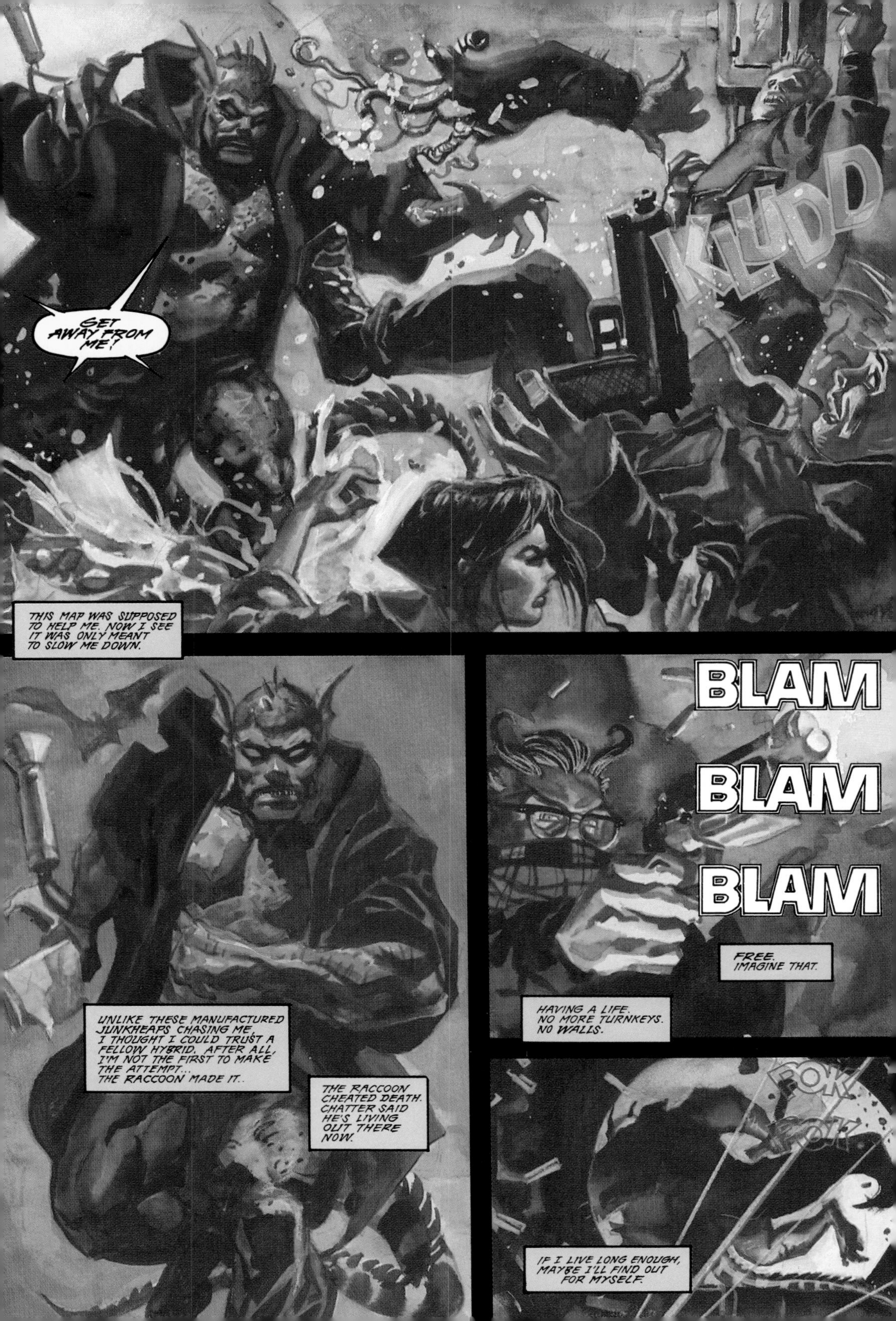
GET AWAY FROM ME!
KLUDD
THIS MAP WAS SUPPOSED TO HELP ME. NOW I SEE IT WAS ONLY MEANT TO SLOW ME DOWN.
UNLIKE THESE MANUFACTURED JUNKHEAPS CHASING ME, I THOUGHT I COULD TRUST A FELLOW HYBRID. AFTER ALL, I'M NOT THE FIRST TO MAKE THE ATTEMPT... THE RACCOON MADE IT..
THE RACCOON CHEATED DEATH. CHATTER SAID HE'S LIVING OUT THERE NOW.
BLAM
BLAM
BLAM
FREE. IMAGINE THAT.
HAVING A LIFE. NO MORE TURNKEYS. NO WALLS.
IF I LIVE LONG ENOUGH, MAYBE I'LL FIND OUT FOR MYSELF.

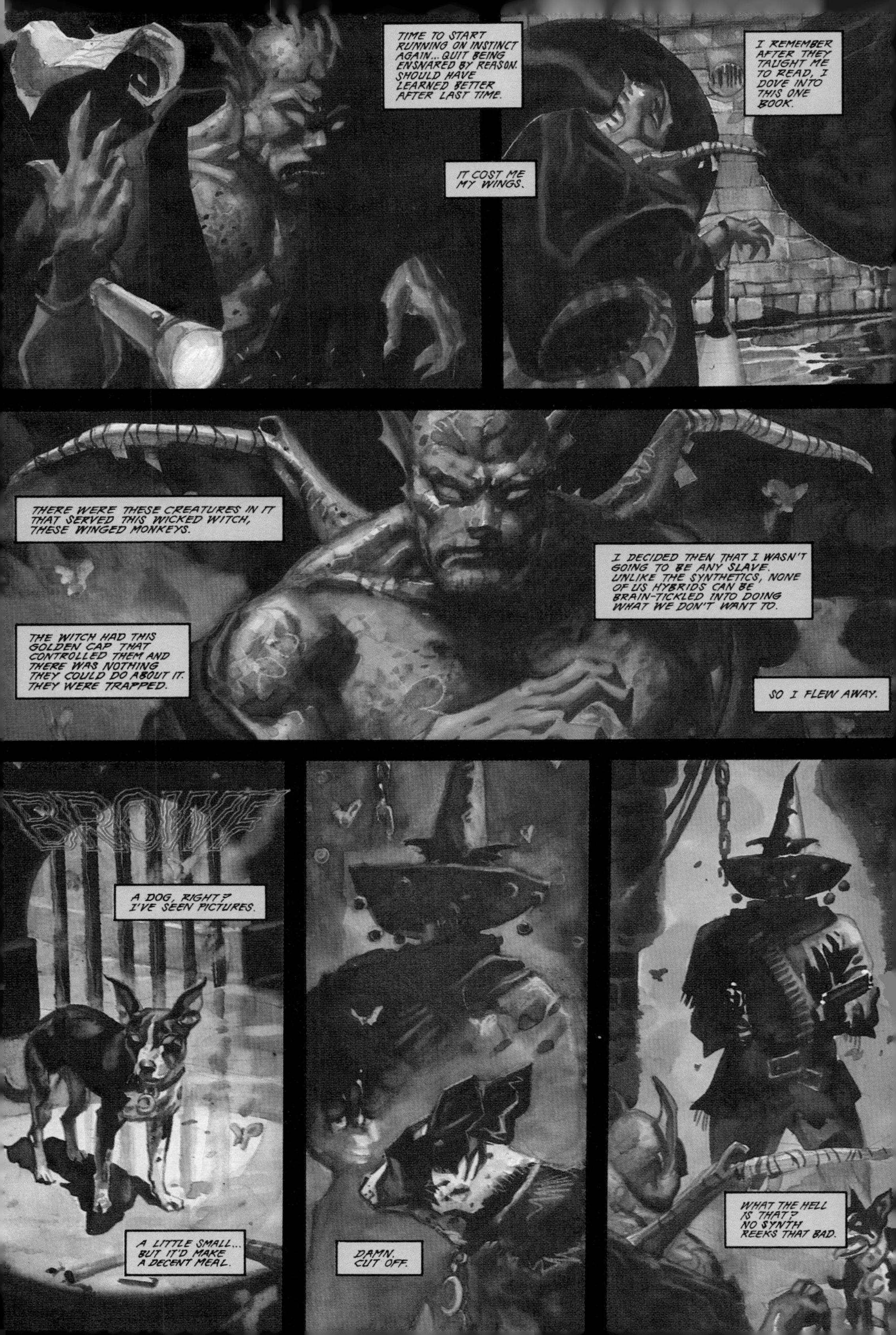
TIME TO START RUNNING ON INSTINCT AGAIN... QUIT BEING ENSNARED BY REASON. SHOULD HAVE LEARNED BETTER AFTER LAST TIME.
IT COST ME MY WINGS.
I REMEMBER AFTER THEY TAUGHT ME TO READ, I DOVE INTO THIS ONE BOOK.
THERE WERE THESE CREATURES IN IT THAT SERVED THIS WICKED WITCH, THESE WINGED MONKEYS.
THE WITCH HAD THIS GOLDEN CAP THAT CONTROLLED THEM AND THERE WAS NOTHING THEY COULD DO ABOUT IT. THEY WERE TRAPPED.
I DECIDED THEN THAT I WASN'T GOING TO BE ANY SLAVE. UNLIKE THE SYNTHETICS, NONE OF US HYBRIDS CAN BE BRAIN-TICKLED INTO DOING WHAT WE DON'T WANT TO.
SO I FLEW AWAY.
BROWF
A DOG, RIGHT? I'VE SEEN PICTURES.
A LITTLE SMALL... BUT IT'D MAKE A DECENT MEAL.
DAMN. CUT OFF.
WHAT THE HELL IS THAT? NO SYNTH REEKS THAT BAD.

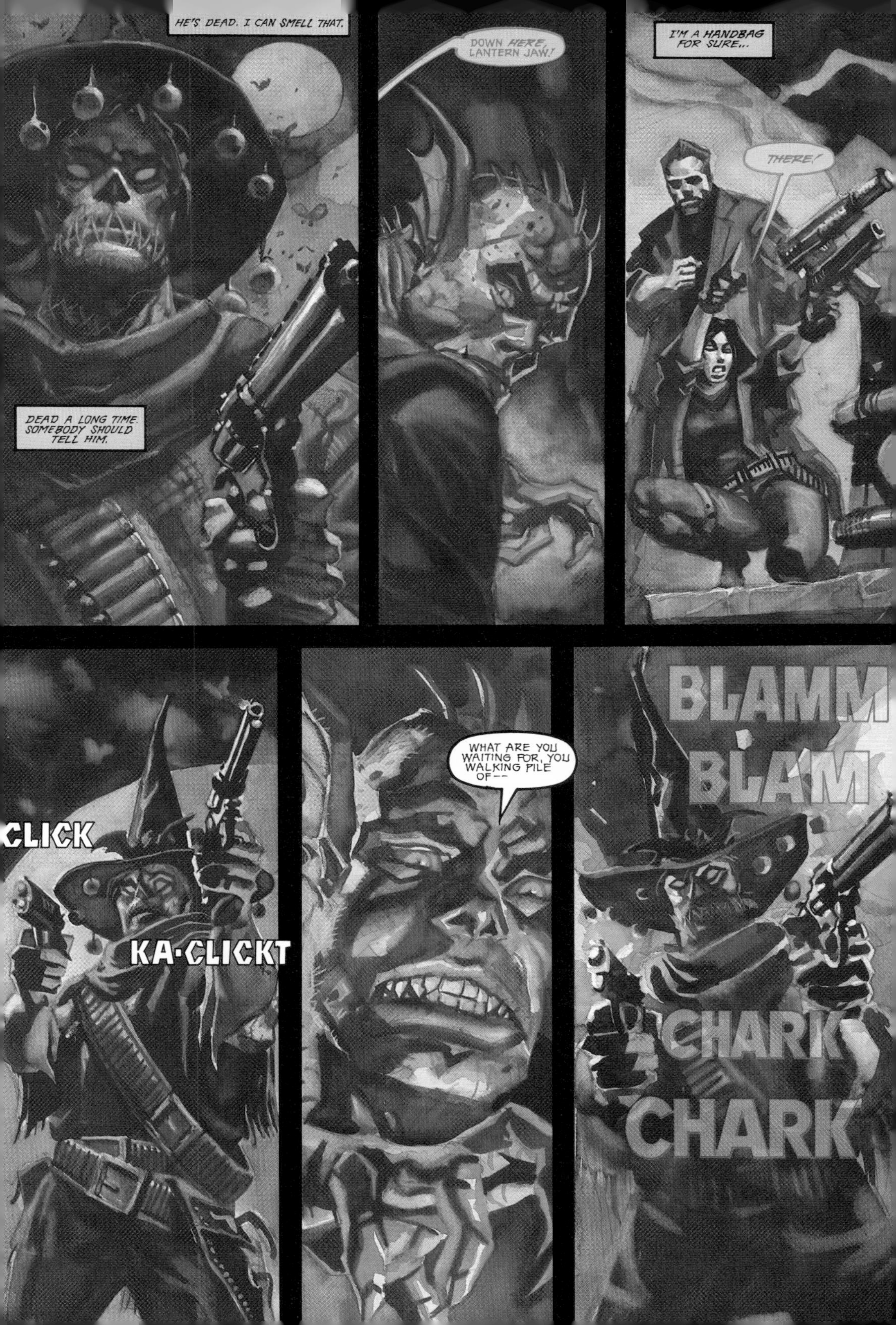
HE'S DEAD. I CAN SMELL THAT.
DEAD A LONG TIME. SOMEBODY SHOULD TELL HIM.
DOWN HERE, LANTERN JAW!
I'M A HANDBAG FOR SURE...
THERE!
CLICK
KA·CLICKT
WHAT ARE YOU WAITING FOR, YOU WALKING PILE OF--
BLAMM
BLAM
CHARK
CHARK

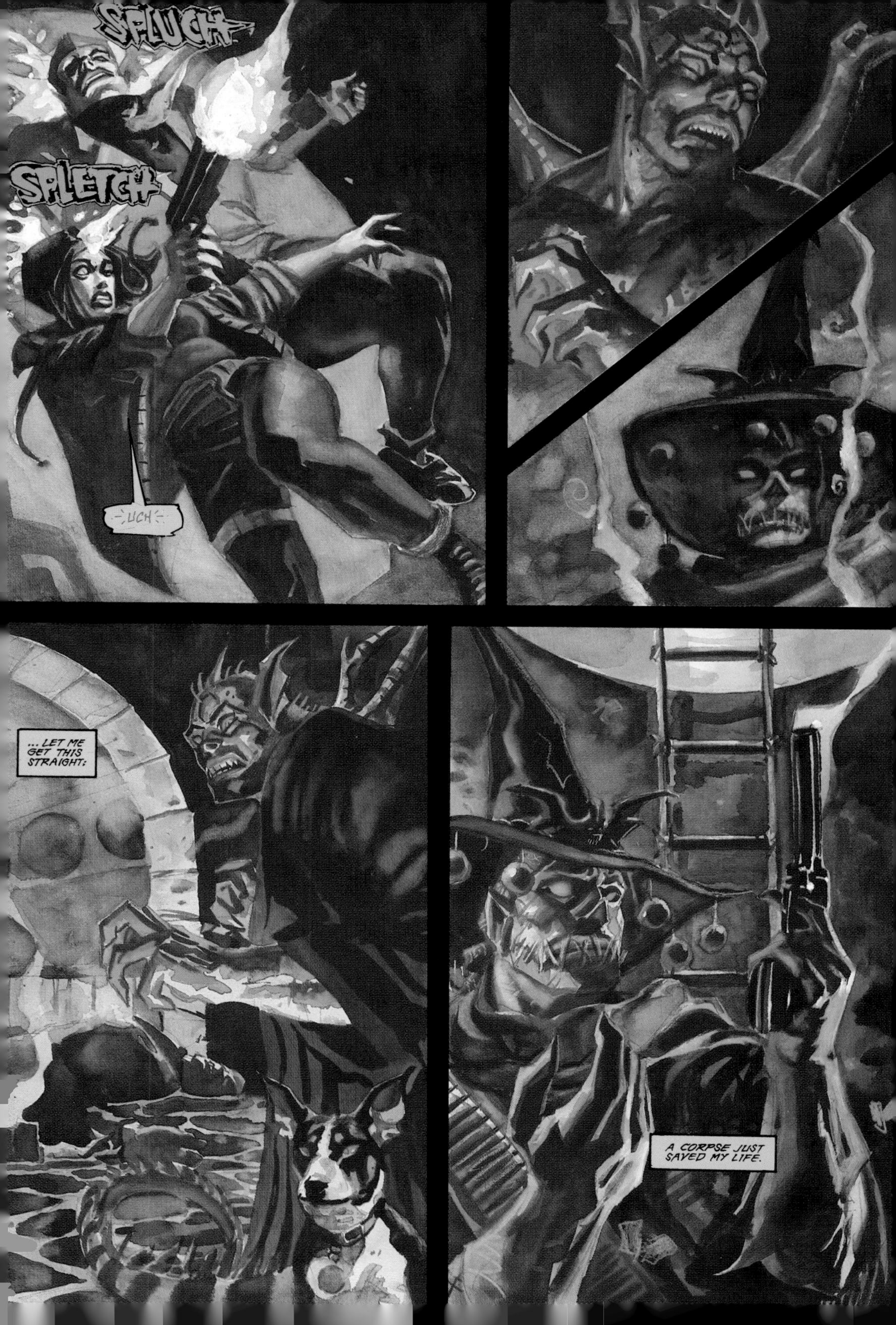
SPLUCH
SPLETCH
UCH
... LET ME GET THIS STRAIGHT:
A CORPSE JUST SAVED MY LIFE.

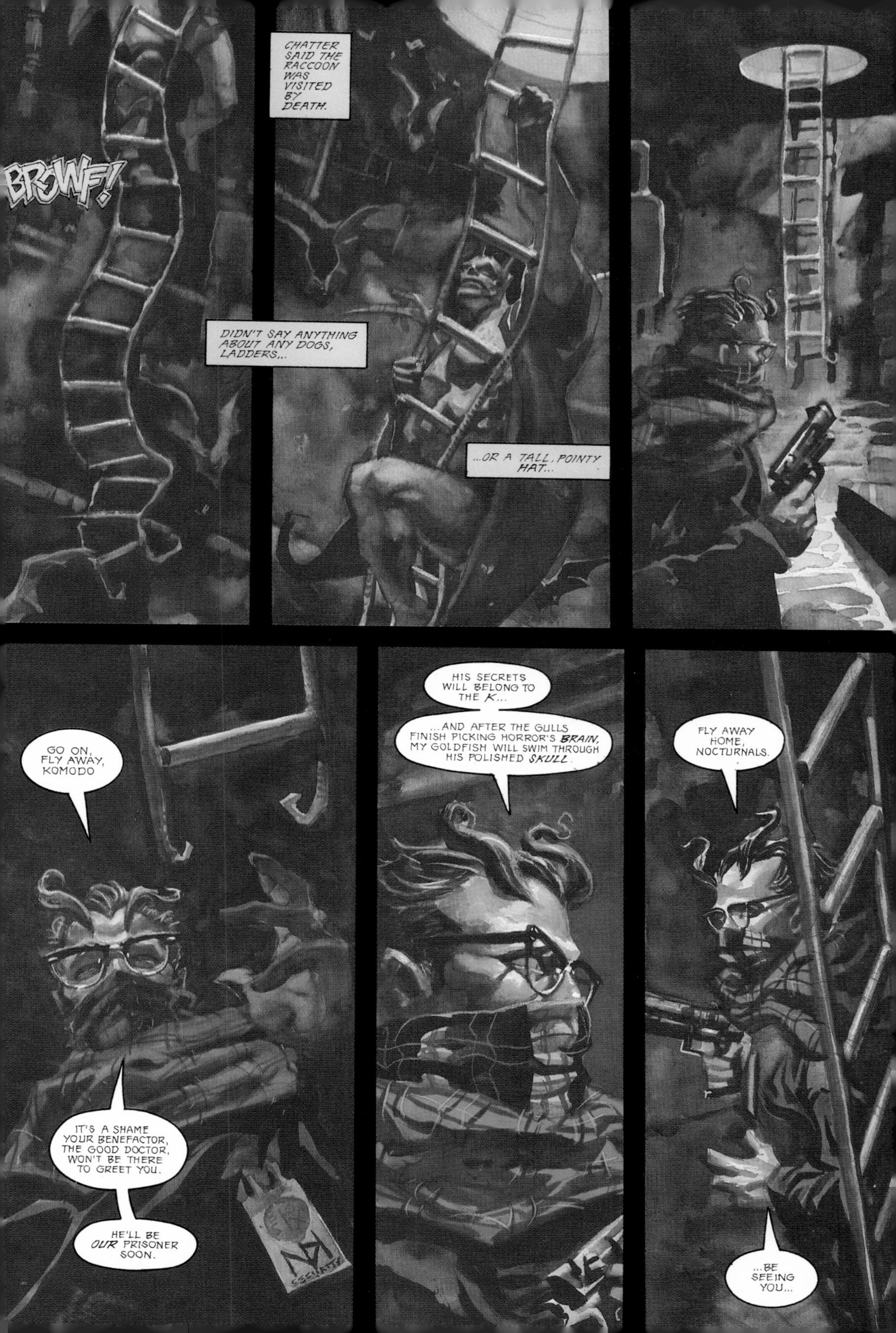
BROWF!
CHATTER SAID THE RACCOON WAS VISITED BY DEATH.
DIDN'T SAY ANYTHING ABOUT ANY DOGS, LADDERS...
...OR A TALL, POINTY HAT...
GO ON, FLY AWAY, KOMODO
IT'S A SHAME YOUR BENEFACTOR, THE GOOD DOCTOR, WON'T BE THERE TO GREET YOU.
HE'LL BE OUR PRISONER SOON.
HIS SECRETS WILL BELONG TO THE K...
...AND AFTER THE GULLS FINISH PICKING HORROR'S BRAIN, MY GOLDFISH WILL SWIM THROUGH HIS POLISHED SKULL.
FLY AWAY HOME, NOCTURNALS.
...BE SEEING YOU...

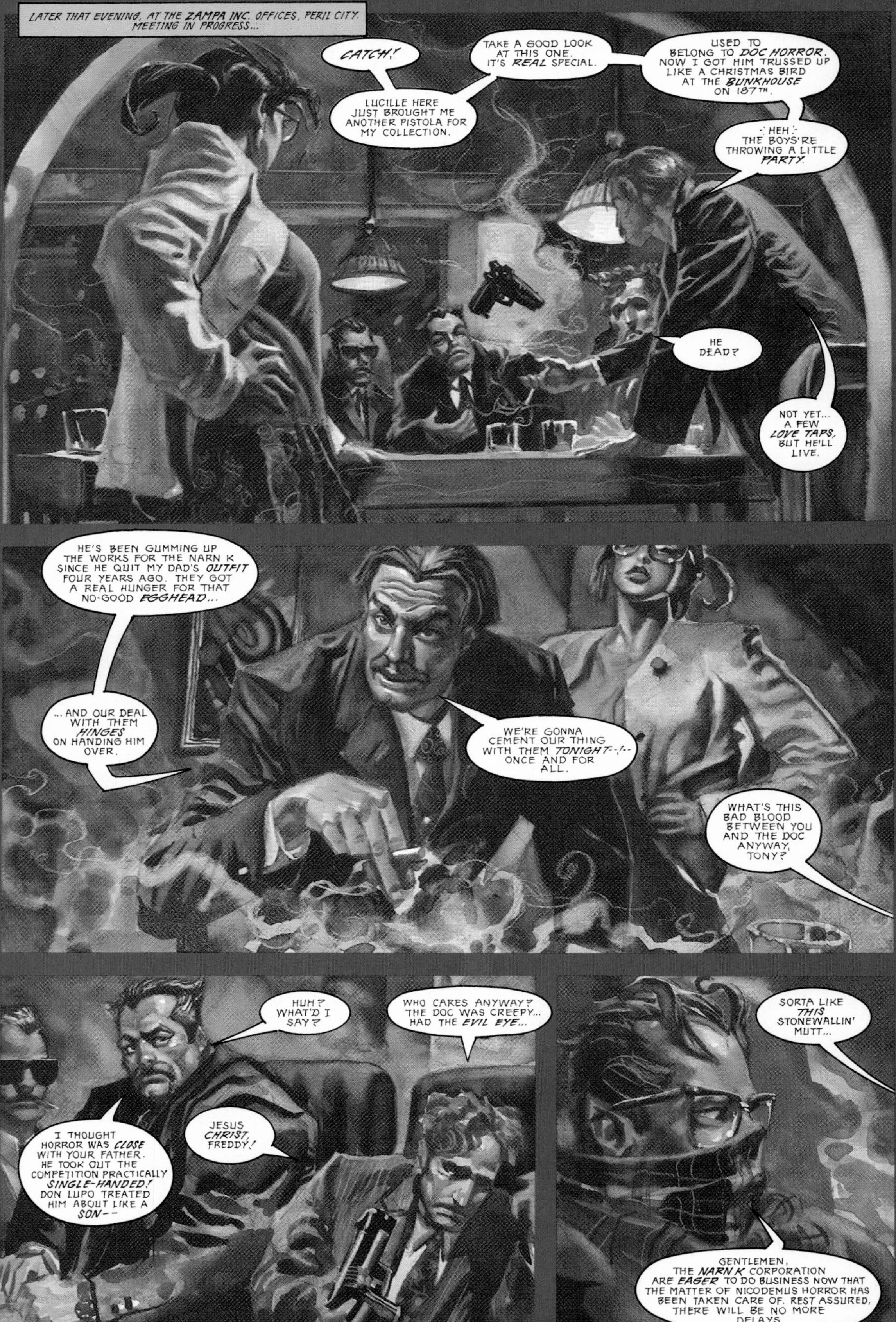
LATER THAT EVENING, AT THE ZAMPA INC. OFFICES, PERIL CITY. MEETING IN PROGRESS...
CATCH!
LUCILLE HERE JUST BROUGHT ME ANOTHER PISTOLA FOR MY COLLECTION.
TAKE A GOOD LOOK AT THIS ONE. IT'S REAL SPECIAL.
USED TO BELONG TO DOC HORROR. NOW I GOT HIM TRUSSED UP LIKE A CHRISTMAS BIRD AT THE BUNKHOUSE ON 187TH.
HEH. THE BOYS'RE THROWING A LITTLE PARTY.
HE DEAD?
NOT YET... A FEW LOVE TAPS, BUT HE'LL LIVE.
HE'S BEEN GUMMING UP THE WORKS FOR THE NARN K SINCE HE QUIT MY DAD'S OUTFIT FOUR YEARS AGO. THEY GOT A REAL HUNGER FOR THAT NO-GOOD EGGHEAD...
...AND OUR DEAL WITH THEM HINGES ON HANDING HIM OVER.
WE'RE GONNA CEMENT OUR THING WITH THEM TONIGHT--!-- ONCE AND FOR ALL.
WHAT'S THIS BAD BLOOD BETWEEN YOU AND THE DOC ANYWAY, TONY?
I THOUGHT HORROR WAS CLOSE WITH YOUR FATHER. HE TOOK OUT THE COMPETITION PRACTICALLY SINGLE-HANDED! DON LUPO TREATED HIM ABOUT LIKE A SON--
JESUS CHRIST, FREDDY!
HUH? WHAT'D I SAY?
WHO CARES ANYWAY? THE DOC WAS CREEPY... HAD THE EVIL EYE...
SORTA LIKE THIS STONEWALLIN' MUTT...
GENTLEMEN, THE NARN K CORPORATION ARE EAGER TO DO BUSINESS NOW THAT THE MATTER OF NICODEMUS HORROR HAS BEEN TAKEN CARE OF. REST ASSURED, THERE WILL BE NO MORE DELAYS.

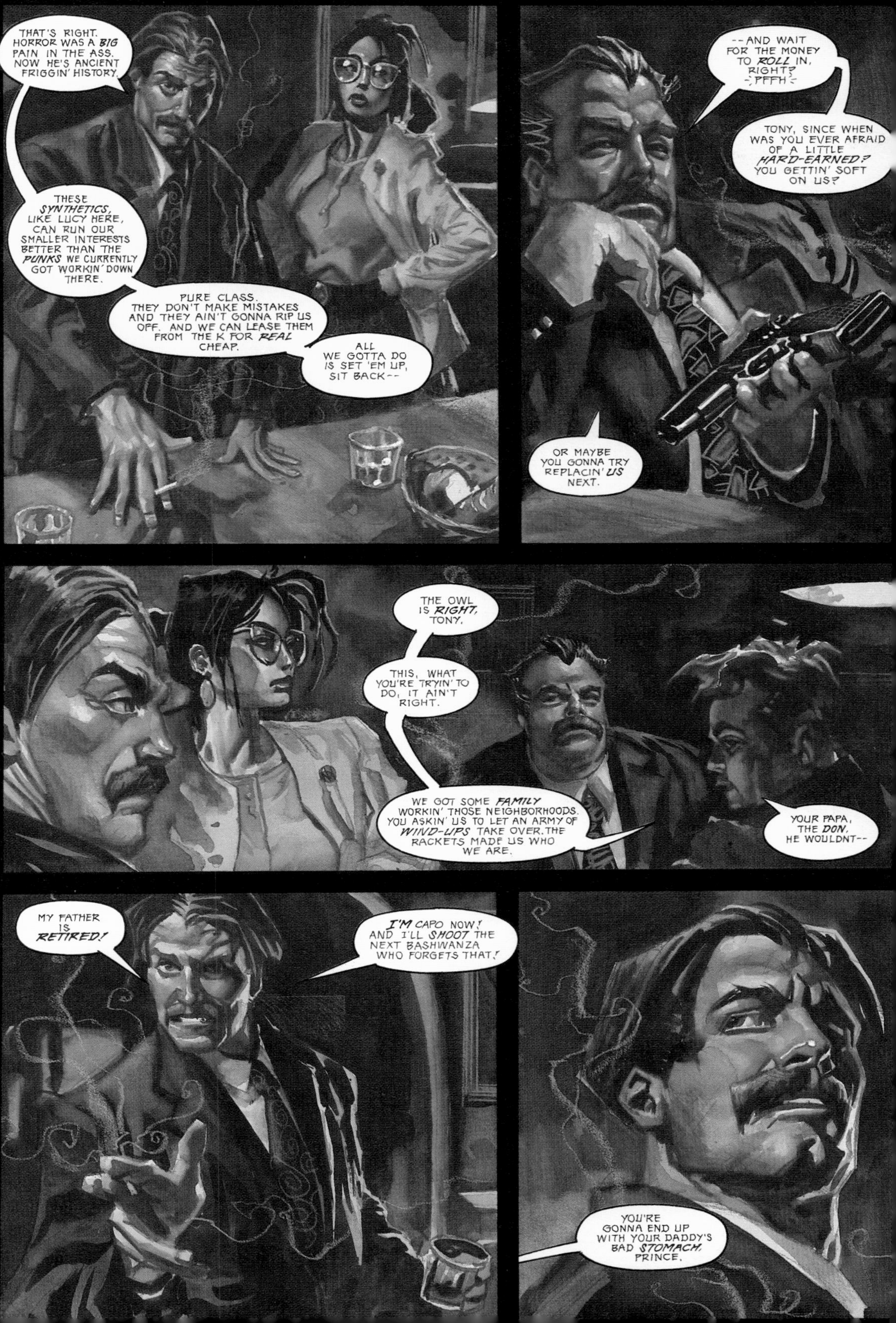
THAT'S RIGHT. HORROR WAS A BIG PAIN IN THE ASS. NOW HE'S ANCIENT FRIGGIN' HISTORY.
THESE SYNTHETICS, LIKE LUCY HERE, CAN RUN OUR SMALLER INTERESTS BETTER THAN THE PUNKS WE CURRENTLY GOT WORKIN' DOWN THERE.
PURE CLASS. THEY DON'T MAKE MISTAKES AND THEY AIN'T GONNA RIP US OFF. AND WE CAN LEASE THEM FROM THE K FOR REAL CHEAP.
ALL WE GOTTA DO IS SET 'EM UP, SIT BACK--
--AND WAIT FOR THE MONEY TO ROLL IN, RIGHT? -PFFH-
TONY, SINCE WHEN WAS YOU EVER AFRAID OF A LITTLE HARD-EARNED? YOU GETTIN' SOFT ON US?
OR MAYBE YOU GONNA TRY REPLACIN' US NEXT.
THE OWL IS RIGHT, TONY.
THIS, WHAT YOU'RE TRYIN' TO DO, IT AIN'T RIGHT.
WE GOT SOME FAMILY WORKIN' THOSE NEIGHBORHOODS. YOU ASKIN' US TO LET AN ARMY OF WIND-UPS TAKE OVER. THE RACKETS MADE US WHO WE ARE.
YOUR PAPA, THE DON, HE WOULDNT--
MY FATHER IS RETIRED!
I'M CAPO NOW! AND I'LL SHOOT THE NEXT BASHWANZA WHO FORGETS THAT!
YOU'RE GONNA END UP WITH YOUR DADDY'S BAD STOMACH, PRINCE.

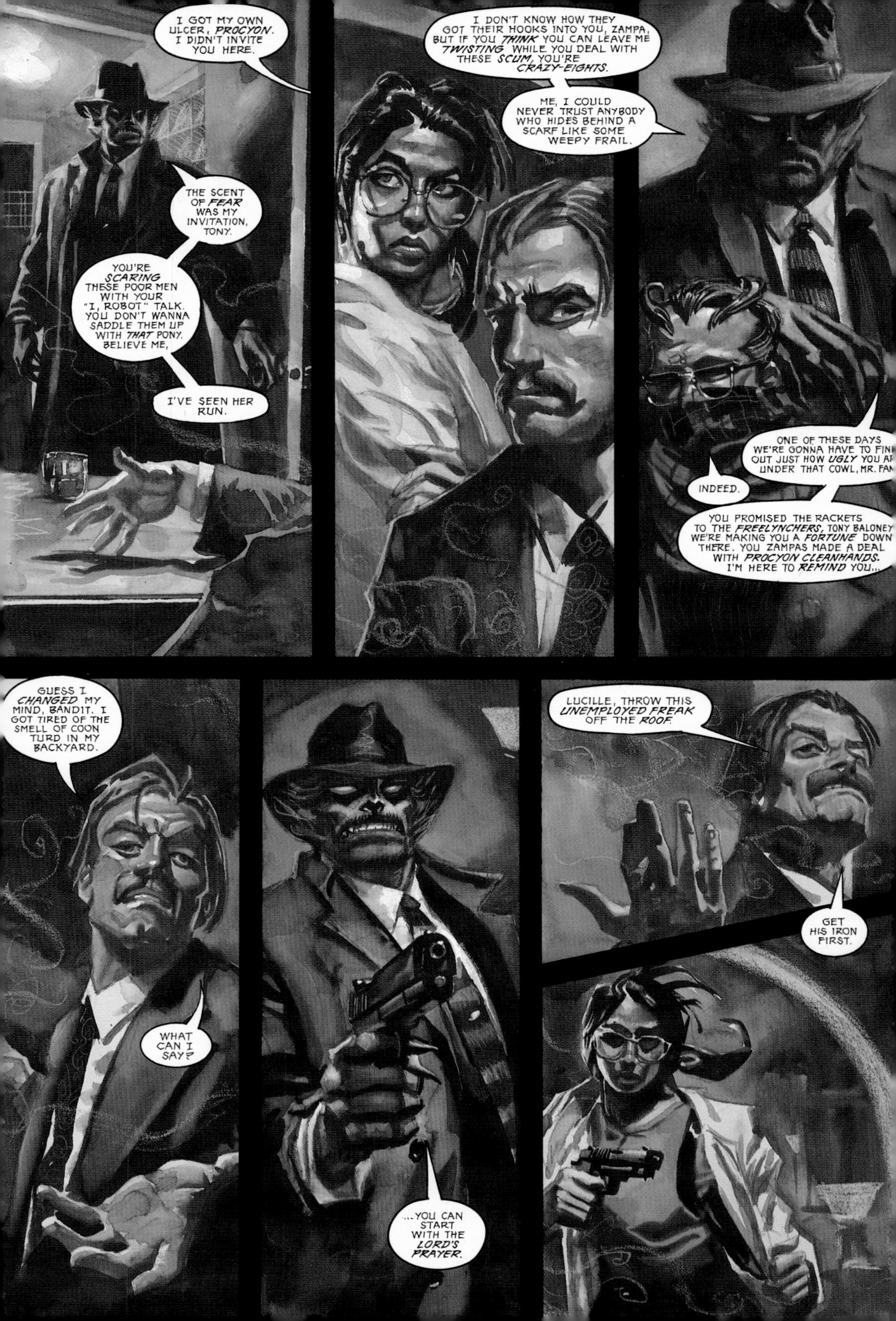
I GOT MY OWN ULCER, PROCYON. I DIDN'T INVITE YOU HERE.
THE SCENT OF FEAR WAS MY INVITATION, TONY.
YOU'RE SCARING THESE POOR MEN WITH YOUR "I, ROBOT" TALK. YOU DON'T WANNA SADDLE THEM UP WITH THAT PONY. BELIEVE ME,
I'VE SEEN HER RUN.
I DON'T KNOW HOW THEY GOT THEIR HOOKS INTO YOU, ZAMPA, BUT IF YOU THINK YOU CAN LEAVE ME TWISTING WHILE YOU DEAL WITH THESE SCUM, YOU'RE CRAZY-EIGHTS.
ME, I COULD NEVER TRUST ANYBODY WHO HIDES BEHIND A SCARF LIKE SOME WEEPY FRAIL.
ONE OF THESE DAYS WE'RE GONNA HAVE TO FIN OUT JUST HOW UGLY YOU AR UNDER THAT COWL, MR. FA
INDEED.
YOU PROMISED THE RACKETS TO THE FREELYNCHERS, TONY BALONEY. WE'RE MAKING YOU A FORTUNE DOWN THERE. YOU ZAMPAS MADE A DEAL WITH PROCYON CLEANHANDS. I'M HERE TO REMIND YOU...
GUESS I CHANGED MY MIND, BANDIT. I GOT TIRED OF THE SMELL OF COON TURD IN MY BACKYARD.
WHAT CAN I SAY?
...YOU CAN START WITH THE LORD'S PRAYER.
LUCILLE, THROW THIS UNEMPLOYED FREAK OFF THE ROOF.
GET HIS IRON FIRST.

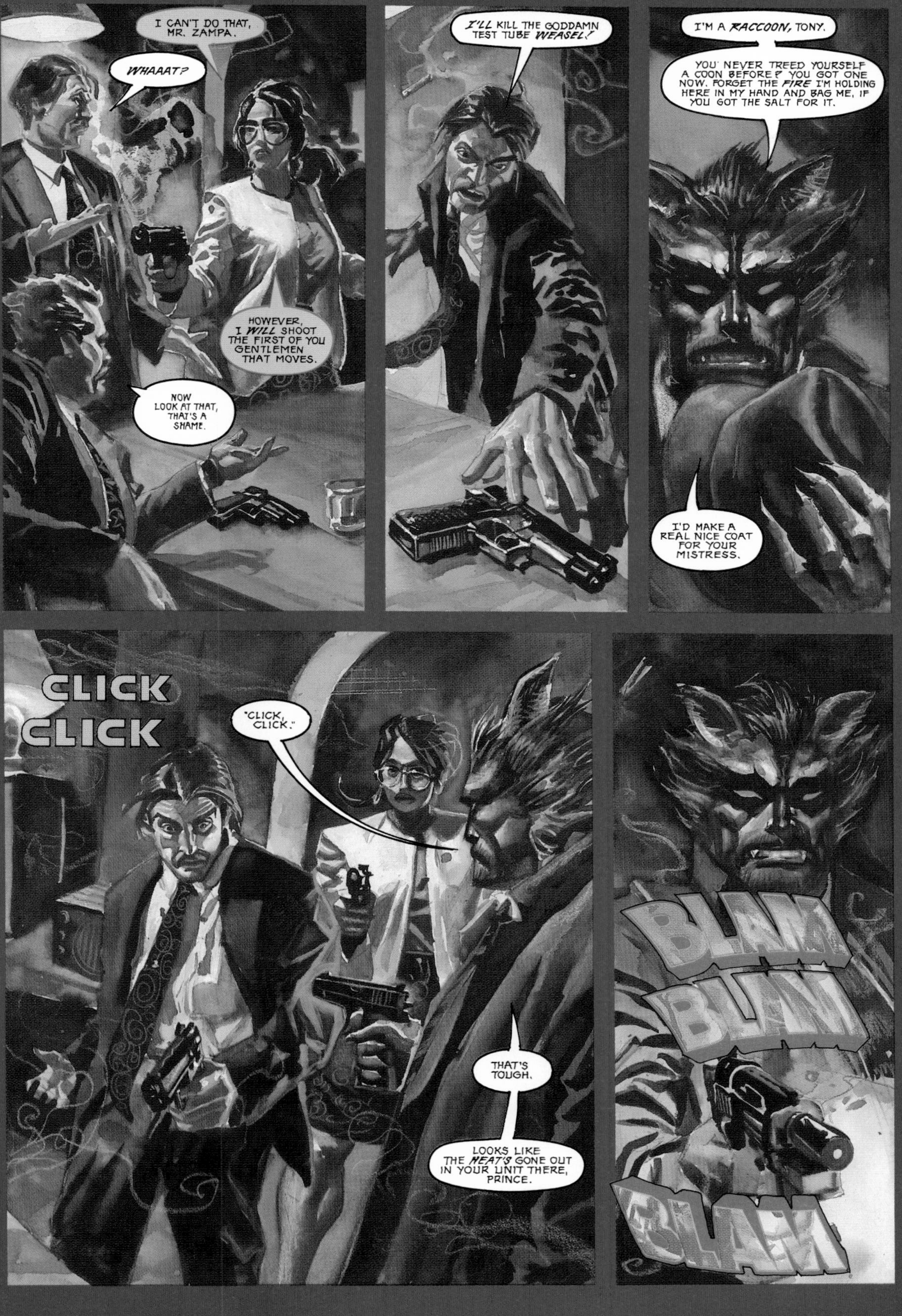

I CAN'T DO THAT, MR. ZAMPA.
WHAAAT?
HOWEVER, I WILL SHOOT THE FIRST OF YOU GENTLEMEN THAT MOVES.
NOW LOOK AT THAT, THAT'S A SHAME.
I'LL KILL THE GODDAMN TEST TUBE WEASEL!
I'M A RACCOON, TONY.
YOU NEVER TREED YOURSELF A COON BEFORE? YOU GOT ONE NOW. FORGET THE FIRE I'M HOLDING HERE IN MY HAND AND BAG ME, IF YOU GOT THE SALT FOR IT.
I'D MAKE A REAL NICE COAT FOR YOUR MISTRESS.
CLICK
CLICK
"CLICK, CLICK."
THAT'S TOUGH.
LOOKS LIKE THE HEAT'S GONE OUT IN YOUR UNIT THERE, PRINCE.
BLAM
BLAM
BLAM

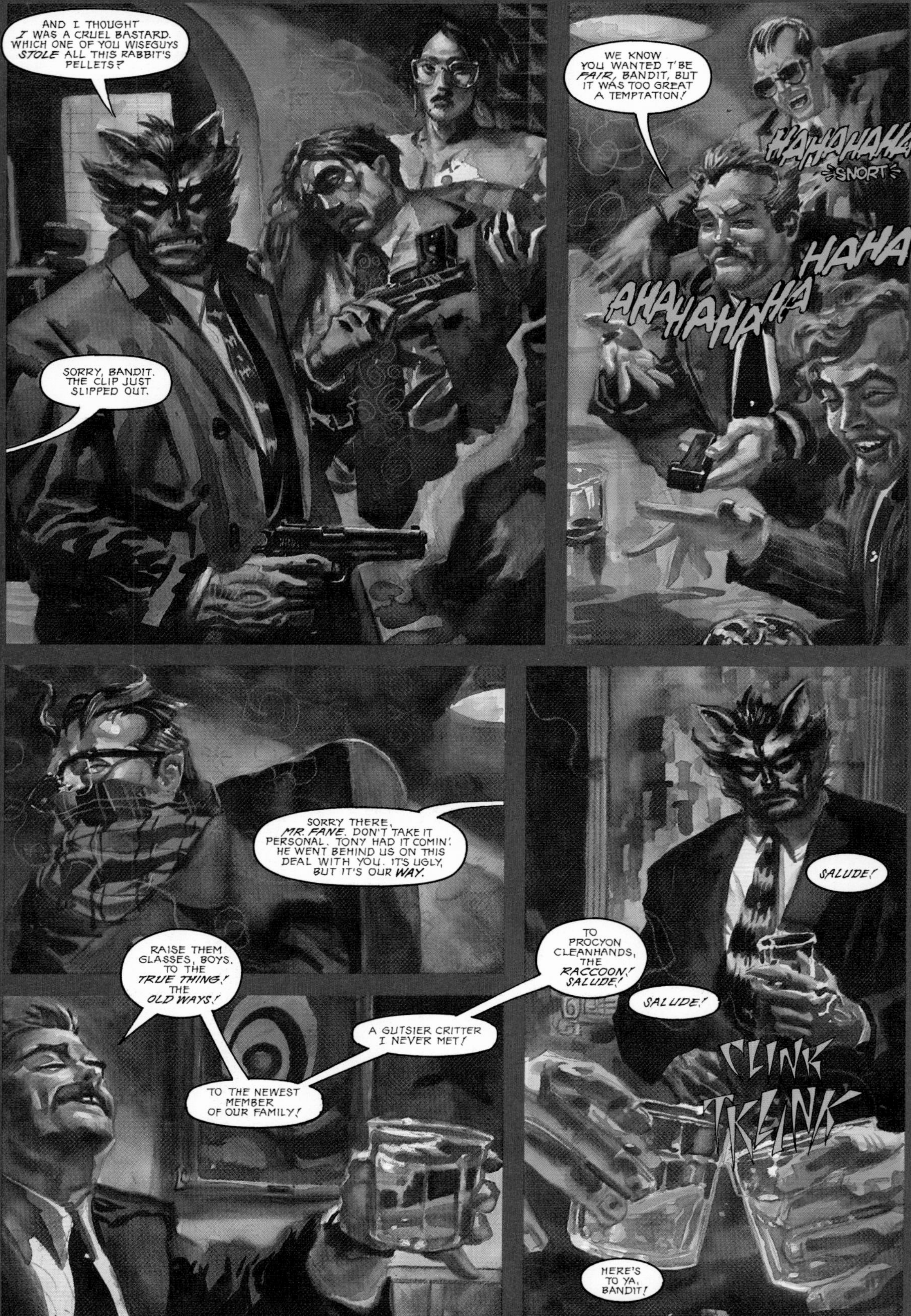
AND I THOUGHT I WAS A CRUEL BASTARD. WHICH ONE OF YOU WISEGUYS STOLE ALL THIS RABBIT'S PELLETS?
SORRY, BANDIT. THE CLIP JUST SLIPPED OUT.
WE KNOW YOU WANTED T'BE FAIR, BANDIT, BUT IT WAS TOO GREAT A TEMPTATION!
HAHAHAHA
SNORT
HAHA
AHAHAHAHAHA
SORRY THERE, MR. FANE. DON'T TAKE IT PERSONAL. TONY HAD IT COMIN'. HE WENT BEHIND US ON THIS DEAL WITH YOU. IT'S UGLY, BUT IT'S OUR WAY.
RAISE THEM GLASSES, BOYS, TO THE TRUE THING! THE OLD WAYS!
TO THE NEWEST MEMBER OF OUR FAMILY!
A GUTSIER CRITTER I NEVER MET!
TO PROCYON CLEANHANDS, THE RACCOON! SALUDE!
SALUDE!
SALUDE!
CLINK
TKLINK
HERE'S TO YA, BANDIT!

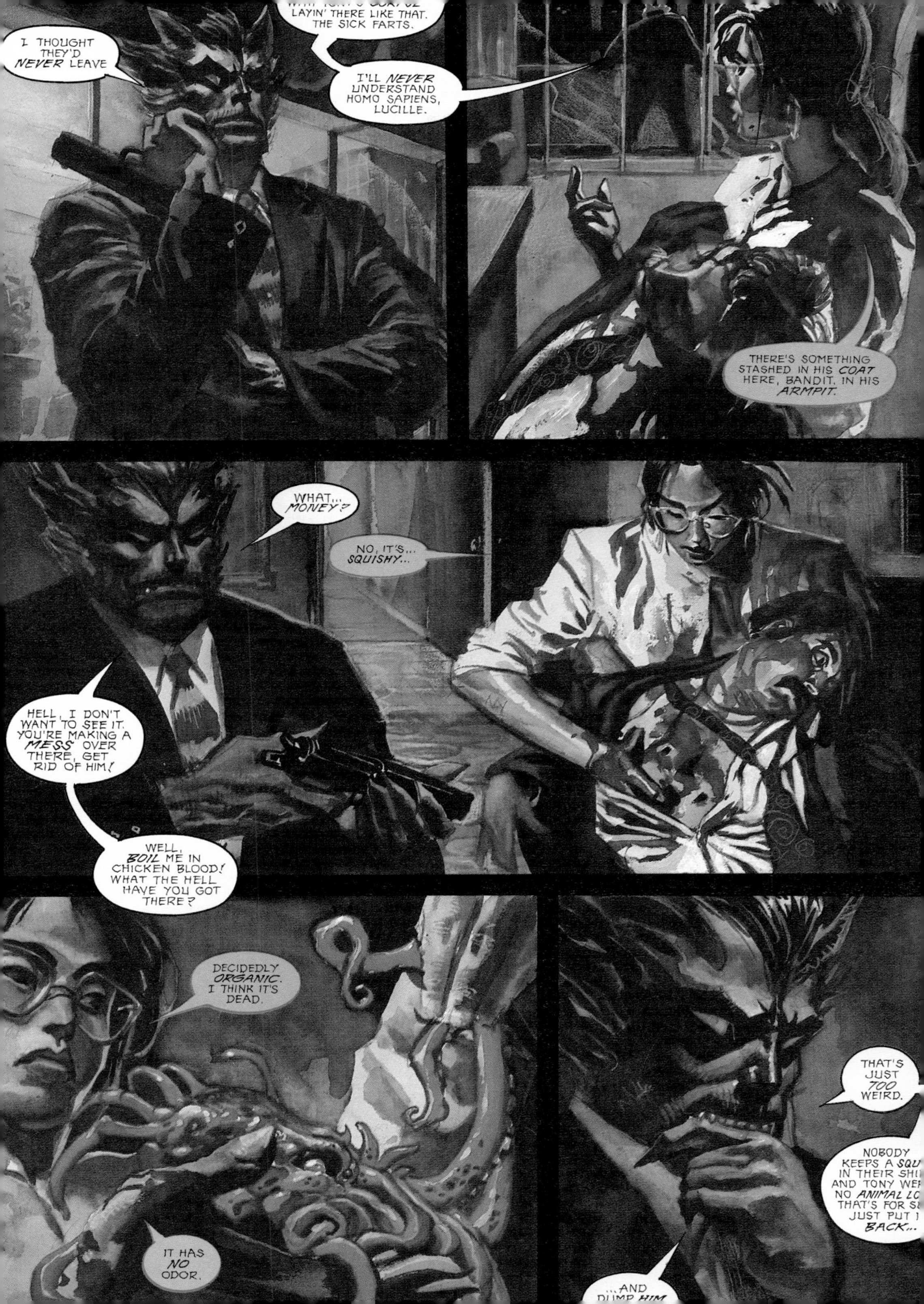

I THOUGHT THEY'D NEVER LEAVE
LAYIN' THERE LIKE THAT. THE SICK FARTS.
I'LL NEVER UNDERSTAND HOMO SAPIENS, LUCILLE.
THERE'S SOMETHING STASHED IN HIS COAT HERE, BANDIT, IN HIS ARMPIT.
WHAT... MONEY?
NO, IT'S... SQUISHY...
HELL, I DON'T WANT TO SEE IT. YOU'RE MAKING A MESS OVER THERE, GET RID OF HIM!
WELL, BOIL ME IN CHICKEN BLOOD! WHAT THE HELL HAVE YOU GOT THERE?
DECIDEDLY ORGANIC. I THINK IT'S DEAD.
IT HAS NO ODOR.
THAT'S JUST TOO WEIRD.
NOBODY KEEPS A
IN THEIR
AND TONY
NO ANIMAL
THAT'S FOR
JUST PUT
BACK...
...AND

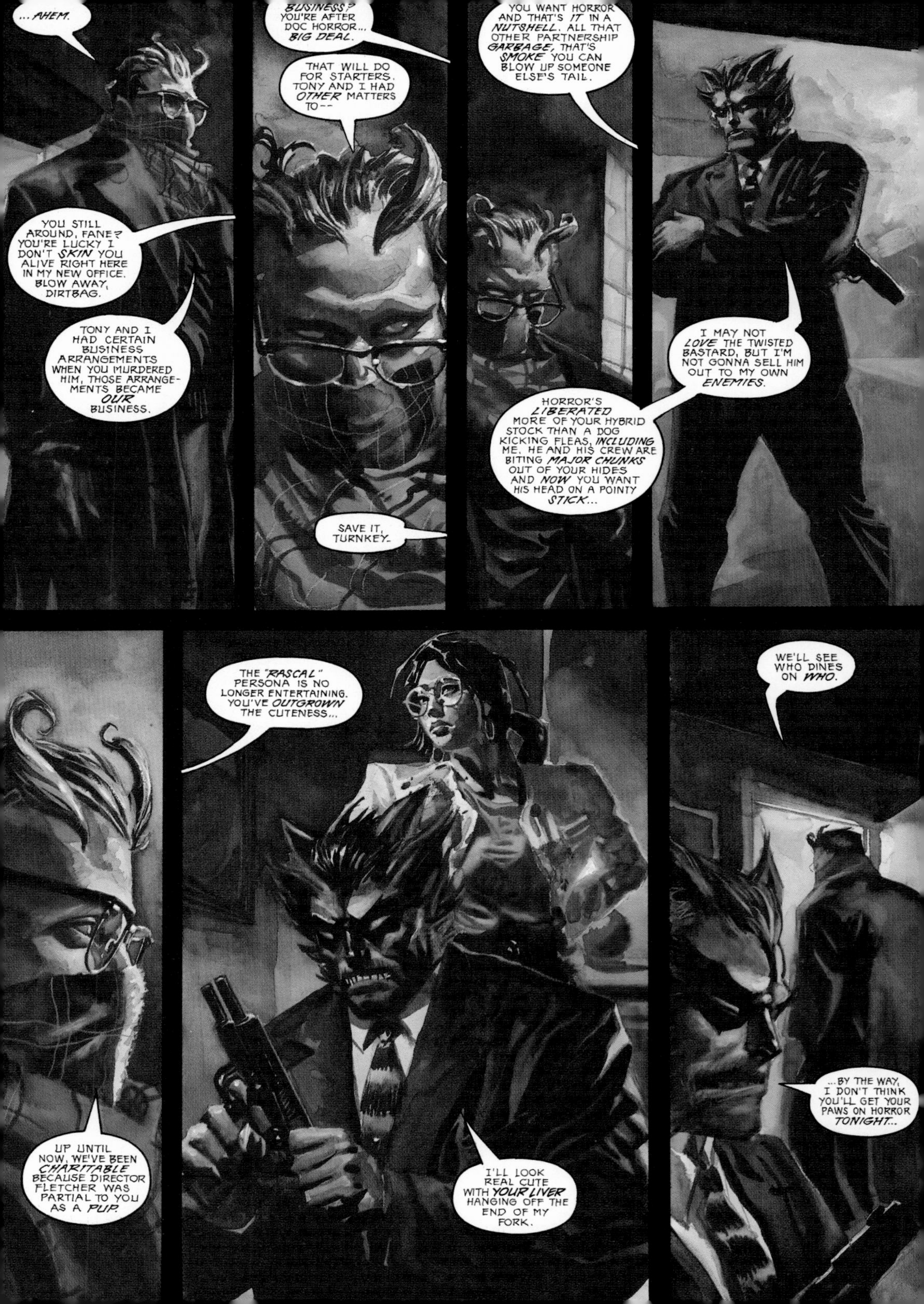
...AHEM.
BUSINESS? YOU'RE AFTER DOC HORROR... BIG DEAL.
THAT WILL DO FOR STARTERS. TONY AND I HAD OTHER MATTERS TO--
YOU WANT HORROR AND THAT'S IT IN A NUTSHELL. ALL THAT OTHER PARTNERSHIP GARBAGE, THAT'S SMOKE YOU CAN BLOW UP SOMEONE ELSE'S TAIL.
YOU STILL AROUND, FANE? YOU'RE LUCKY I DON'T SKIN YOU ALIVE RIGHT HERE IN MY NEW OFFICE. BLOW AWAY, DIRTBAG.
TONY AND I HAD CERTAIN BUSINESS ARRANGEMENTS WHEN YOU MURDERED HIM, THOSE ARRANGE-MENTS BECAME OUR BUSINESS.
SAVE IT, TURNKEY.
HORROR'S LIBERATED MORE OF YOUR HYBRID STOCK THAN A DOG KICKING FLEAS, INCLUDING ME. HE AND HIS CREW ARE BITING MAJOR CHUNKS OUT OF YOUR HIDES AND NOW YOU WANT HIS HEAD ON A POINTY STICK...
I MAY NOT LOVE THE TWISTED BASTARD, BUT I'M NOT GONNA SELL HIM OUT TO MY OWN ENEMIES.
UP UNTIL NOW, WE'VE BEEN CHARITABLE BECAUSE DIRECTOR FLETCHER WAS PARTIAL TO YOU AS A PUP.
THE "RASCAL" PERSONA IS NO LONGER ENTERTAINING. YOU'VE OUTGROWN THE CUTENESS...
I'LL LOOK REAL CUTE WITH YOUR LIVER HANGING OFF THE END OF MY FORK.
WE'LL SEE WHO DINES ON WHO.
...BY THE WAY, I DON'T THINK YOU'LL GET YOUR PAWS ON HORROR TONIGHT...

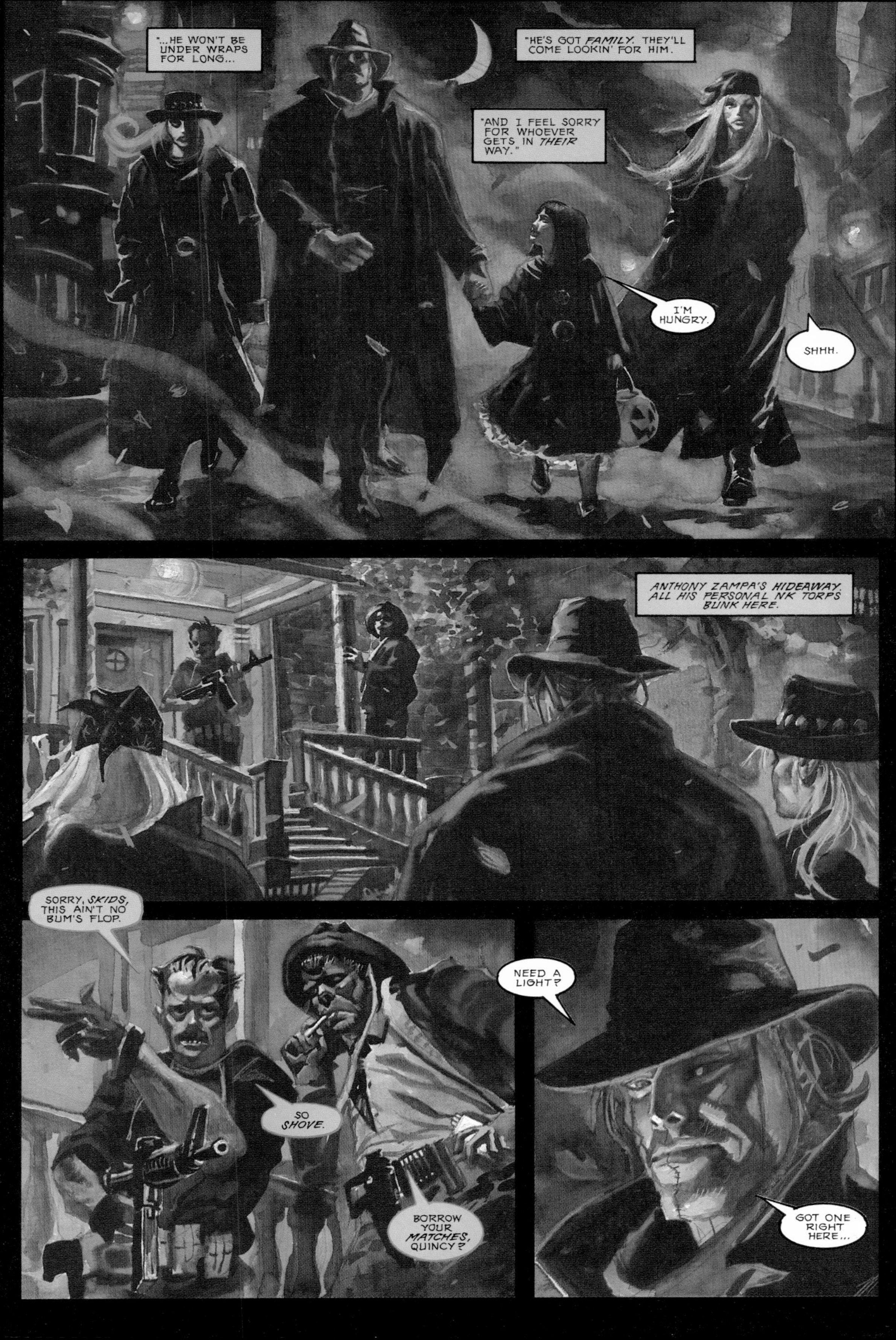
"...HE WON'T BE UNDER WRAPS FOR LONG...
"HE'S GOT *FAMILY*. THEY'LL COME LOOKIN' FOR HIM.
"AND I FEEL SORRY FOR WHOEVER GETS IN *THEIR* WAY."
I'M HUNGRY.
SHHH.
ANTHONY ZAMPA'S HIDEAWAY. ALL HIS PERSONAL NK TORPS BUNK HERE.
SORRY, *SKIDS*, THIS AIN'T NO BUM'S FLOP.
SO *SHOVE*.
BORROW YOUR *MATCHES*, QUINCY?
NEED A LIGHT?
GOT ONE RIGHT HERE...

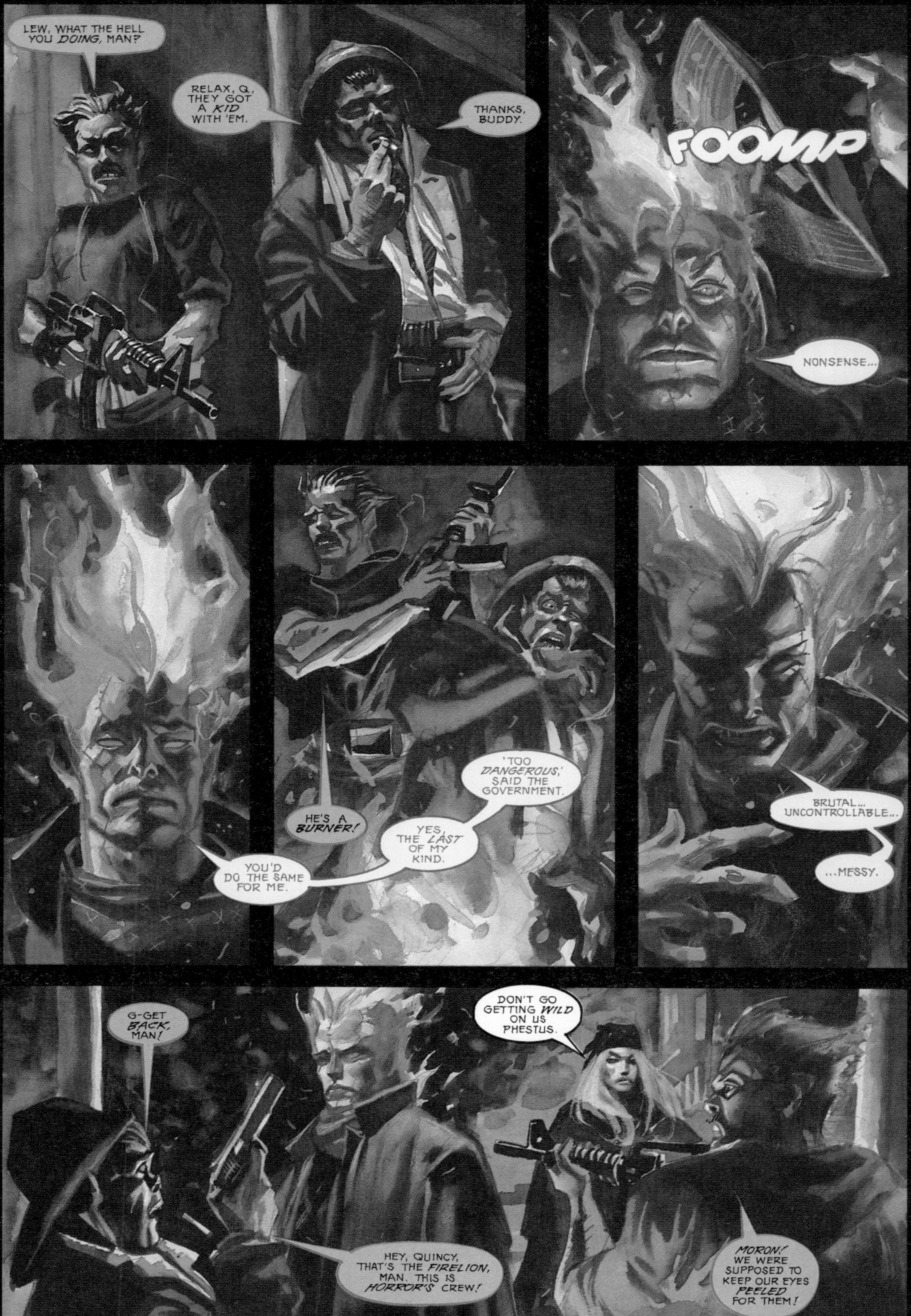
LEW, WHAT THE HELL YOU *DOING*, MAN?
RELAX, Q, THEY GOT A *KID* WITH 'EM.
THANKS, BUDDY.
FOOMP
NONSENSE...
YOU'D DO THE SAME FOR ME.
HE'S A *BURNER!*
YES, THE *LAST* OF MY KIND.
'TOO *DANGEROUS*,' SAID THE GOVERNMENT.
BRUTAL... UNCONTROLLABLE...
...MESSY.
G-GET *BACK*, MAN!
DON'T GO GETTING *WILD* ON US PHESTUS.
HEY, QUINCY, THAT'S THE *FIRELION*, MAN. THIS IS *HORROR'S* CREW!
MORON! WE WERE SUPPOSED TO KEEP OUR EYES *PEELED* FOR THEM!

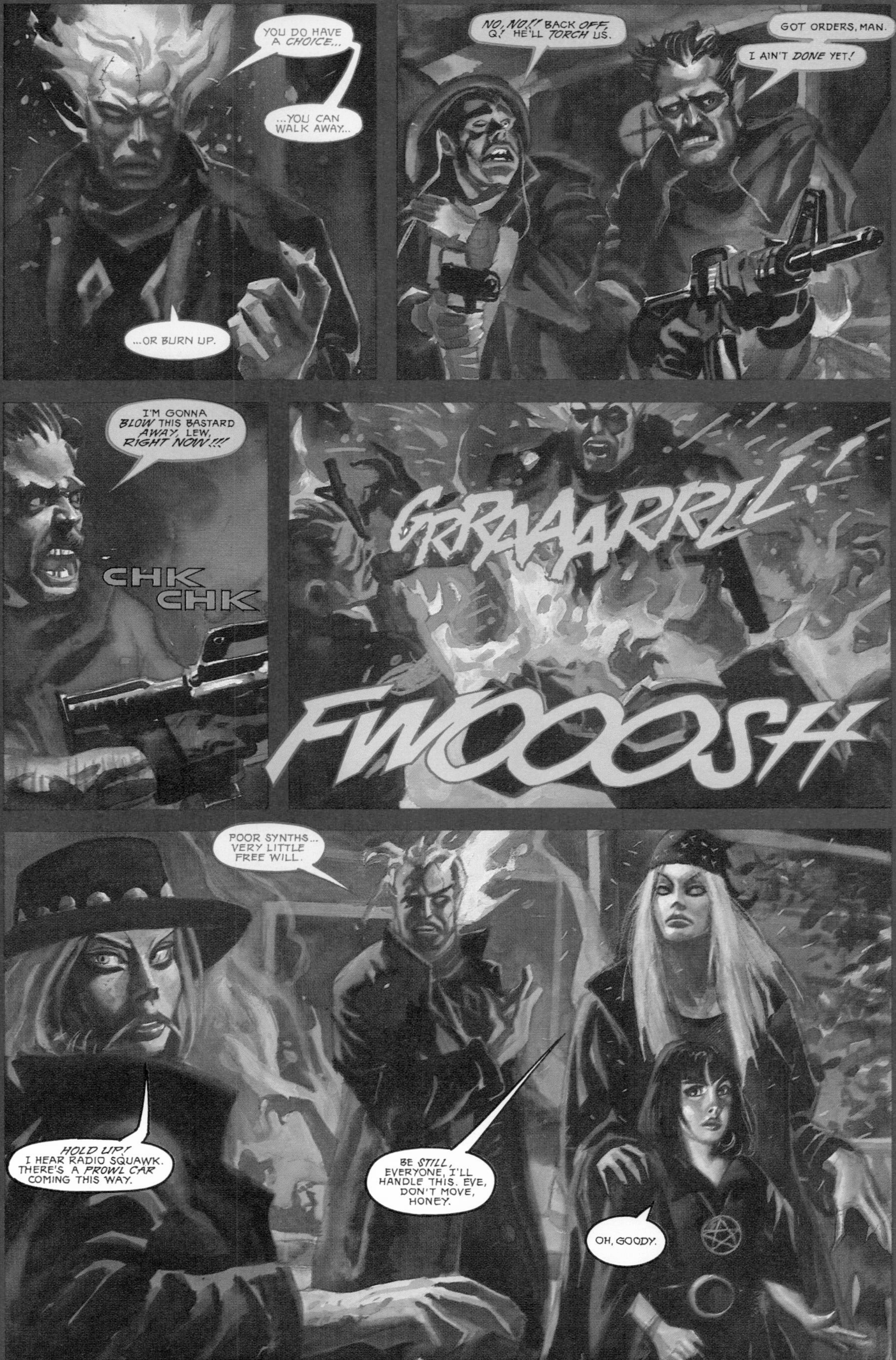
YOU DO HAVE A *CHOICE*...
...YOU CAN WALK AWAY...
...OR BURN UP.
NO, NO!! BACK *OFF*, Q! HE'LL *TORCH* US.
GOT ORDERS, MAN.
I AIN'T *DONE* YET!
I'M GONNA *BLOW* THIS BASTARD *AWAY*, LEW, *RIGHT NOW!!!*
CHK CHK
GRRAAARRRL!
FWOOOSH
POOR SYNTHS... VERY LITTLE FREE WILL.
HOLD UP! I HEAR RADIO SQUAWK. THERE'S A *PROWL CAR* COMING THIS WAY.
BE *STILL*, EVERYONE, I'LL HANDLE THIS. EVE, DON'T MOVE, HONEY.
OH, GOODY.

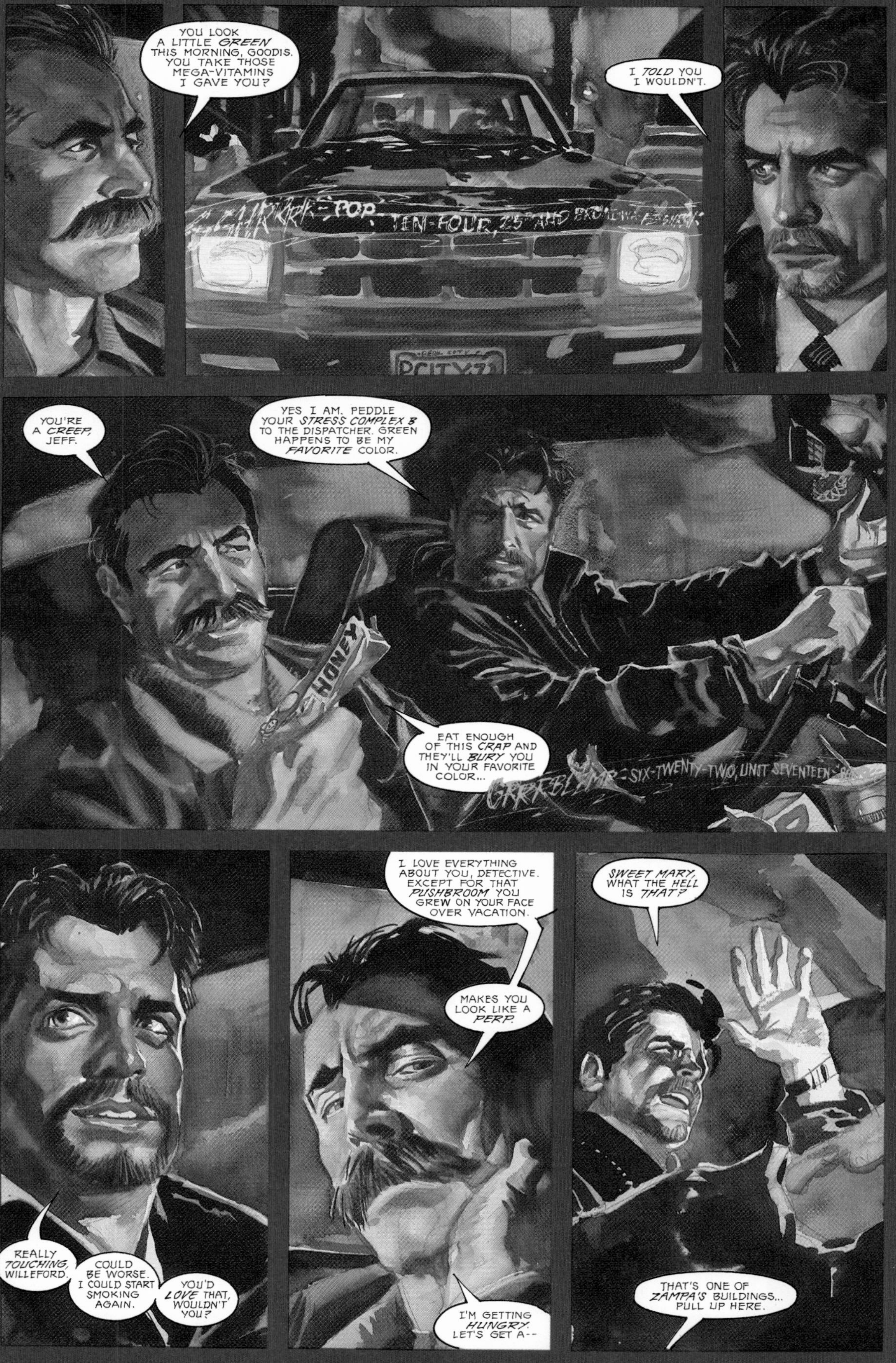
YOU LOOK A LITTLE *GREEN* THIS MORNING, GOODIS. YOU TAKE THOSE MEGA-VITAMINS I GAVE YOU?
POP. TEN-FOUR, 25TH AND
I *TOLD* YOU I WOULDN'T.
YOU'RE A *CREEP*, JEFF.
YES I AM. PEDDLE YOUR *STRESS COMPLEX B* TO THE DISPATCHER. GREEN HAPPENS TO BE MY *FAVORITE* COLOR.
HONEY
EAT ENOUGH OF THIS *CRAP* AND THEY'LL *BURY* YOU IN YOUR FAVORITE COLOR...
GRRRBLEMP - SIX-TWENTY-TWO, UNIT SEVENTEEN
REALLY *TOUCHING*, WILLEFORD.
COULD BE WORSE. I COULD START SMOKING AGAIN.
YOU'D *LOVE* THAT, WOULDN'T YOU?
I LOVE EVERYTHING ABOUT YOU, DETECTIVE. EXCEPT FOR THAT *PUSHBROOM* YOU GREW ON YOUR FACE OVER VACATION.
MAKES YOU LOOK LIKE A *PERP*.
I'M GETTING *HUNGRY*. LET'S GET A--
SWEET MARY, WHAT THE *HELL* IS *THAT*?
THAT'S ONE OF *ZAMPA'S* BUILDINGS... PULL UP HERE.

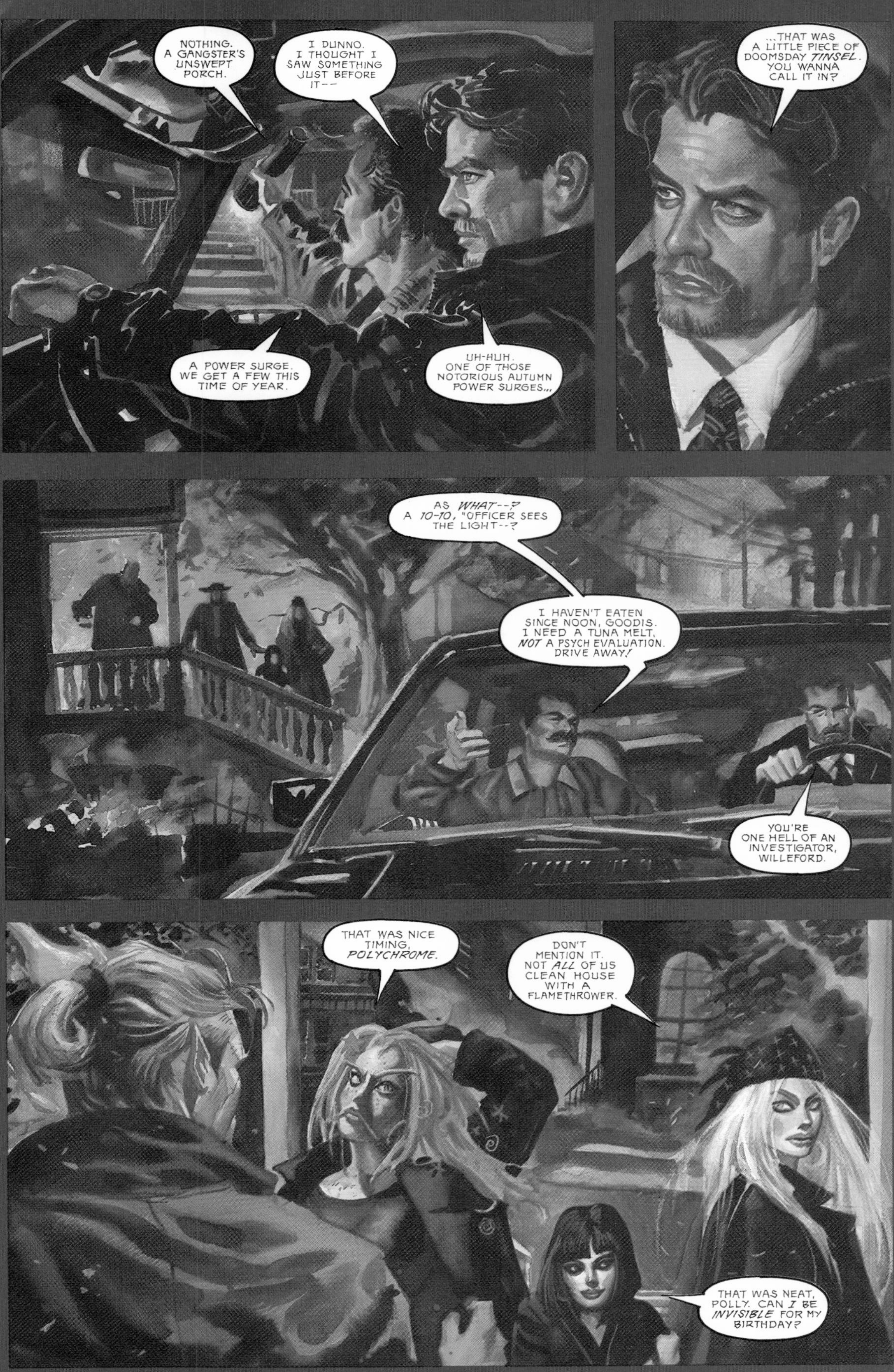
NOTHING. A GANGSTER'S UNSWEPT PORCH.
I DUNNO. I THOUGHT I SAW SOMETHING JUST BEFORE IT--
A POWER SURGE. WE GET A FEW THIS TIME OF YEAR.
UH-HUH. ONE OF THOSE NOTORIOUS AUTUMN POWER SURGES...
...THAT WAS A LITTLE PIECE OF DOOMSDAY TINSEL. YOU WANNA CALL IT IN?
AS WHAT--? A 10-10, "OFFICER SEES THE LIGHT--?
I HAVEN'T EATEN SINCE NOON, GOODIS. I NEED A TUNA MELT, NOT A PSYCH EVALUATION. DRIVE AWAY!
YOU'RE ONE HELL OF AN INVESTIGATOR, WILLEFORD.
THAT WAS NICE TIMING, POLYCHROME.
DON'T MENTION IT. NOT ALL OF US CLEAN HOUSE WITH A FLAMETHROWER.
THAT WAS NEAT, POLLY. CAN I BE INVISIBLE FOR MY BIRTHDAY?

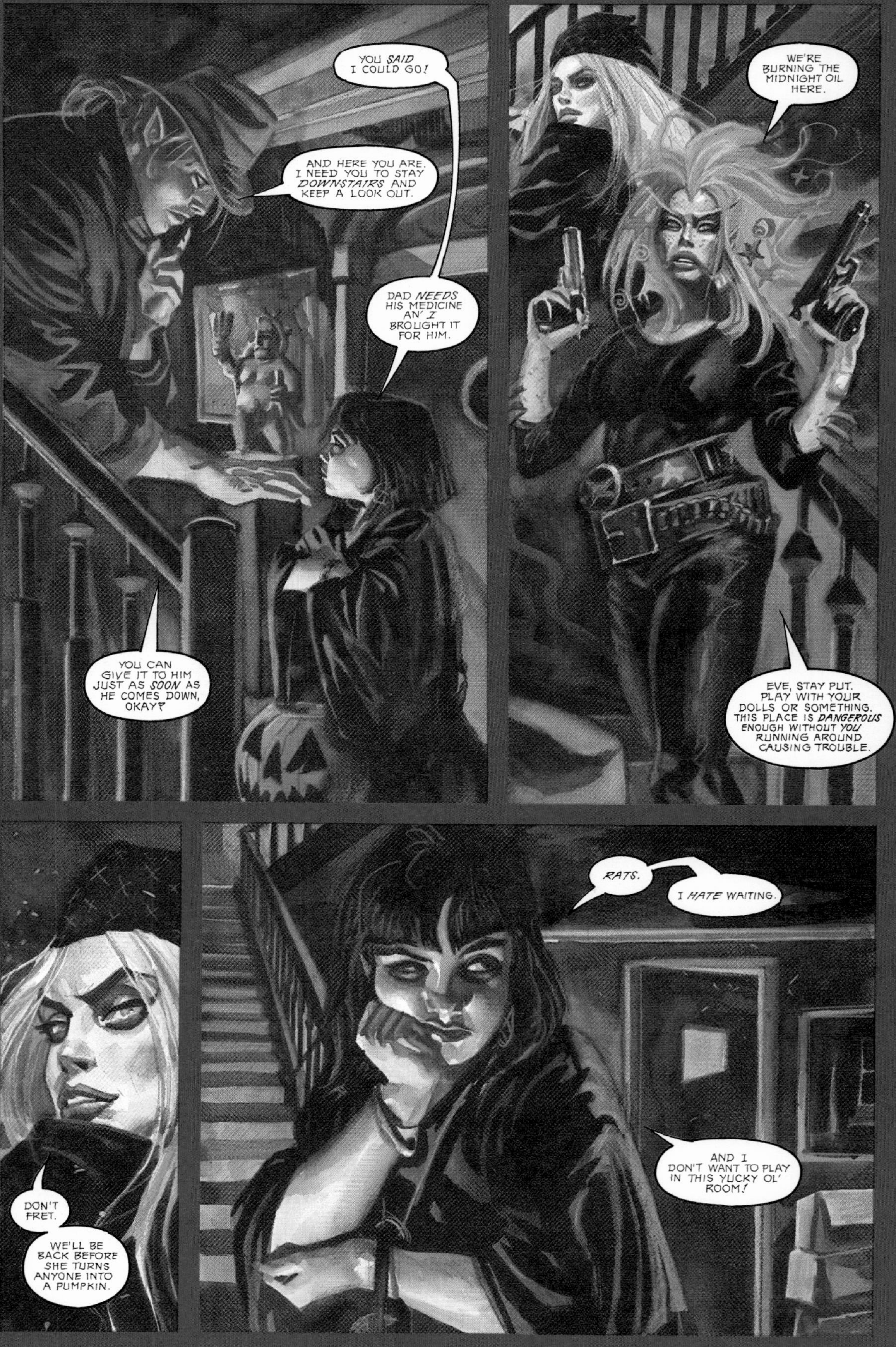

YOU SAID I COULD GO!
AND HERE YOU ARE. I NEED YOU TO STAY DOWNSTAIRS AND KEEP A LOOK OUT.
DAD NEEDS HIS MEDICINE AN' I BROUGHT IT FOR HIM.
YOU CAN GIVE IT TO HIM JUST AS SOON AS HE COMES DOWN, OKAY?
WE'RE BURNING THE MIDNIGHT OIL HERE.
EVE, STAY PUT. PLAY WITH YOUR DOLLS OR SOMETHING. THIS PLACE IS DANGEROUS ENOUGH WITHOUT YOU RUNNING AROUND CAUSING TROUBLE.
DON'T FRET.
WE'LL BE BACK BEFORE SHE TURNS ANYONE INTO A PUMPKIN.
RATS.
I HATE WAITING.
AND I DON'T WANT TO PLAY IN THIS YUCKY OL' ROOM!

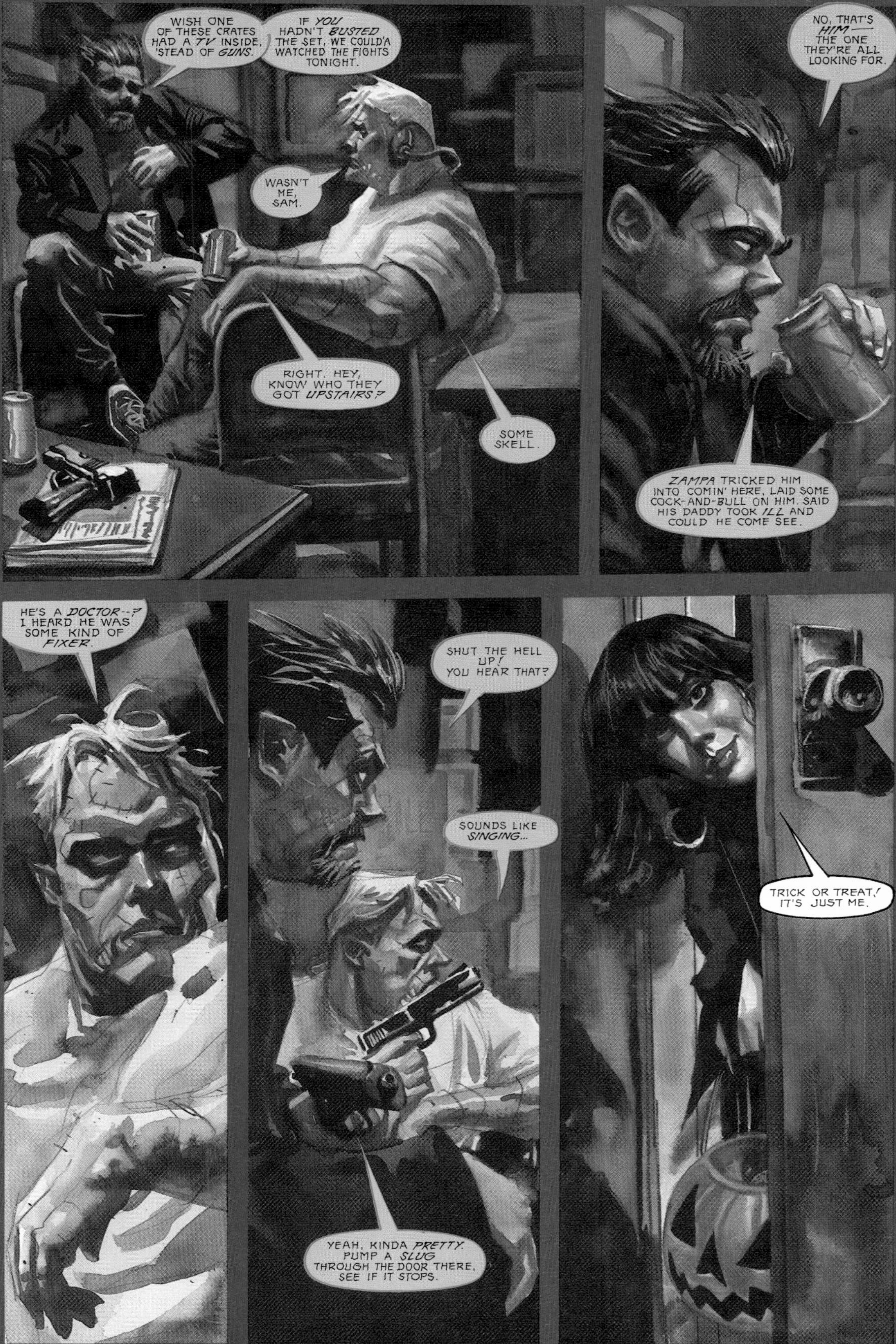

WISH ONE OF THESE CRATES HAD A TV INSIDE, 'STEAD OF GUNS.
IF YOU HADN'T BUSTED THE SET, WE COULD'A WATCHED THE FIGHTS TONIGHT.
WASN'T ME, SAM.
RIGHT. HEY, KNOW WHO THEY GOT UPSTAIRS?
SOME SKELL.
NO, THAT'S HIM— THE ONE THEY'RE ALL LOOKING FOR.
ZAMPA TRICKED HIM INTO COMIN' HERE, LAID SOME COCK-AND-BULL ON HIM. SAID HIS DADDY TOOK ILL AND COULD HE COME SEE.
HE'S A DOCTOR--? I HEARD HE WAS SOME KIND OF FIXER.
SHUT THE HELL UP! YOU HEAR THAT?
SOUNDS LIKE SINGING...
YEAH, KINDA PRETTY. PUMP A SLUG THROUGH THE DOOR THERE, SEE IF IT STOPS.
TRICK OR TREAT! IT'S JUST ME.

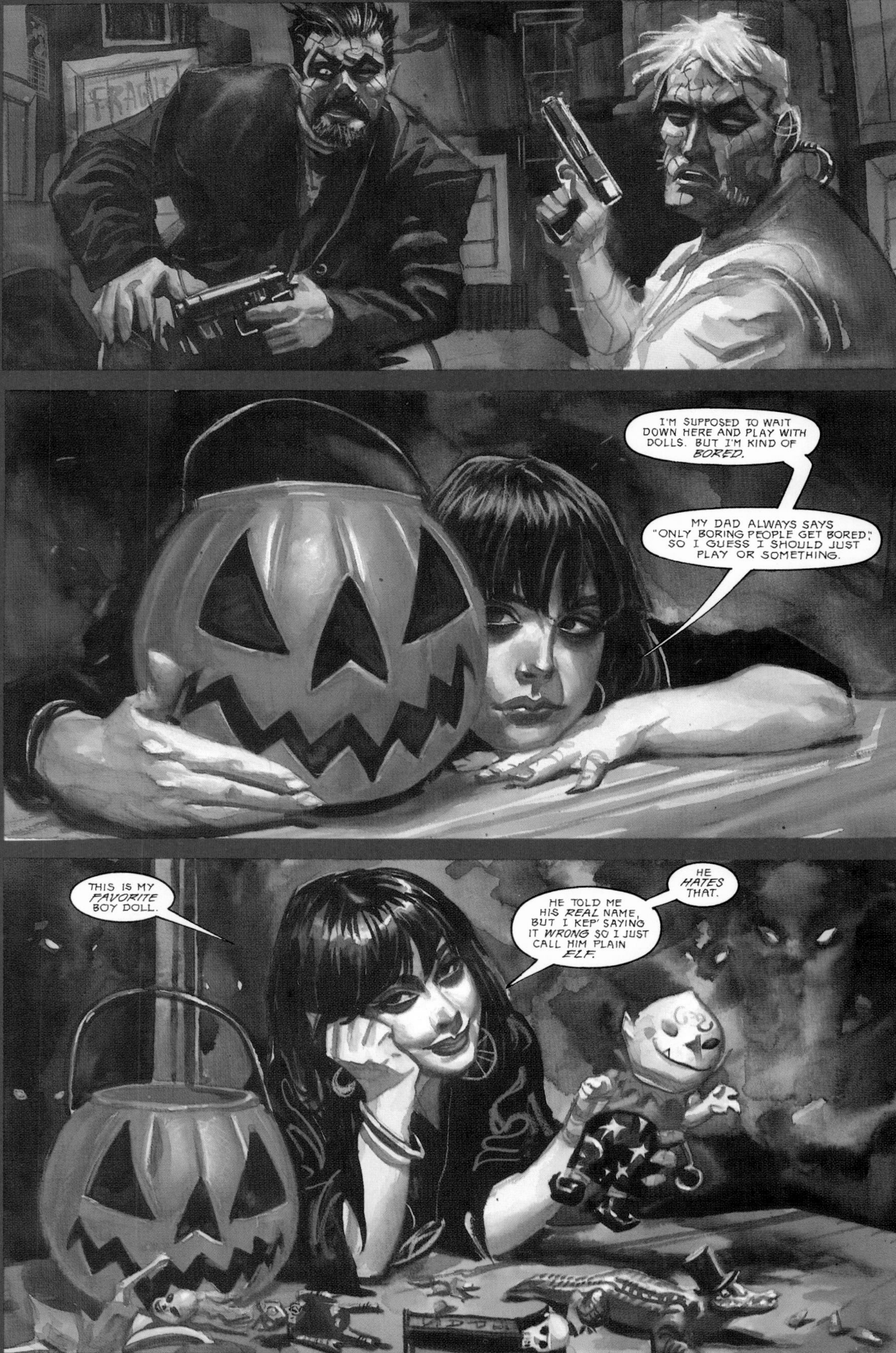
FRAGILE
I'M SUPPOSED TO WAIT DOWN HERE AND PLAY WITH DOLLS. BUT I'M KIND OF *BORED.*
MY DAD ALWAYS SAYS "ONLY BORING PEOPLE GET BORED," SO I GUESS I SHOULD JUST PLAY OR SOMETHING.
THIS IS MY *FAVORITE* BOY DOLL.
HE TOLD ME HIS *REAL* NAME, BUT I KEP' SAYING IT *WRONG* SO I JUST CALL HIM PLAIN *ELF.*
HE *HATES* THAT.

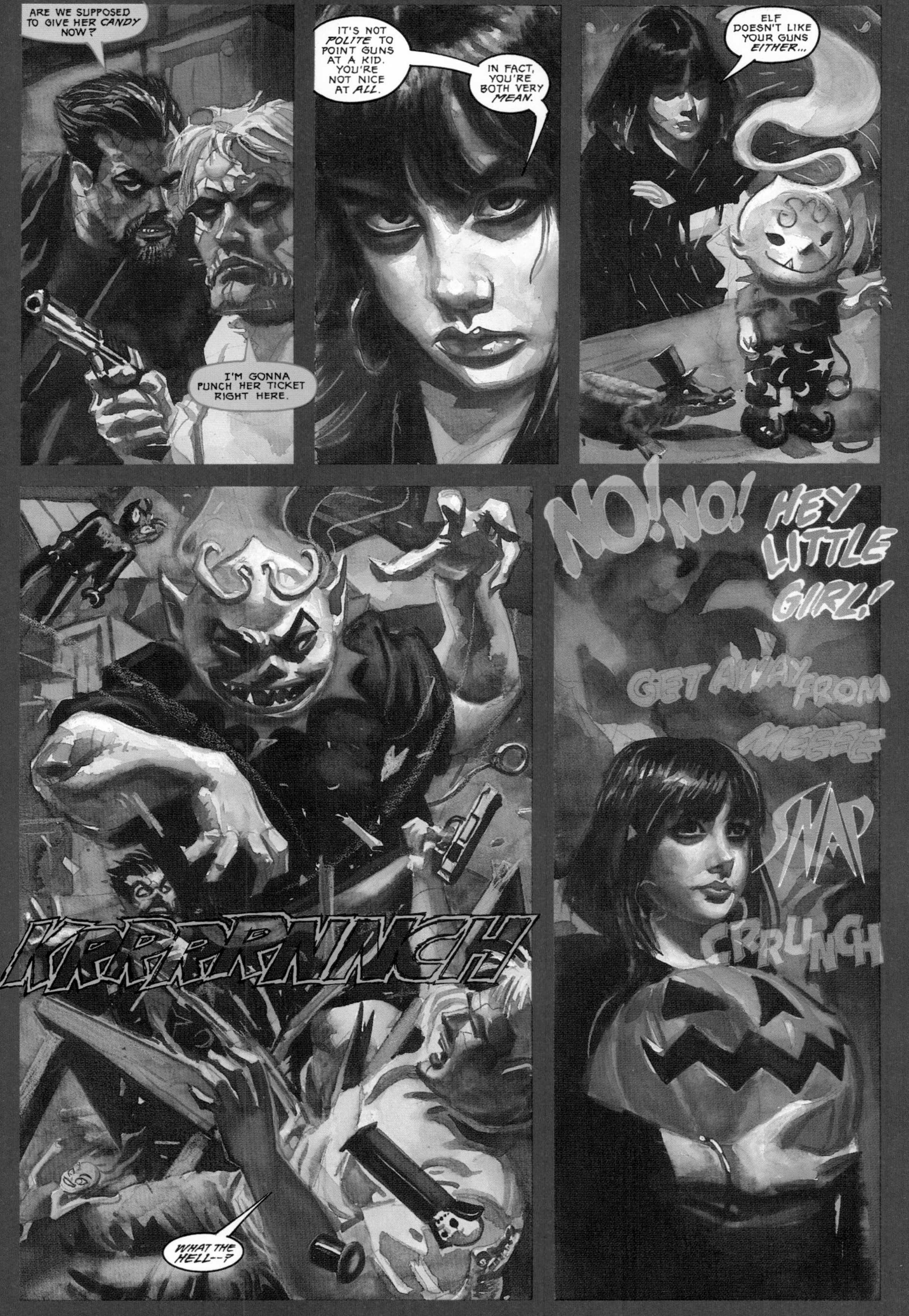
ARE WE SUPPOSED TO GIVE HER *CANDY* NOW?
I'M GONNA PUNCH HER TICKET RIGHT HERE.
IT'S NOT *POLITE* TO POINT GUNS AT A KID. YOU'RE NOT NICE AT *ALL*.
IN FACT, YOU'RE BOTH VERY *MEAN*.
ELF DOESN'T LIKE YOUR GUNS *EITHER*...
KRRRRNNCH
WHAT THE HELL--?
NO! NO! HEY LITTLE GIRL!
GET AWAY FROM MEEEE
SNAP
CRRUNCH

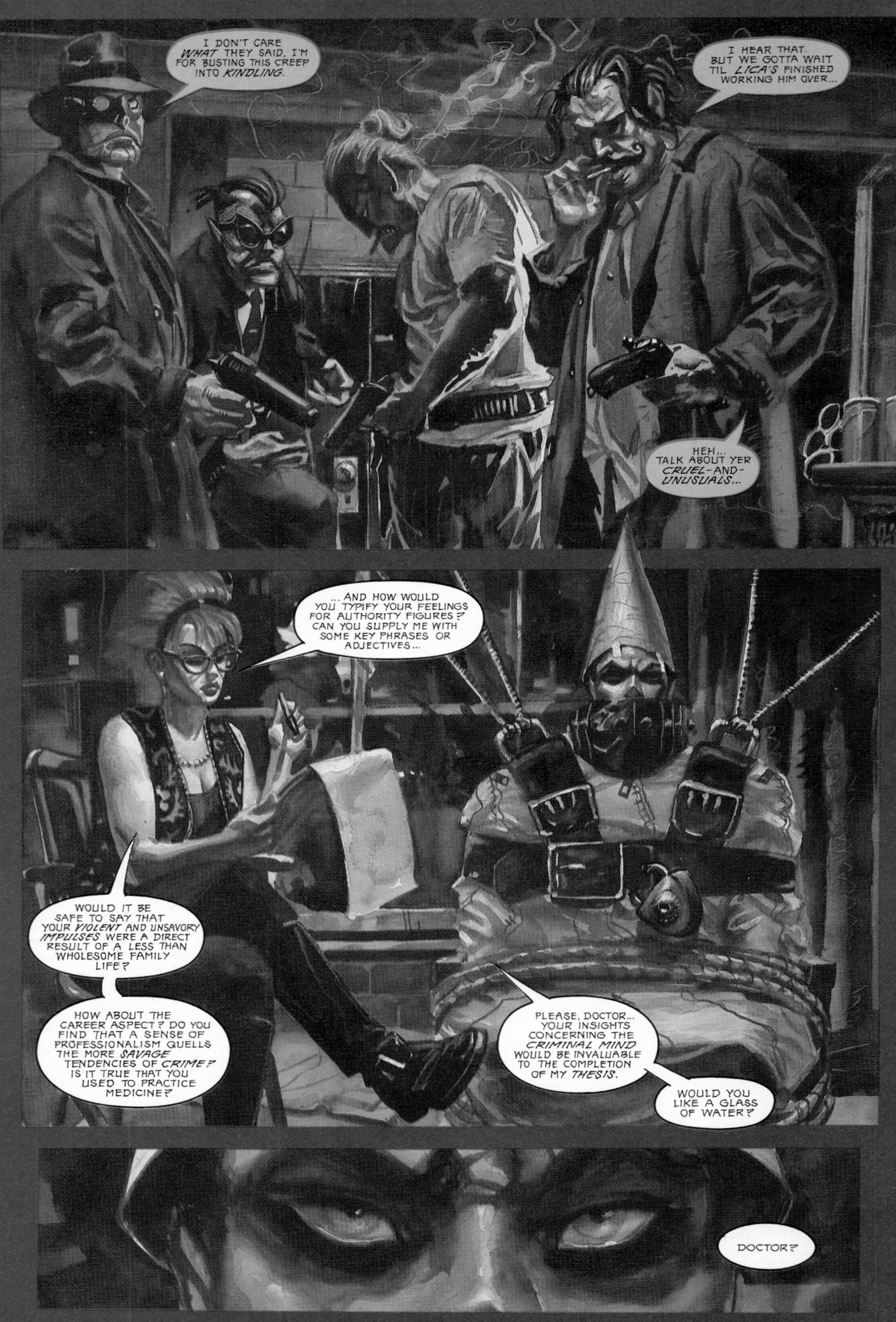

I DON'T CARE *WHAT* THEY SAID, I'M FOR BUSTING THIS CREEP INTO *KINDLING*.
I HEAR THAT. BUT WE GOTTA WAIT TIL *LICA'S* FINISHED WORKING HIM OVER...
HEH... TALK ABOUT YER *CRUEL*-AND-*UNUSUALS*...
... AND HOW WOULD YOU TYPIFY YOUR FEELINGS FOR AUTHORITY FIGURES? CAN YOU SUPPLY ME WITH SOME KEY PHRASES OR ADJECTIVES...
WOULD IT BE SAFE TO SAY THAT YOUR *VIOLENT* AND UNSAVORY *IMPULSES* WERE A DIRECT RESULT OF A LESS THAN WHOLESOME FAMILY LIFE?
HOW ABOUT THE CAREER ASPECT? DO YOU FIND THAT A SENSE OF PROFESSIONALISM QUELLS THE MORE *SAVAGE* TENDENCIES OF *CRIME*? IS IT TRUE THAT YOU USED TO PRACTICE MEDICINE?
PLEASE, DOCTOR... YOUR INSIGHTS CONCERNING THE *CRIMINAL MIND* WOULD BE INVALUABLE TO THE COMPLETION OF MY *THESIS*.
WOULD YOU LIKE A GLASS OF WATER?
DOCTOR?

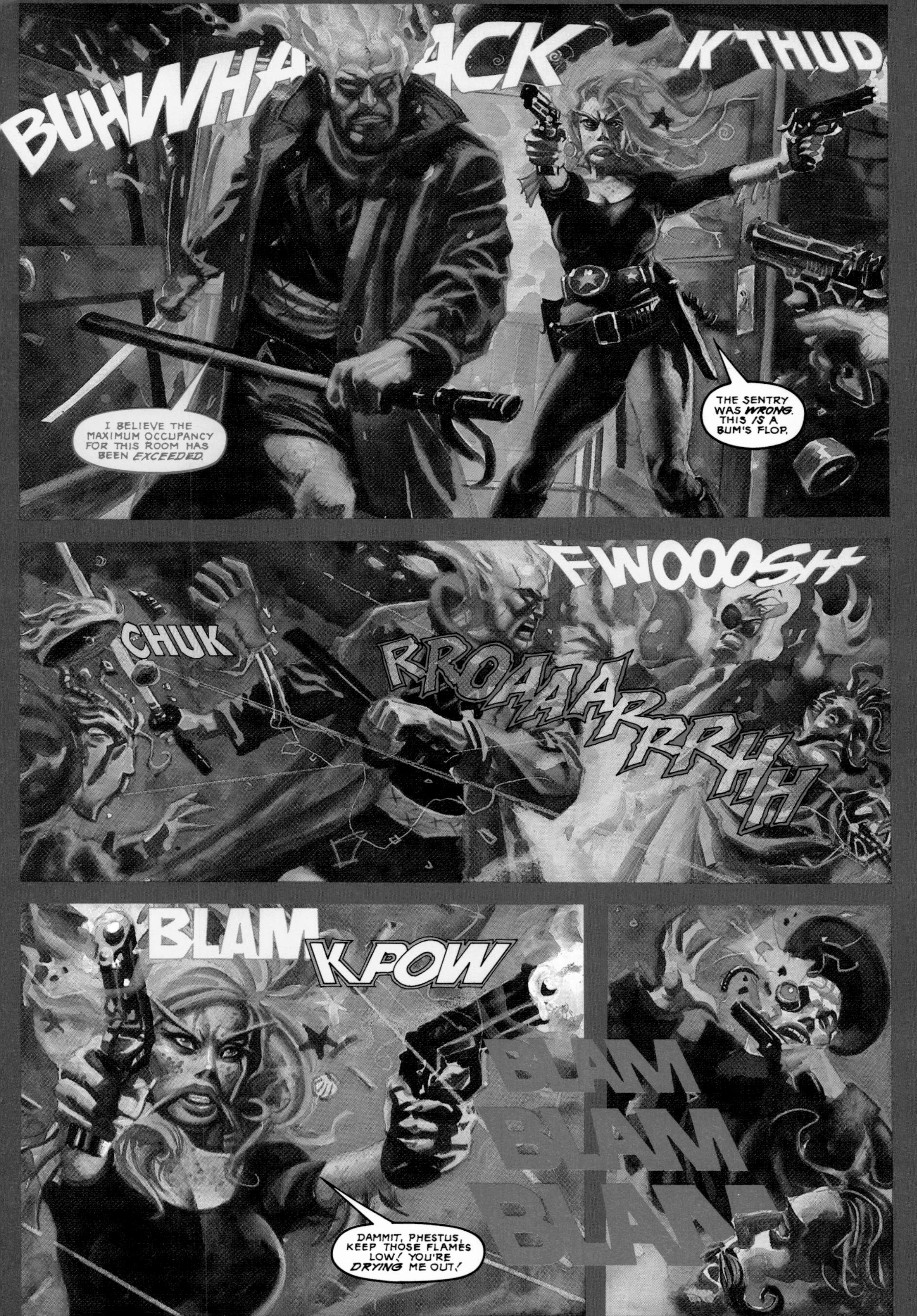
BUHWHA ACK
K THUD
I BELIEVE THE MAXIMUM OCCUPANCY FOR THIS ROOM HAS BEEN *EXCEEDED*.
THE SENTRY WAS *WRONG*. THIS *IS* A BUM'S FLOP.
FWOOOSH
CHUK
RROAAARRRHH
BLAM
KPOW
BLAM
BLAM
DAMMIT, PHESTUS, KEEP THOSE FLAMES LOW! YOU'RE *DRYING* ME OUT!

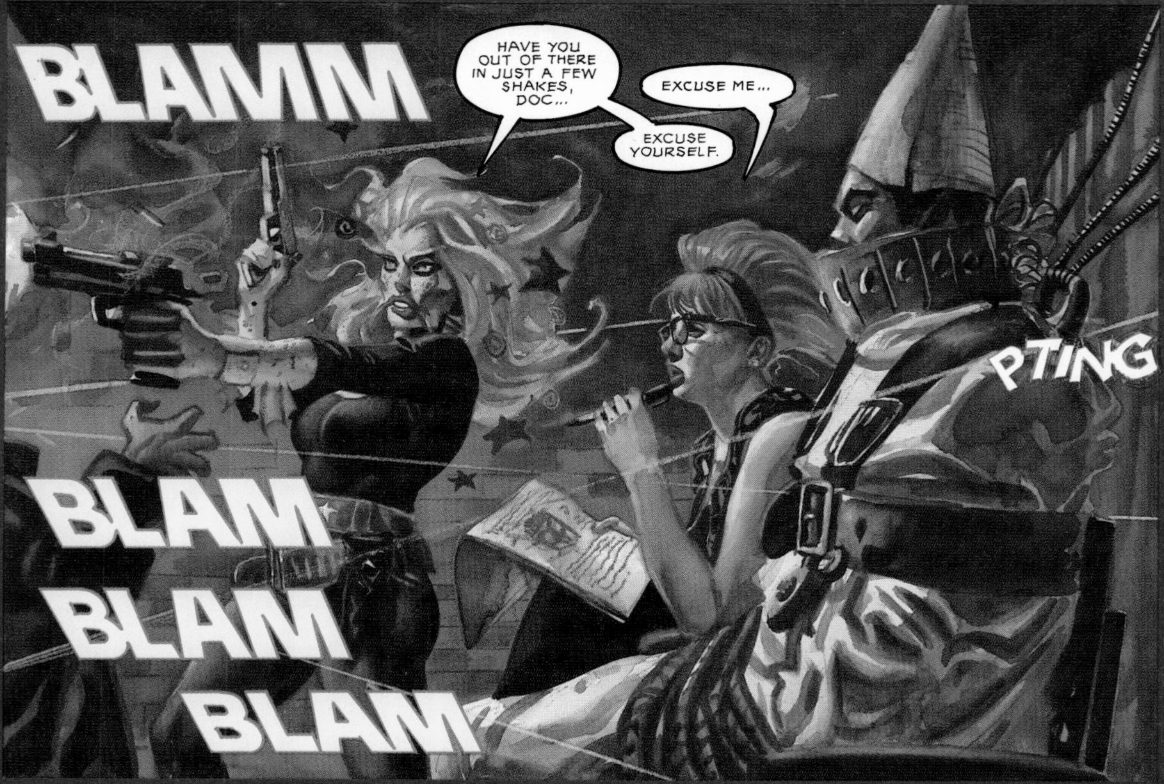
BLAMM
HAVE YOU OUT OF THERE IN JUST A FEW SHAKES, DOC...
EXCUSE ME...
EXCUSE YOURSELF.
PTING
BLAM
BLAM
BLAM

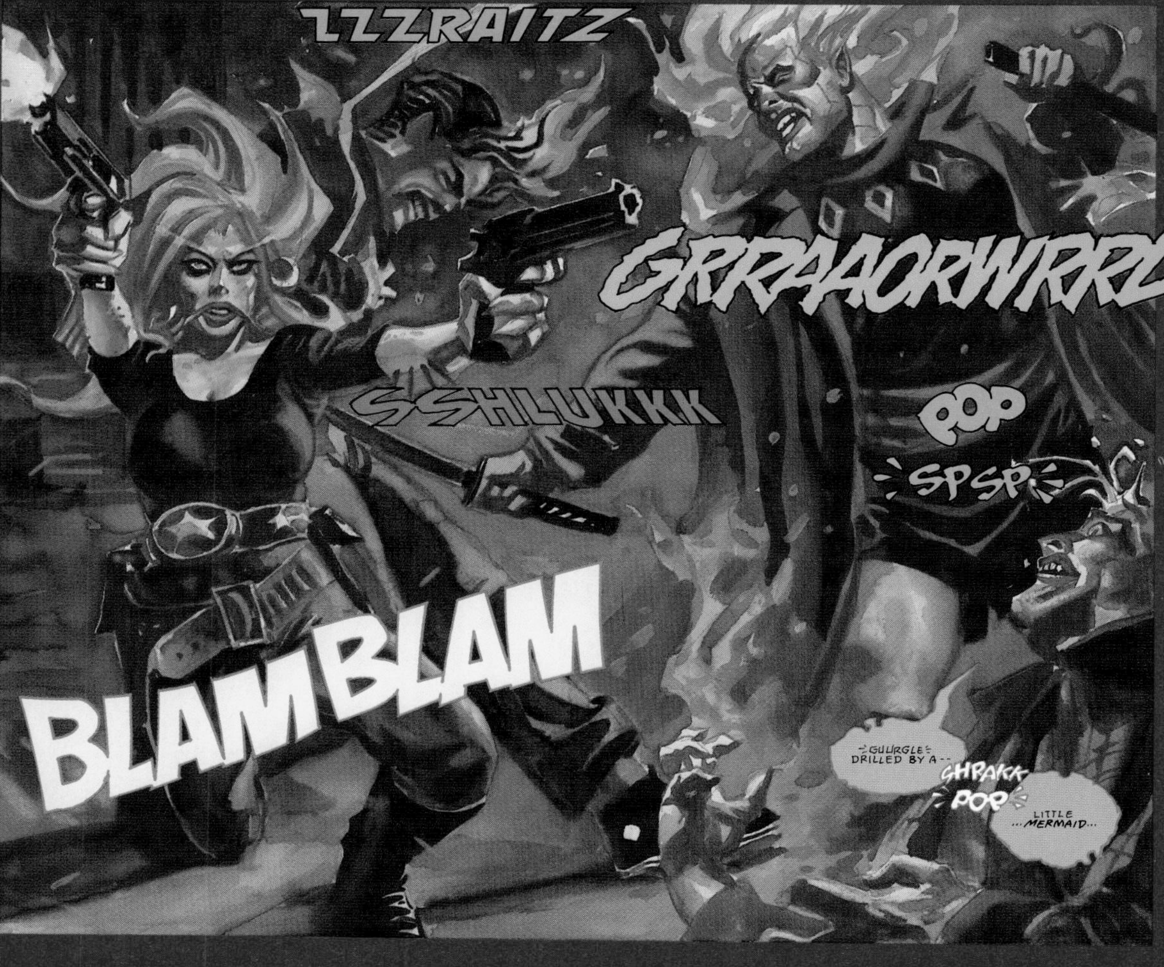
ZZZRAITZ
GRRAAORWRRRL
SSHLUKKK
POP
SPSP
BLAM BLAM
GUURGLE DRILLED BY A--
SHRAKK
POP
LITTLE ...MERMAID...

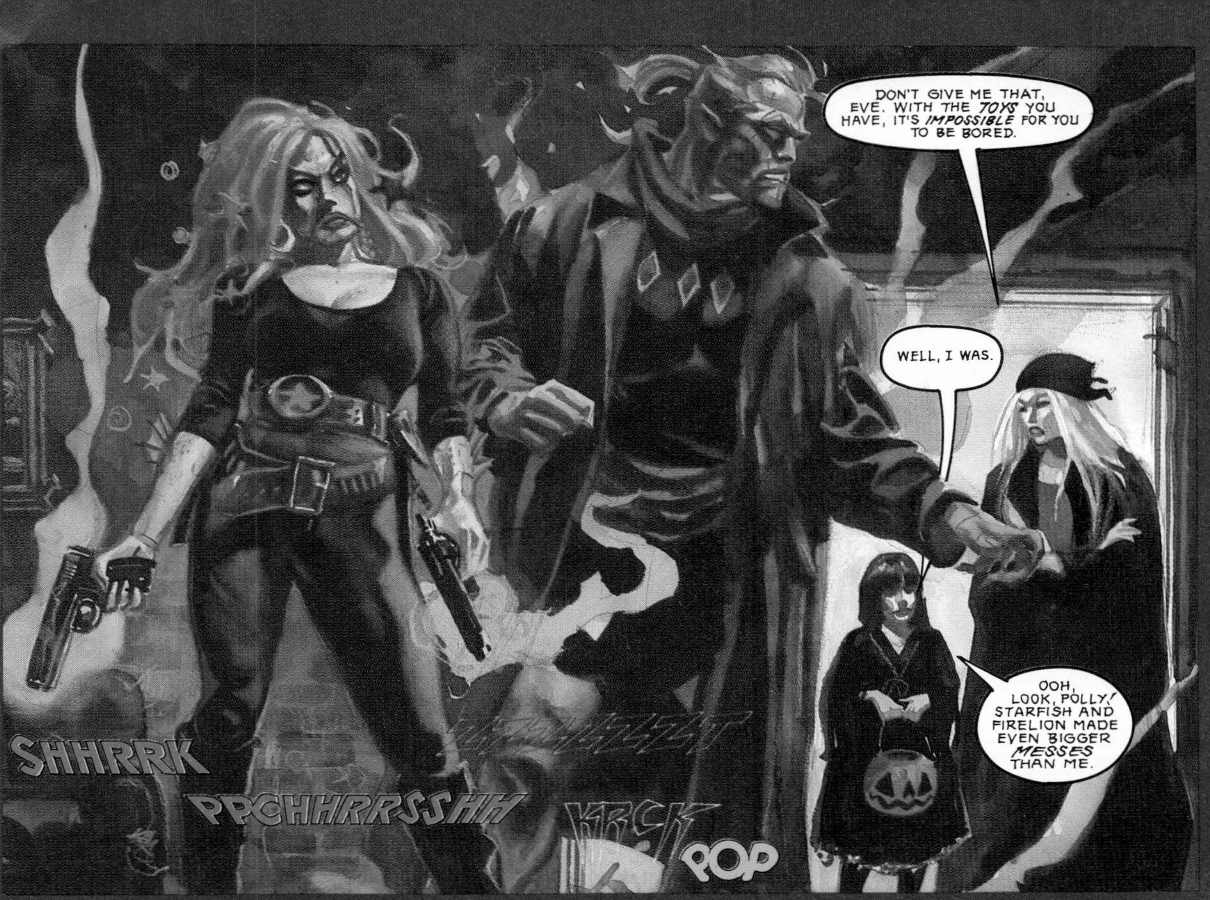
DON'T GIVE ME THAT, EVE. WITH THE *TOYS* YOU HAVE, IT'S *IMPOSSIBLE* FOR YOU TO BE BORED.
WELL, I WAS.
OOH, LOOK, POLLY! STARFISH AND FIRELION MADE EVEN BIGGER *MESSES* THAN ME.
SHHRRK
PPCHHRRSSHH
KRCK
POP

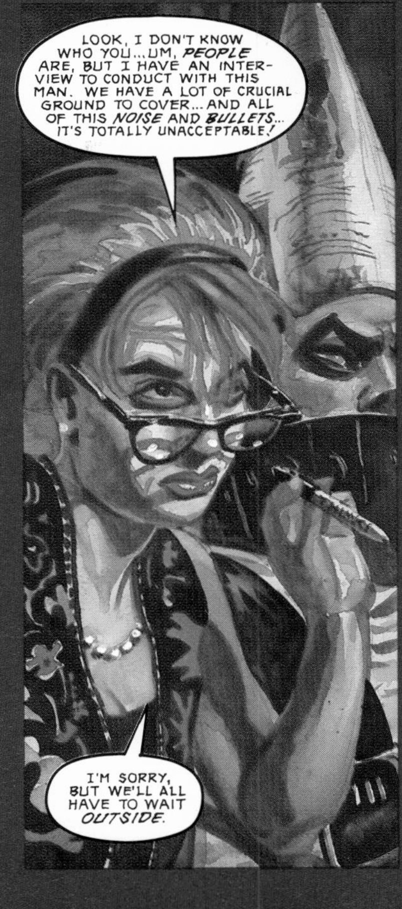
LOOK, I DON'T KNOW WHO YOU...UM, *PEOPLE* ARE, BUT I HAVE AN INTER-VIEW TO CONDUCT WITH THIS MAN. WE HAVE A LOT OF CRUCIAL GROUND TO COVER... AND ALL OF THIS *NOISE* AND *BULLETS*... IT'S TOTALLY UNACCEPTABLE!
I'M SORRY, BUT WE'LL ALL HAVE TO WAIT *OUTSIDE*.

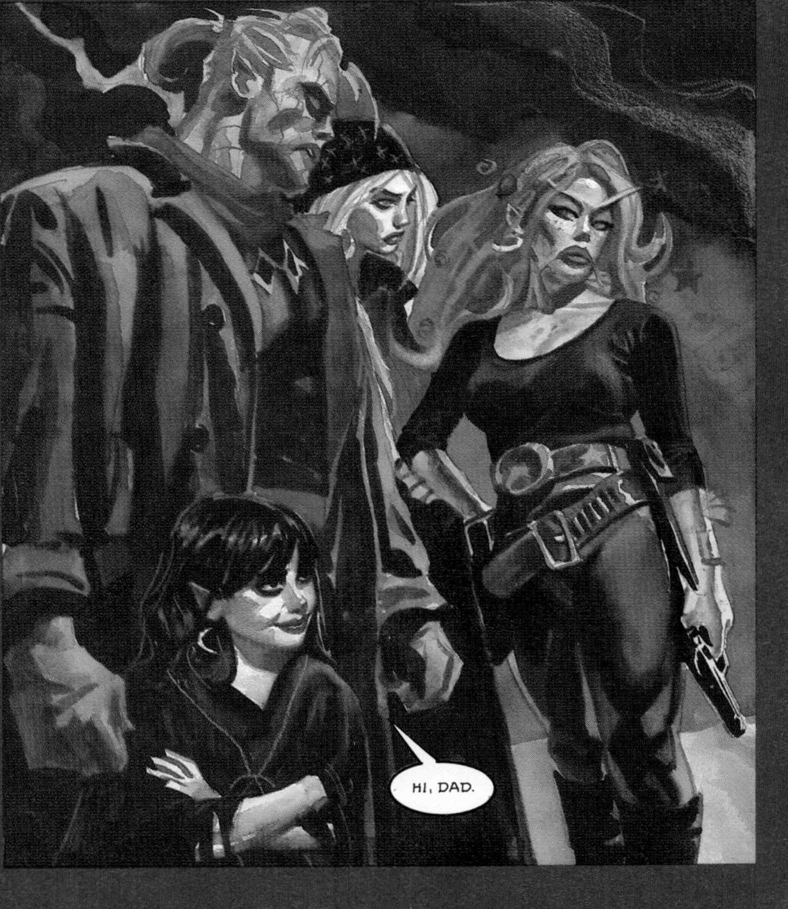
HI, DAD.

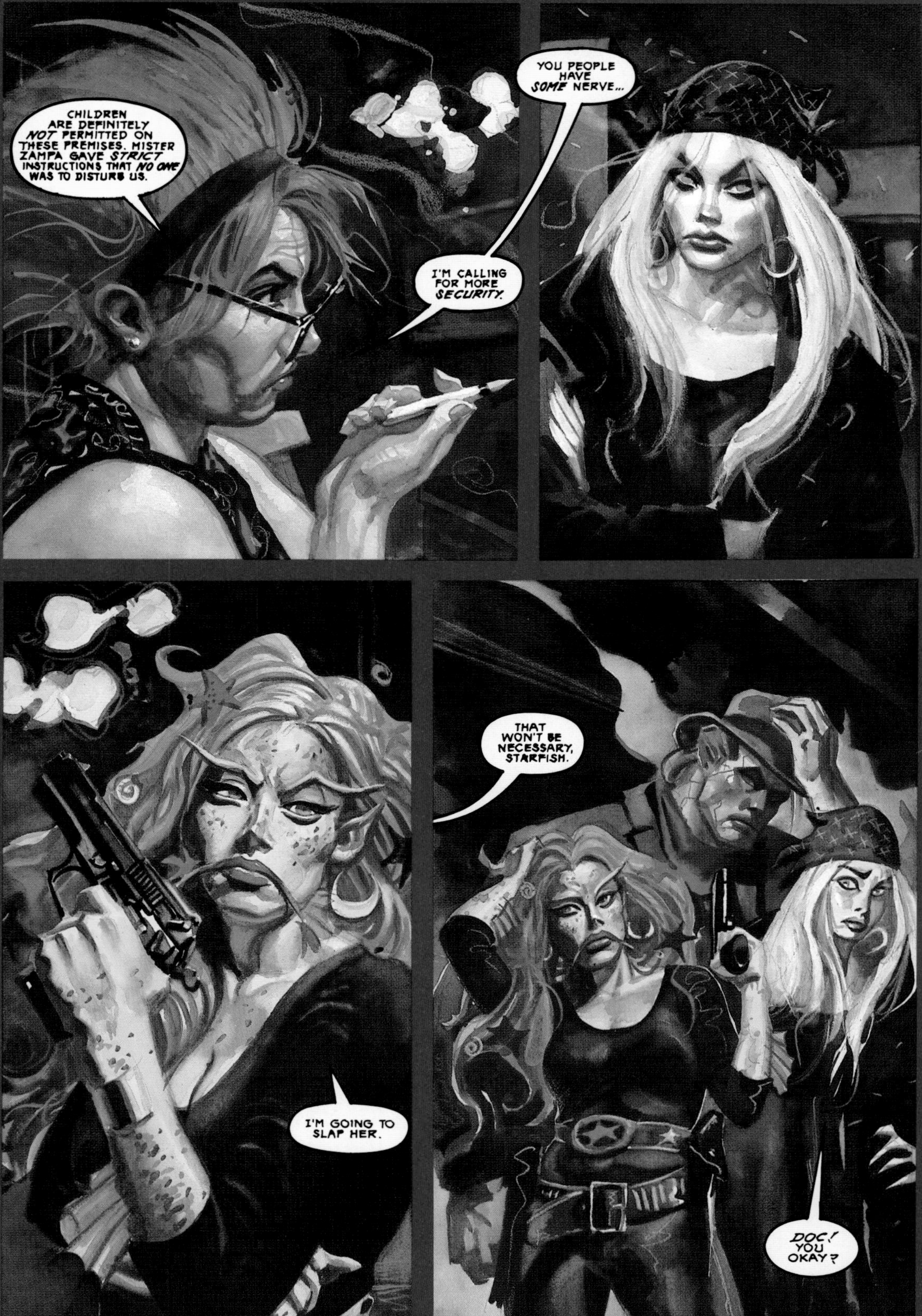
CHILDREN ARE DEFINITELY *NOT* PERMITTED ON THESE PREMISES. MISTER ZAMPA GAVE *STRICT* INSTRUCTIONS THAT *NO ONE* WAS TO DISTURB US.
YOU PEOPLE HAVE *SOME* NERVE...
I'M CALLING FOR MORE *SECURITY*.
I'M GOING TO SLAP HER.
THAT WON'T BE NECESSARY, STARFISH.
DOC! YOU OKAY?

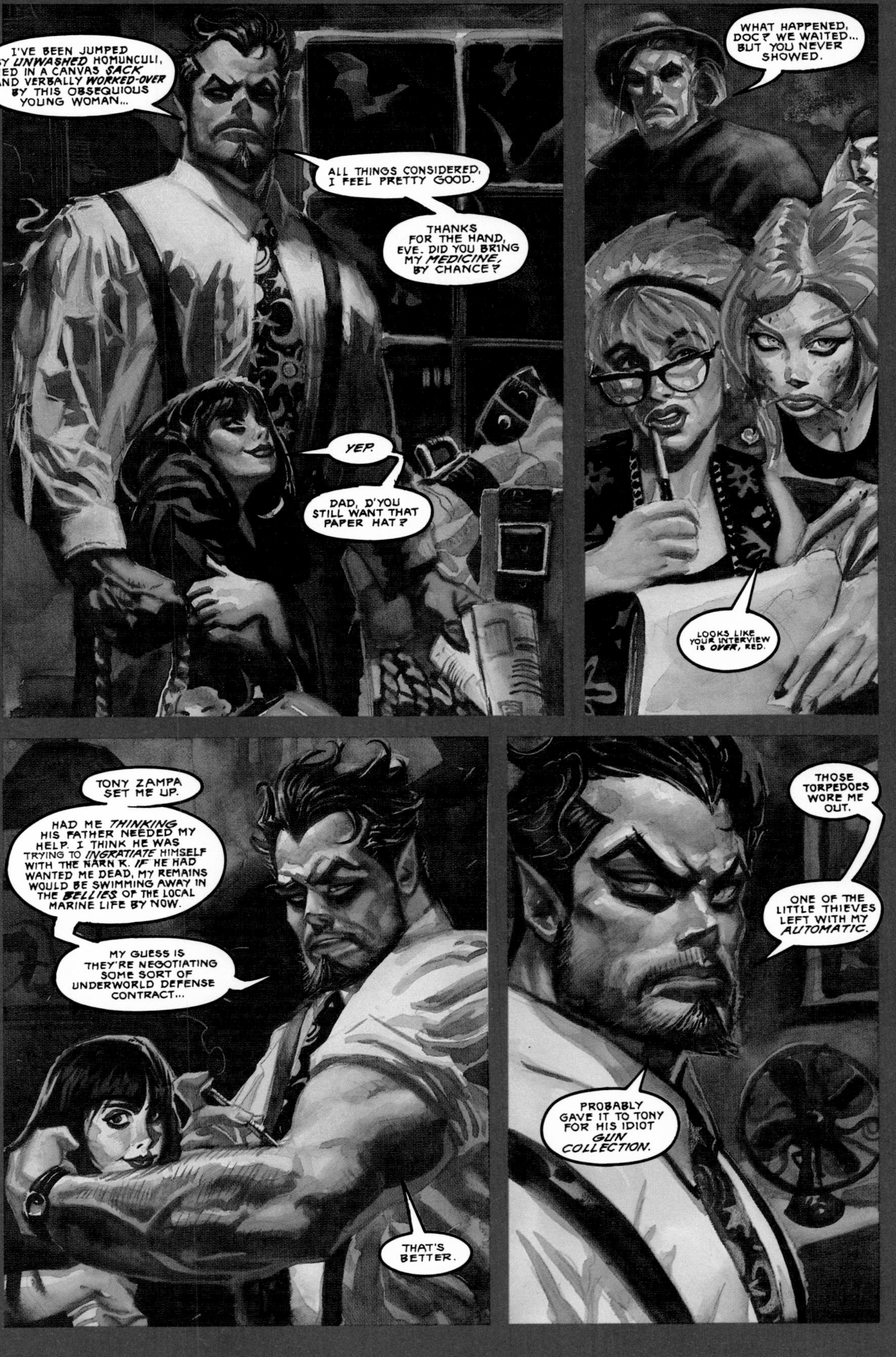

I'VE BEEN JUMPED BY *UNWASHED* HOMUNCULI, TIED IN A CANVAS *SACK* AND VERBALLY *WORKED-OVER* BY THIS OBSEQUIOUS YOUNG WOMAN...
ALL THINGS CONSIDERED, I FEEL PRETTY GOOD.
THANKS FOR THE HAND, EVE. DID YOU BRING MY *MEDICINE*, BY CHANCE?
YEP.
DAD, D'YOU STILL WANT THAT PAPER HAT?
WHAT HAPPENED, DOC? WE WAITED... BUT YOU NEVER SHOWED.
LOOKS LIKE YOUR INTERVIEW IS *OVER*, RED.
TONY ZAMPA SET ME UP.
HAD ME *THINKING* HIS FATHER NEEDED MY HELP. I THINK HE WAS TRYING TO *INGRATIATE* HIMSELF WITH THE NARN K. *IF* HE HAD WANTED ME DEAD, MY REMAINS WOULD BE SWIMMING AWAY IN THE *BELLIES* OF THE LOCAL MARINE LIFE BY NOW.
MY GUESS IS THEY'RE NEGOTIATING SOME SORT OF UNDERWORLD DEFENSE CONTRACT...
THAT'S BETTER.
THOSE TORPEDOES WORE ME OUT.
ONE OF THE LITTLE THIEVES LEFT WITH MY *AUTOMATIC*.
PROBABLY GAVE IT TO TONY FOR HIS IDIOT *GUN COLLECTION*.

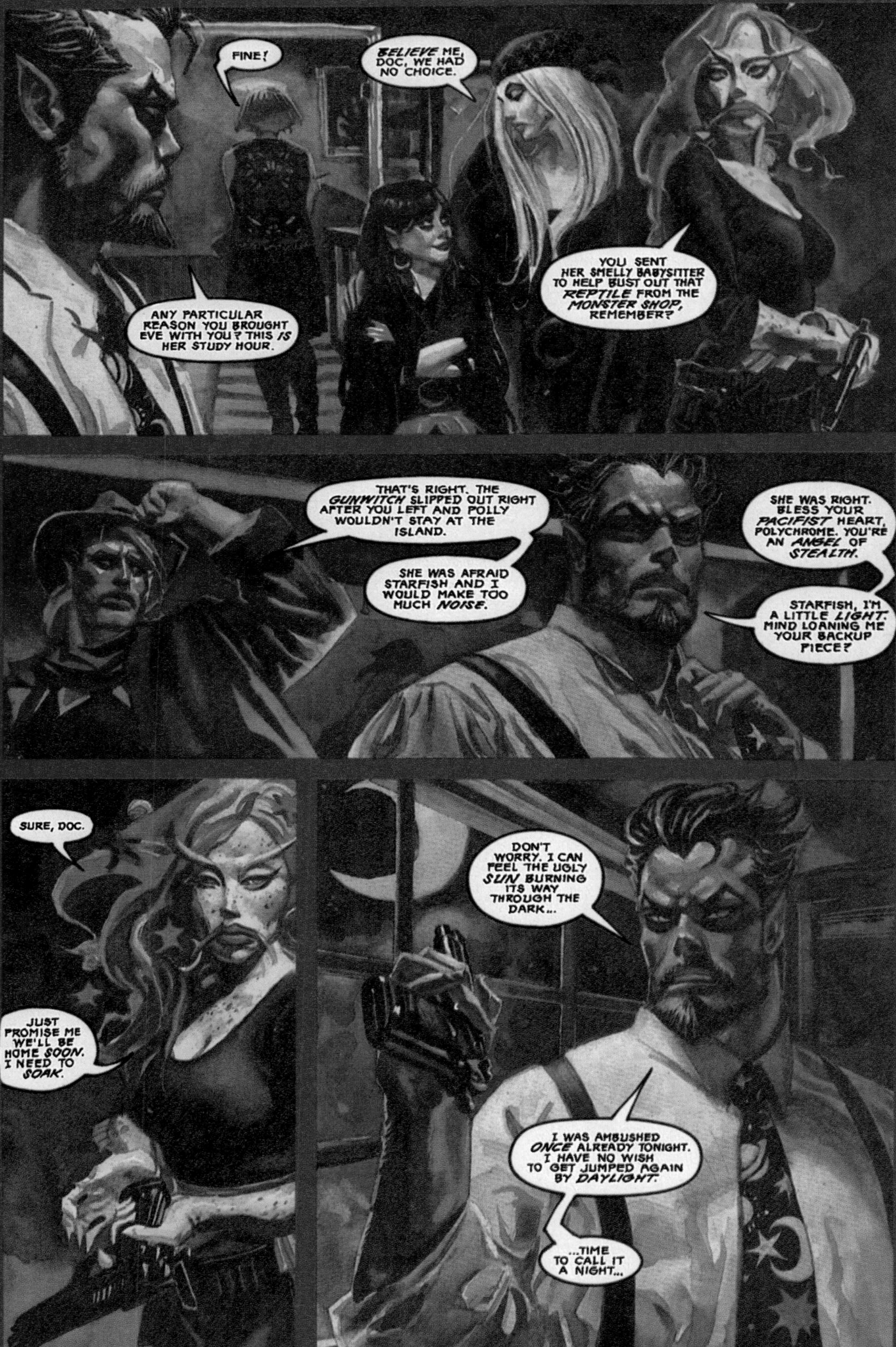
FINE!
BELIEVE ME, DOC, WE HAD NO CHOICE.
ANY PARTICULAR REASON YOU BROUGHT EVE WITH YOU? THIS IS HER STUDY HOUR.
YOU SENT HER SMELLY BABYSITTER TO HELP BUST OUT THAT REPTILE FROM THE MONSTER SHOP, REMEMBER?
THAT'S RIGHT. THE GUNWITCH SLIPPED OUT RIGHT AFTER YOU LEFT AND POLLY WOULDN'T STAY AT THE ISLAND.
SHE WAS AFRAID STARFISH AND I WOULD MAKE TOO MUCH NOISE.
SHE WAS RIGHT. BLESS YOUR PACIFIST HEART, POLYCHROME. YOU'RE AN ANGEL OF STEALTH.
STARFISH, I'M A LITTLE LIGHT. MIND LOANING ME YOUR BACKUP PIECE?
SURE, DOC.
JUST PROMISE ME WE'LL BE HOME SOON. I NEED TO SOAK.
DON'T WORRY. I CAN FEEL THE UGLY SUN BURNING ITS WAY THROUGH THE DARK...
I WAS AMBUSHED ONCE ALREADY TONIGHT. I HAVE NO WISH TO GET JUMPED AGAIN BY DAYLIGHT.
...TIME TO CALL IT A NIGHT...

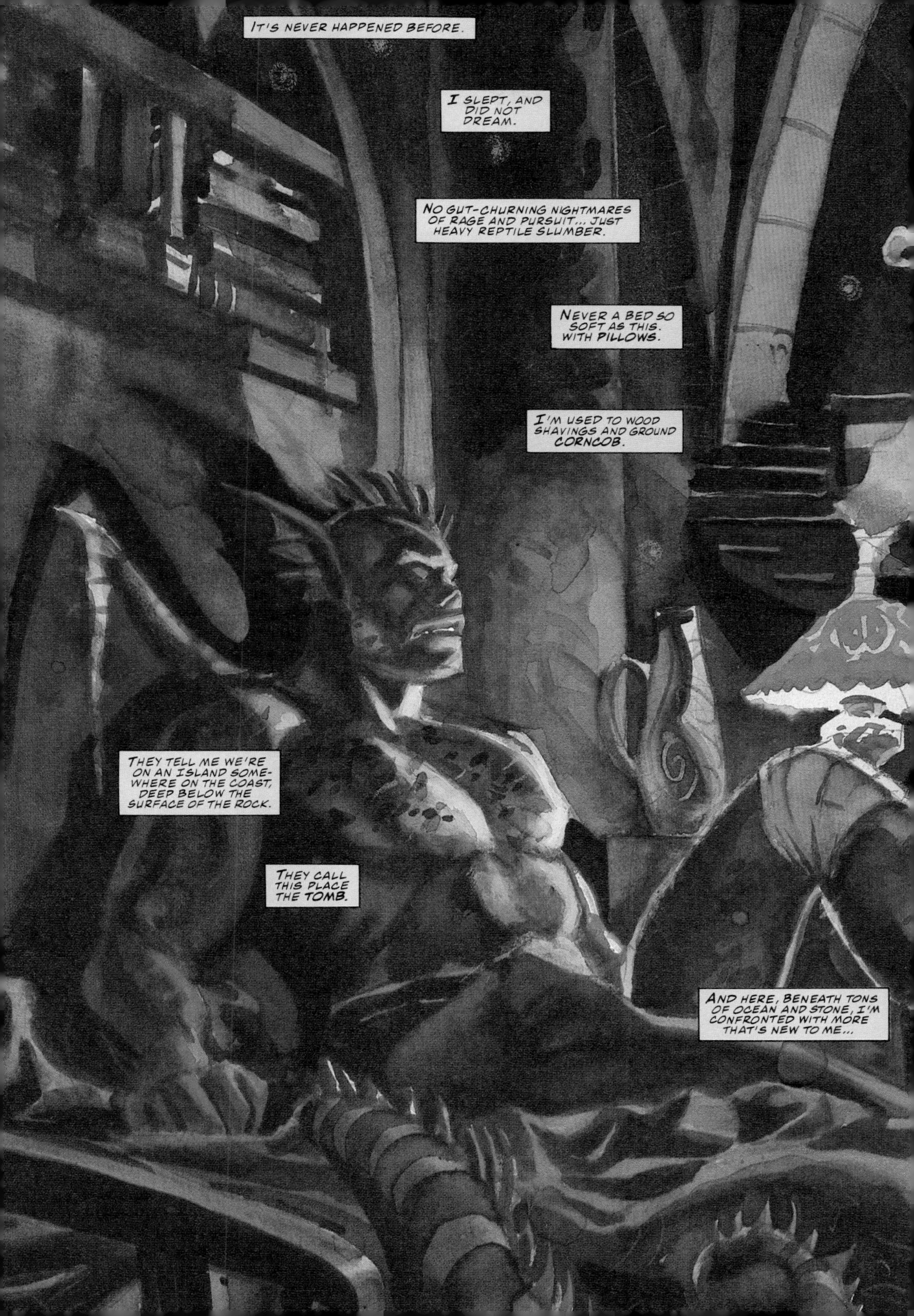
It's never happened before.
I slept, and did not dream.
No gut-churning nightmares of rage and pursuit... just heavy reptile slumber.
Never a bed so soft as this. With pillows.
I'm used to wood shavings and ground corncob.
They tell me we're on an island somewhere on the coast, deep below the surface of the Rock.
They call this place the Tomb.
And here, beneath tons of ocean and stone, I'm confronted with more that's new to me...

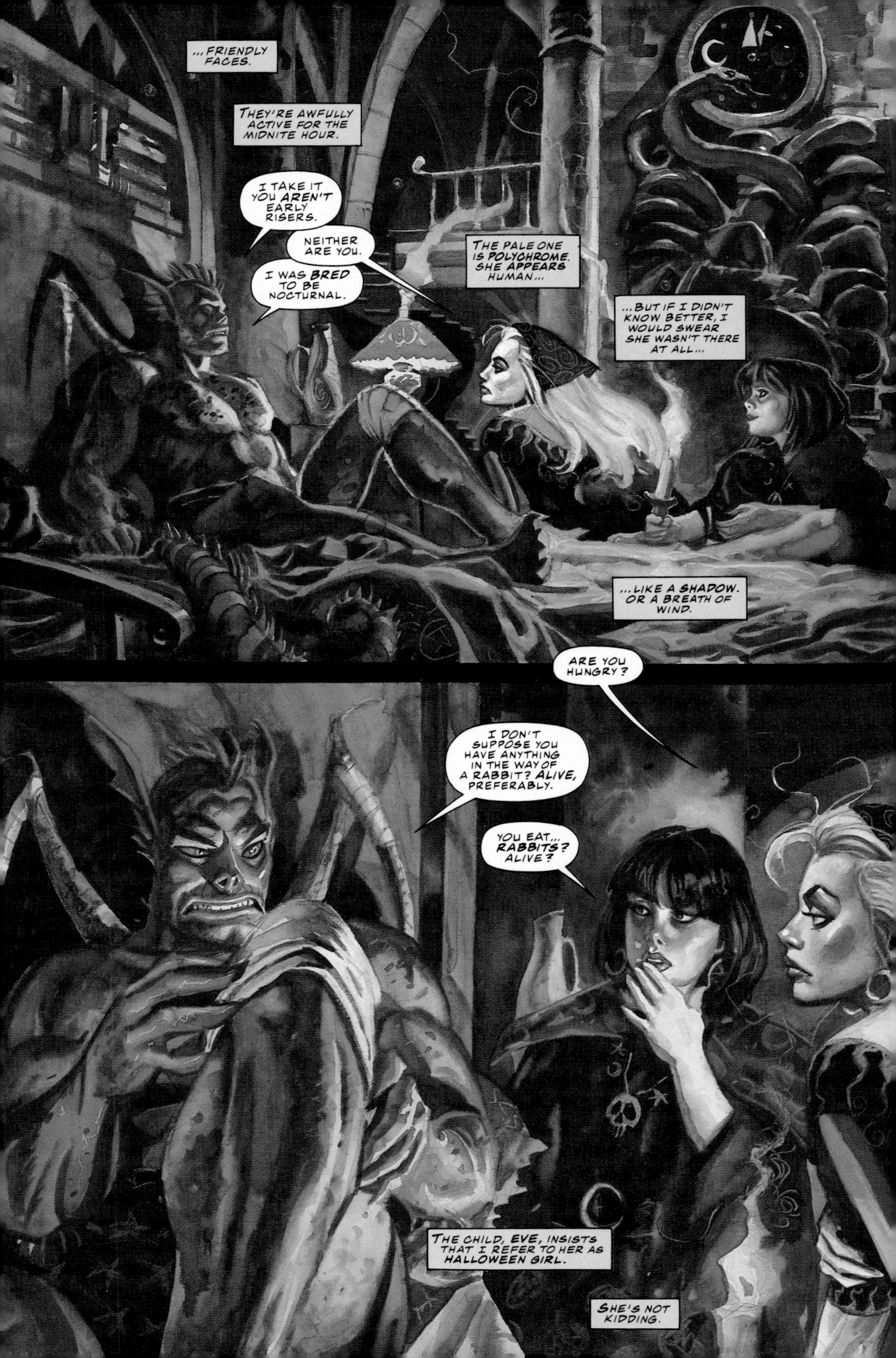
...FRIENDLY FACES.
THEY'RE AWFULLY ACTIVE FOR THE MIDNITE HOUR.
I TAKE IT YOU AREN'T EARLY RISERS.
NEITHER ARE YOU.
I WAS BRED TO BE NOCTURNAL.
THE PALE ONE IS POLYCHROME. SHE APPEARS HUMAN...
...BUT IF I DIDN'T KNOW BETTER, I WOULD SWEAR SHE WASN'T THERE AT ALL...
...LIKE A SHADOW. OR A BREATH OF WIND.
ARE YOU HUNGRY?
I DON'T SUPPOSE YOU HAVE ANYTHING IN THE WAY OF A RABBIT? ALIVE, PREFERABLY.
YOU EAT... RABBITS? ALIVE?
THE CHILD, EVE, INSISTS THAT I REFER TO HER AS HALLOWEEN GIRL.
SHE'S NOT KIDDING.

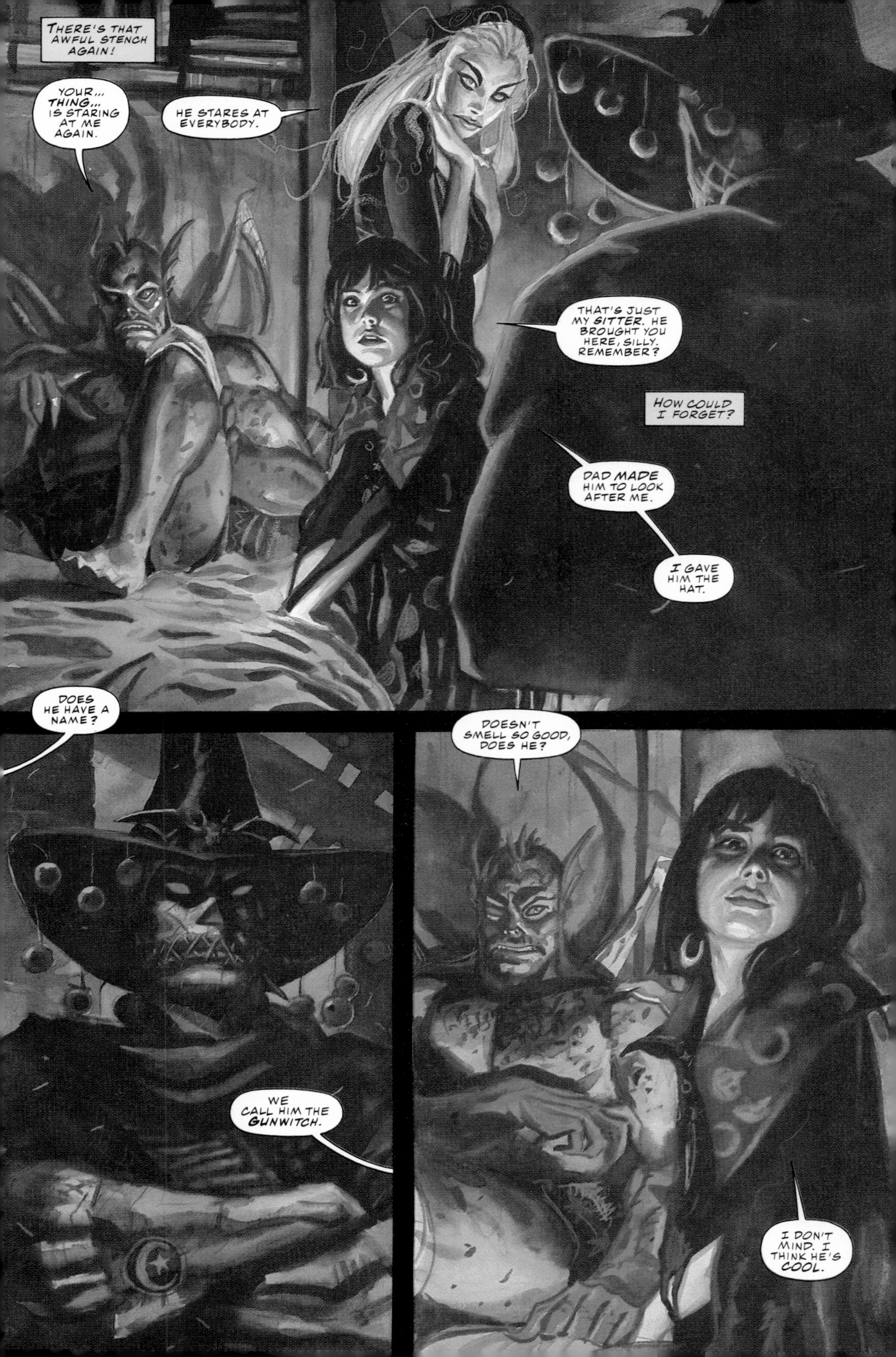

THERE'S THAT AWFUL STENCH AGAIN!
YOUR... THING... IS STARING AT ME AGAIN.
HE STARES AT EVERYBODY.
THAT'S JUST MY SITTER. HE BROUGHT YOU HERE, SILLY. REMEMBER?
HOW COULD I FORGET?
DAD MADE HIM TO LOOK AFTER ME.
I GAVE HIM THE HAT.
DOES HE HAVE A NAME?
WE CALL HIM THE GUNWITCH.
DOESN'T SMELL SO GOOD, DOES HE?
I DON'T MIND. I THINK HE'S COOL.

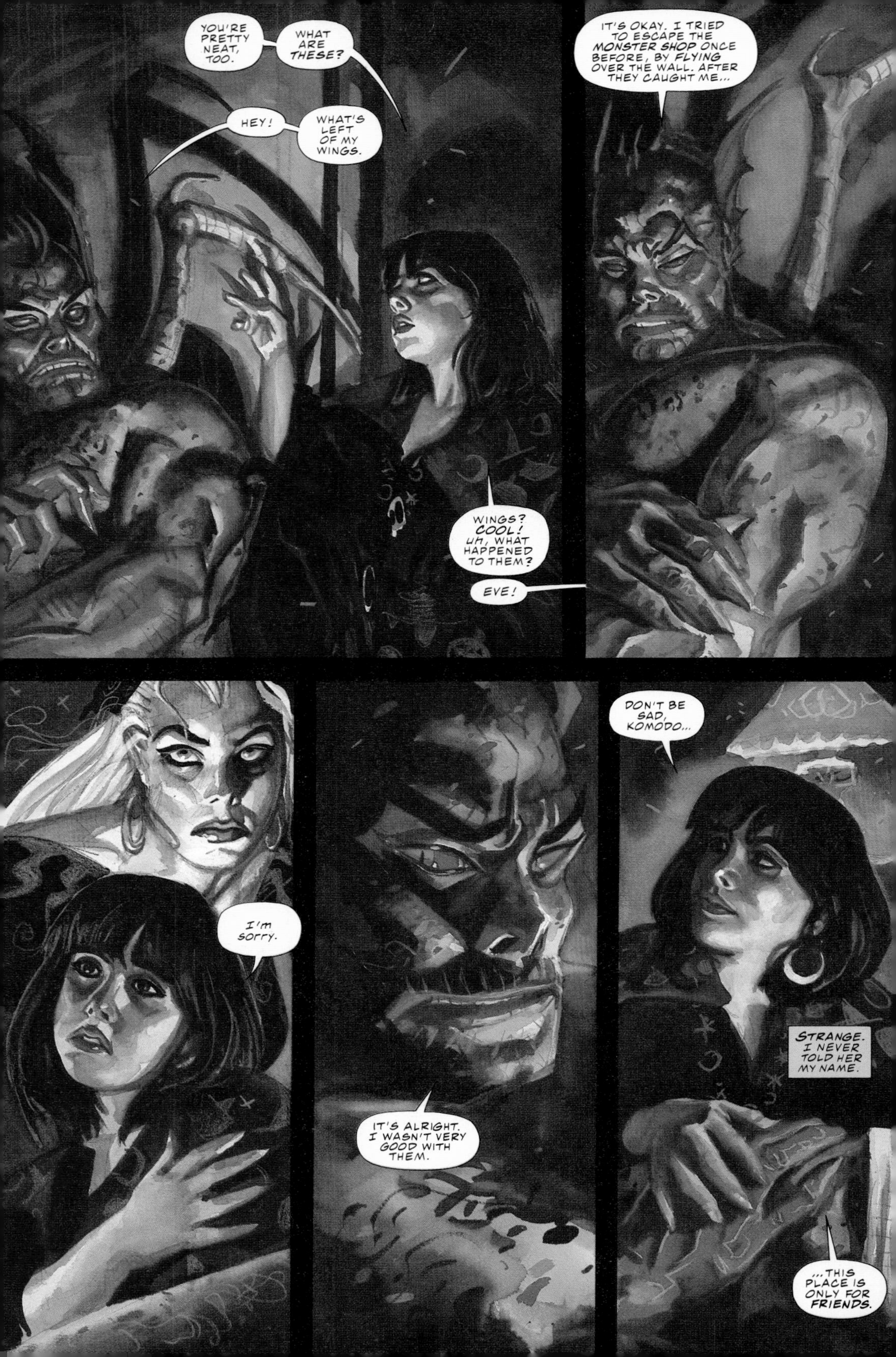

YOU'RE PRETTY NEAT, TOO.
WHAT ARE THESE?
HEY!
WHAT'S LEFT OF MY WINGS.
WINGS? COOL! uh, WHAT HAPPENED TO THEM?
EVE!
IT'S OKAY. I TRIED TO ESCAPE THE MONSTER SHOP ONCE BEFORE, BY FLYING OVER THE WALL. AFTER THEY CAUGHT ME...
I'm sorry.
IT'S ALRIGHT. I WASN'T VERY GOOD WITH THEM.
DON'T BE SAD, KOMODO...
STRANGE. I NEVER TOLD HER MY NAME.
...THIS PLACE IS ONLY FOR FRIENDS.

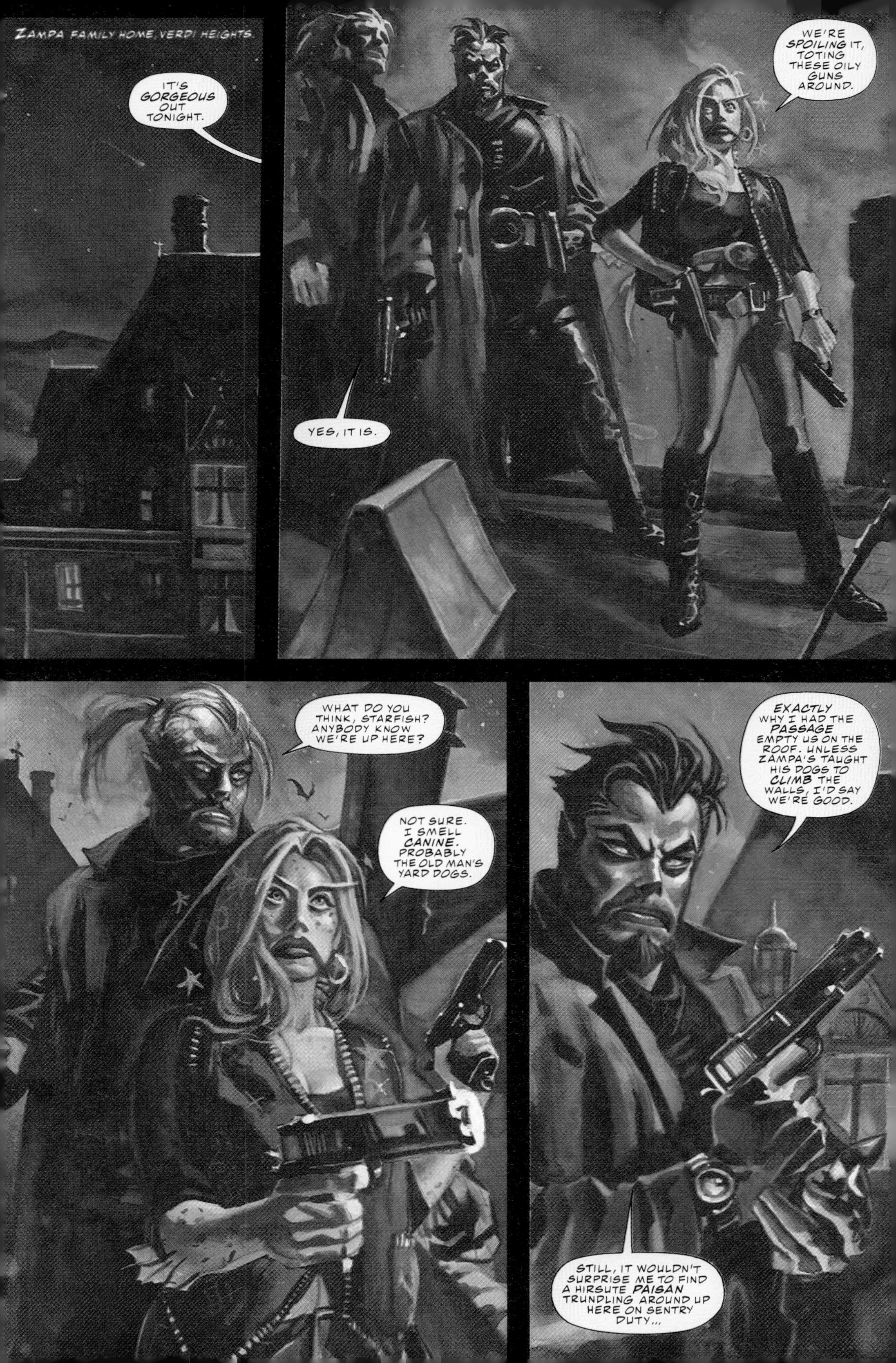
ZAMPA FAMILY HOME, VERDI HEIGHTS.
IT'S GORGEOUS OUT TONIGHT.
YES, IT IS.
WE'RE SPOILING IT, TOTING THESE OILY GUNS AROUND.
WHAT DO YOU THINK, STARFISH? ANYBODY KNOW WE'RE UP HERE?
NOT SURE. I SMELL CANINE. PROBABLY THE OLD MAN'S YARD DOGS.
EXACTLY WHY I HAD THE PASSAGE EMPTY US ON THE ROOF. UNLESS ZAMPA'S TAUGHT HIS DOGS TO CLIMB THE WALLS, I'D SAY WE'RE GOOD.
STILL, IT WOULDN'T SURPRISE ME TO FIND A HIRSUTE PAISAN TRUNDLING AROUND UP HERE ON SENTRY DUTY...

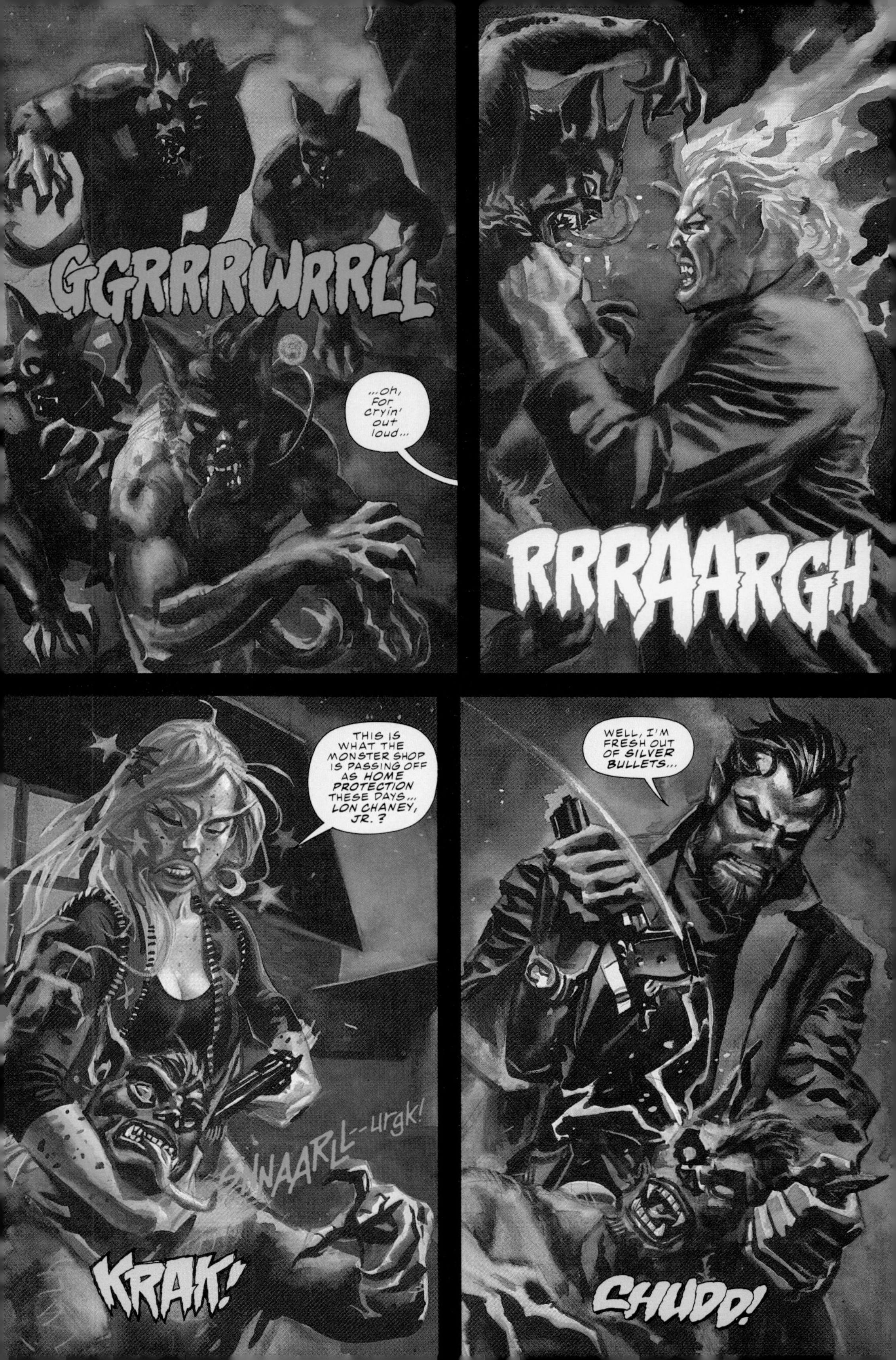
GGRRRWRRLL
...oh, for cryin' out loud...
RRRAARGH
THIS IS WHAT THE MONSTER SHOP IS PASSING OFF AS HOME PROTECTION THESE DAYS... LON CHANEY, JR.?
SNAARLL--urgk!
KRAK!
WELL, I'M FRESH OUT OF SILVER BULLETS...
CHUDD!

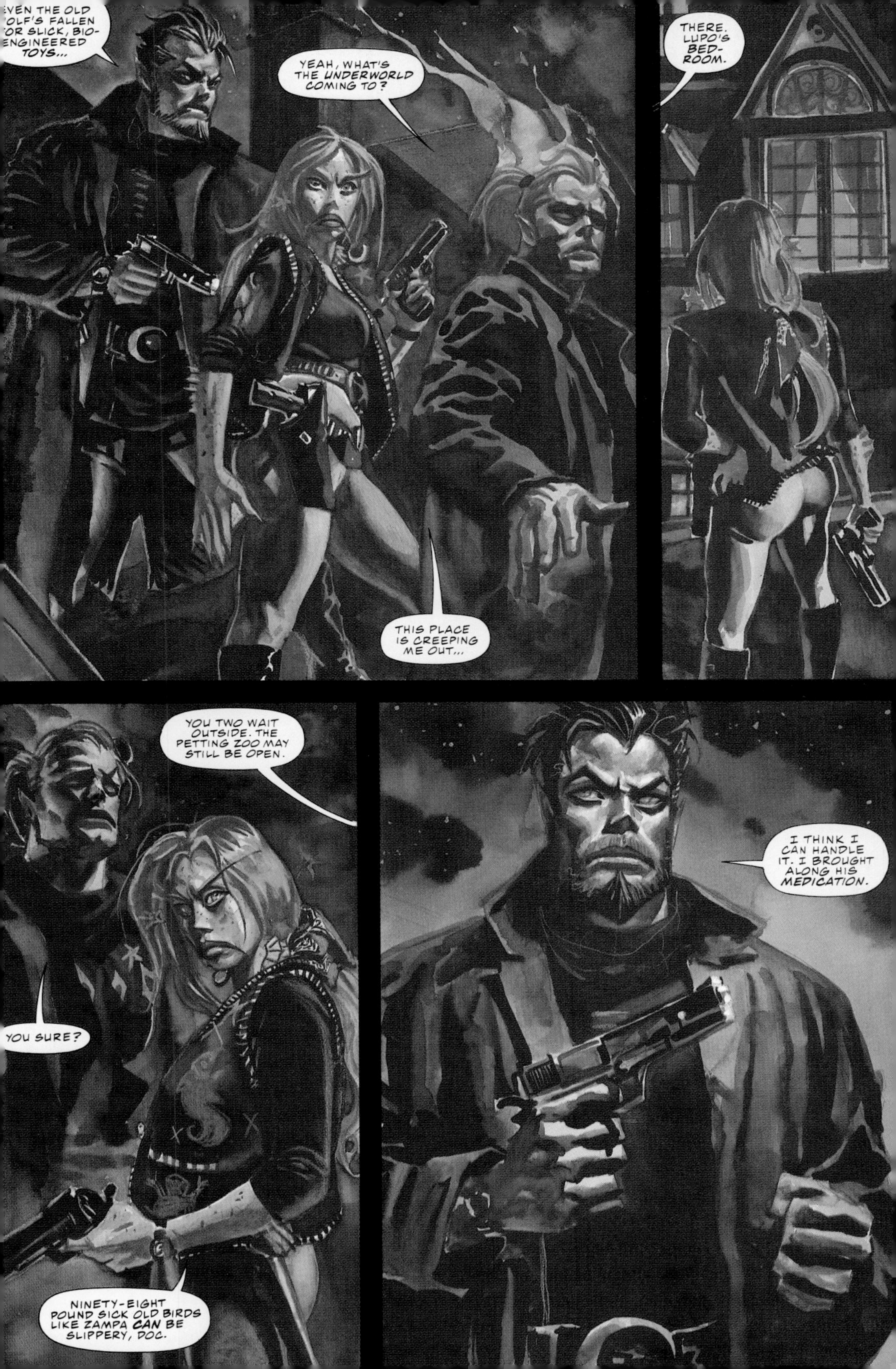
EVEN THE OLD WOLF'S FALLEN FOR SLICK, BIO-ENGINEERED TOYS...
YEAH, WHAT'S THE UNDERWORLD COMING TO?
THIS PLACE IS CREEPING ME OUT...
THERE. LUPO'S BED-ROOM.
YOU TWO WAIT OUTSIDE. THE PETTING ZOO MAY STILL BE OPEN.
YOU SURE?
NINETY-EIGHT POUND SICK OLD BIRDS LIKE ZAMPA CAN BE SLIPPERY, DOC.
I THINK I CAN HANDLE IT. I BROUGHT ALONG HIS MEDICATION.

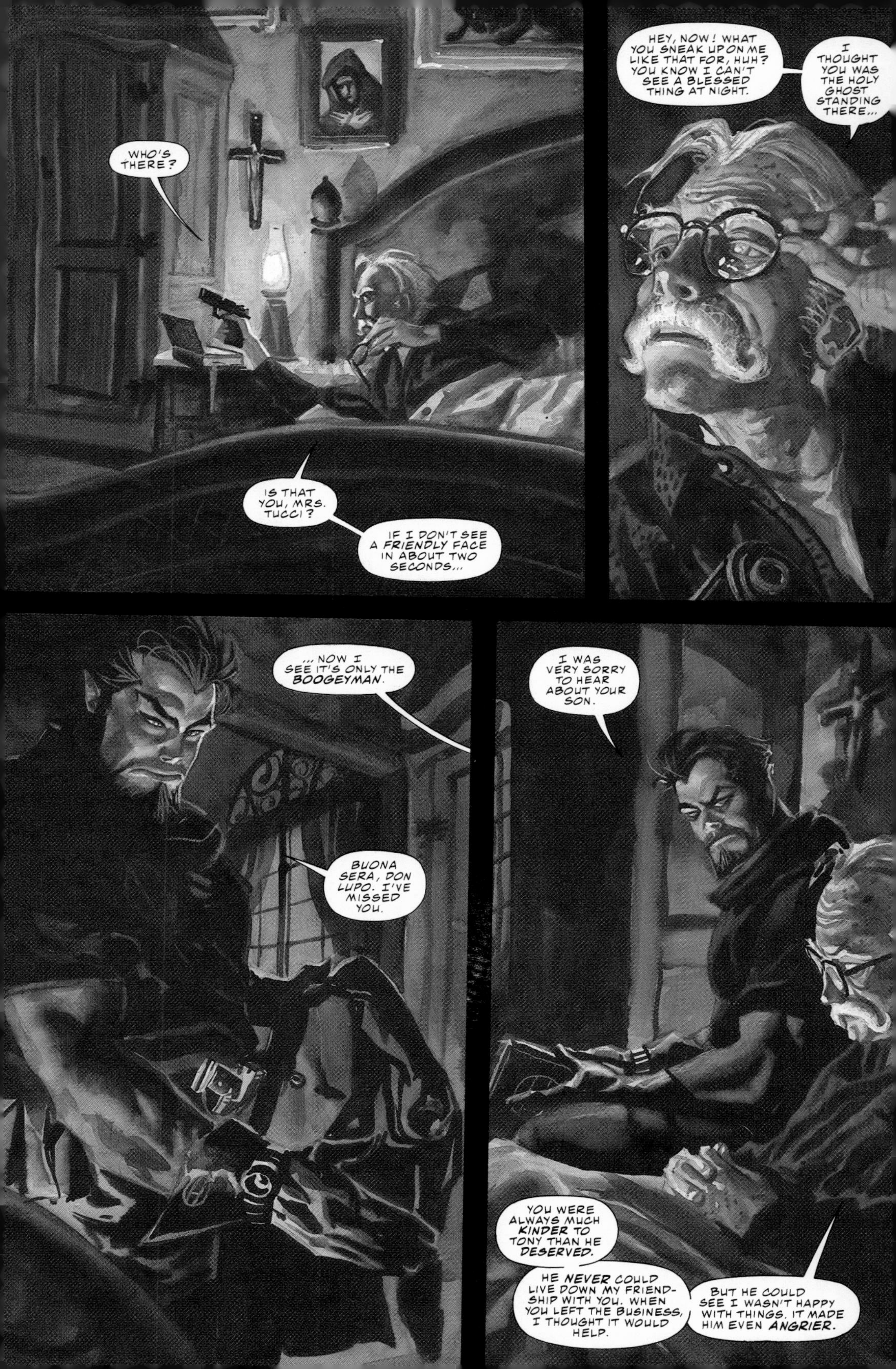
WHO'S THERE?
IS THAT YOU, MRS. TUCCI?
IF I DON'T SEE A FRIENDLY FACE IN ABOUT TWO SECONDS...
HEY, NOW! WHAT YOU SNEAK UPON ME LIKE THAT FOR, HUH? YOU KNOW I CAN'T SEE A BLESSED THING AT NIGHT.
I THOUGHT YOU WAS THE HOLY GHOST STANDING THERE...
...NOW I SEE IT'S ONLY THE BOOGEYMAN.
BUONA SERA, DON LUPO. I'VE MISSED YOU.
I WAS VERY SORRY TO HEAR ABOUT YOUR SON.
YOU WERE ALWAYS MUCH KINDER TO TONY THAN HE DESERVED.
HE NEVER COULD LIVE DOWN MY FRIENDSHIP WITH YOU. WHEN YOU LEFT THE BUSINESS, I THOUGHT IT WOULD HELP.
BUT HE COULD SEE I WASN'T HAPPY WITH THINGS. IT MADE HIM EVEN ANGRIER.

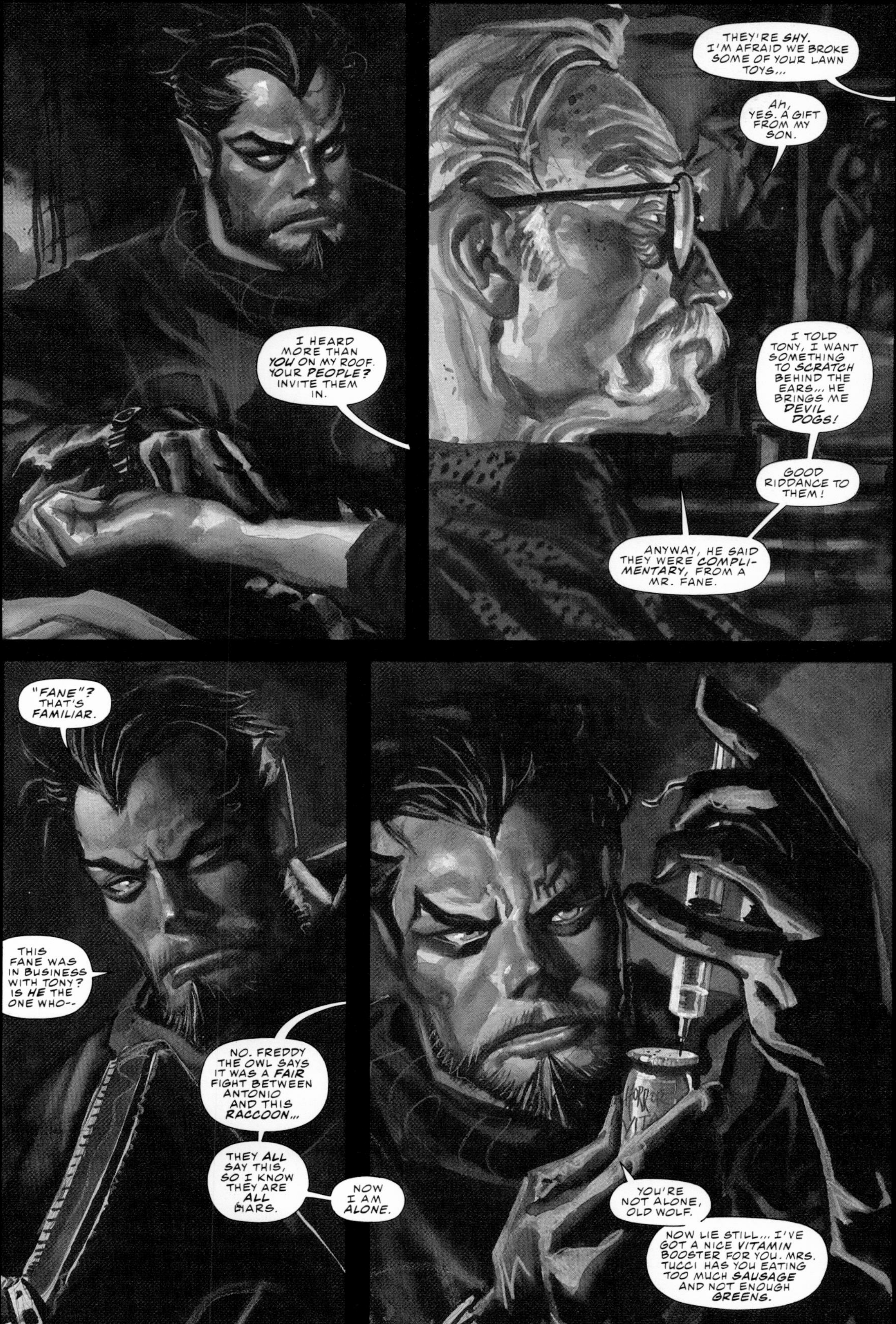
I HEARD MORE THAN YOU ON MY ROOF. YOUR PEOPLE? INVITE THEM IN.
THEY'RE SHY. I'M AFRAID WE BROKE SOME OF YOUR LAWN TOYS...
AH, YES. A GIFT FROM MY SON.
I TOLD TONY, I WANT SOMETHING TO SCRATCH BEHIND THE EARS... HE BRINGS ME DEVIL DOGS!
GOOD RIDDANCE TO THEM!
ANYWAY, HE SAID THEY WERE COMPLI-MENTARY, FROM A MR. FANE.
"FANE"? THAT'S FAMILIAR.
THIS FANE WAS IN BUSINESS WITH TONY? IS HE THE ONE WHO--
NO. FREDDY THE OWL SAYS IT WAS A FAIR FIGHT BETWEEN ANTONIO AND THIS RACCOON...
THEY ALL SAY THIS, SO I KNOW THEY ARE ALL LIARS.
NOW I AM ALONE.
YOU'RE NOT ALONE, OLD WOLF.
NOW LIE STILL... I'VE GOT A NICE VITAMIN BOOSTER FOR YOU. MRS. TUCCI HAS YOU EATING TOO MUCH SAUSAGE AND NOT ENOUGH GREENS.

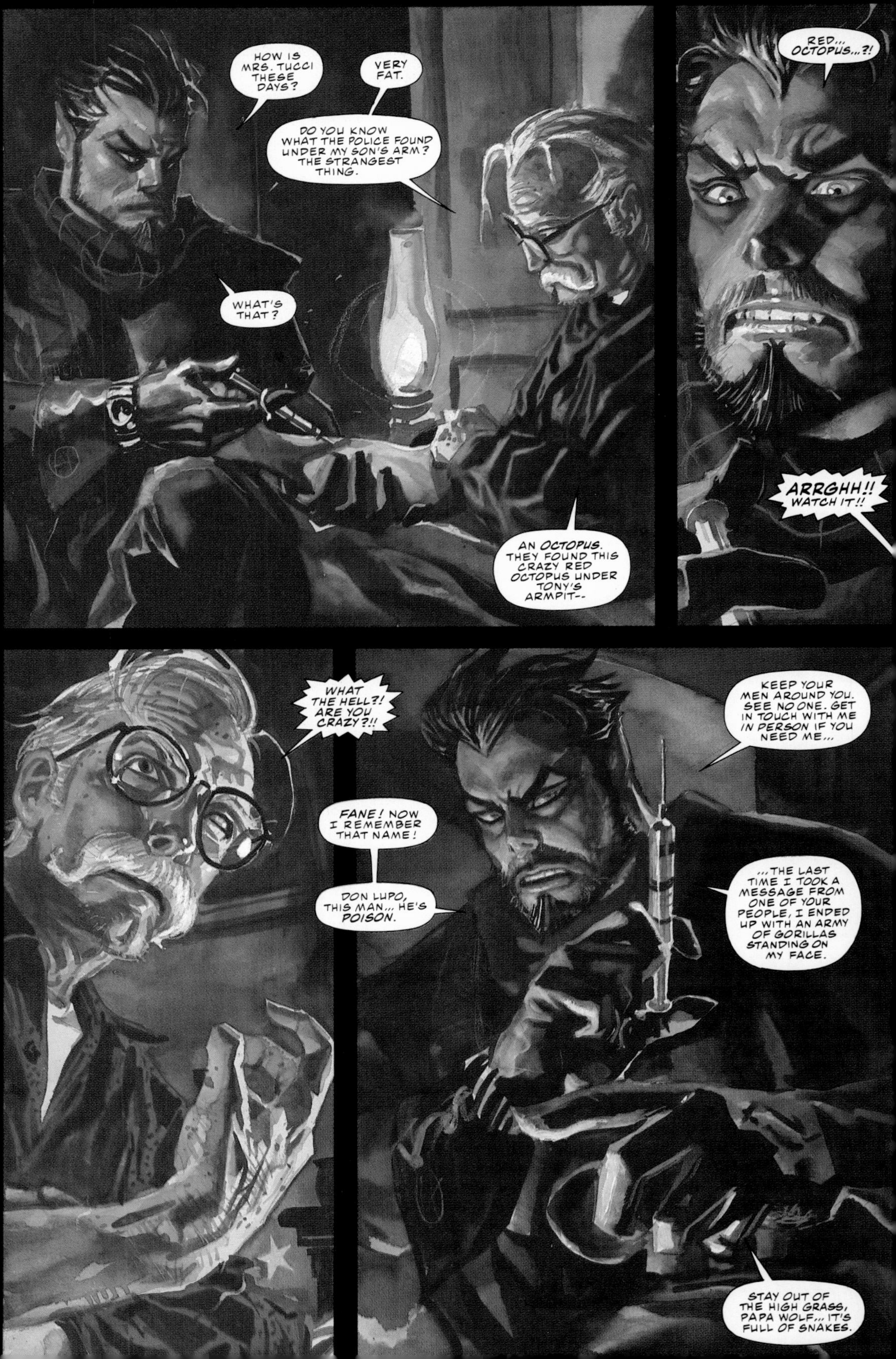
HOW IS MRS. TUCCI THESE DAYS?
VERY FAT.
DO YOU KNOW WHAT THE POLICE FOUND UNDER MY SON'S ARM? THE STRANGEST THING.
WHAT'S THAT?
AN OCTOPUS. THEY FOUND THIS CRAZY RED OCTOPUS UNDER TONY'S ARMPIT--
RED... OCTOPUS...?!
ARRGHH!! WATCH IT!!
WHAT THE HELL?! ARE YOU CRAZY?!!
FANE! NOW I REMEMBER THAT NAME!
DON LUPO, THIS MAN... HE'S POISON.
KEEP YOUR MEN AROUND YOU. SEE NO ONE. GET IN TOUCH WITH ME IN PERSON IF YOU NEED ME...
...THE LAST TIME I TOOK A MESSAGE FROM ONE OF YOUR PEOPLE, I ENDED UP WITH AN ARMY OF GORILLAS STANDING ON MY FACE.
STAY OUT OF THE HIGH GRASS, PAPA WOLF... IT'S FULL OF SNAKES.

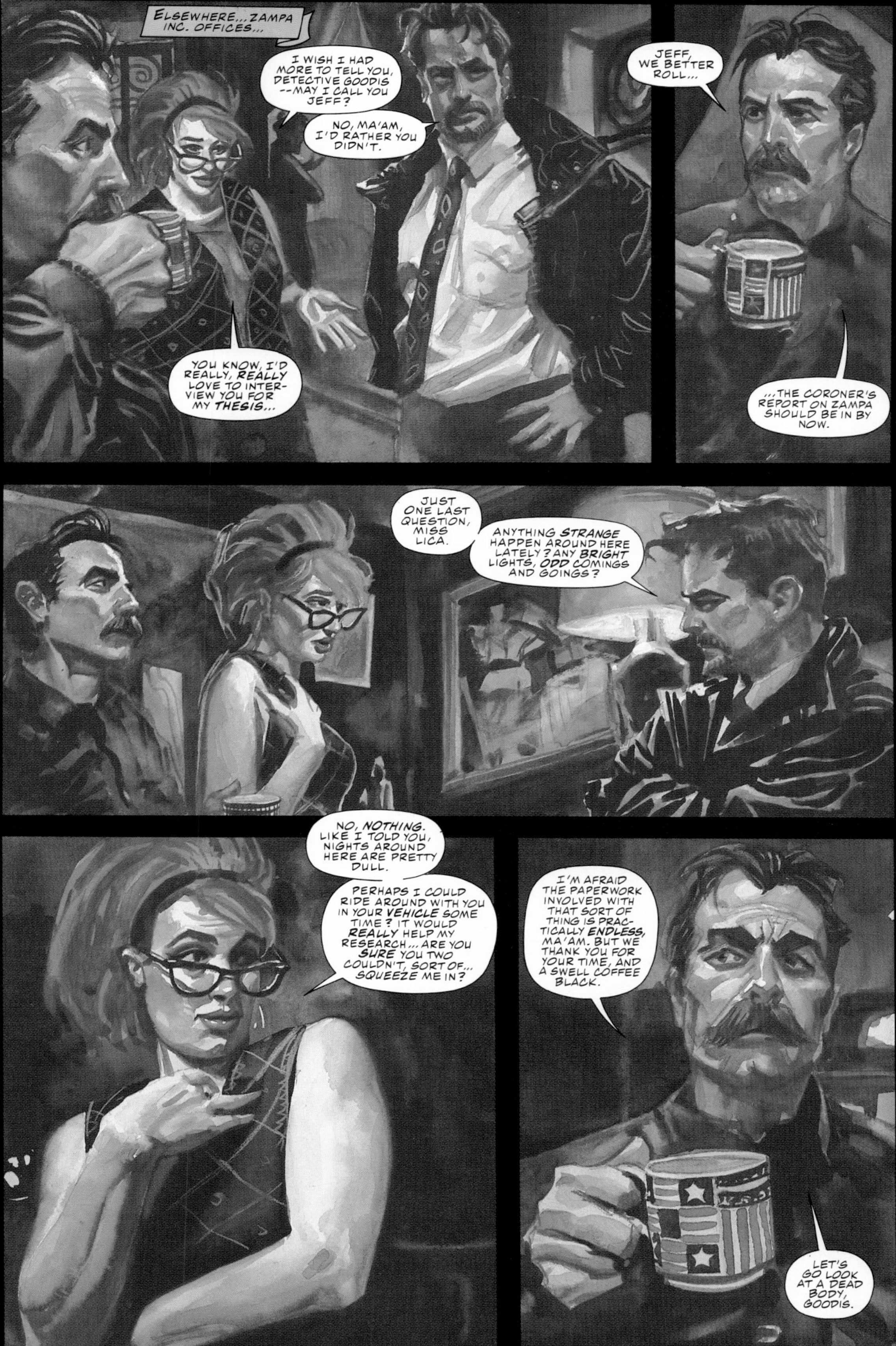
ELSEWHERE... ZAMPA INC. OFFICES...
I WISH I HAD MORE TO TELL YOU, DETECTIVE GOODIS --MAY I CALL YOU JEFF?
NO, MA'AM, I'D RATHER YOU DIDN'T.
YOU KNOW, I'D REALLY, REALLY LOVE TO INTER-VIEW YOU FOR MY THESIS...
JEFF, WE BETTER ROLL...
...THE CORONER'S REPORT ON ZAMPA SHOULD BE IN BY NOW.
JUST ONE LAST QUESTION, MISS LICA.
ANYTHING STRANGE HAPPEN AROUND HERE LATELY? ANY BRIGHT LIGHTS, ODD COMINGS AND GOINGS?
NO, NOTHING. LIKE I TOLD YOU, NIGHTS AROUND HERE ARE PRETTY DULL.
PERHAPS I COULD RIDE AROUND WITH YOU IN YOUR VEHICLE SOME TIME? IT WOULD REALLY HELP MY RESEARCH... ARE YOU SURE YOU TWO COULDN'T, SORT OF... SQUEEZE ME IN?
I'M AFRAID THE PAPERWORK INVOLVED WITH THAT SORT OF THING IS PRAC-TICALLY ENDLESS, MA'AM. BUT WE THANK YOU FOR YOUR TIME, AND A SWELL COFFEE BLACK.
LET'S GO LOOK AT A DEAD BODY, GOODIS.

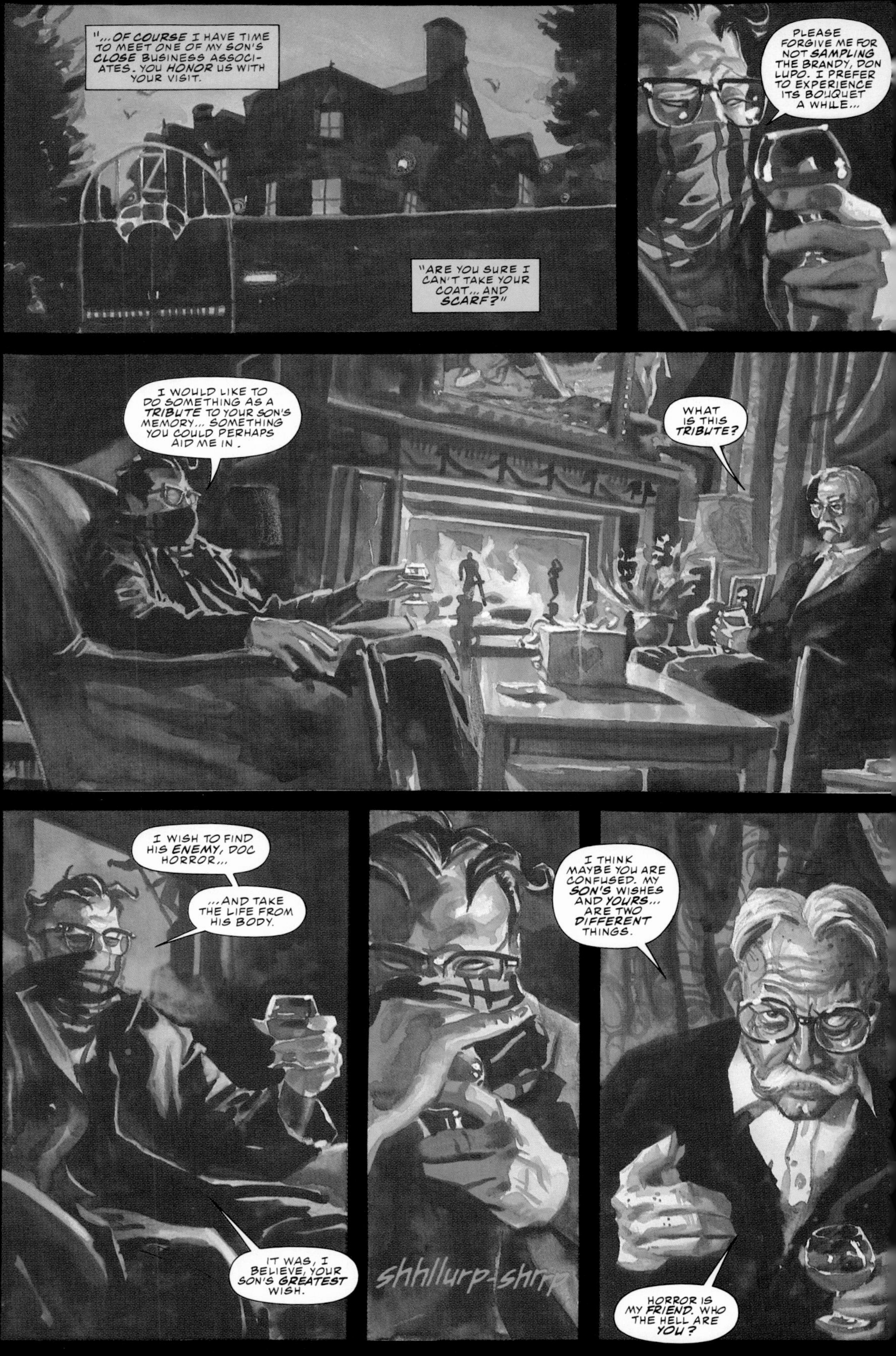
"...OF COURSE I HAVE TIME TO MEET ONE OF MY SON'S CLOSE BUSINESS ASSOCIATES. YOU HONOR US WITH YOUR VISIT.
"ARE YOU SURE I CAN'T TAKE YOUR COAT... AND SCARF?"
PLEASE FORGIVE ME FOR NOT SAMPLING THE BRANDY, DON LUPO. I PREFER TO EXPERIENCE ITS BOUQUET A WHILE...
I WOULD LIKE TO DO SOMETHING AS A TRIBUTE TO YOUR SON'S MEMORY... SOMETHING YOU COULD PERHAPS AID ME IN.
WHAT IS THIS TRIBUTE?
I WISH TO FIND HIS ENEMY, DOC HORROR...
...AND TAKE THE LIFE FROM HIS BODY.
IT WAS, I BELIEVE, YOUR SON'S GREATEST WISH.
shhllurp-shrrp
I THINK MAYBE YOU ARE CONFUSED. MY SON'S WISHES AND YOURS... ARE TWO DIFFERENT THINGS.
HORROR IS MY FRIEND. WHO THE HELL ARE YOU?

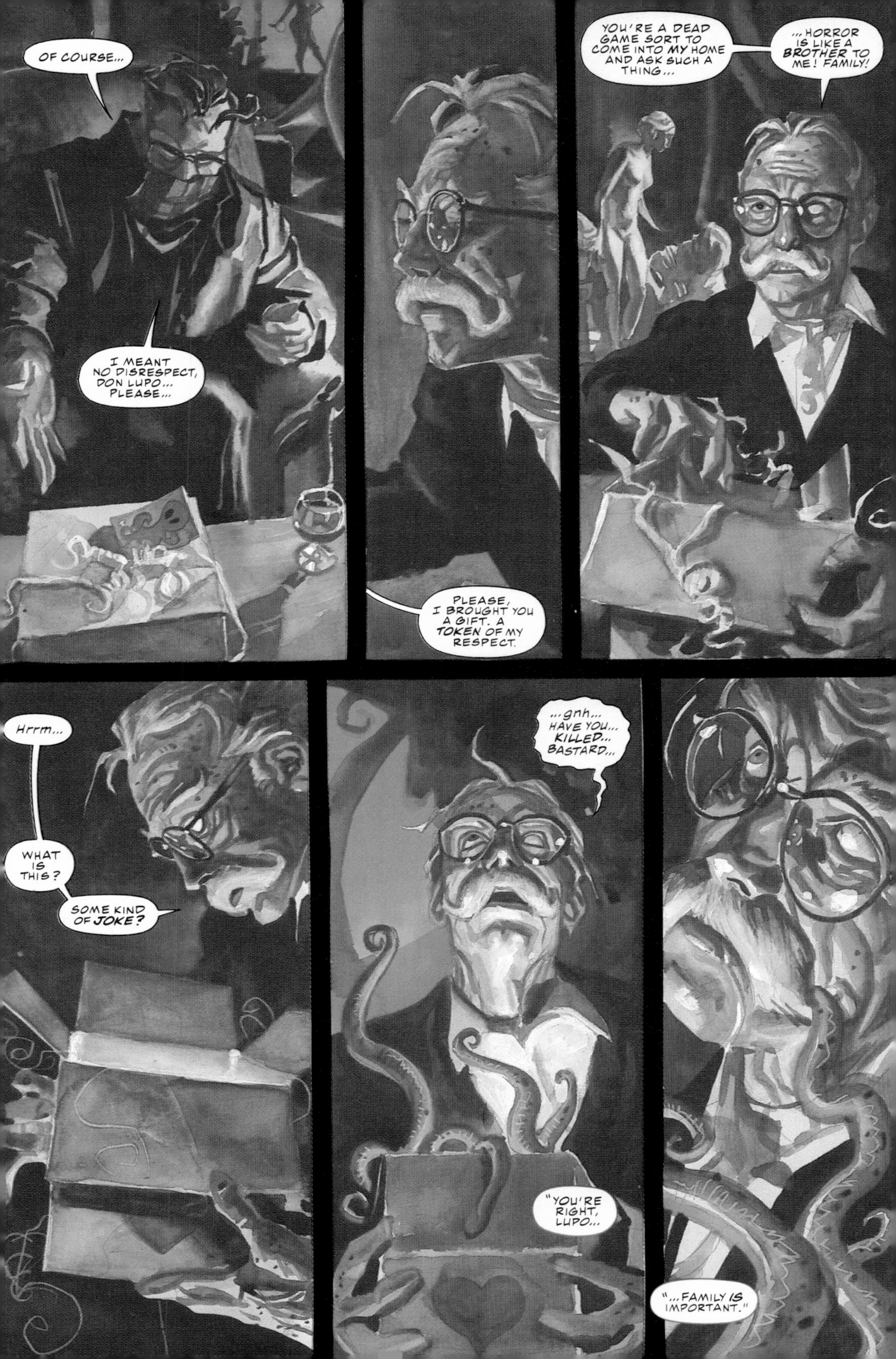
OF COURSE...
I MEANT NO DISRESPECT, DON LUPO... PLEASE...
PLEASE, I BROUGHT YOU A GIFT. A TOKEN OF MY RESPECT.
YOU'RE A DEAD GAME SORT TO COME INTO MY HOME AND ASK SUCH A THING...
...HORROR IS LIKE A BROTHER TO ME! FAMILY!
Hrrm...
WHAT IS THIS?
SOME KIND OF JOKE?
...gnh... HAVE YOU... KILLED... BASTARD...
"YOU'RE RIGHT, LUPO...
"...FAMILY IS IMPORTANT."

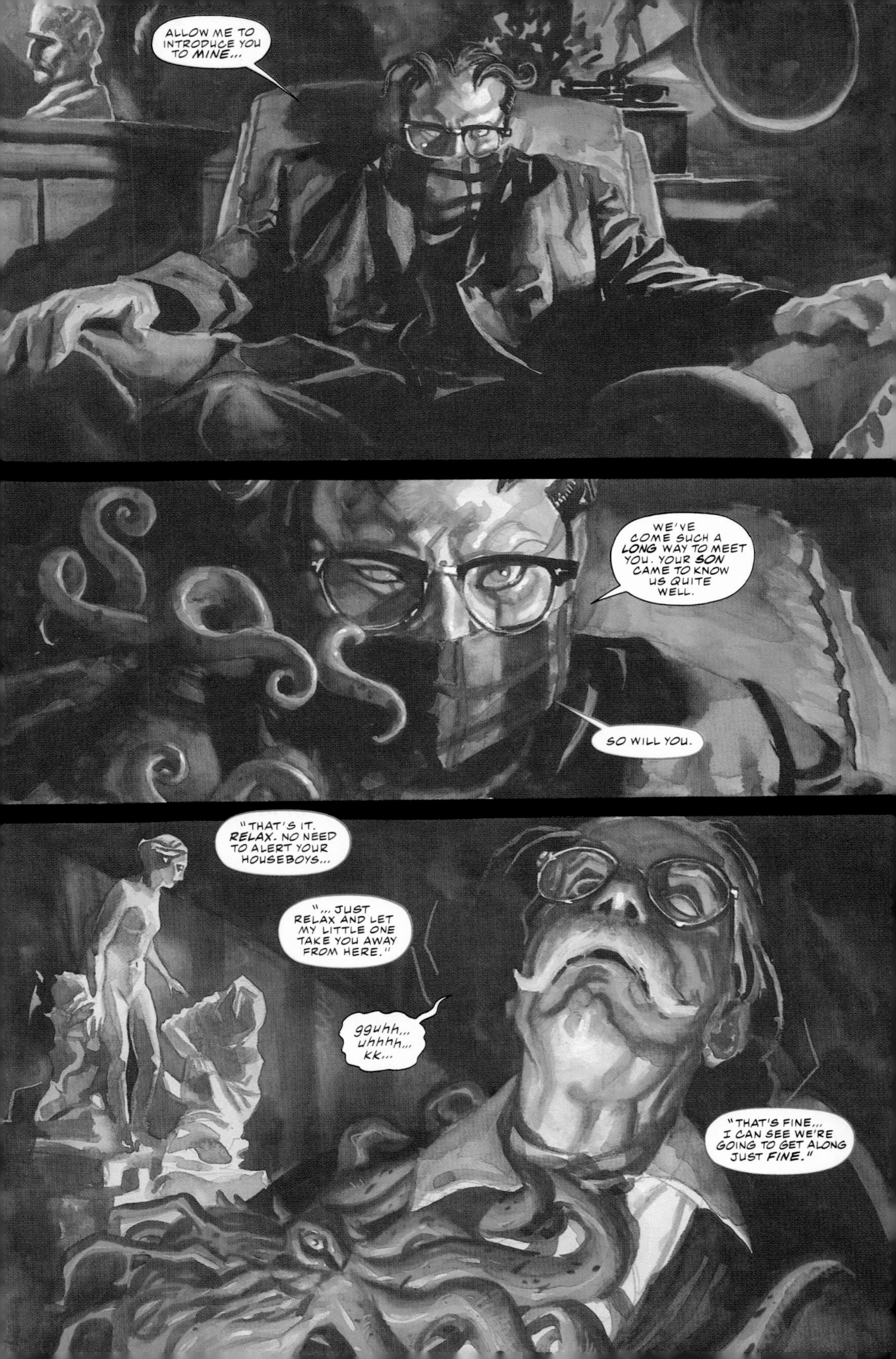
ALLOW ME TO INTRODUCE YOU TO *MINE*...
WE'VE COME SUCH A *LONG* WAY TO MEET YOU. YOUR *SON* CAME TO KNOW US QUITE WELL.
SO WILL YOU.
"THAT'S IT. *RELAX*. NO NEED TO ALERT YOUR HOUSEBOYS...
"... JUST RELAX AND LET MY LITTLE ONE TAKE YOU AWAY FROM HERE."
gguhh... uhhhh... kk...
"THAT'S FINE... I CAN SEE WE'RE GOING TO GET ALONG JUST *FINE*."

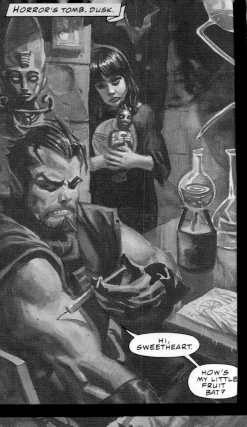

HI, SWEETHEART.

HOW'S MY LITTLE FRUIT BAT?

...FINE...

DAD, DO YOU TAKE YOUR MEDICINE TO KEEP FROM HURTING PEOPLE?

WHO TOLD YOU THAT?!

NOBODY, I MEAN JUST THE TOYS DID.

YOU SHOULDN'T TALK TO SPIRITS WITHOUT CONSULTING YOUR FATHER FIRST, EVENING.

THE TRUTH IS, HONEY, I PICKED UP A PRETTY NASTY VIRUS ON ONE OF MY EXPLORATIONS.

I WAS GETTING VERY SICK. IF I HADN'T COME UP WITH THIS SERUM WHEN I DID...

...WELL, I MIGHT HAVE HURT A LOT OF PEOPLE.

AS IT IS, I'VE KEPT IT UNDER CONTROL.

SO EVERYTHING IS REALLY OKAY?

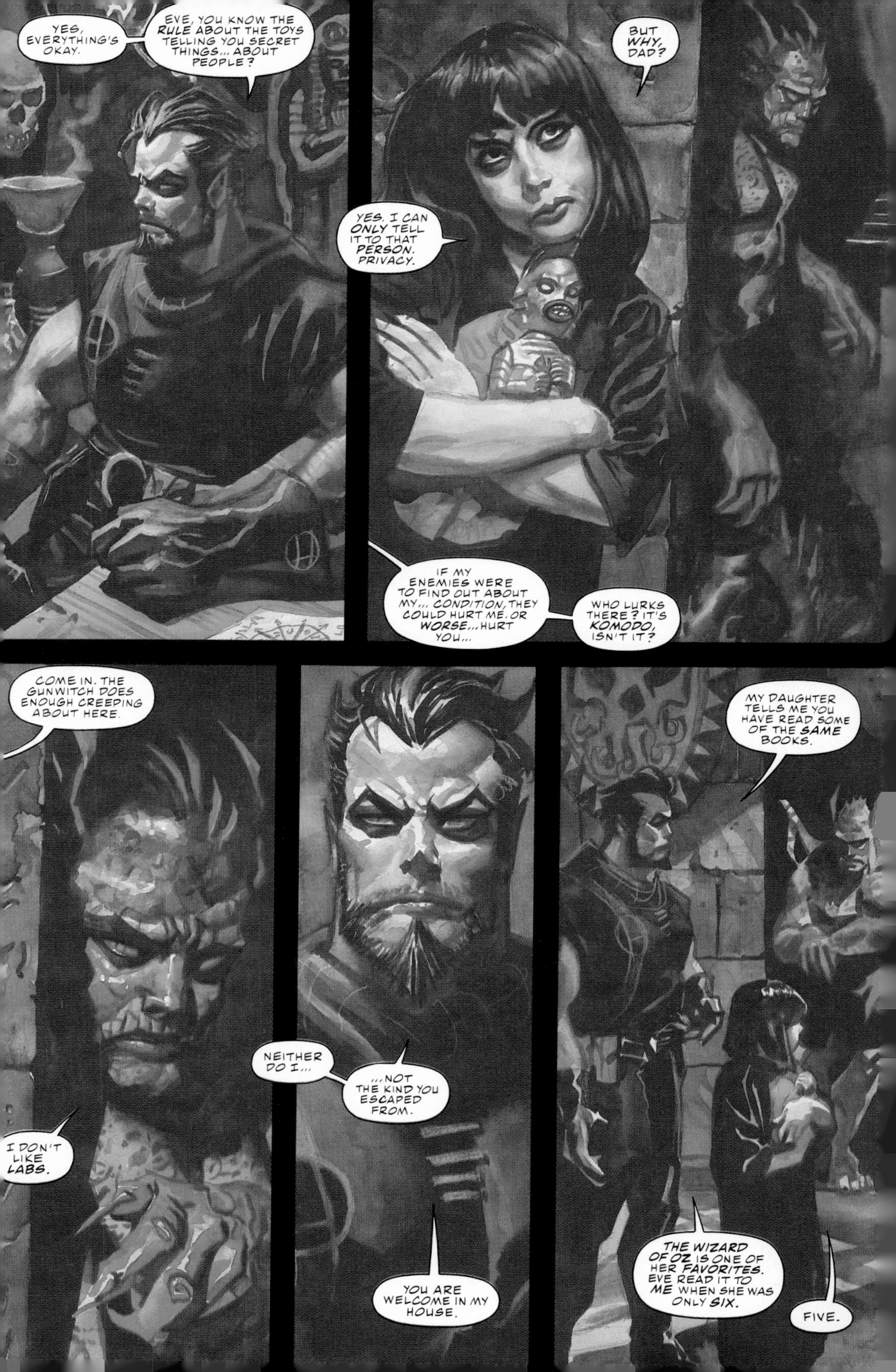

YES, EVERYTHING'S OKAY.
EVE, YOU KNOW THE RULE ABOUT THE TOYS TELLING YOU SECRET THINGS... ABOUT PEOPLE?
BUT WHY, DAD?
YES. I CAN ONLY TELL IT TO THAT PERSON. PRIVACY.
IF MY ENEMIES WERE TO FIND OUT ABOUT MY... CONDITION, THEY COULD HURT ME. OR WORSE... HURT YOU...
WHO LURKS THERE? IT'S KOMODO, ISN'T IT?
COME IN. THE GUNWITCH DOES ENOUGH CREEPING ABOUT HERE.
I DON'T LIKE LABS.
NEITHER DO I...
...NOT THE KIND YOU ESCAPED FROM.
YOU ARE WELCOME IN MY HOUSE.
MY DAUGHTER TELLS ME YOU HAVE READ SOME OF THE SAME BOOKS.
THE WIZARD OF OZ IS ONE OF HER FAVORITES. EVE READ IT TO ME WHEN SHE WAS ONLY SIX.
FIVE.

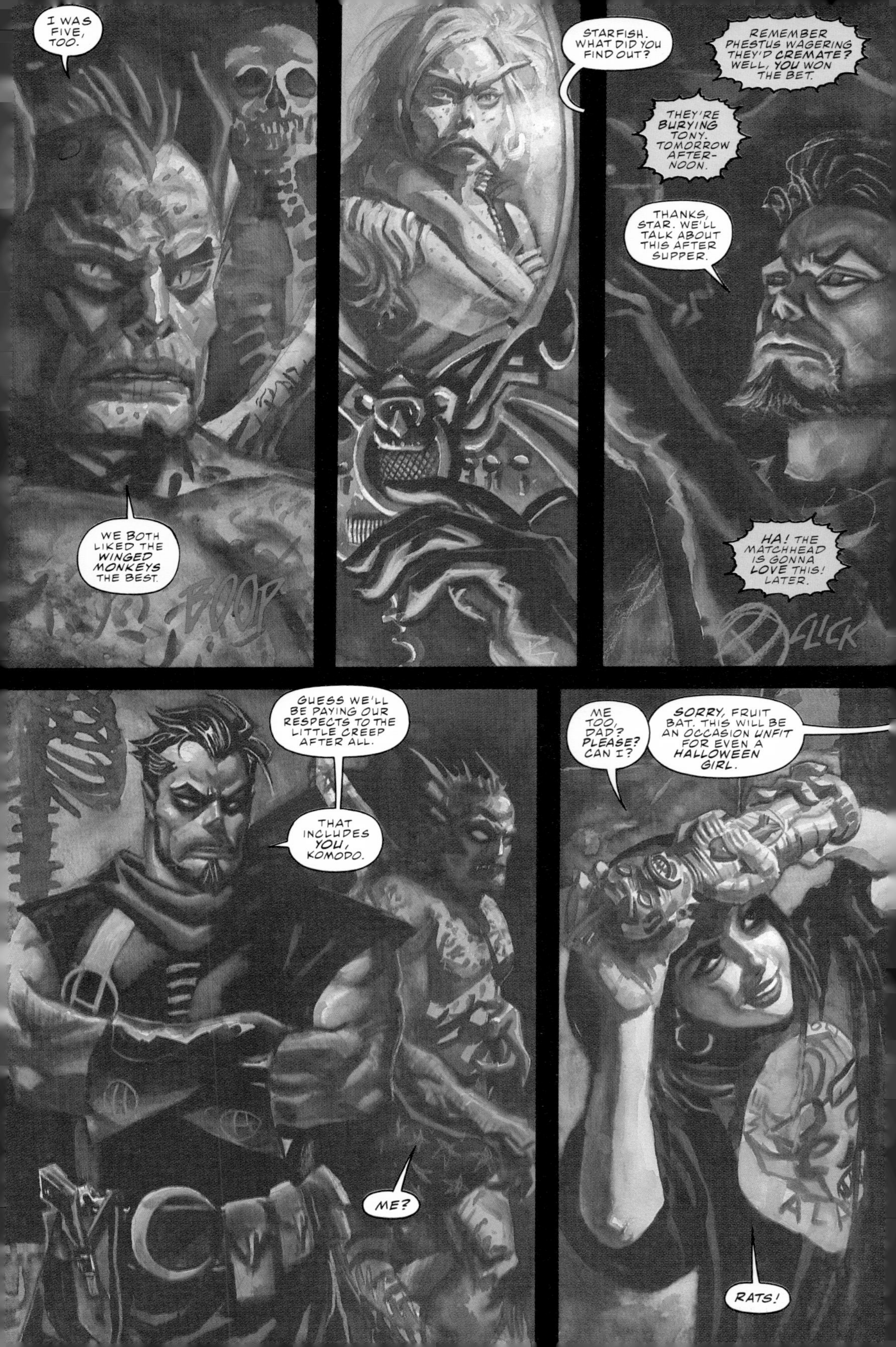

I WAS FIVE, TOO.
WE BOTH LIKED THE WINGED MONKEYS THE BEST.
BOOP
STARFISH. WHAT DID YOU FIND OUT?
REMEMBER PHESTUS WAGERING THEY'D CREMATE? WELL, YOU WON THE BET.
THEY'RE BURYING TONY. TOMORROW AFTER-NOON.
THANKS, STAR. WE'LL TALK ABOUT THIS AFTER SUPPER.
HA! THE MATCHHEAD IS GONNA LOVE THIS! LATER.
CLICK
GUESS WE'LL BE PAYING OUR RESPECTS TO THE LITTLE CREEP AFTER ALL.
THAT INCLUDES YOU, KOMODO.
ME?
ME TOO, DAD? PLEASE? CAN I?
SORRY, FRUIT BAT. THIS WILL BE AN OCCASION UNFIT FOR EVEN A HALLOWEEN GIRL.
RATS!

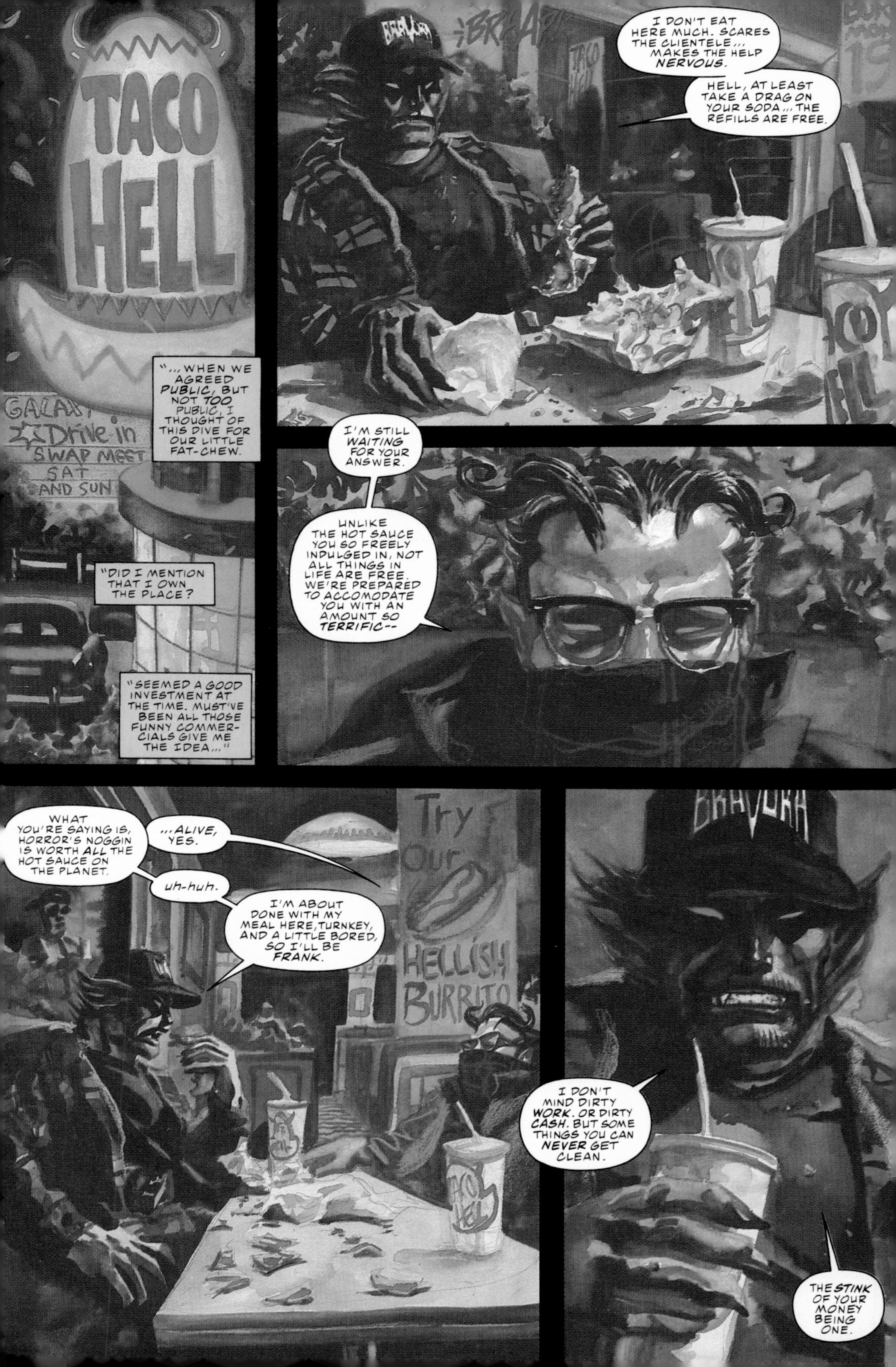
TACO HELL
GALAXY Drive in
SWAP MEET SAT AND SUN
¡BRAAP!
I DON'T EAT HERE MUCH. SCARES THE CLIENTELE... MAKES THE HELP NERVOUS.
HELL, AT LEAST TAKE A DRAG ON YOUR SODA... THE REFILLS ARE FREE.
"...WHEN WE AGREED PUBLIC, BUT NOT TOO PUBLIC, I THOUGHT OF THIS DIVE FOR OUR LITTLE FAT-CHEW.
"DID I MENTION THAT I OWN THE PLACE?
"SEEMED A GOOD INVESTMENT AT THE TIME. MUST'VE BEEN ALL THOSE FUNNY COMMERCIALS GIVE ME THE IDEA..."
I'M STILL WAITING FOR YOUR ANSWER.
UNLIKE THE HOT SAUCE YOU SO FREELY INDULGED IN, NOT ALL THINGS IN LIFE ARE FREE. WE'RE PREPARED TO ACCOMODATE YOU WITH AN AMOUNT SO TERRIFIC--
WHAT YOU'RE SAYING IS, HORROR'S NOGGIN IS WORTH ALL THE HOT SAUCE ON THE PLANET.
...ALIVE, YES.
uh-huh.
I'M ABOUT DONE WITH MY MEAL HERE, TURNKEY, AND A LITTLE BORED, SO I'LL BE FRANK.
Try Our
HELLISH BURRITO
BRAVURA
I DON'T MIND DIRTY WORK, OR DIRTY CASH. BUT SOME THINGS YOU CAN NEVER GET CLEAN.
THE STINK OF YOUR MONEY BEING ONE.

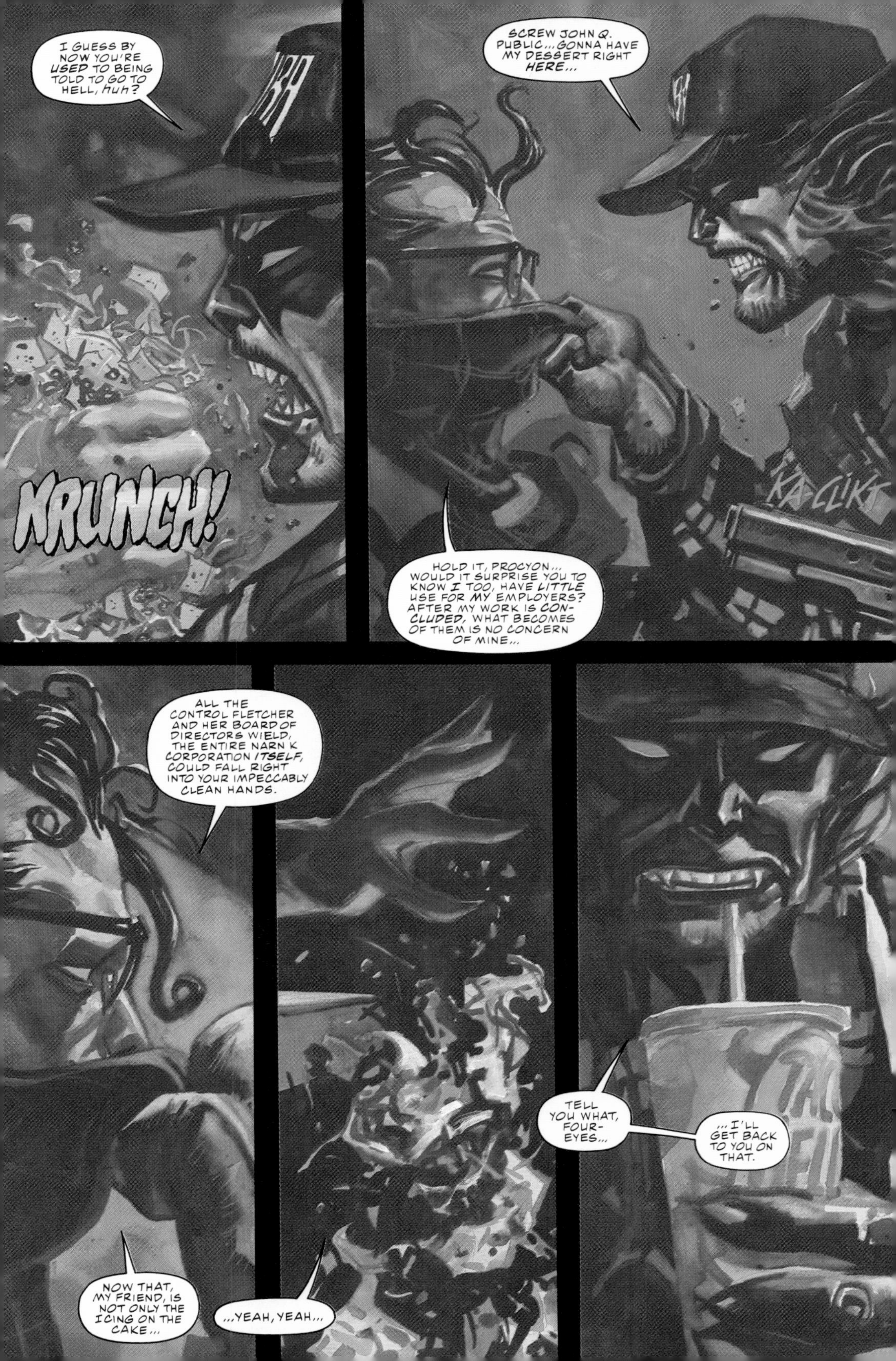
I GUESS BY NOW YOU'RE USED TO BEING TOLD TO GO TO HELL, HUH?
KRUNCH!
SCREW JOHN Q. PUBLIC... GONNA HAVE MY DESSERT RIGHT HERE...
KA-CLIK
HOLD IT, PROCYON... WOULD IT SURPRISE YOU TO KNOW I TOO, HAVE LITTLE USE FOR MY EMPLOYERS? AFTER MY WORK IS CONCLUDED, WHAT BECOMES OF THEM IS NO CONCERN OF MINE...
ALL THE CONTROL FLETCHER AND HER BOARD OF DIRECTORS WIELD, THE ENTIRE NARN K CORPORATION ITSELF, COULD FALL RIGHT INTO YOUR IMPECCABLY CLEAN HANDS.
NOW THAT, MY FRIEND, IS NOT ONLY THE ICING ON THE CAKE...
...YEAH, YEAH...
TELL YOU WHAT, FOUR-EYES...
...I'LL GET BACK TO YOU ON THAT.

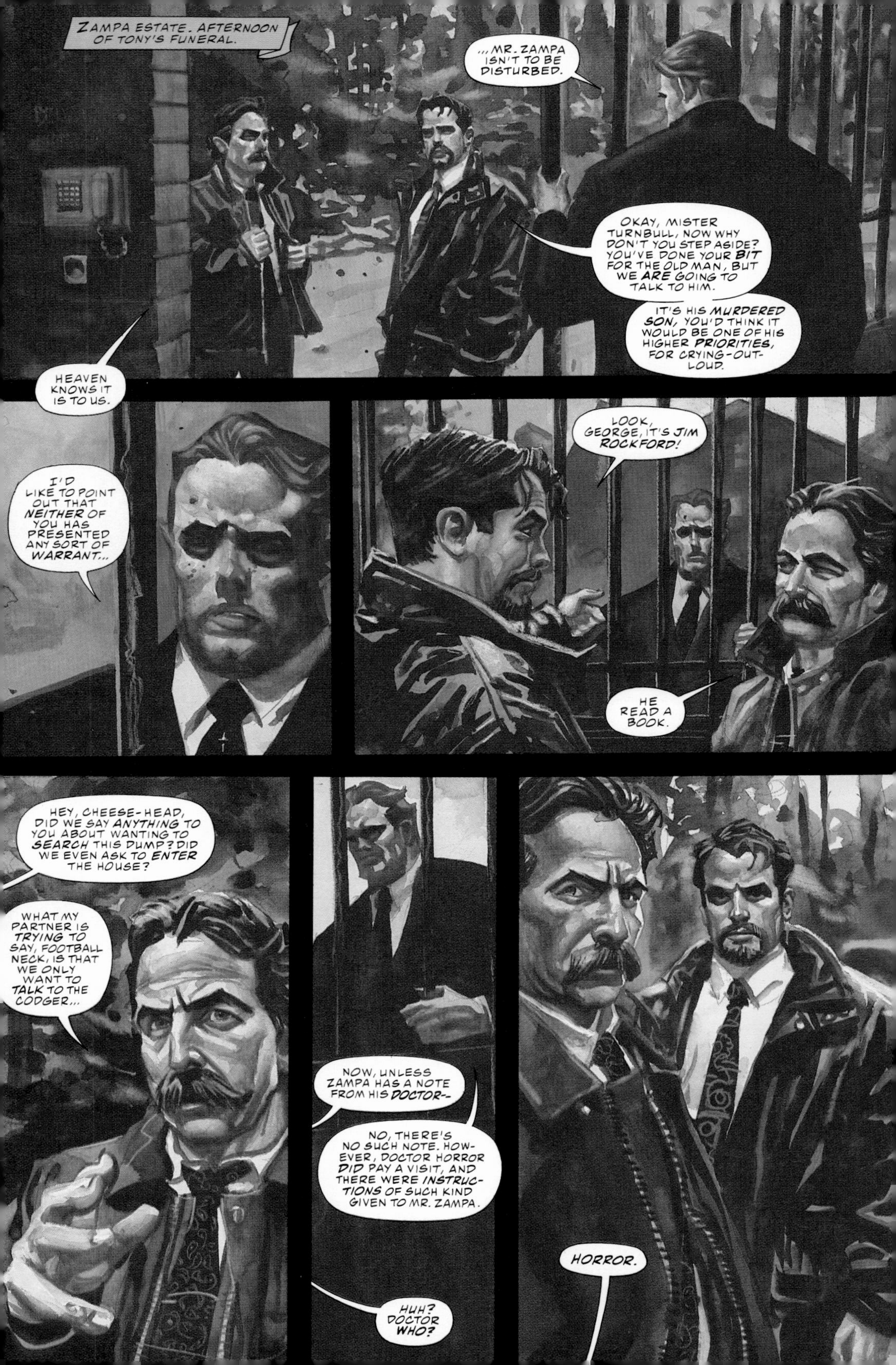
ZAMPA ESTATE. AFTERNOON OF TONY'S FUNERAL.
...MR. ZAMPA ISN'T TO BE DISTURBED.
OKAY, MISTER TURNBULL, NOW WHY DON'T YOU STEP ASIDE? YOU'VE DONE YOUR BIT FOR THE OLD MAN, BUT WE ARE GOING TO TALK TO HIM.
IT'S HIS MURDERED SON, YOU'D THINK IT WOULD BE ONE OF HIS HIGHER PRIORITIES, FOR CRYING-OUT-LOUD.
HEAVEN KNOWS IT IS TO US.
I'D LIKE TO POINT OUT THAT NEITHER OF YOU HAS PRESENTED ANY SORT OF WARRANT...
LOOK, GEORGE, IT'S JIM ROCKFORD!
HE READ A BOOK.
HEY, CHEESE-HEAD, DID WE SAY ANYTHING TO YOU ABOUT WANTING TO SEARCH THIS DUMP? DID WE EVEN ASK TO ENTER THE HOUSE?
WHAT MY PARTNER IS TRYING TO SAY, FOOTBALL NECK, IS THAT WE ONLY WANT TO TALK TO THE CODGER...
NOW, UNLESS ZAMPA HAS A NOTE FROM HIS DOCTOR--
NO, THERE'S NO SUCH NOTE. HOWEVER, DOCTOR HORROR DID PAY A VISIT, AND THERE WERE INSTRUCTIONS OF SUCH KIND GIVEN TO MR. ZAMPA.
HUH? DOCTOR WHO?
HORROR.

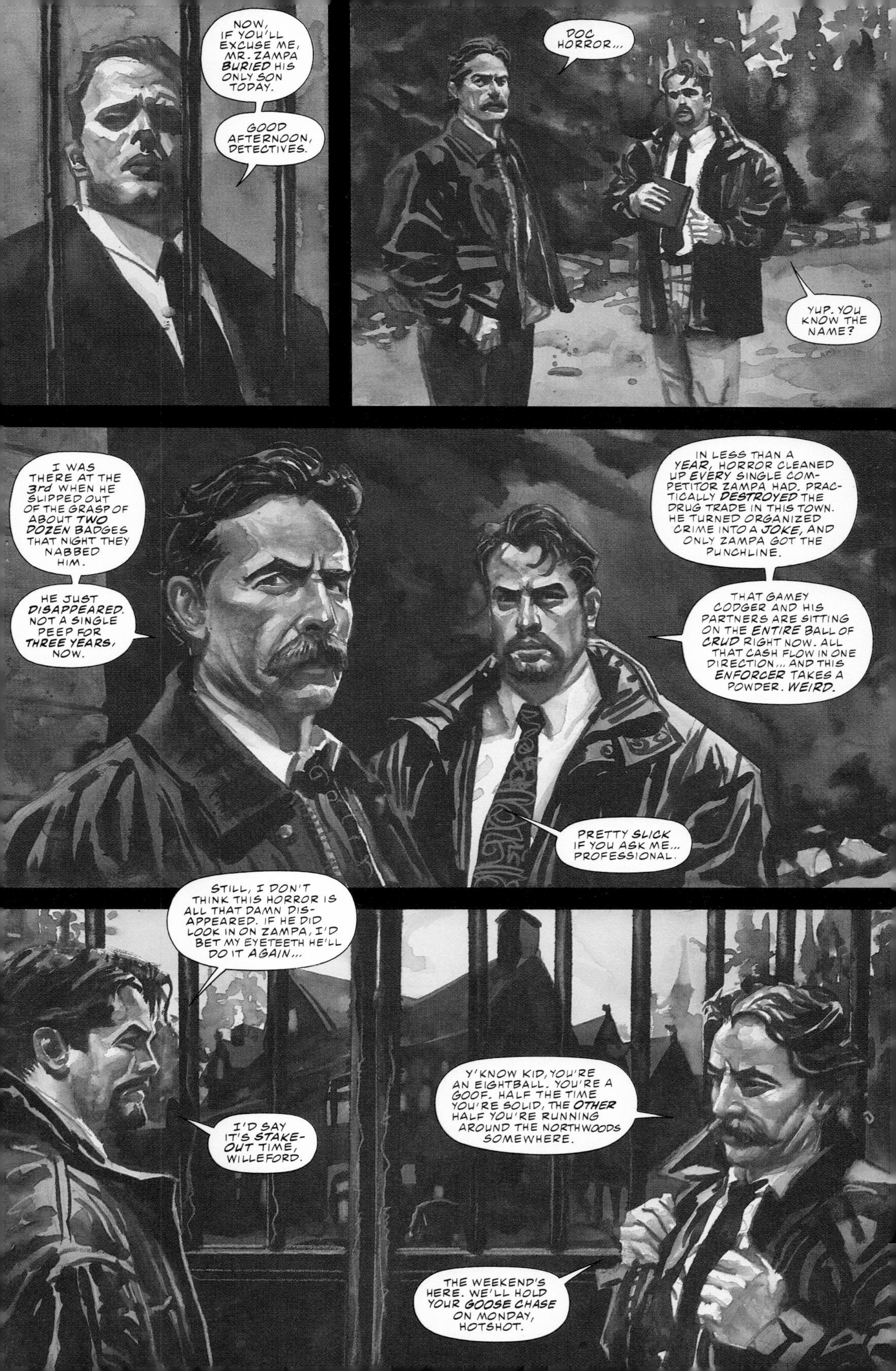
NOW, IF YOU'LL EXCUSE ME, MR. ZAMPA BURIED HIS ONLY SON TODAY.
GOOD AFTERNOON, DETECTIVES.
DOC HORROR...
YUP. YOU KNOW THE NAME?
I WAS THERE AT THE 3rd WHEN HE SLIPPED OUT OF THE GRASP OF ABOUT TWO DOZEN BADGES THAT NIGHT THEY NABBED HIM.
HE JUST DISAPPEARED. NOT A SINGLE PEEP FOR THREE YEARS, NOW.
IN LESS THAN A YEAR, HORROR CLEANED UP EVERY SINGLE COMPETITOR ZAMPA HAD. PRACTICALLY DESTROYED THE DRUG TRADE IN THIS TOWN. HE TURNED ORGANIZED CRIME INTO A JOKE, AND ONLY ZAMPA GOT THE PUNCHLINE.
THAT GAMEY CODGER AND HIS PARTNERS ARE SITTING ON THE ENTIRE BALL OF CRUD RIGHT NOW. ALL THAT CASH FLOW IN ONE DIRECTION... AND THIS ENFORCER TAKES A POWDER. WEIRD.
PRETTY SLICK IF YOU ASK ME... PROFESSIONAL.
STILL, I DON'T THINK THIS HORROR IS ALL THAT DAMN DISAPPEARED. IF HE DID LOOK IN ON ZAMPA, I'D BET MY EYETEETH HE'LL DO IT AGAIN...
I'D SAY IT'S STAKE-OUT TIME, WILLEFORD.
Y'KNOW KID, YOU'RE AN EIGHTBALL. YOU'RE A GOOF. HALF THE TIME YOU'RE SOLID, THE OTHER HALF YOU'RE RUNNING AROUND THE NORTHWOODS SOMEWHERE.
THE WEEKEND'S HERE. WE'LL HOLD YOUR GOOSE CHASE ON MONDAY, HOTSHOT.

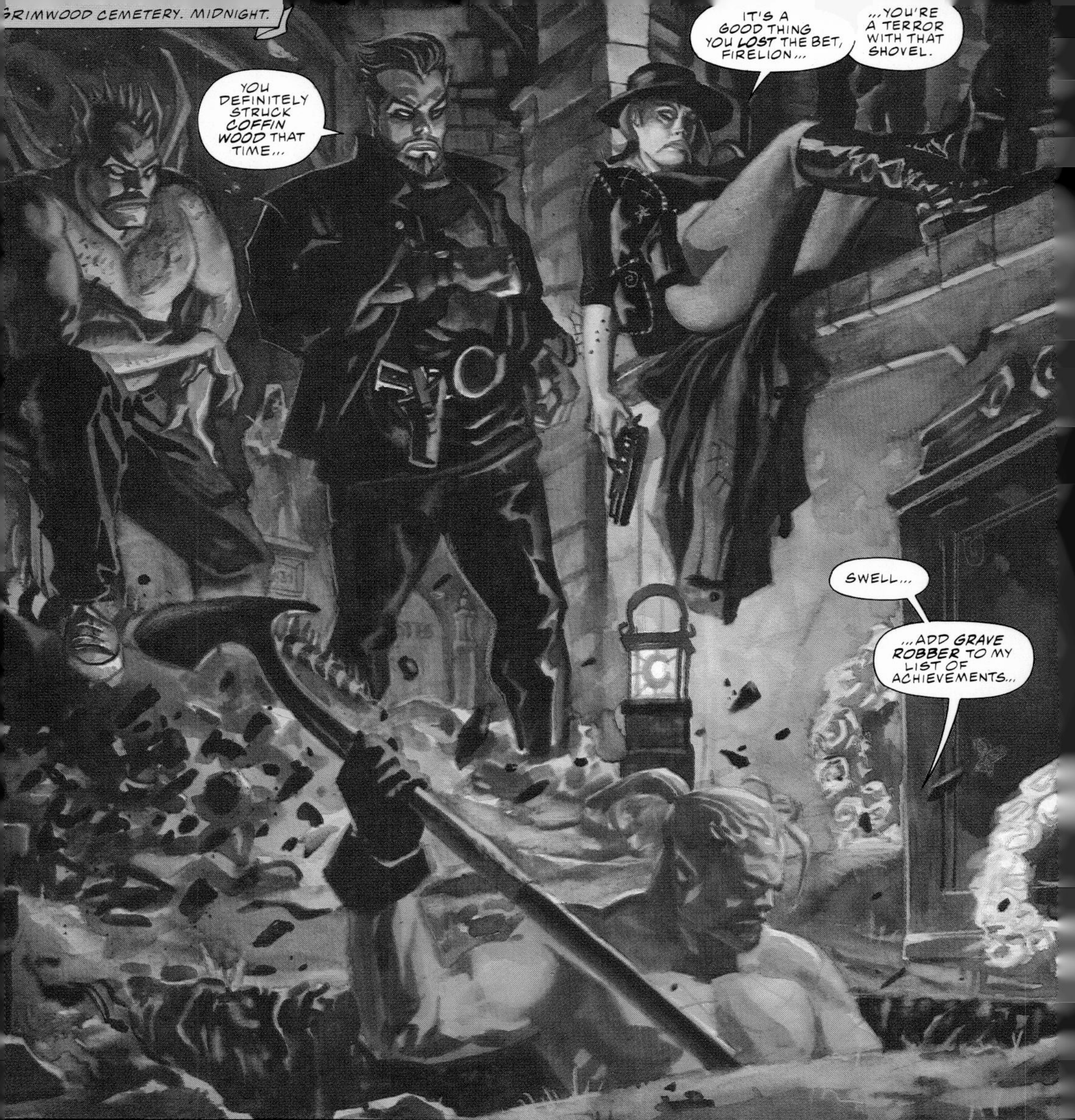
GRIMWOOD CEMETERY. MIDNIGHT.
YOU DEFINITELY STRUCK COFFIN WOOD THAT TIME...
IT'S A GOOD THING YOU LOST THE BET, FIRELION...
...YOU'RE A TERROR WITH THAT SHOVEL.
SWELL...
...ADD GRAVE ROBBER TO MY LIST OF ACHIEVEMENTS...

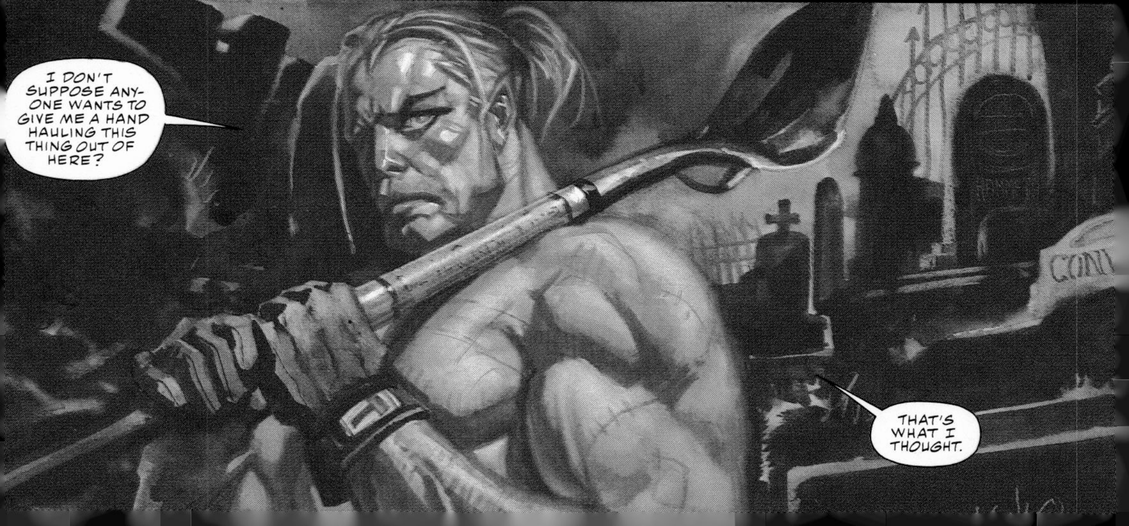
I DON'T SUPPOSE ANYONE WANTS TO GIVE ME A HAND HAULING THIS THING OUT OF HERE?
THAT'S WHAT I THOUGHT.

SO THEY FOUND A CREEPY-CRAWLY CLINGING TO TONY'S BODY... WHAT THE HELL'S THAT GOT TO DO WITH US?
SINCE WHEN DID WE BECOME THE HYGIENE POLICE?
I KNOW YOU SAID YOU'D EXPLAIN EVERYTHING ONCE WE EXHUMED THE PRINCE OF TURD HILL, BUT DIGGING UP A CORPSE...?
...MISTER, THAT'S KINDA SICK. EVEN FOR US.
LET'S GET THIS OVER WITH...
HSSSSS
NO...
HEY. SOMETHING'S MOVING IN THERE...
CRREEEEAAAKK!

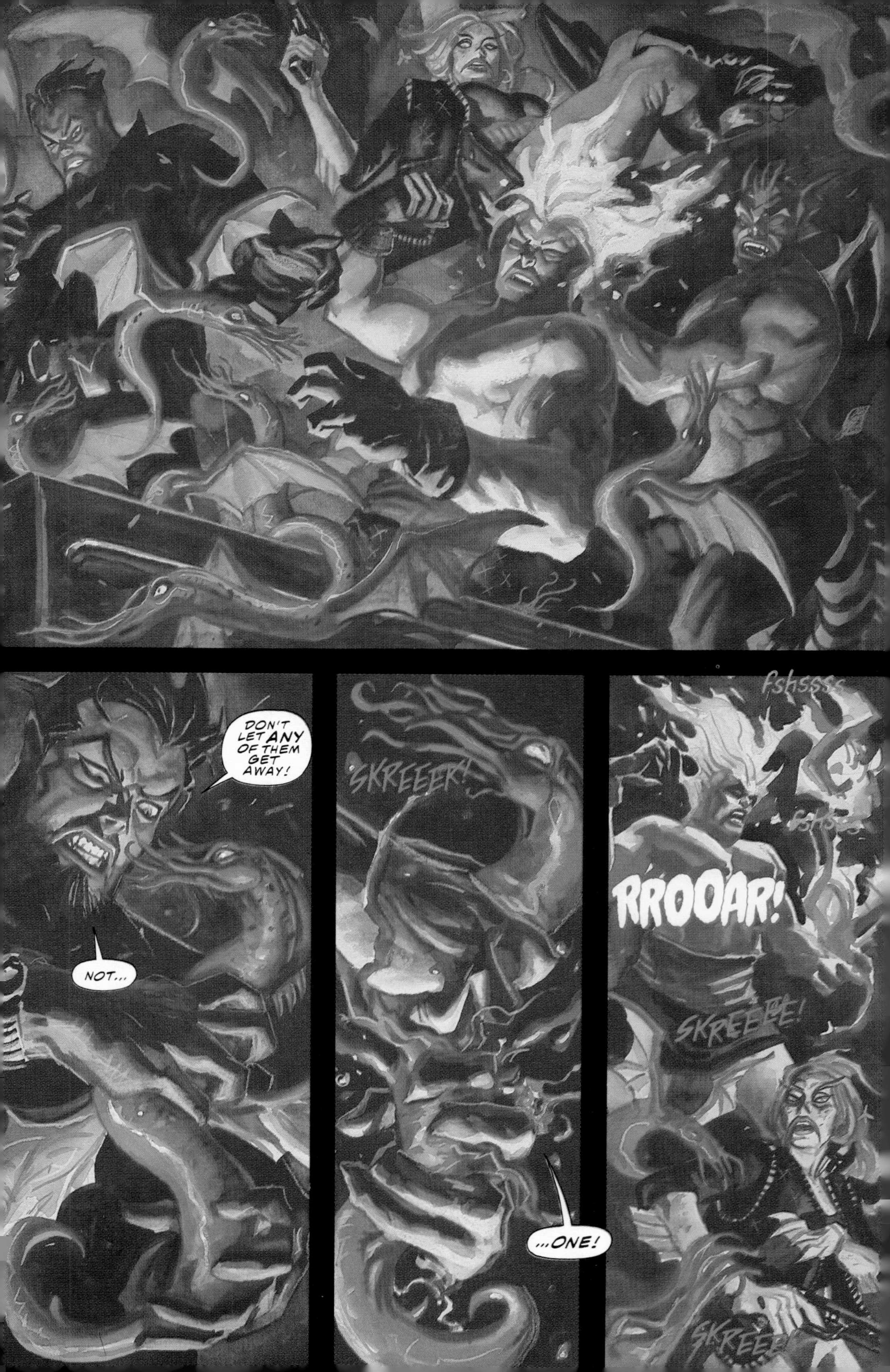
DON'T LET ANY OF THEM GET AWAY!
NOT...
SKREEEER!
...ONE!
fshssss
RROOAR!

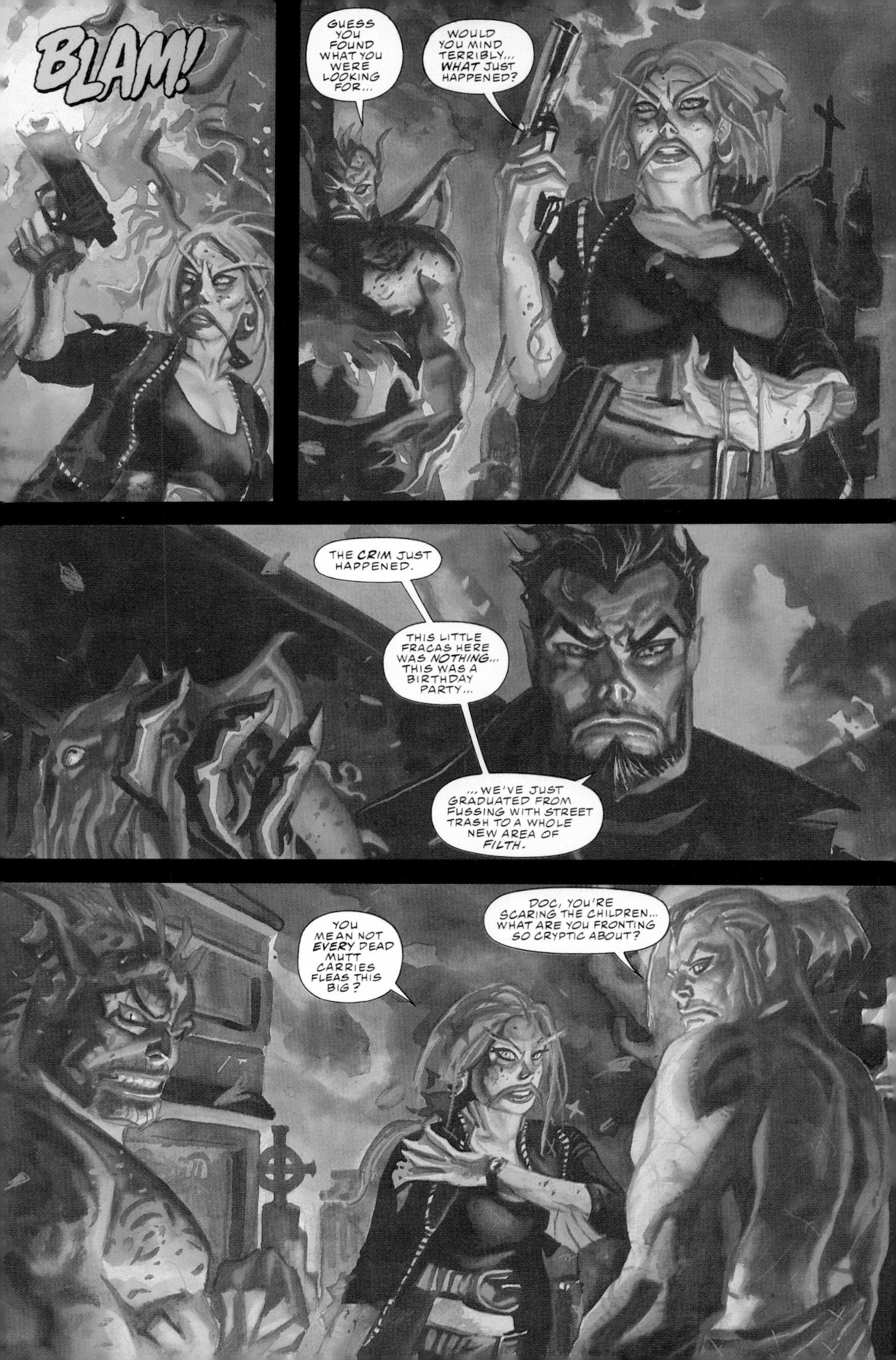
BLAM!
GUESS YOU FOUND WHAT YOU WERE LOOKING FOR...
WOULD YOU MIND TERRIBLY... WHAT JUST HAPPENED?
THE CRIM JUST HAPPENED.
THIS LITTLE FRACAS HERE WAS NOTHING... THIS WAS A BIRTHDAY PARTY...
...WE'VE JUST GRADUATED FROM FUSSING WITH STREET TRASH TO A WHOLE NEW AREA OF FILTH.
YOU MEAN NOT EVERY DEAD MUTT CARRIES FLEAS THIS BIG?
DOC, YOU'RE SCARING THE CHILDREN... WHAT ARE YOU FRONTING SO CRYPTIC ABOUT?

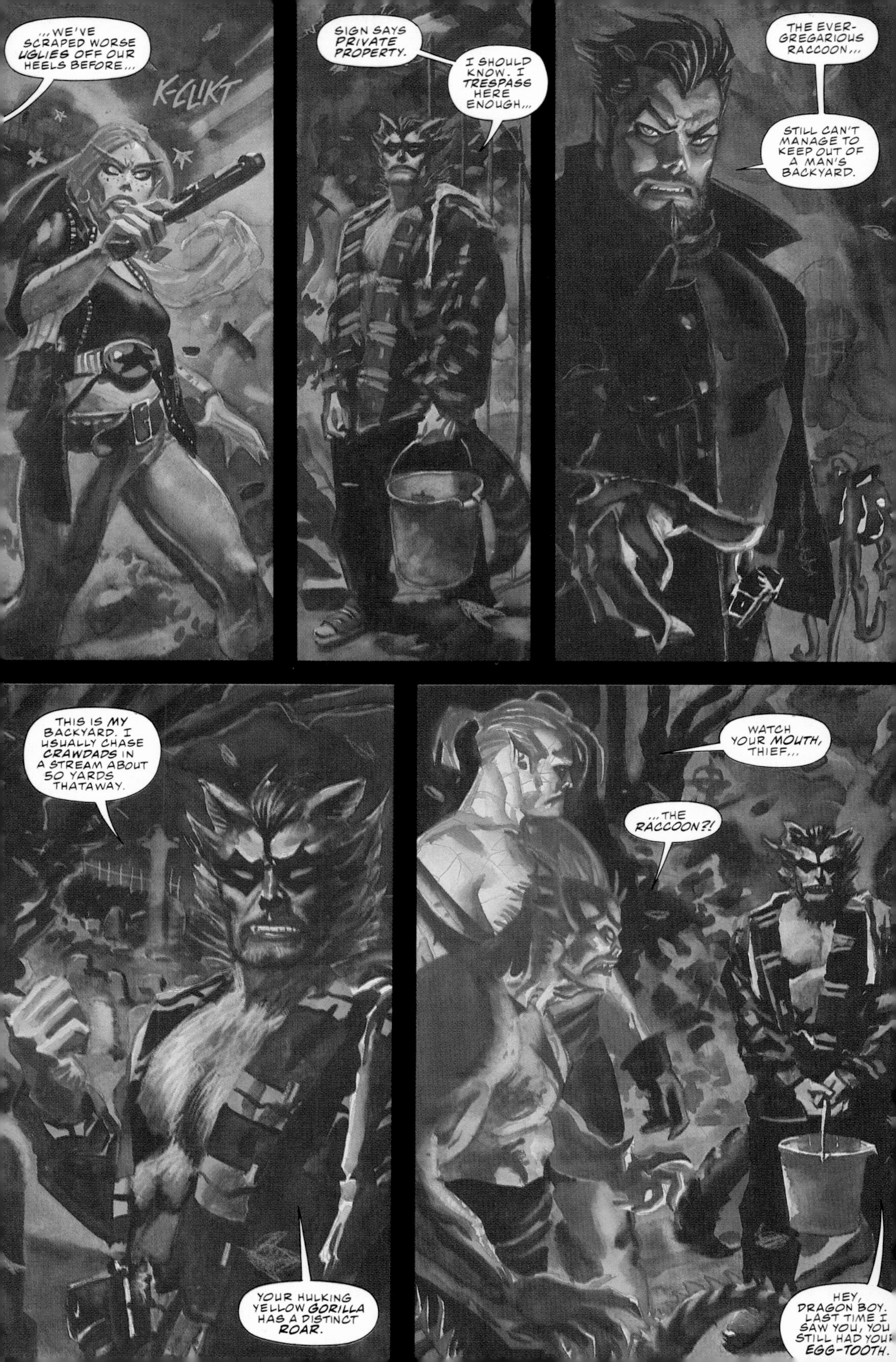
...WE'VE SCRAPED WORSE UGLIES OFF OUR HEELS BEFORE...
K-CLIKT
SIGN SAYS PRIVATE PROPERTY.
I SHOULD KNOW. I TRESPASS HERE ENOUGH...
THE EVER-GREGARIOUS RACCOON...
STILL CAN'T MANAGE TO KEEP OUT OF A MAN'S BACKYARD.
THIS IS MY BACKYARD. I USUALLY CHASE CRAWDADS IN A STREAM ABOUT 50 YARDS THATAWAY.
YOUR HULKING YELLOW GORILLA HAS A DISTINCT ROAR.
WATCH YOUR MOUTH, THIEF...
...THE RACCOON?!
HEY, DRAGON BOY. LAST TIME I SAW YOU, YOU STILL HAD YOUR EGG-TOOTH.

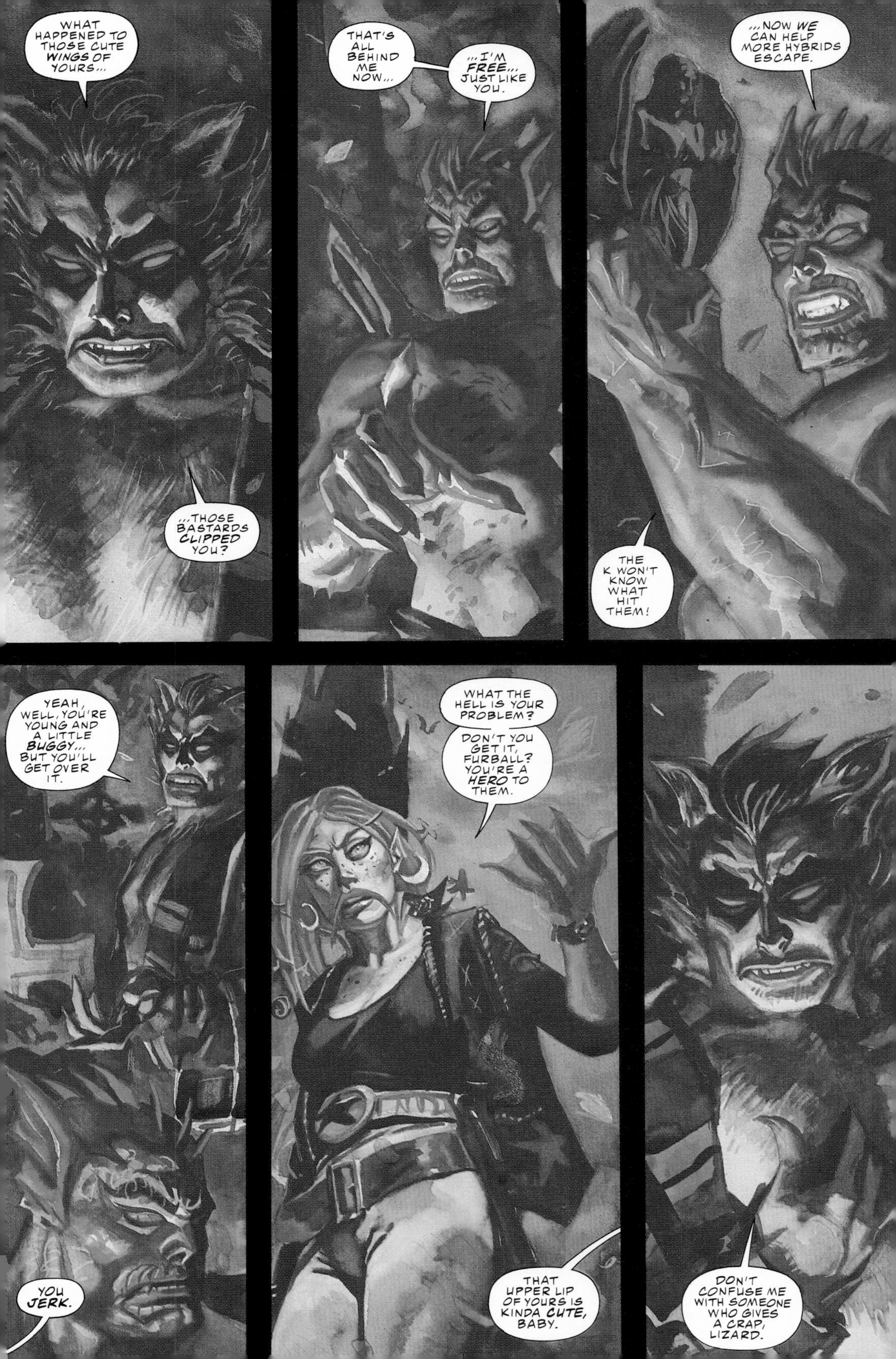
WHAT HAPPENED TO THOSE CUTE WINGS OF YOURS...
...THOSE BASTARDS CLIPPED YOU?
THAT'S ALL BEHIND ME NOW...
...I'M FREE... JUST LIKE YOU.
...NOW WE CAN HELP MORE HYBRIDS ESCAPE.
THE K WON'T KNOW WHAT HIT THEM!
YEAH, WELL, YOU'RE YOUNG AND A LITTLE BUGGY... BUT YOU'LL GET OVER IT.
YOU JERK.
WHAT THE HELL IS YOUR PROBLEM?
DON'T YOU GET IT, FURBALL? YOU'RE A HERO TO THEM.
THAT UPPER LIP OF YOURS IS KINDA CUTE, BABY.
DON'T CONFUSE ME WITH SOMEONE WHO GIVES A CRAP, LIZARD.

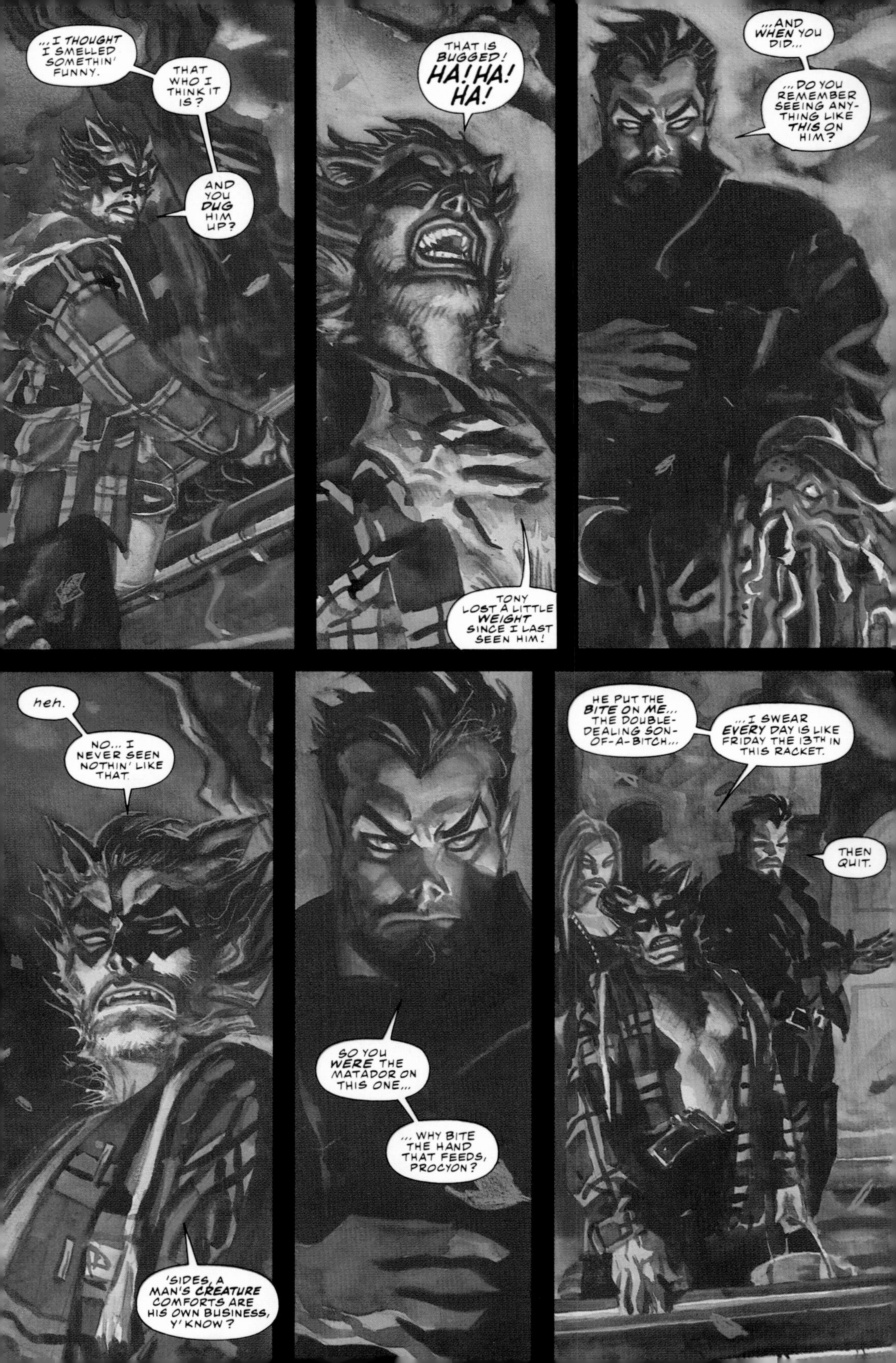
...I THOUGHT I SMELLED SOMETHIN' FUNNY.
THAT WHO I THINK IT IS?
AND YOU DUG HIM UP?
THAT IS BUGGED! HA! HA! HA!
TONY LOST A LITTLE WEIGHT SINCE I LAST SEEN HIM!
...AND WHEN YOU DID...
...DO YOU REMEMBER SEEING ANY-THING LIKE THIS ON HIM?
heh.
NO... I NEVER SEEN NOTHIN' LIKE THAT.
'SIDES, A MAN'S CREATURE COMFORTS ARE HIS OWN BUSINESS, Y'KNOW?
SO YOU WERE THE MATADOR ON THIS ONE...
...WHY BITE THE HAND THAT FEEDS, PROCYON?
HE PUT THE BITE ON ME... THE DOUBLE-DEALING SON-OF-A-BITCH...
...I SWEAR EVERY DAY IS LIKE FRIDAY THE 13TH IN THIS RACKET.
THEN QUIT.

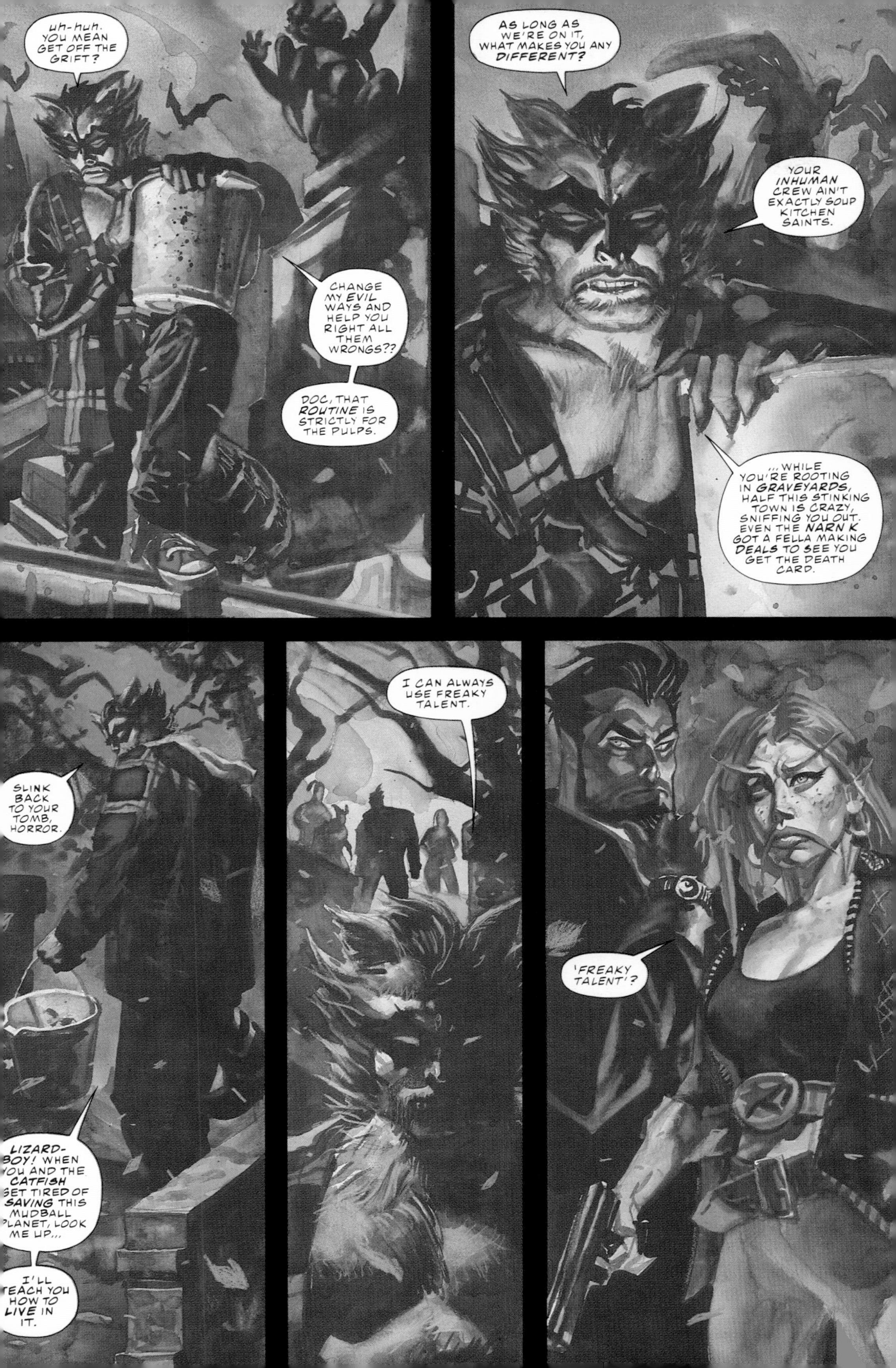

UH-HUH. YOU MEAN GET OFF THE GRIFT?
CHANGE MY EVIL WAYS AND HELP YOU RIGHT ALL THEM WRONGS??
DOC, THAT ROUTINE IS STRICTLY FOR THE PULPS.
AS LONG AS WE'RE ON IT, WHAT MAKES YOU ANY DIFFERENT?
YOUR INHUMAN CREW AIN'T EXACTLY SOUP KITCHEN SAINTS.
...WHILE YOU'RE ROOTING IN GRAVEYARDS, HALF THIS STINKING TOWN IS CRAZY, SNIFFING YOU OUT. EVEN THE NARN K GOT A FELLA MAKING DEALS TO SEE YOU GET THE DEATH CARD.
SLINK BACK TO YOUR TOMB, HORROR.
LIZARD-BOY! WHEN YOU AND THE CATFISH GET TIRED OF SAVING THIS MUDBALL PLANET, LOOK ME UP...
I'LL TEACH YOU HOW TO LIVE IN IT.
I CAN ALWAYS USE FREAKY TALENT.
'FREAKY TALENT'?

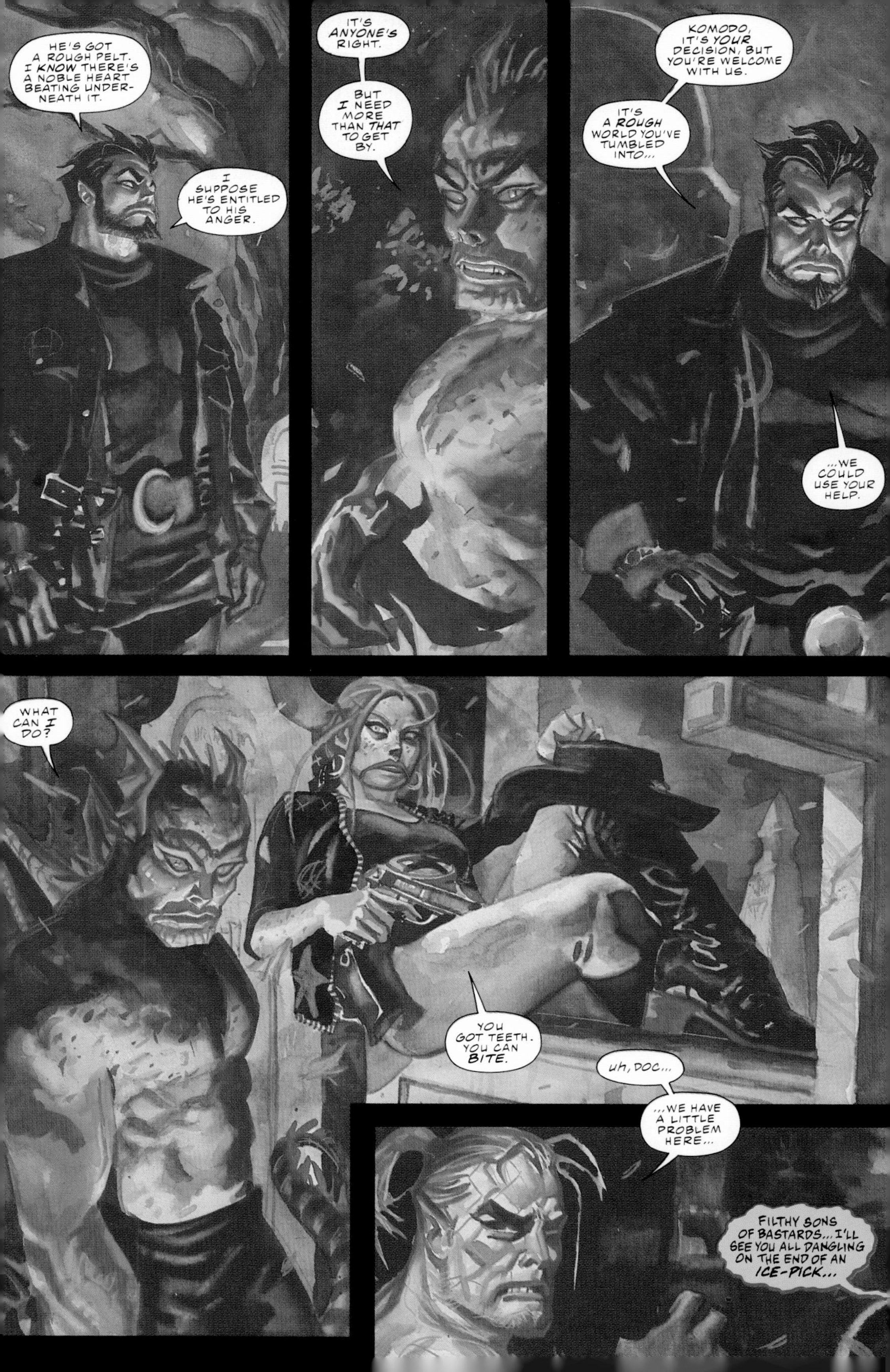
HE'S GOT A ROUGH PELT. I KNOW THERE'S A NOBLE HEART BEATING UNDERNEATH IT.
I SUPPOSE HE'S ENTITLED TO HIS ANGER.
IT'S ANYONE'S RIGHT.
BUT I NEED MORE THAN THAT TO GET BY.
KOMODO, IT'S YOUR DECISION, BUT YOU'RE WELCOME WITH US.
IT'S A ROUGH WORLD YOU'VE TUMBLED INTO...
...WE COULD USE YOUR HELP.
WHAT CAN I DO?
YOU GOT TEETH. YOU CAN BITE.
UH, DOC...
...WE HAVE A LITTLE PROBLEM HERE...
FILTHY SONS OF BASTARDS... I'LL SEE YOU ALL DANGLING ON THE END OF AN ICE-PICK...

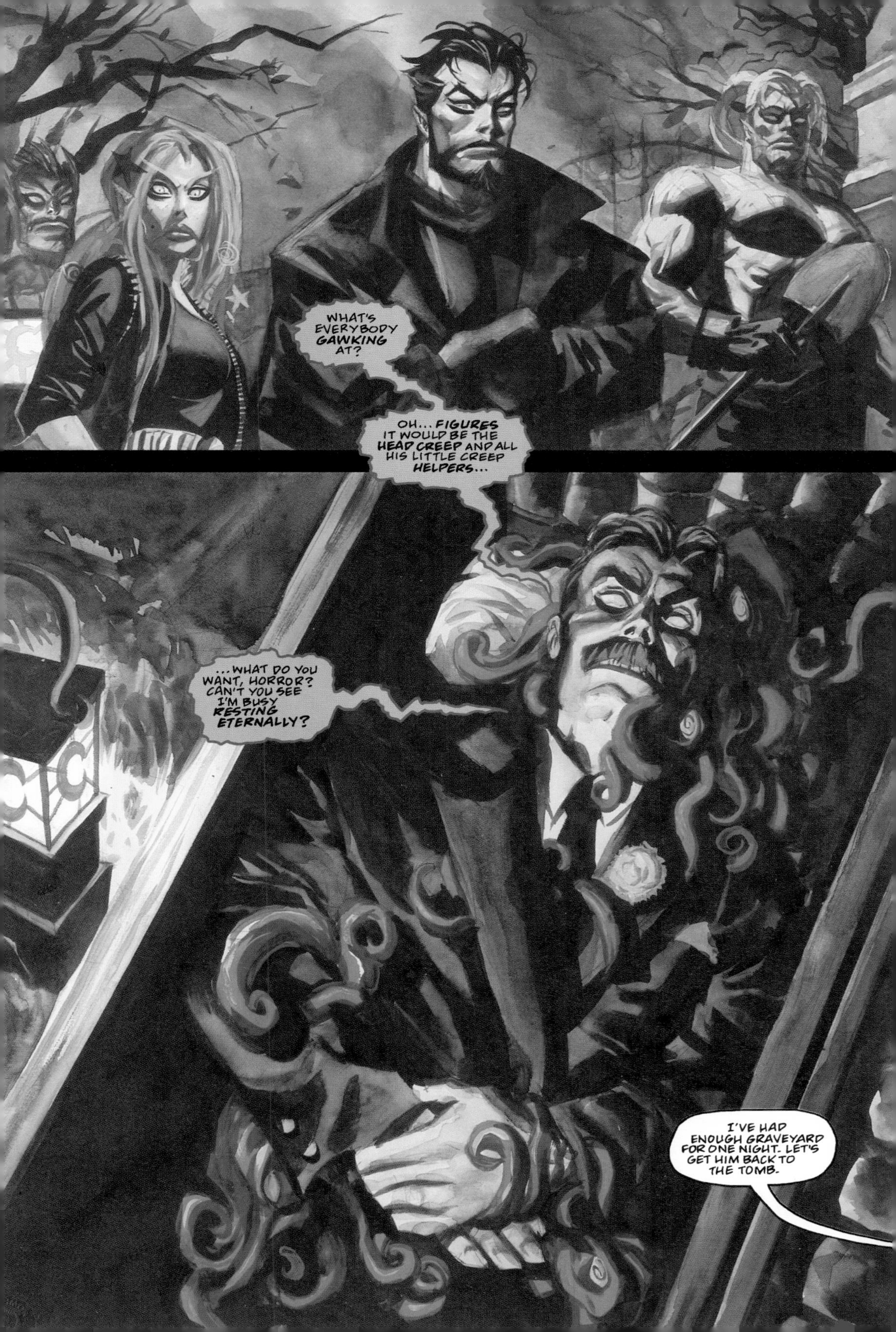
WHAT'S EVERYBODY GAWKING AT?
OH... FIGURES IT WOULD BE THE HEAD CREEP AND ALL HIS LITTLE CREEP HELPERS...
...WHAT DO YOU WANT, HORROR? CAN'T YOU SEE I'M BUSY RESTING ETERNALLY?
I'VE HAD ENOUGH GRAVEYARD FOR ONE NIGHT. LET'S GET HIM BACK TO THE TOMB.

...I FEEL... LIKE A BAG OF WET CEMENT...
YOU SMELL LIKE A BAG OF WET SOMETHING, BUT YOU SHOULDN'T FEEL ANYTHING.
AFTER ALL, YOU'RE A CORPSE.
...YEAH... SORTA HAD THAT PART FIGURED... I SWEAR TO CHRIST, HORROR... IF THIS IS YOUR DOING...
OH NO... I'D NEVER BRING YOU BACK FROM THE DEAD...
...I'LL GET THE BACKSTABBERS THAT DEALT ME THIS DIRT...
...MY SO-CALLED PARTNERS. THOSE CRUSTY MOUSTACHE PETES SET THE TABLE, AND THE RACCOON DISHED IT OUT...
BASTARDS.
STILL... IT DON'T EXPLAIN WHY I'M HERE NOW... A TALKING STIFF...
YOU HAVE ANOTHER CONFEDERATE TO THANK FOR THAT.

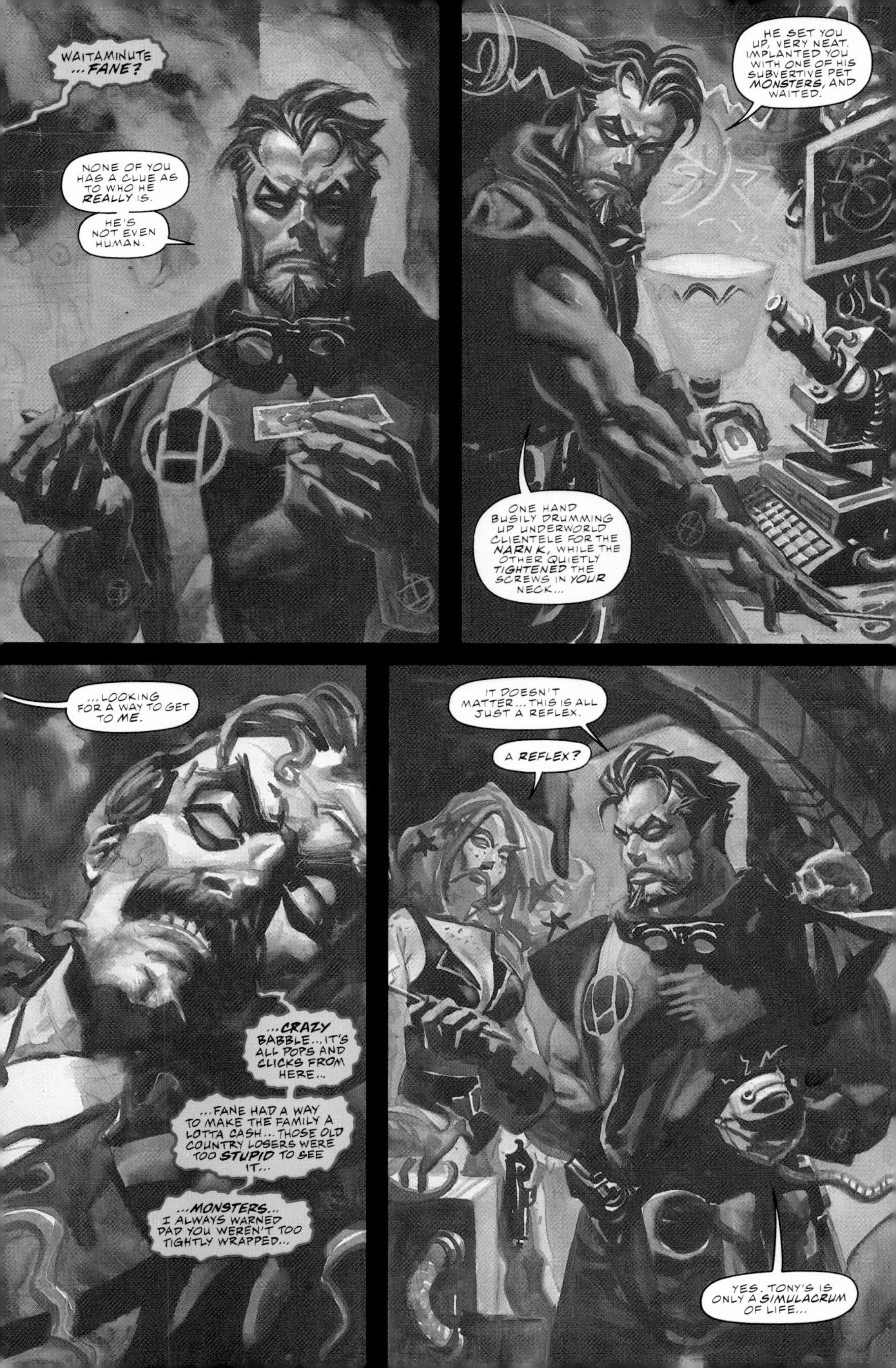
WAITAMINUTE ...FANE?
NONE OF YOU HAS A CLUE AS TO WHO HE REALLY IS.
HE'S NOT EVEN HUMAN.
HE SET YOU UP, VERY NEAT. IMPLANTED YOU WITH ONE OF HIS SUBVERTIVE PET MONSTERS, AND WAITED.
ONE HAND BUSILY DRUMMING UP UNDERWORLD CLIENTELE FOR THE NARN K, WHILE THE OTHER QUIETLY TIGHTENED THE SCREWS IN YOUR NECK...
...LOOKING FOR A WAY TO GET TO ME.
...CRAZY BABBLE... IT'S ALL POPS AND CLICKS FROM HERE...
...FANE HAD A WAY TO MAKE THE FAMILY A LOTTA CASH... THOSE OLD COUNTRY LOSERS WERE TOO STUPID TO SEE IT...
...MONSTERS... I ALWAYS WARNED DAD YOU WEREN'T TOO TIGHTLY WRAPPED...
IT DOESN'T MATTER... THIS IS ALL JUST A REFLEX.
A REFLEX?
YES. TONY'S IS ONLY A SIMULACRUM OF LIFE...

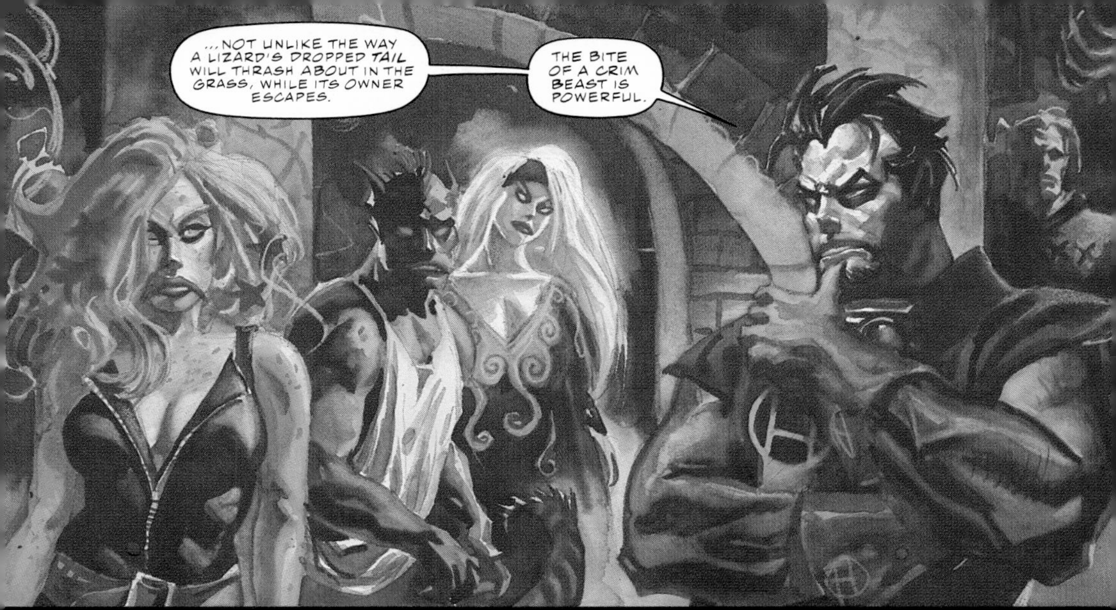
...NOT UNLIKE THE WAY A LIZARD'S DROPPED TAIL WILL THRASH ABOUT IN THE GRASS, WHILE ITS OWNER ESCAPES.
THE BITE OF A CRIM BEAST IS POWERFUL.

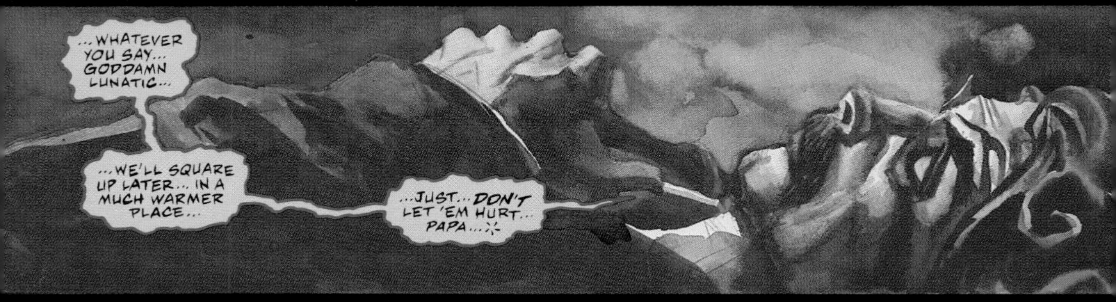
...WHATEVER YOU SAY... GODDAMN LUNATIC...
...WE'LL SQUARE UP LATER... IN A MUCH WARMER PLACE...
...JUST... DON'T LET 'EM HURT... PAPA...

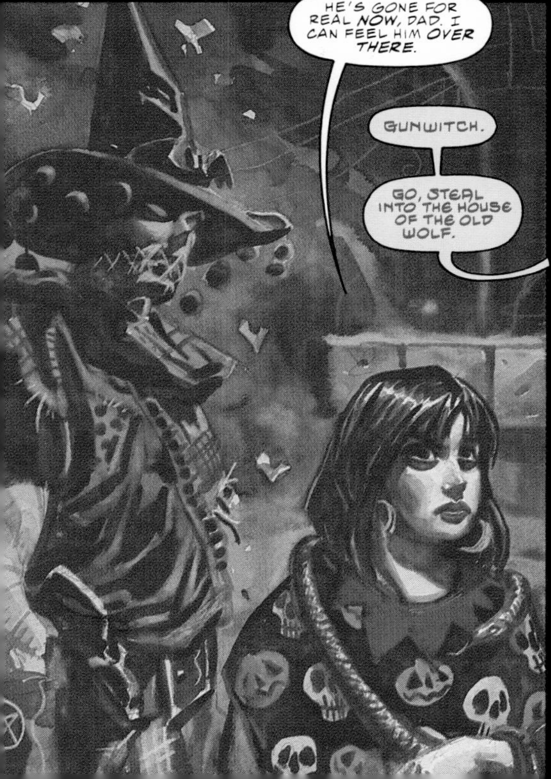
HE'S GONE FOR REAL NOW, DAD. I CAN FEEL HIM OVER THERE.
GUNWITCH.
GO, STEAL INTO THE HOUSE OF THE OLD WOLF.

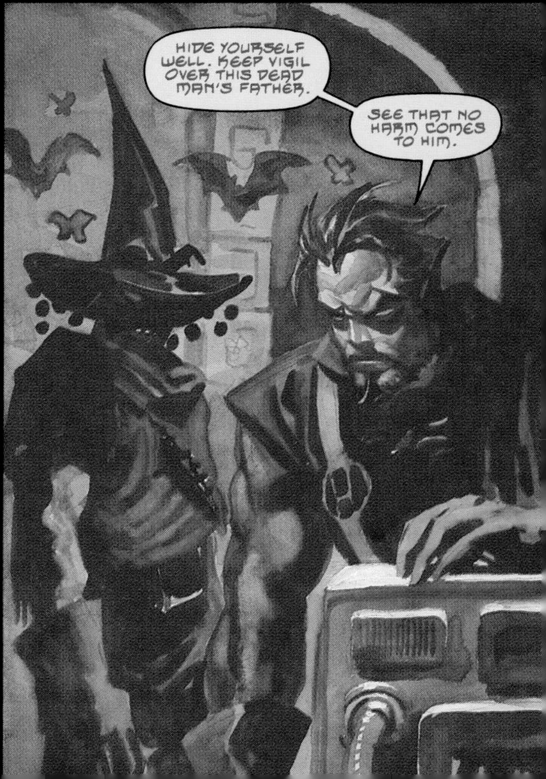
HIDE YOURSELF WELL. KEEP VIGIL OVER THIS DEAD MAN'S FATHER.
SEE THAT NO HARM COMES TO HIM.

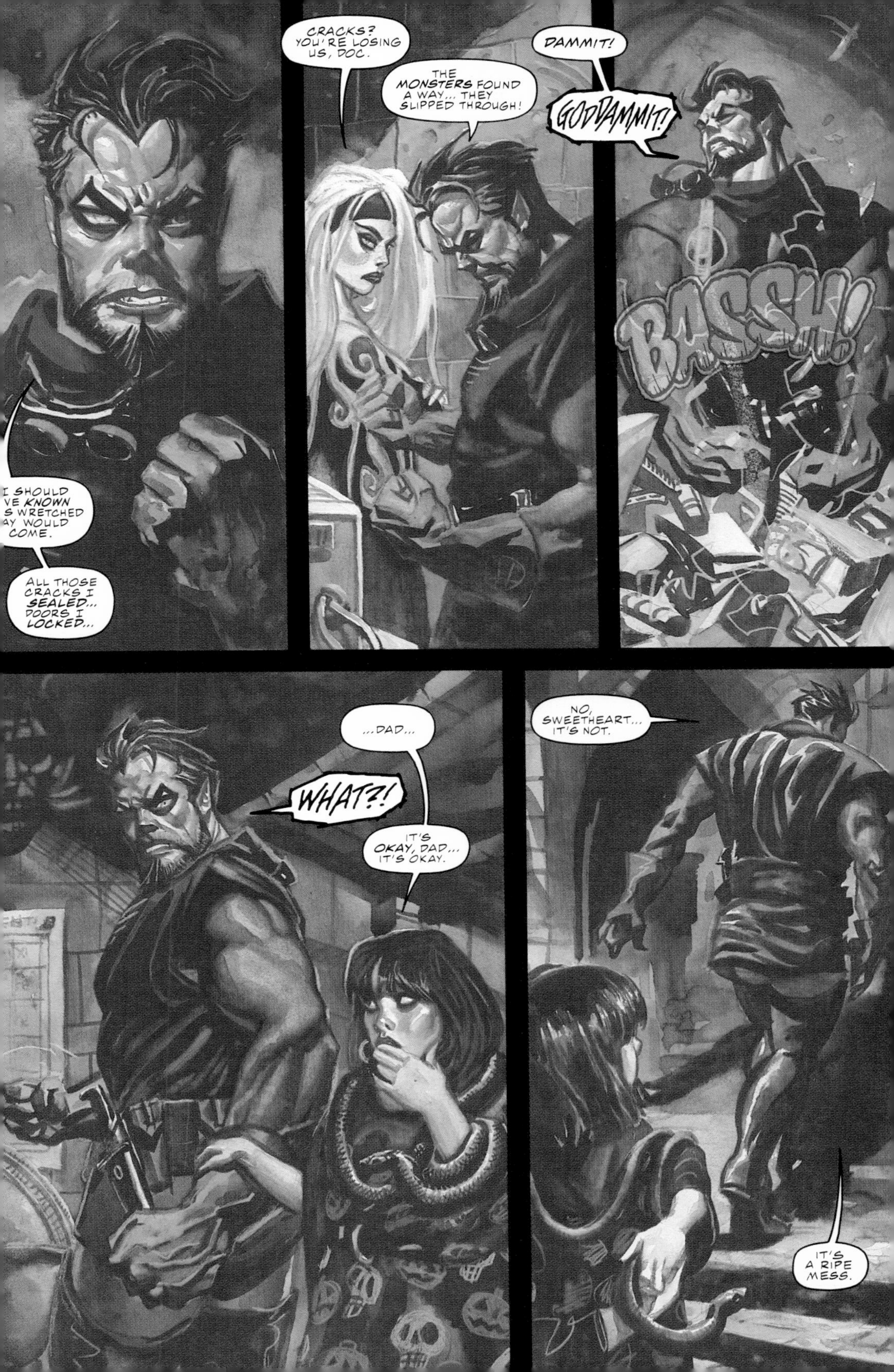

I SHOULD VE KNOWN S WRETCHED AY WOULD COME.
ALL THOSE CRACKS I SEALED... DOORS I LOCKED...
CRACKS? YOU'RE LOSING US, DOC.
THE MONSTERS FOUND A WAY... THEY SLIPPED THROUGH!
DAMMIT!
GODDAMMIT!
BASSH!
...DAD...
WHAT?!
IT'S OKAY, DAD... IT'S OKAY.
NO, SWEETHEART... IT'S NOT.
IT'S A RIPE MESS.

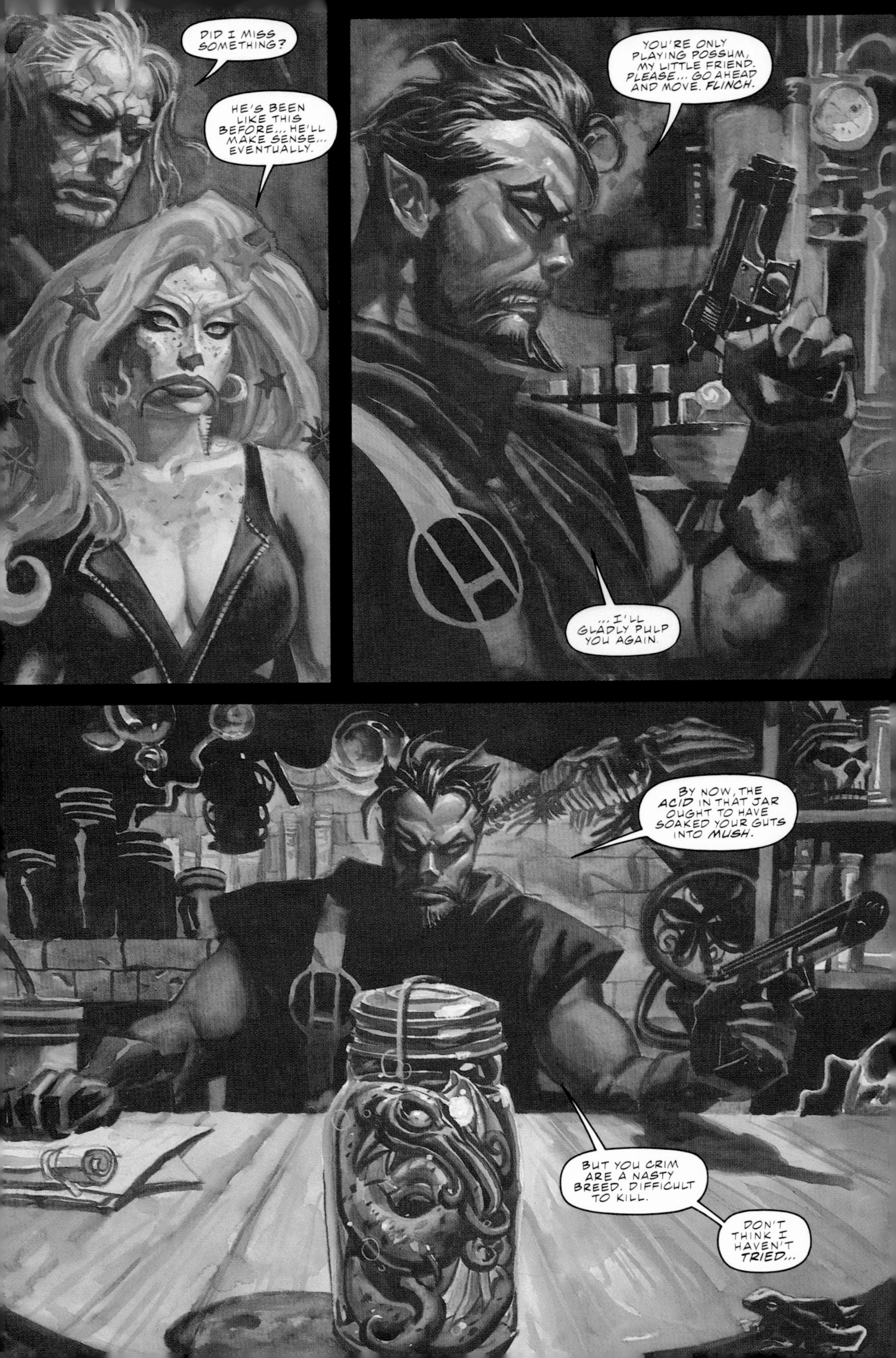
DID I MISS SOMETHING?
HE'S BEEN LIKE THIS BEFORE... HE'LL MAKE SENSE... EVENTUALLY.
YOU'RE ONLY PLAYING POSSUM, MY LITTLE FRIEND. PLEASE... GO AHEAD AND MOVE. FLINCH.
...I'LL GLADLY PULP YOU AGAIN.
BY NOW, THE ACID IN THAT JAR OUGHT TO HAVE SOAKED YOUR GUTS INTO MUSH.
BUT YOU CRIM ARE A NASTY BREED. DIFFICULT TO KILL.
DON'T THINK I HAVEN'T TRIED...

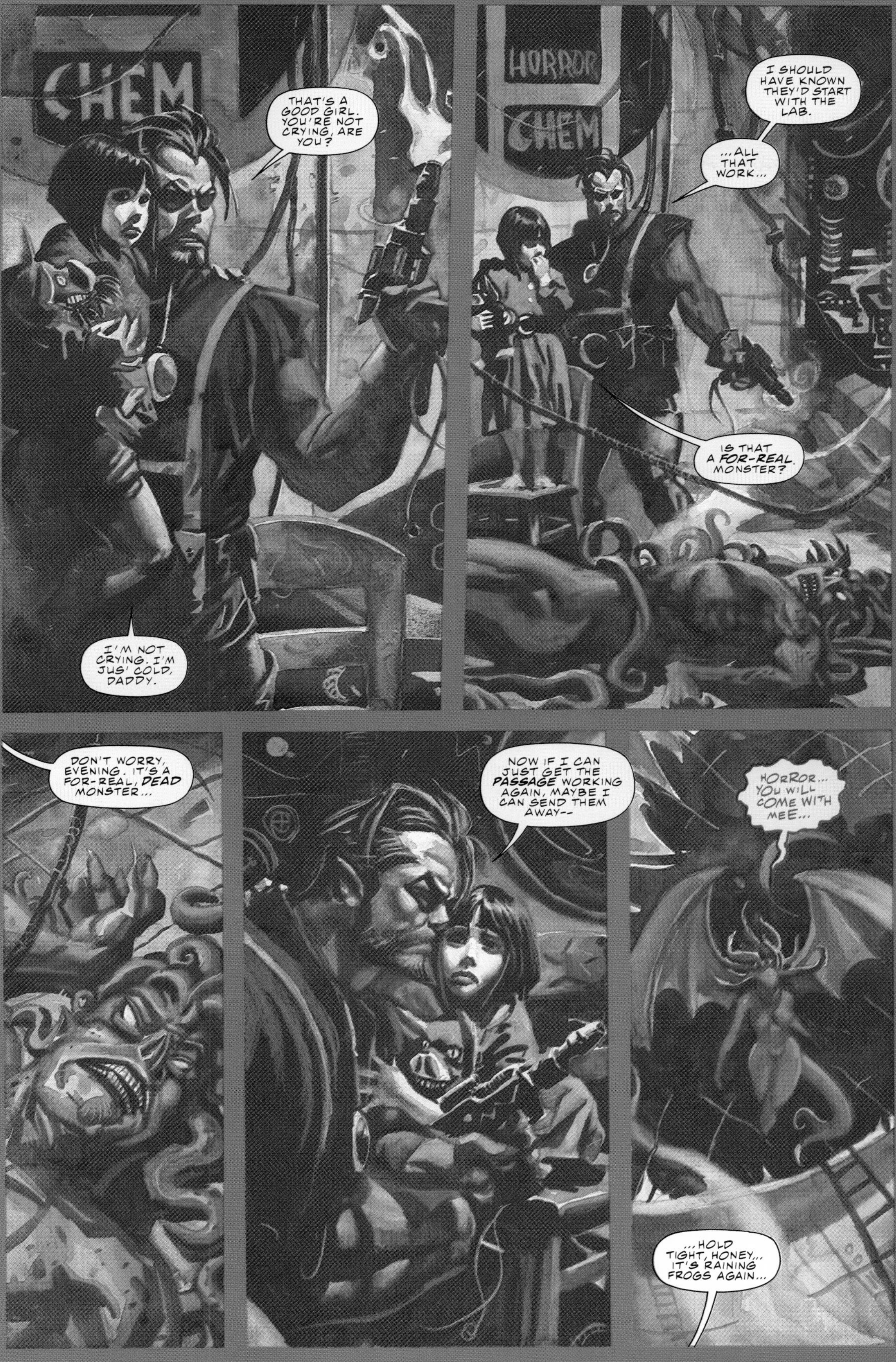
CHEM
THAT'S A GOOD GIRL. YOU'RE NOT CRYING, ARE YOU?
I'M NOT CRYING. I'M JUS' COLD, DADDY.
HORROR
CHEM
I SHOULD HAVE KNOWN THEY'D START WITH THE LAB.
...ALL THAT WORK...
IS THAT A FOR-REAL MONSTER?
DON'T WORRY, EVENING. IT'S A FOR-REAL, DEAD MONSTER...
NOW IF I CAN JUST GET THE PASSAGE WORKING AGAIN, MAYBE I CAN SEND THEM AWAY--
HORROR... YOU WILL COME WITH MEE...
...HOLD TIGHT, HONEY... IT'S RAINING FROGS AGAIN...

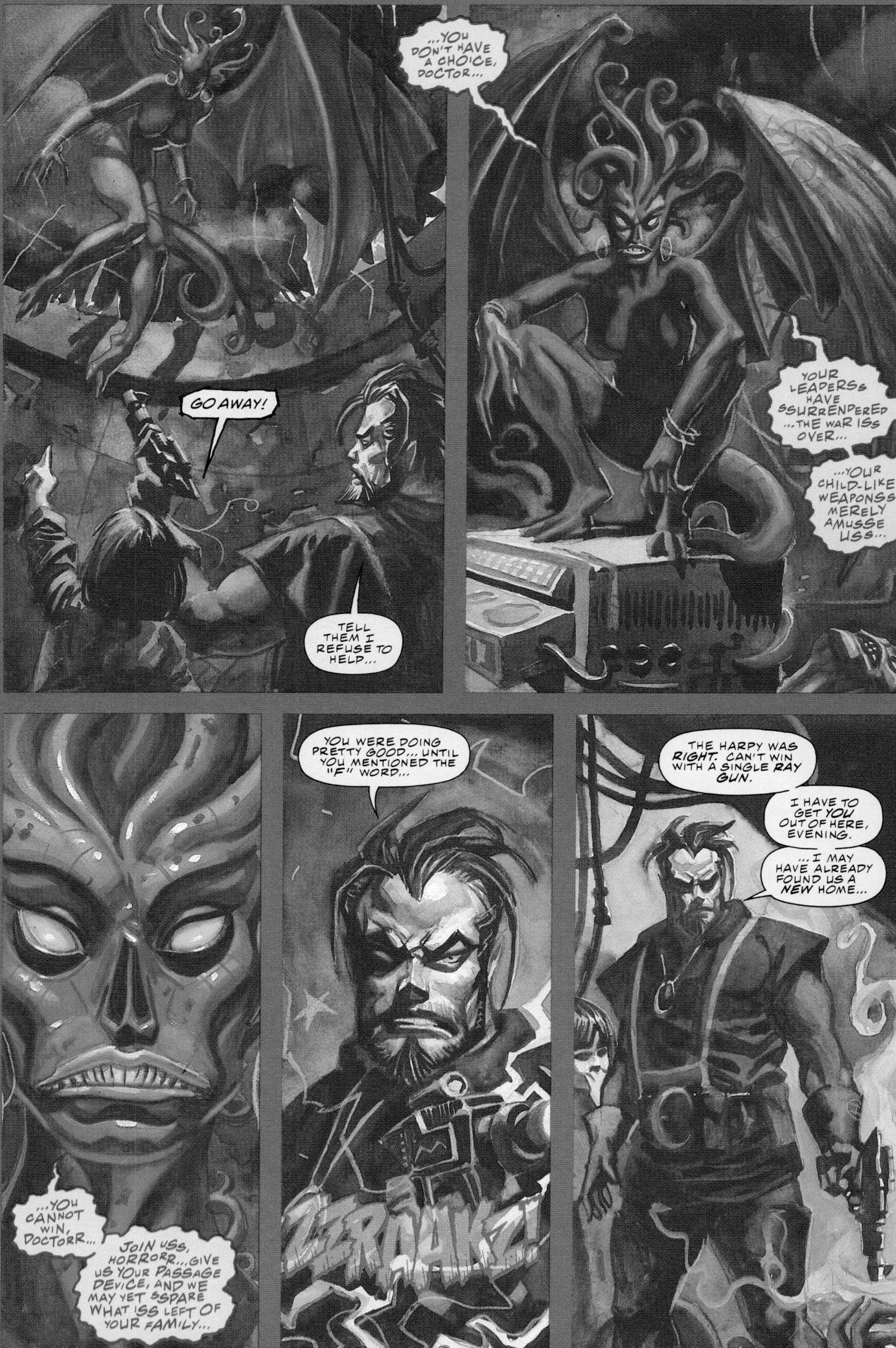
...YOU DON'T HAVE A CHOICE, DOCTOR...
GO AWAY!
TELL THEM I REFUSE TO HELP...
YOUR LEADERSS HAVE SSURRENDERED ...THE WAR ISS OVER...
...YOUR CHILD-LIKE WEAPONSS MERELY AMUSSE USS...
...YOU CANNOT WIN, DOCTORR...
JOIN USS, HORRORR... GIVE US YOUR PASSAGE DEVICE, AND WE MAY YET SSPARE WHAT ISS LEFT OF YOUR FAMILY...
YOU WERE DOING PRETTY GOOD... UNTIL YOU MENTIONED THE "F" WORD...
THE HARPY WAS RIGHT. CAN'T WIN WITH A SINGLE RAY GUN.
I HAVE TO GET YOU OUT OF HERE, EVENING.
...I MAY HAVE ALREADY FOUND US A NEW HOME...

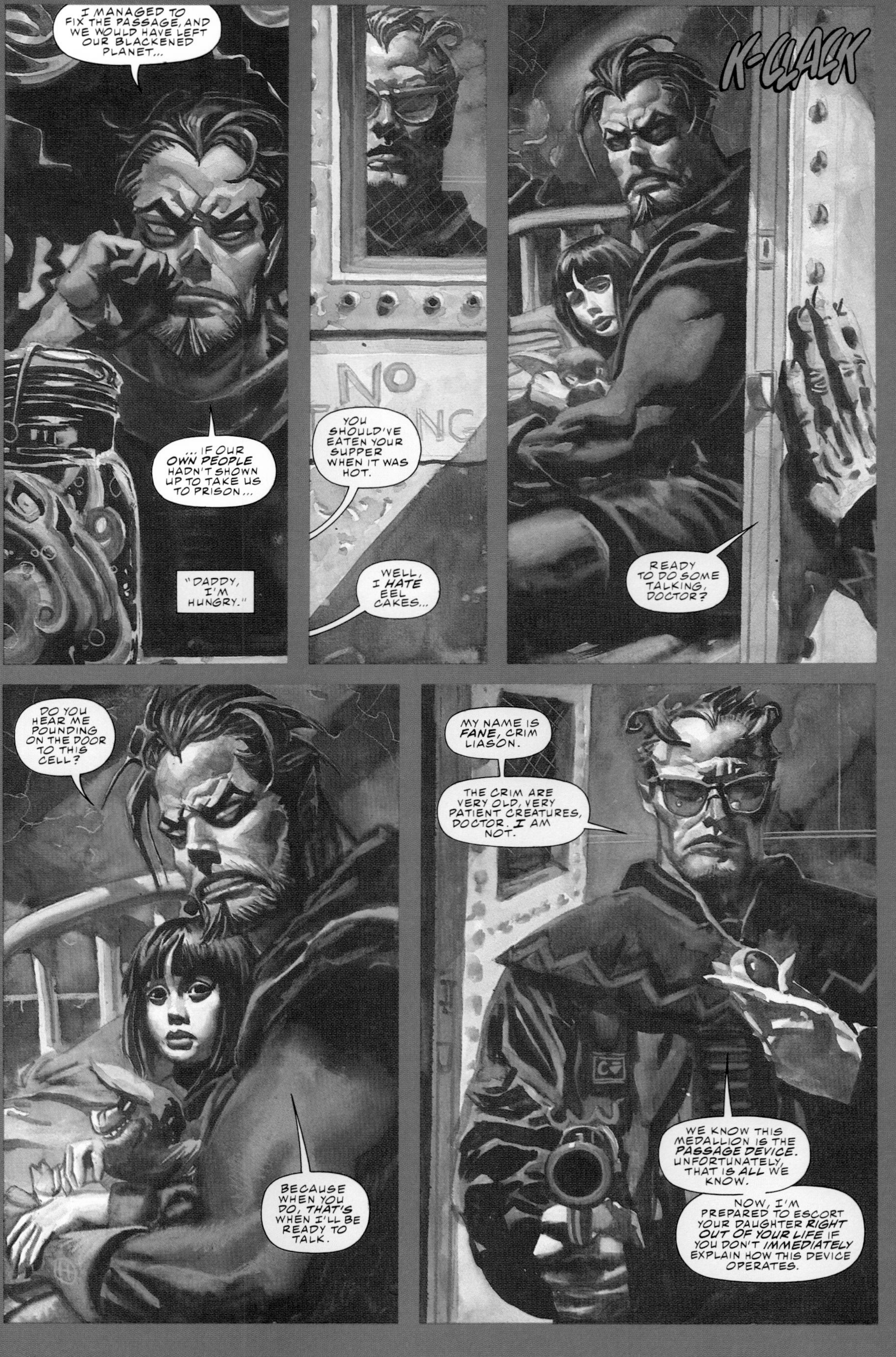

I MANAGED TO FIX THE PASSAGE, AND WE WOULD HAVE LEFT OUR BLACKENED PLANET...
... IF OUR ***OWN PEOPLE*** HADN'T SHOWN UP TO TAKE US TO PRISON...
"DADDY, I'M HUNGRY."
NO
YOU SHOULD'VE EATEN YOUR SUPPER WHEN IT WAS HOT.
WELL, I ***HATE*** EEL CAKES...
K-CLACK
READY TO DO SOME TALKING, DOCTOR?
DO YOU HEAR ME POUNDING ON THE DOOR TO THIS CELL?
BECAUSE WHEN YOU ***DO***, ***THAT'S*** WHEN I'LL BE READY TO TALK.
MY NAME IS ***FANE***, CRIM LIASON.
THE CRIM ARE VERY OLD, VERY PATIENT CREATURES, DOCTOR. ***I*** AM NOT.
WE KNOW THIS MEDALLION IS THE ***PASSAGE DEVICE***. UNFORTUNATELY, THAT IS ***ALL*** WE KNOW.
NOW, I'M PREPARED TO ESCORT YOUR DAUGHTER ***RIGHT OUT OF YOUR LIFE*** IF YOU DON'T ***IMMEDIATELY*** EXPLAIN HOW THIS DEVICE OPERATES.

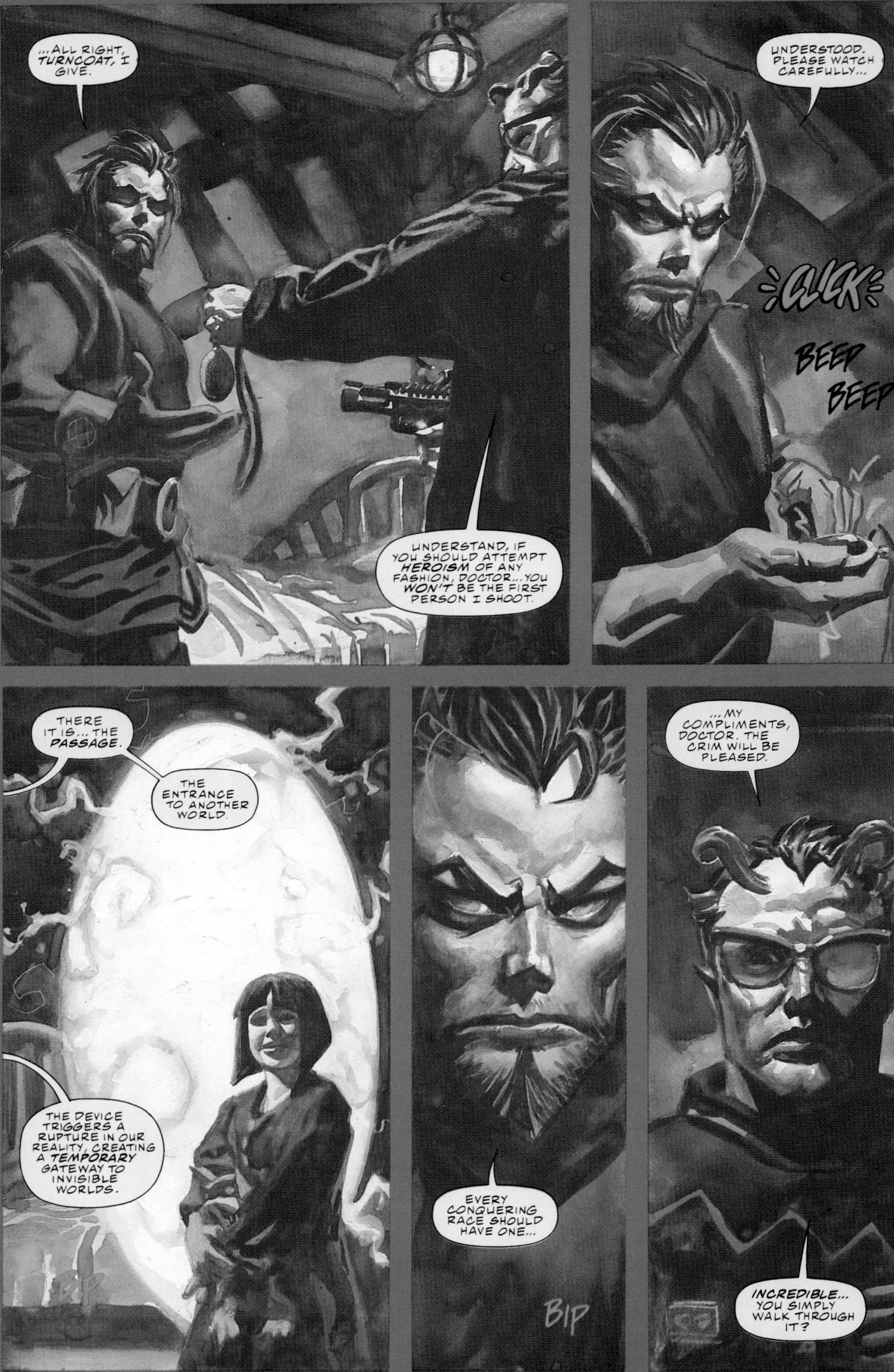
...ALL RIGHT, TURNCOAT, I GIVE.
UNDERSTAND, IF YOU SHOULD ATTEMPT HEROISM OF ANY FASHION, DOCTOR... YOU WON'T BE THE FIRST PERSON I SHOOT.
UNDERSTOOD. PLEASE WATCH CAREFULLY...
CLICK
BEEP BEEP
THERE IT IS... THE PASSAGE.
THE ENTRANCE TO ANOTHER WORLD.
THE DEVICE TRIGGERS A RUPTURE IN OUR REALITY, CREATING A TEMPORARY GATEWAY TO INVISIBLE WORLDS.
EVERY CONQUERING RACE SHOULD HAVE ONE...
...MY COMPLIMENTS, DOCTOR. THE CRIM WILL BE PLEASED.
INCREDIBLE... YOU SIMPLY WALK THROUGH IT?

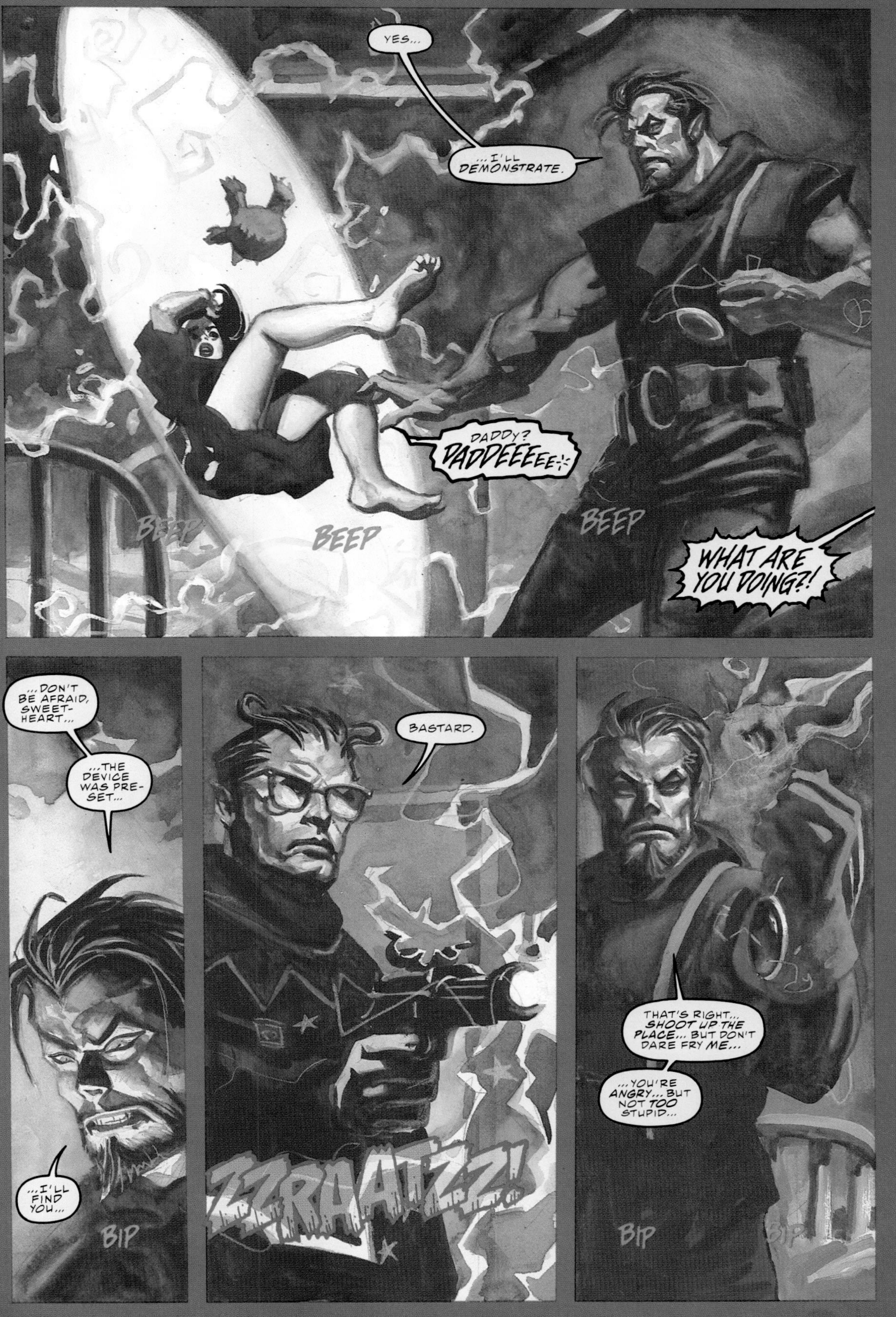
YES...
...I'LL DEMONSTRATE.
DADDY? DADDEEEEEE-!
BEEP
BEEP
BEEP
WHAT ARE YOU DOING?!
...DON'T BE AFRAID, SWEET-HEART...
...THE DEVICE WAS PRE-SET...
...I'LL FIND YOU...
BIP
BASTARD.
ZZRAATZZ!
THAT'S RIGHT... SHOOT UP THE PLACE... BUT DON'T DARE FRY ME...
...YOU'RE ANGRY... BUT NOT TOO STUPID...
BIP
BIP

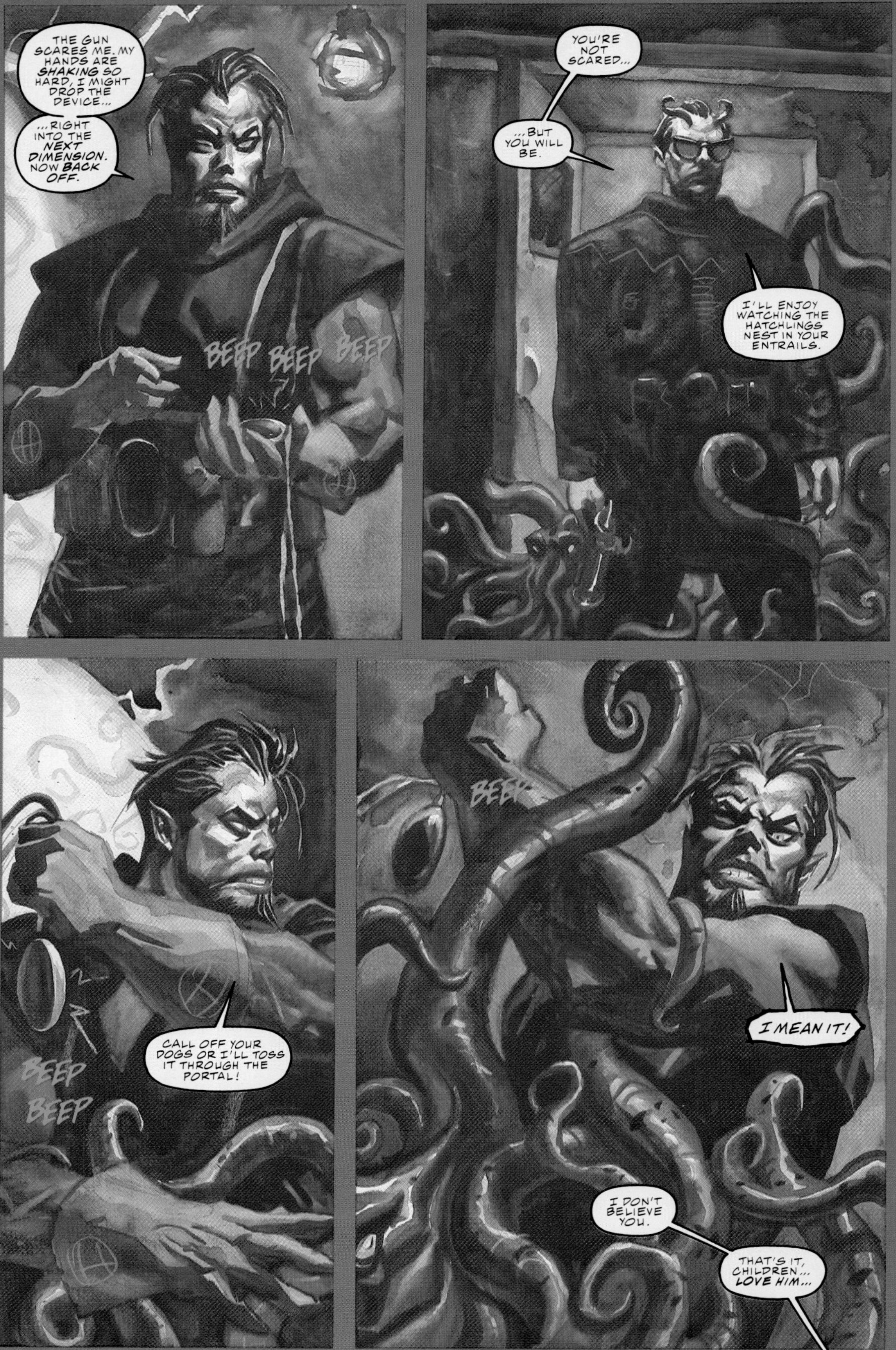

THE GUN SCARES ME. MY HANDS ARE SHAKING SO HARD, I MIGHT DROP THE DEVICE...
...RIGHT INTO THE NEXT DIMENSION. NOW BACK OFF.
BEEP BEEP BEEP
YOU'RE NOT SCARED...
...BUT YOU WILL BE.
I'LL ENJOY WATCHING THE HATCHLINGS NEST IN YOUR ENTRAILS.
BEEP BEEP
CALL OFF YOUR DOGS OR I'LL TOSS IT THROUGH THE PORTAL!
BEEP
I MEAN IT!
I DON'T BELIEVE YOU.
THAT'S IT, CHILDREN... LOVE HIM...

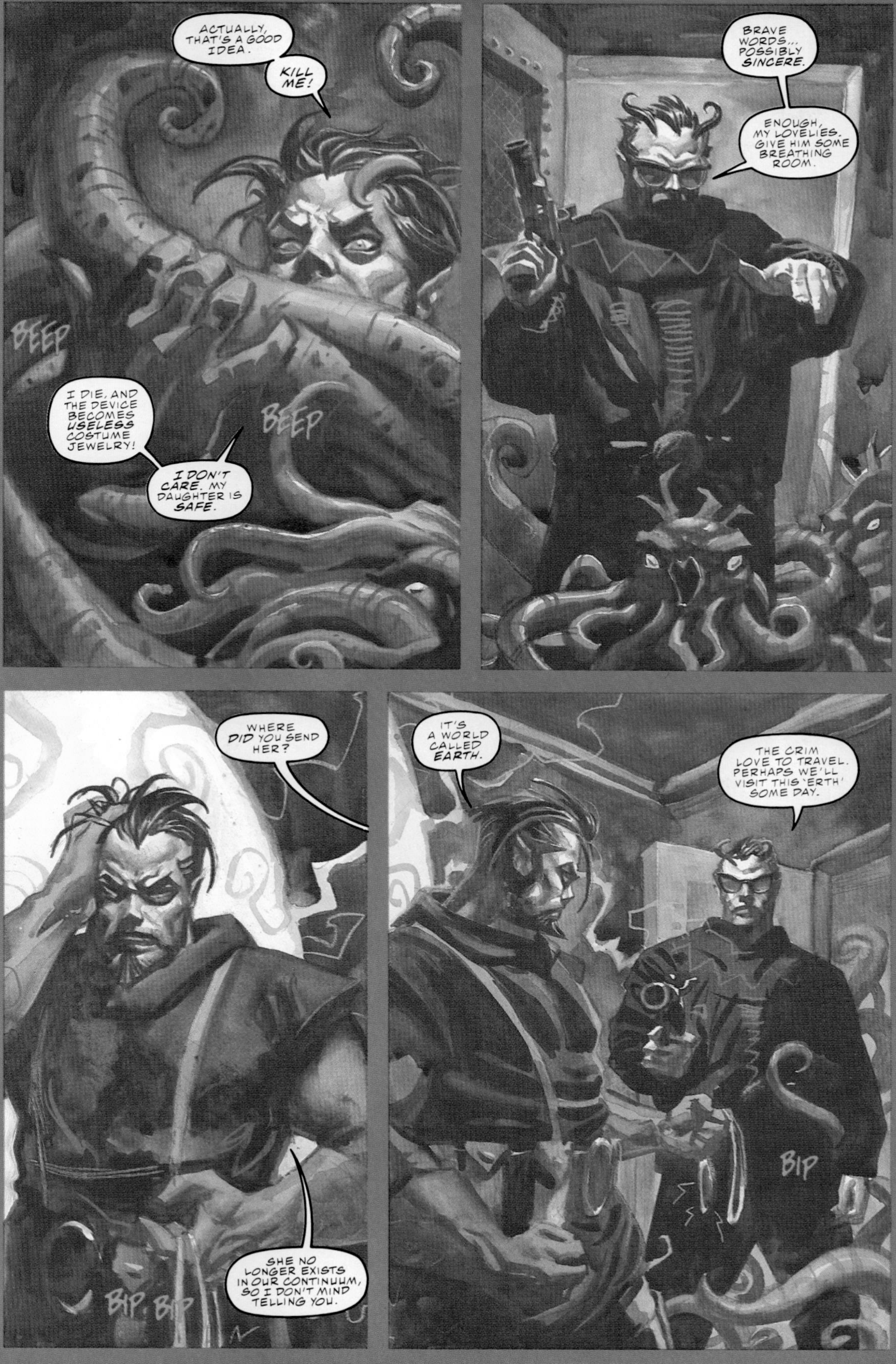
ACTUALLY, THAT'S A GOOD IDEA.
KILL ME!
BEEP
I DIE, AND THE DEVICE BECOMES USELESS COSTUME JEWELRY!
BEEP
I DON'T CARE. MY DAUGHTER IS SAFE.
BRAVE WORDS... POSSIBLY SINCERE.
ENOUGH, MY LOVELIES. GIVE HIM SOME BREATHING ROOM.
WHERE DID YOU SEND HER?
SHE NO LONGER EXISTS IN OUR CONTINUUM, SO I DON'T MIND TELLING YOU.
BIP BIP
IT'S A WORLD CALLED EARTH.
THE CRIM LOVE TO TRAVEL. PERHAPS WE'LL VISIT THIS 'ERTH' SOME DAY.
BIP

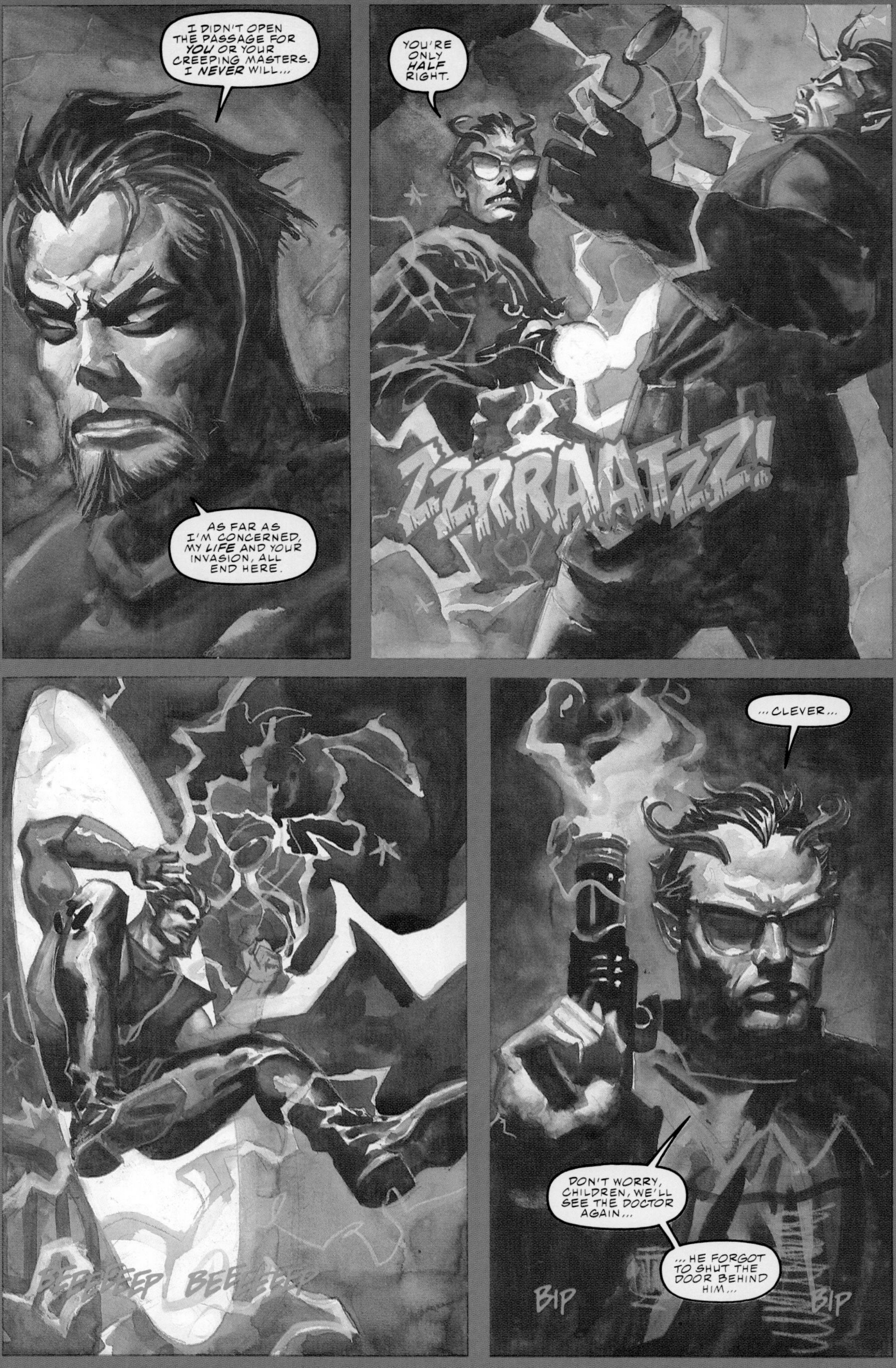

I DIDN'T OPEN THE PASSAGE FOR *YOU* OR YOUR CREEPING MASTERS. I *NEVER* WILL...
AS FAR AS I'M CONCERNED, MY *LIFE* AND YOUR INVASION, ALL END HERE.
YOU'RE ONLY *HALF* RIGHT.
BIP
ZZRAAATZZ!
BEEBEEP BEEBEEP
...CLEVER...
DON'T WORRY, CHILDREN, WE'LL SEE THE DOCTOR AGAIN...
...HE FORGOT TO SHUT THE DOOR BEHIND HIM...
BIP BIP

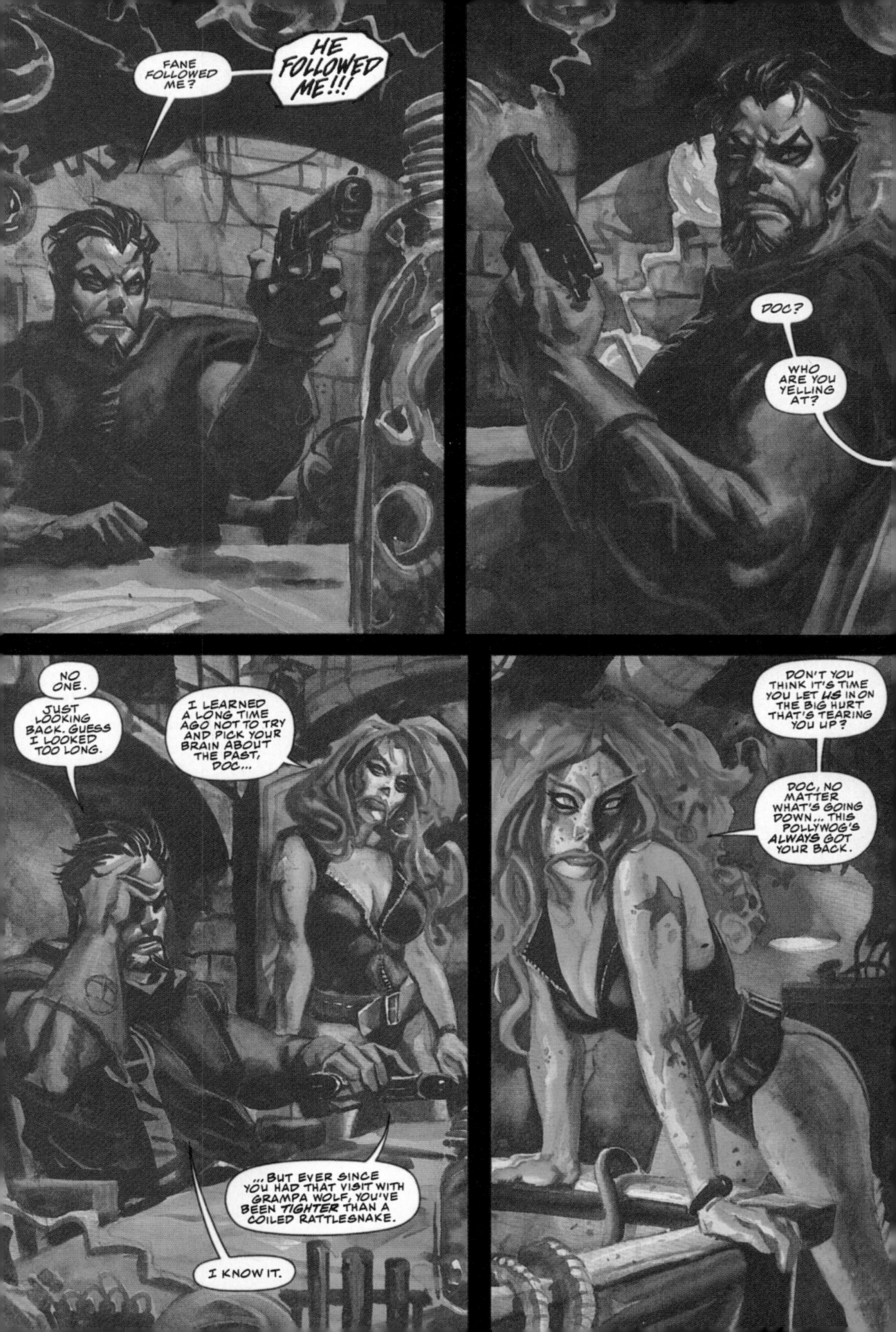
FANE FOLLOWED ME?
HE FOLLOWED ME!!!
DOC?
WHO ARE YOU YELLING AT?
NO ONE.
JUST LOOKING BACK. GUESS I LOOKED TOO LONG.
I LEARNED A LONG TIME AGO NOT TO TRY AND PICK YOUR BRAIN ABOUT THE PAST, DOC...
...BUT EVER SINCE YOU HAD THAT VISIT WITH GRAMPA WOLF, YOU'VE BEEN TIGHTER THAN A COILED RATTLESNAKE.
I KNOW IT.
DON'T YOU THINK IT'S TIME YOU LET US IN ON THE BIG HURT THAT'S TEARING YOU UP?
DOC, NO MATTER WHAT'S GOING DOWN... THIS POLLYWOG'S ALWAYS GOT YOUR BACK.

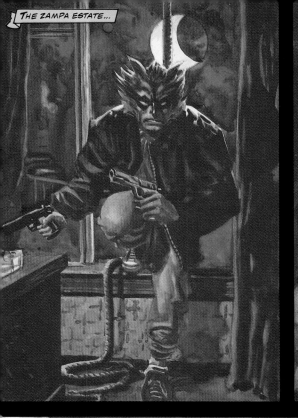

KA-CLIK!

FREEZE, YOU CRAZY HUMP.

WHAT'S YOUR STORY, PAL?

THE THREE LITTLE PIGS.

BLAM! BLAM!

BLAM!

OHGAADGK!

IT'S CLEANHANDS!

POW!

KEE-RIST! WHERE'D HE COME FROM?!

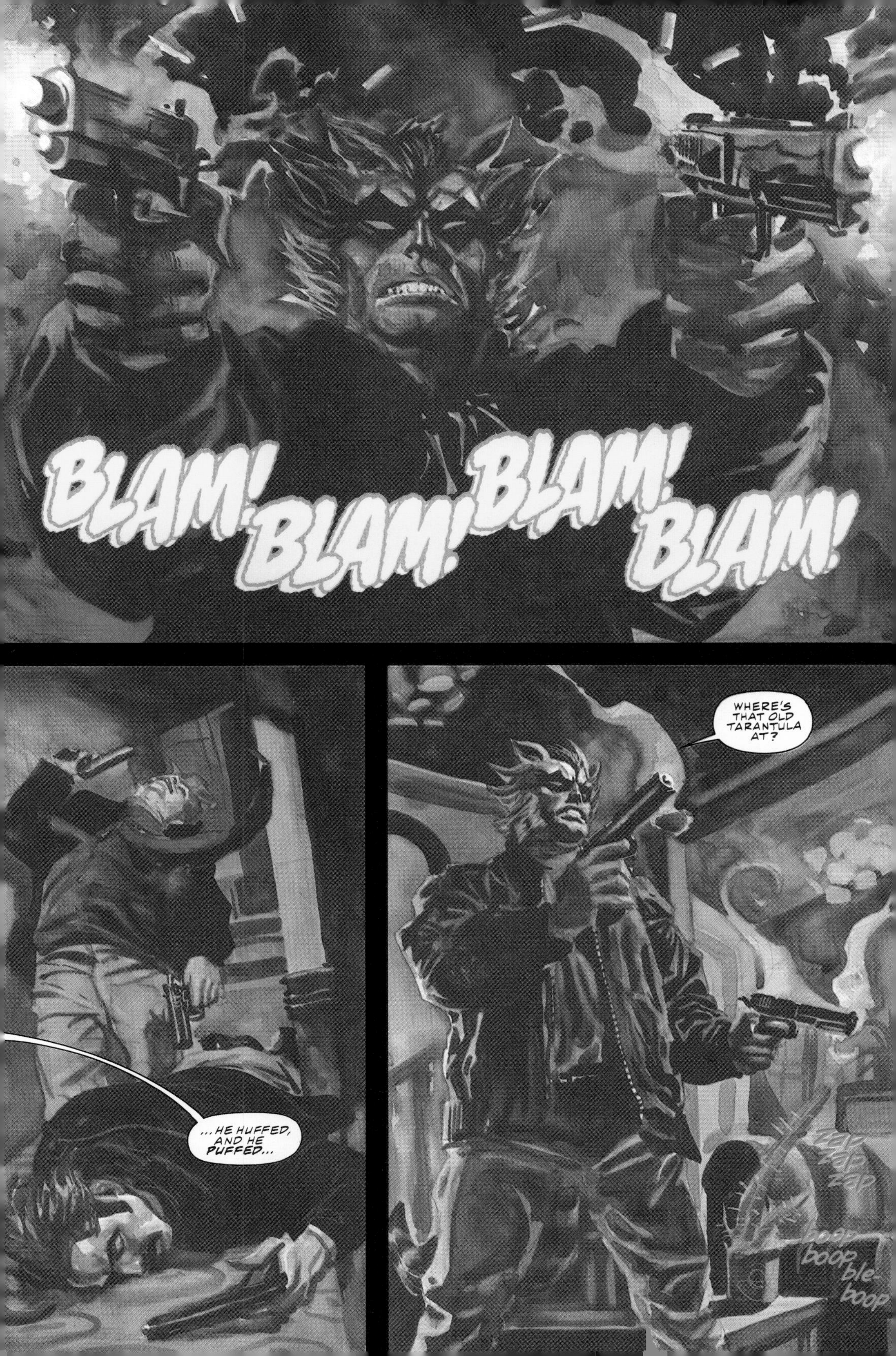
BLAM! BLAM! BLAM! BLAM!
...HE HUFFED, AND HE PUFFED...
WHERE'S THAT OLD TARANTULA AT?
zap zap zap
boop boop ble-boop

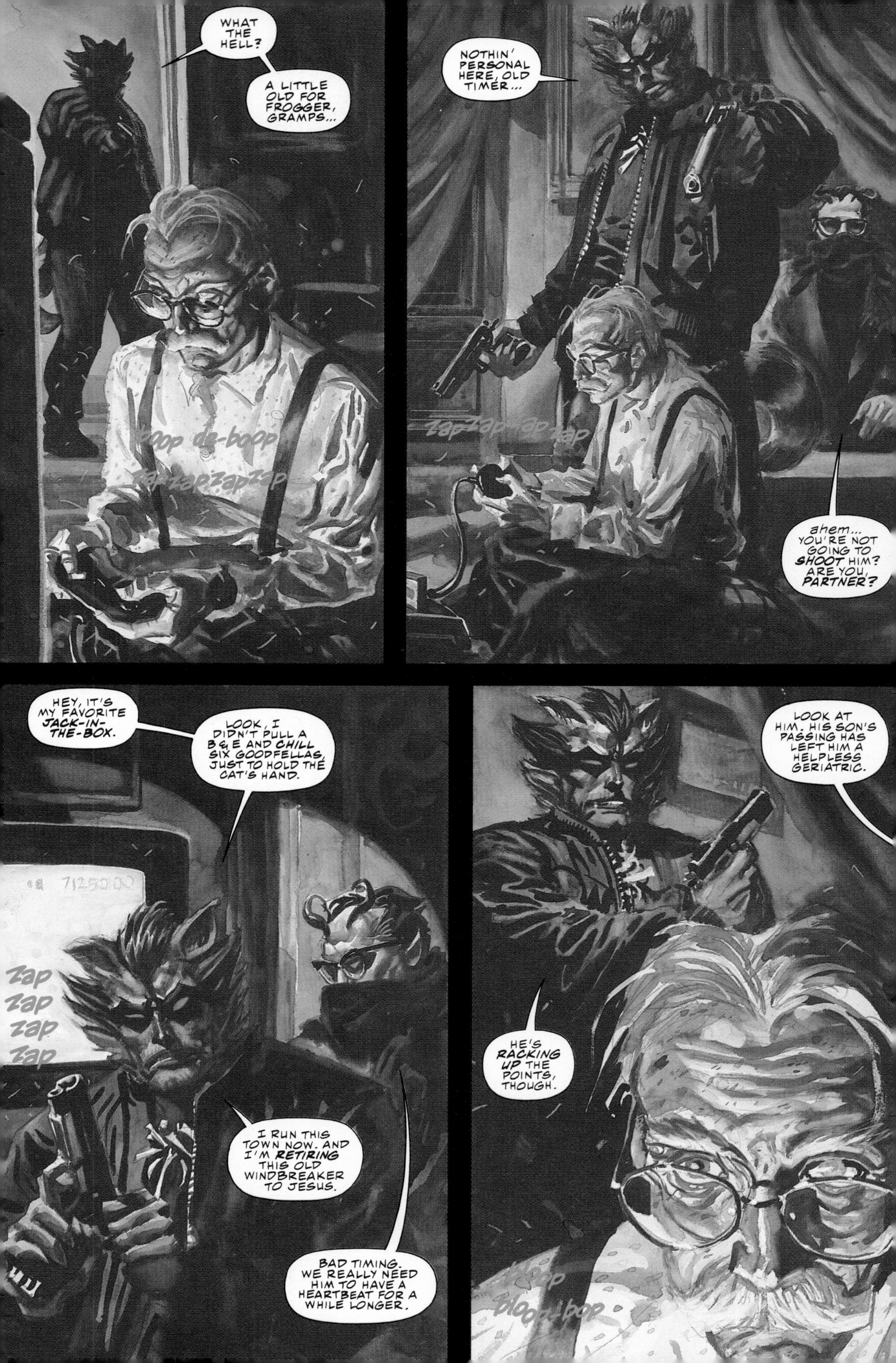
WHAT THE HELL?
A LITTLE OLD FOR FROGGER, GRAMPS...
boop de-boop
zap zap zap zap
NOTHIN' PERSONAL HERE, OLD TIMER...
zap zap zap zap
ahem... YOU'RE NOT GOING TO SHOOT HIM? ARE YOU, PARTNER?
HEY, IT'S MY FAVORITE JACK-IN-THE-BOX.
LOOK, I DIDN'T PULL A B&E AND CHILL SIX GOODFELLAS, JUST TO HOLD THE CAT'S HAND.
7125000
zap zap zap zap
I RUN THIS TOWN NOW. AND I'M RETIRING THIS OLD WINDBREAKER TO JESUS.
BAD TIMING. WE REALLY NEED HIM TO HAVE A HEARTBEAT FOR A WHILE LONGER.
LOOK AT HIM. HIS SON'S PASSING HAS LEFT HIM A HELPLESS GERIATRIC.
HE'S RACKING UP THE POINTS, THOUGH.
bloop bloop bop

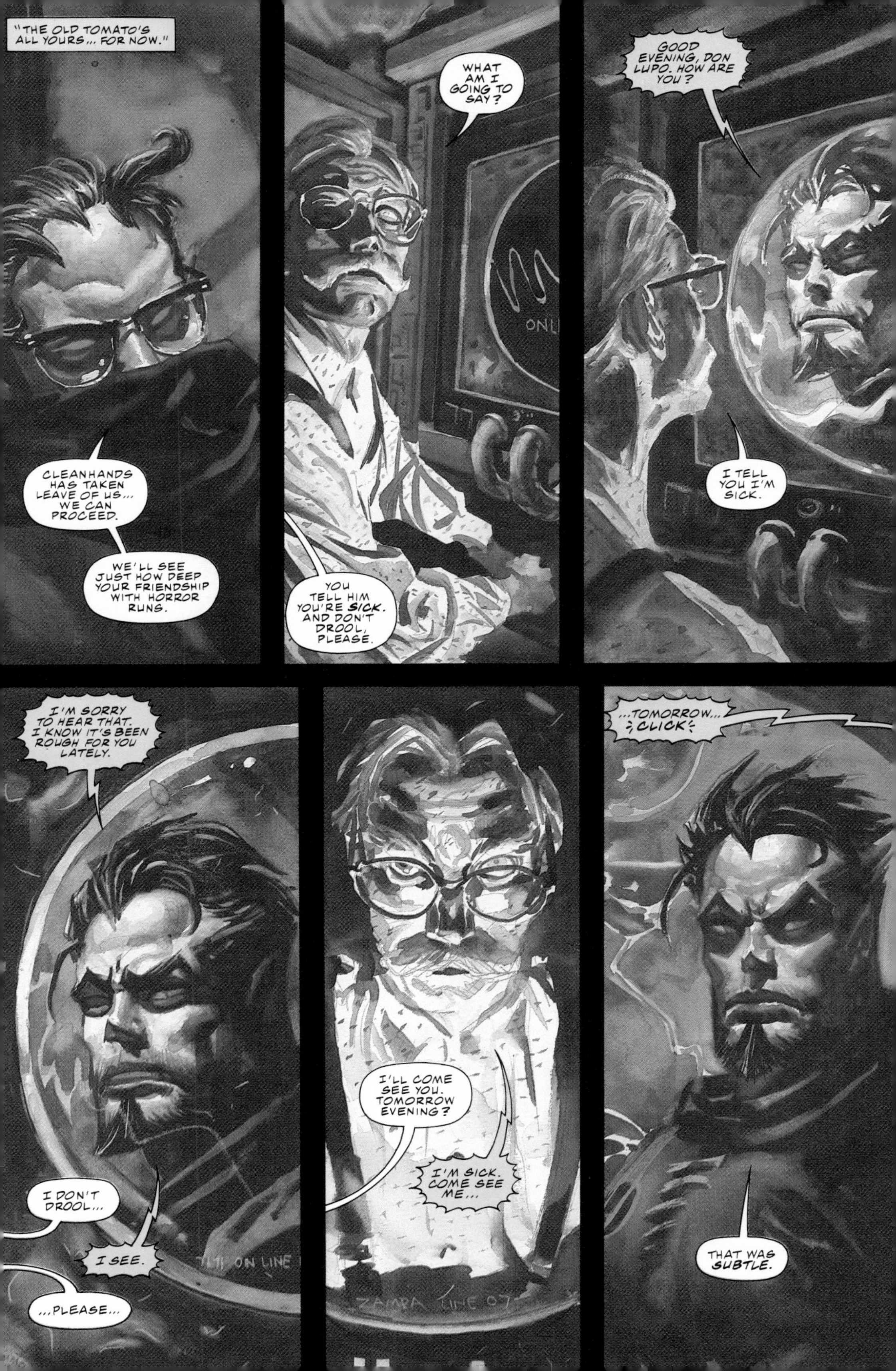
"THE OLD TOMATO'S ALL YOURS... FOR NOW."
CLEANHANDS HAS TAKEN LEAVE OF US... WE CAN PROCEED.
WE'LL SEE JUST HOW DEEP YOUR FRIENDSHIP WITH HORROR RUNS.
WHAT AM I GOING TO SAY?
YOU TELL HIM YOU'RE SICK. AND DON'T DROOL, PLEASE.
ONLI
GOOD EVENING, DON LUPO. HOW ARE YOU?
I TELL YOU I'M SICK.
I'M SORRY TO HEAR THAT. I KNOW IT'S BEEN ROUGH FOR YOU LATELY.
I DON'T DROOL...
I SEE.
...PLEASE...
ON LINE
I'LL COME SEE YOU. TOMORROW EVENING?
I'M SICK. COME SEE ME...
ZAMPA LINE 07
...TOMORROW... CLICK
THAT WAS SUBTLE.

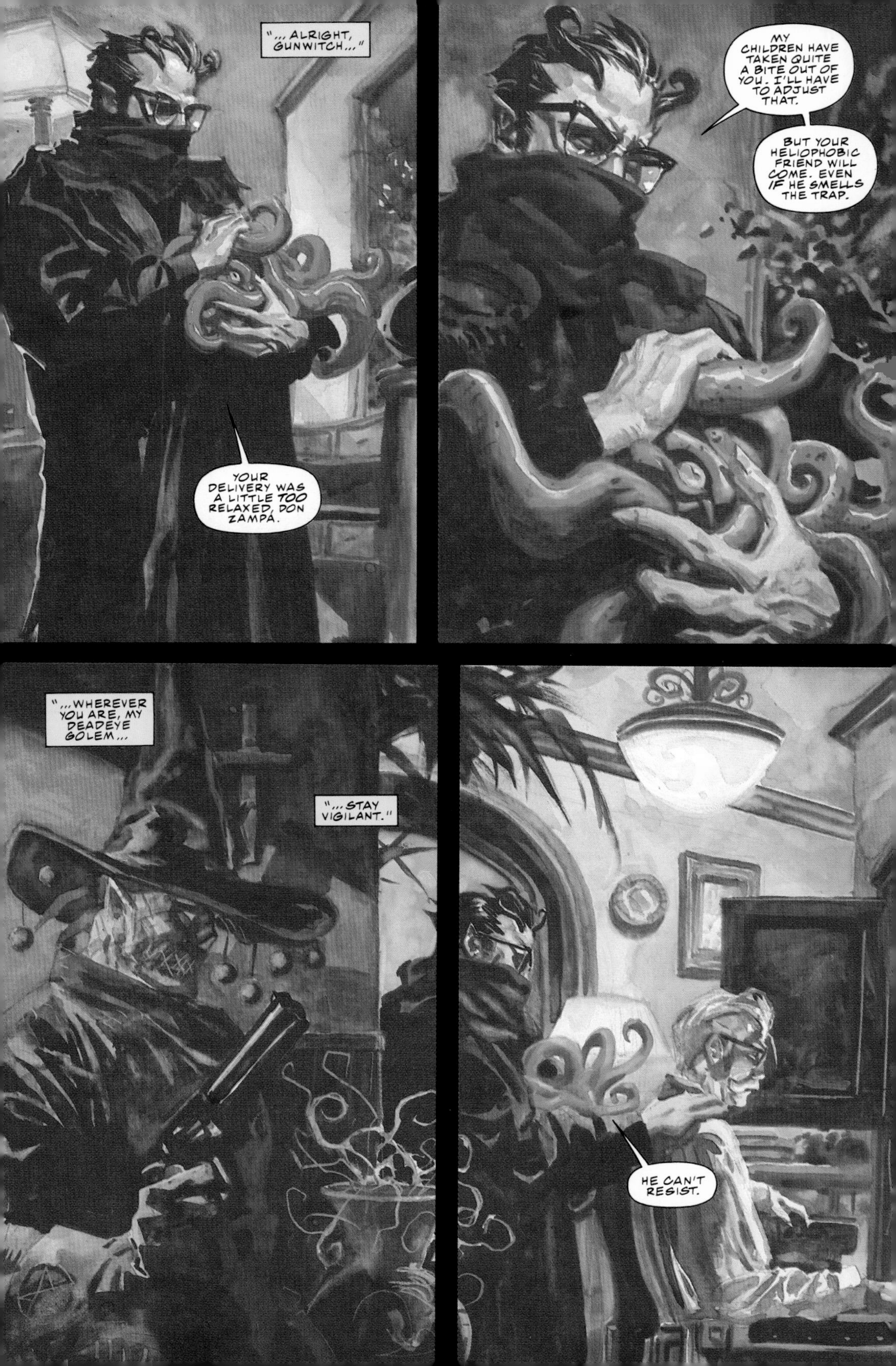
"... ALRIGHT, GUNWITCH..."
YOUR DELIVERY WAS A LITTLE TOO RELAXED, DON ZAMPA.
MY CHILDREN HAVE TAKEN QUITE A BITE OUT OF YOU. I'LL HAVE TO ADJUST THAT.
BUT YOUR HELIOPHOBIC FRIEND WILL COME. EVEN IF HE SMELLS THE TRAP.
"...WHEREVER YOU ARE, MY DEADEYE GOLEM...
"... STAY VIGILANT."
HE CAN'T RESIST.

AND JUST OUTSIDE...
PARTNERS... LIKE HELL.
THE BASTARD'S STRINGING ME.
HE'S GOT THE GEEZER IN HIS POCKET, SOMEHOW. DOESN'T NEED ME ANY-MORE.
SOON AS THIS BUSINESS IS OVER, FANE...
...I'LL SERVE YOUR GUTS WITH BLACKBIRD PIE.
FIRST TONY Z GETS CUTE. NOW THIS CREEP.
SECOND TIME, SHAME ON ME.
I SHOULDN'T COMPLAIN. WITH OR WITHOUT MY HELP, HE'LL NEVER BAG HORROR.
NOT THAT I GIVE A RAT'S LEFT ARM WHAT HAPPENS TO THE DOC.
SO WHY THIS PIT IN MY STOMACH?

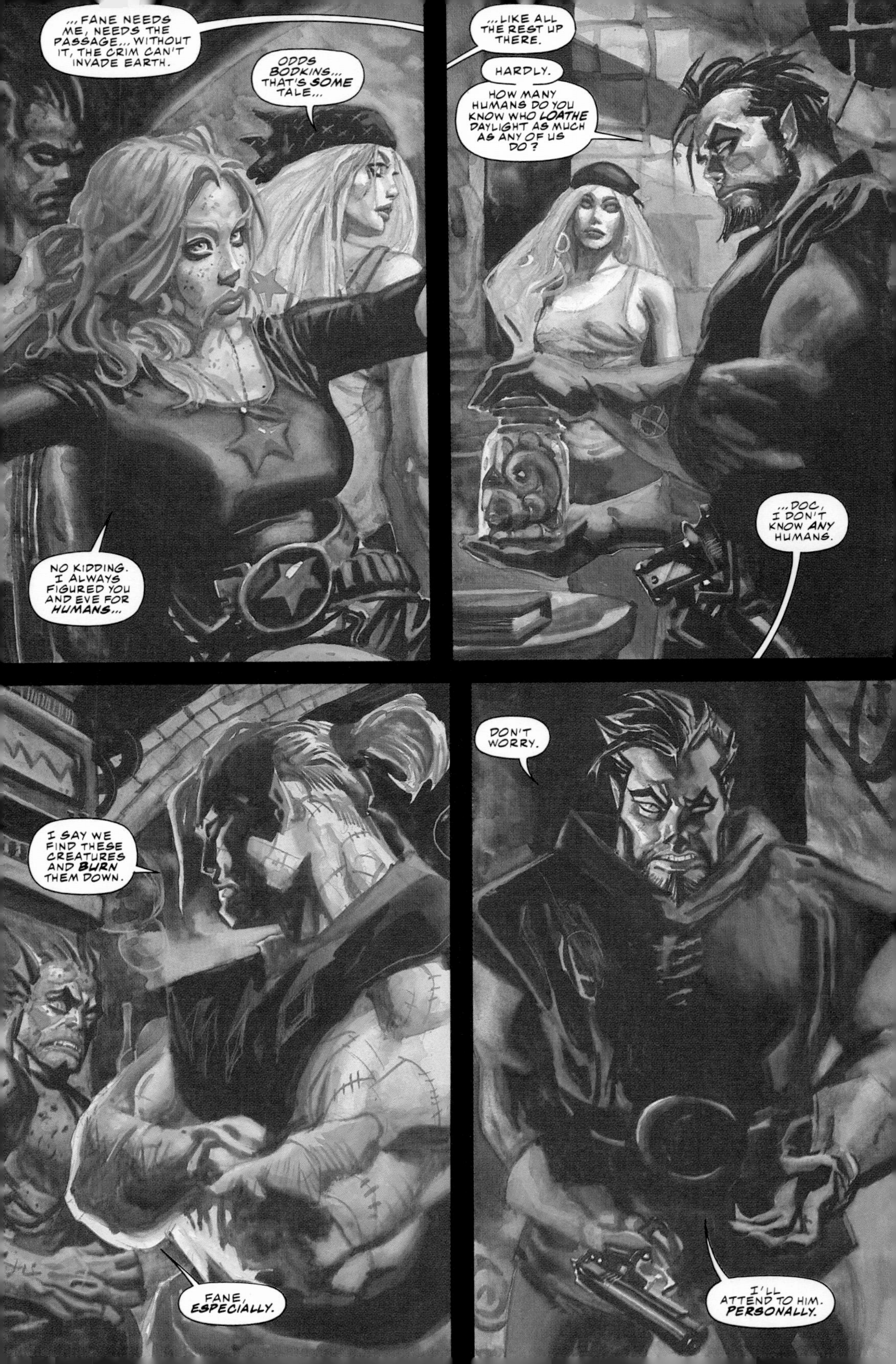
...FANE NEEDS ME, NEEDS THE PASSAGE... WITHOUT IT, THE CRIM CAN'T INVADE EARTH.
ODDS BODKINS... THAT'S SOME TALE...
NO KIDDING. I ALWAYS FIGURED YOU AND EVE FOR HUMANS...
...LIKE ALL THE REST UP THERE.
HARDLY.
HOW MANY HUMANS DO YOU KNOW WHO LOATHE DAYLIGHT AS MUCH AS ANY OF US DO?
...DOC, I DON'T KNOW ANY HUMANS.
I SAY WE FIND THESE CREATURES AND BURN THEM DOWN.
FANE, ESPECIALLY.
DON'T WORRY.
I'LL ATTEND TO HIM. PERSONALLY.

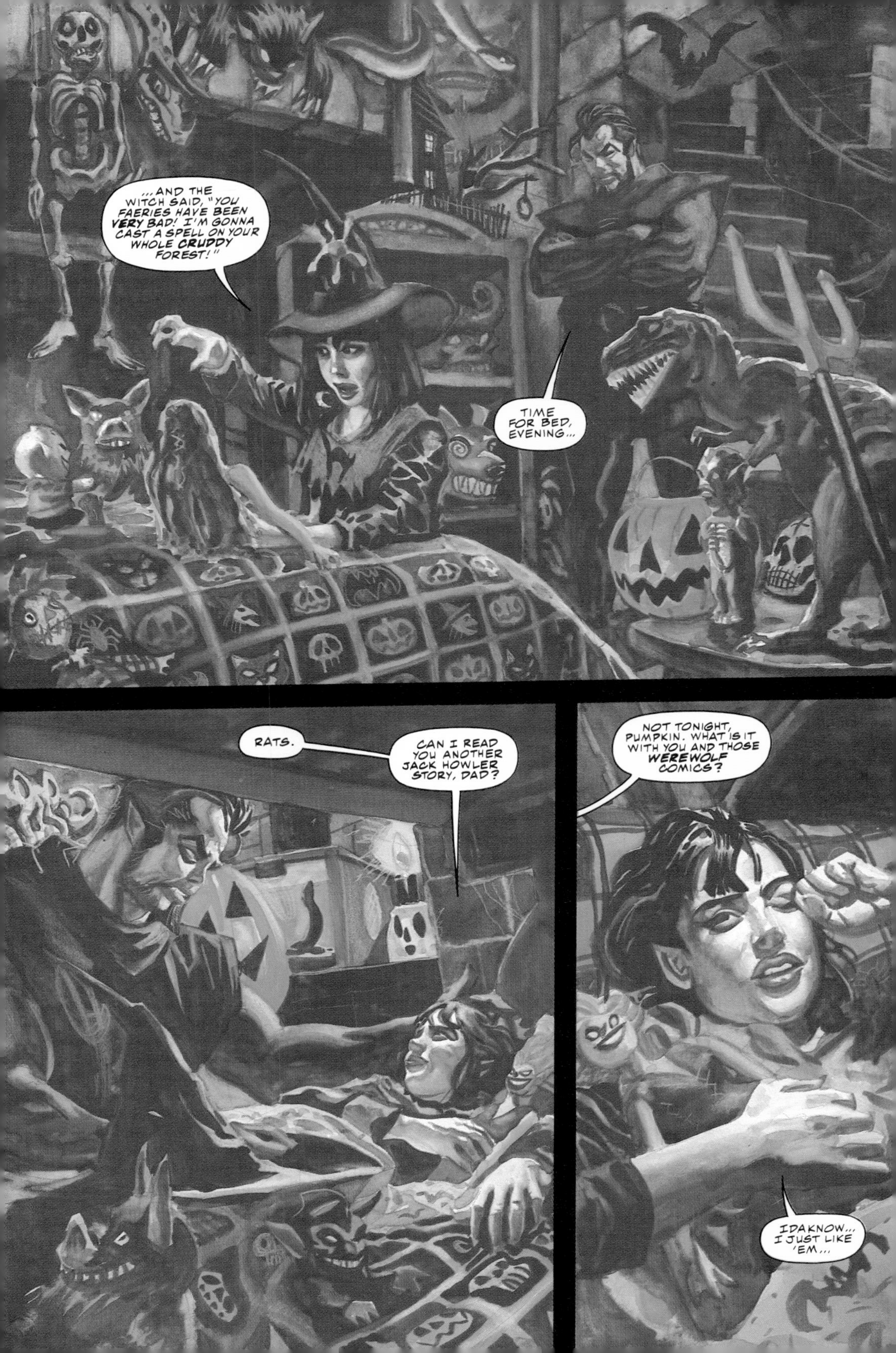
...AND THE WITCH SAID, "YOU FAERIES HAVE BEEN VERY BAD! I'M GONNA CAST A SPELL ON YOUR WHOLE CRUDDY FOREST!"
TIME FOR BED, EVENING...
RATS.
CAN I READ YOU ANOTHER JACK HOWLER STORY, DAD?
NOT TONIGHT, PUMPKIN. WHAT IS IT WITH YOU AND THOSE WEREWOLF COMICS?
IDAKNOW... I JUST LIKE 'EM...

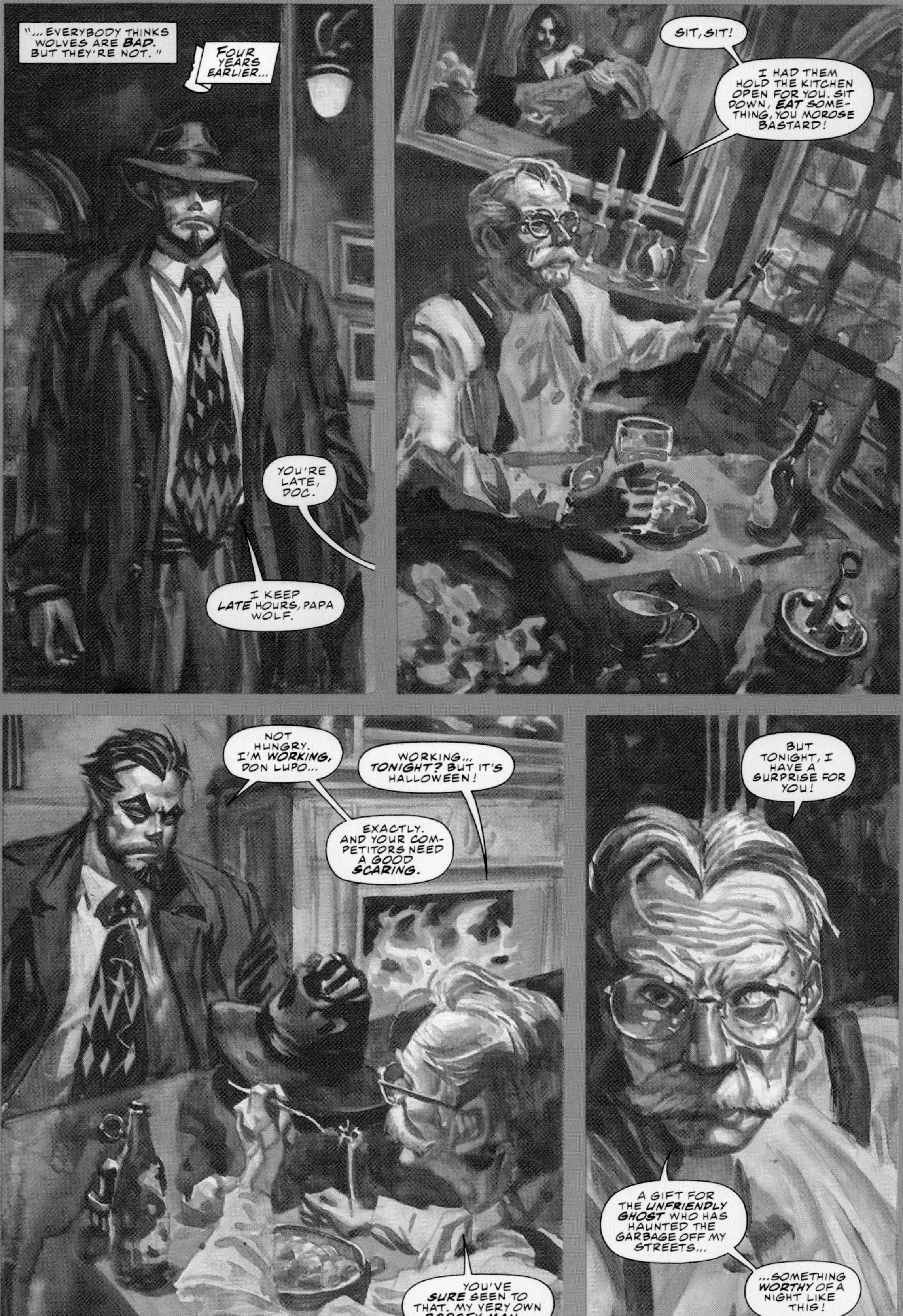
"...EVERYBODY THINKS WOLVES ARE BAD. BUT THEY'RE NOT."
FOUR YEARS EARLIER...
YOU'RE LATE, DOC.
I KEEP LATE HOURS, PAPA WOLF.
SIT, SIT!
I HAD THEM HOLD THE KITCHEN OPEN FOR YOU. SIT DOWN, EAT SOME-THING, YOU MOROSE BASTARD!
NOT HUNGRY. I'M WORKING, DON LUPO...
WORKING... TONIGHT? BUT IT'S HALLOWEEN!
EXACTLY. AND YOUR COM-PETITORS NEED A GOOD SCARING.
YOU'VE SURE SEEN TO THAT. MY VERY OWN BOOGEY MAN.
BUT TONIGHT, I HAVE A SURPRISE FOR YOU!
A GIFT FOR THE UNFRIENDLY GHOST WHO HAS HAUNTED THE GARBAGE OFF MY STREETS...
...SOMETHING WORTHY OF A NIGHT LIKE THIS!

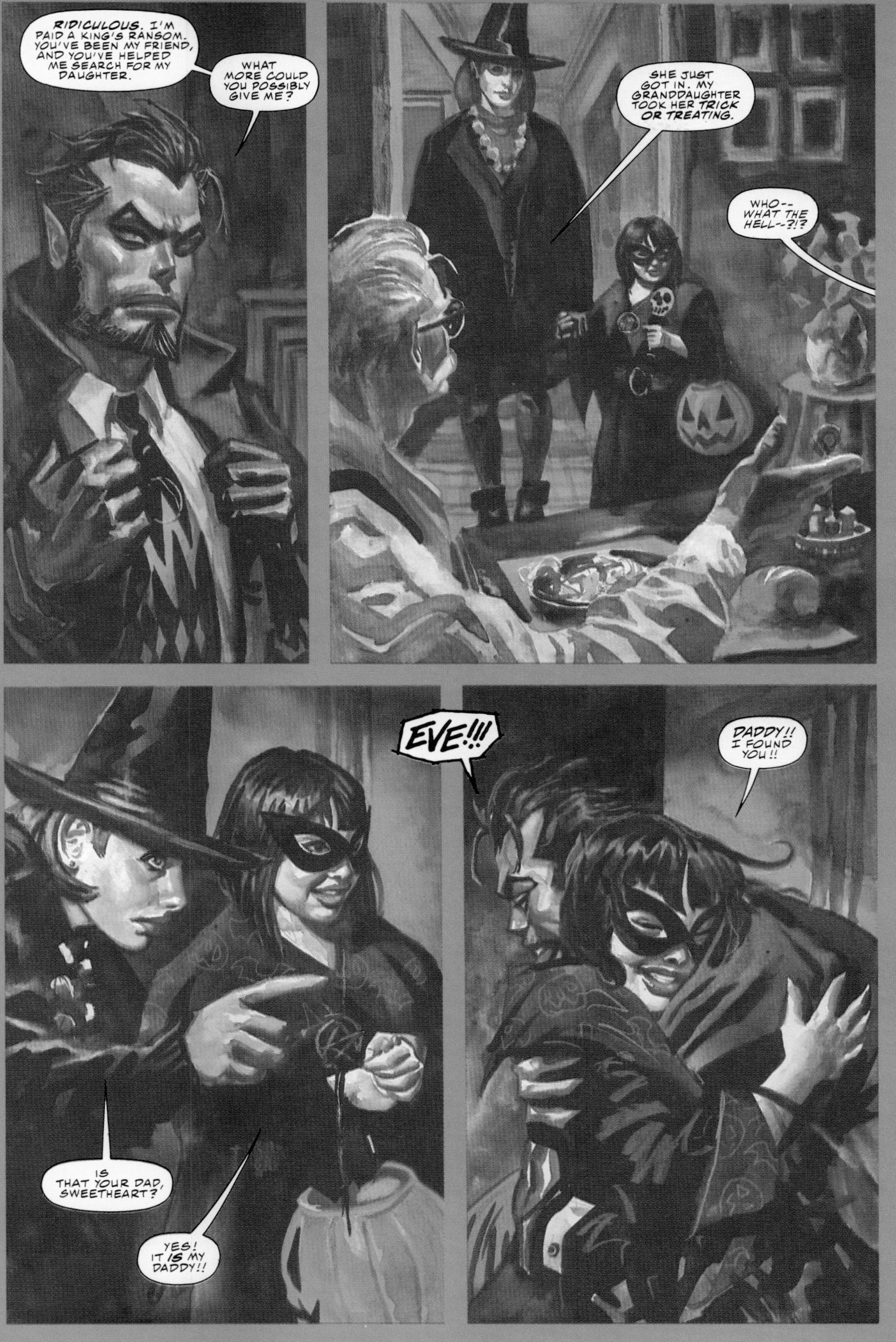
RIDICULOUS. I'M PAID A KING'S RANSOM. YOU'VE BEEN MY FRIEND, AND YOU'VE HELPED ME SEARCH FOR MY DAUGHTER.
WHAT MORE COULD YOU POSSIBLY GIVE ME?
SHE JUST GOT IN. MY GRANDDAUGHTER TOOK HER TRICK OR TREATING.
WHO-- WHAT THE HELL--?!?
IS THAT YOUR DAD, SWEETHEART?
YES! IT IS MY DADDY!!
EVE!!!
DADDY!! I FOUND YOU!!

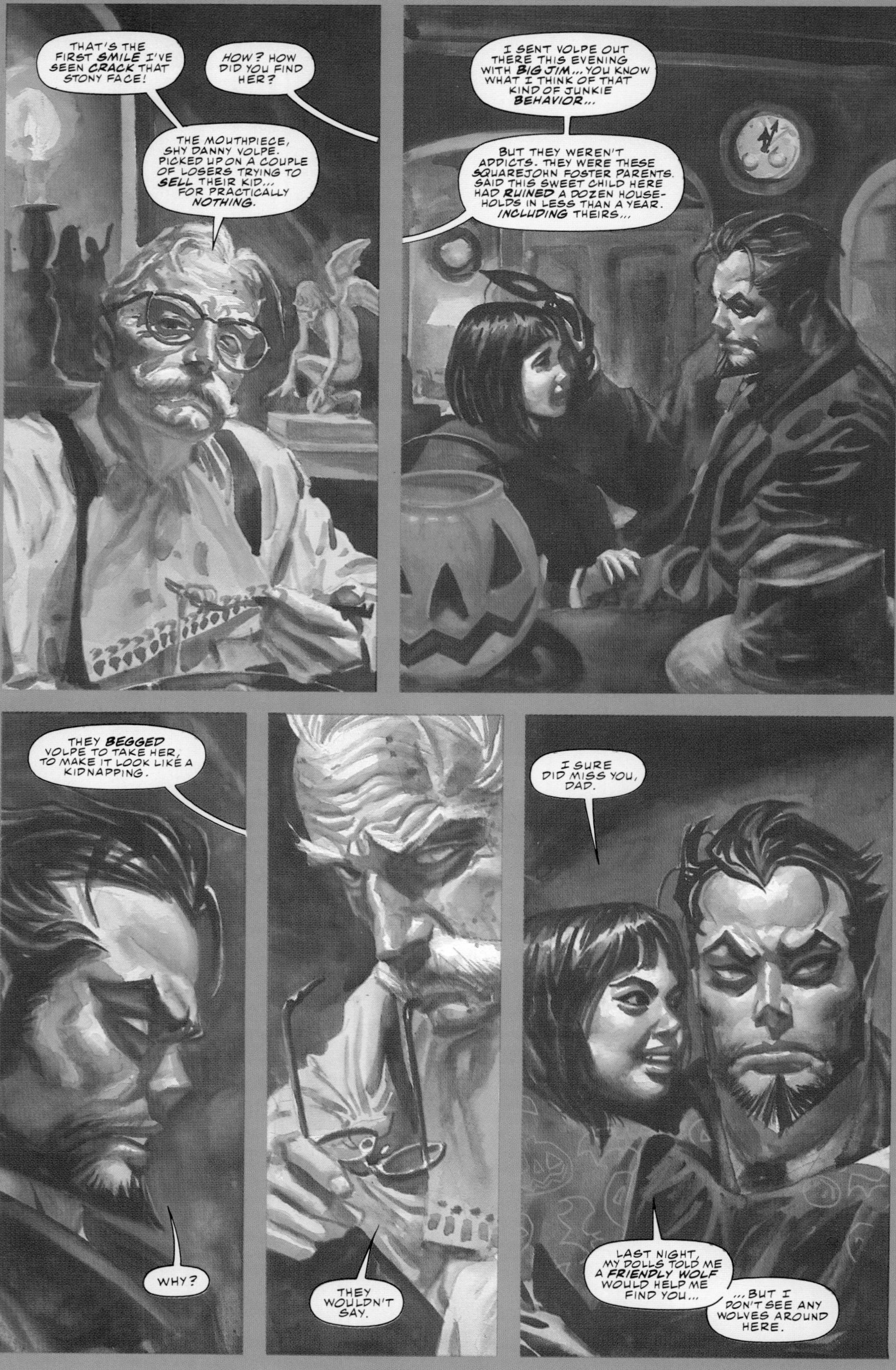
THAT'S THE FIRST SMILE I'VE SEEN CRACK THAT STONY FACE!
HOW? HOW DID YOU FIND HER?
THE MOUTHPIECE, SHY DANNY VOLPE. PICKED UP ON A COUPLE OF LOSERS TRYING TO SELL THEIR KID... FOR PRACTICALLY NOTHING.
I SENT VOLPE OUT THERE THIS EVENING WITH BIG JIM... YOU KNOW WHAT I THINK OF THAT KIND OF JUNKIE BEHAVIOR...
BUT THEY WEREN'T ADDICTS. THEY WERE THESE SQUAREJOHN FOSTER PARENTS. SAID THIS SWEET CHILD HERE HAD RUINED A DOZEN HOUSEHOLDS IN LESS THAN A YEAR. INCLUDING THEIRS...
THEY BEGGED VOLPE TO TAKE HER, TO MAKE IT LOOK LIKE A KIDNAPPING.
WHY?
THEY WOULDN'T SAY.
I SURE DID MISS YOU, DAD.
LAST NIGHT, MY DOLLS TOLD ME A FRIENDLY WOLF WOULD HELP ME FIND YOU...
...BUT I DON'T SEE ANY WOLVES AROUND HERE.

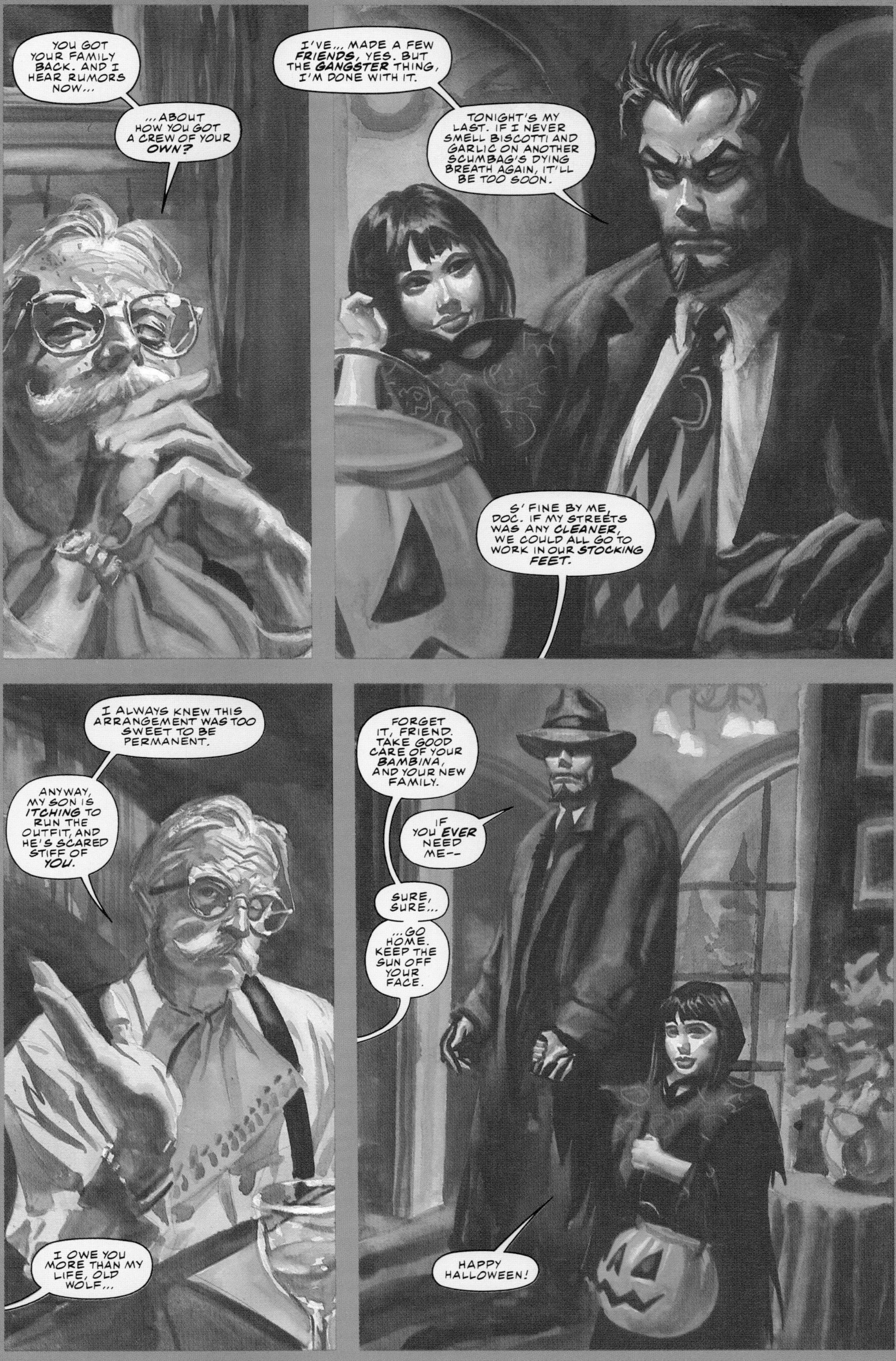
YOU GOT YOUR FAMILY BACK. AND I HEAR RUMORS NOW...
...ABOUT HOW YOU GOT A CREW OF YOUR OWN?
I'VE... MADE A FEW FRIENDS, YES. BUT THE GANGSTER THING, I'M DONE WITH IT.
TONIGHT'S MY LAST. IF I NEVER SMELL BISCOTTI AND GARLIC ON ANOTHER SCUMBAG'S DYING BREATH AGAIN, IT'LL BE TOO SOON.
S' FINE BY ME, DOC. IF MY STREETS WAS ANY CLEANER, WE COULD ALL GO TO WORK IN OUR STOCKING FEET.
I ALWAYS KNEW THIS ARRANGEMENT WAS TOO SWEET TO BE PERMANENT.
ANYWAY, MY SON IS ITCHING TO RUN THE OUTFIT, AND HE'S SCARED STIFF OF YOU.
I OWE YOU MORE THAN MY LIFE, OLD WOLF...
FORGET IT, FRIEND. TAKE GOOD CARE OF YOUR BAMBINA, AND YOUR NEW FAMILY.
IF YOU EVER NEED ME--
SURE, SURE...
...GO HOME. KEEP THE SUN OFF YOUR FACE.
HAPPY HALLOWEEN!

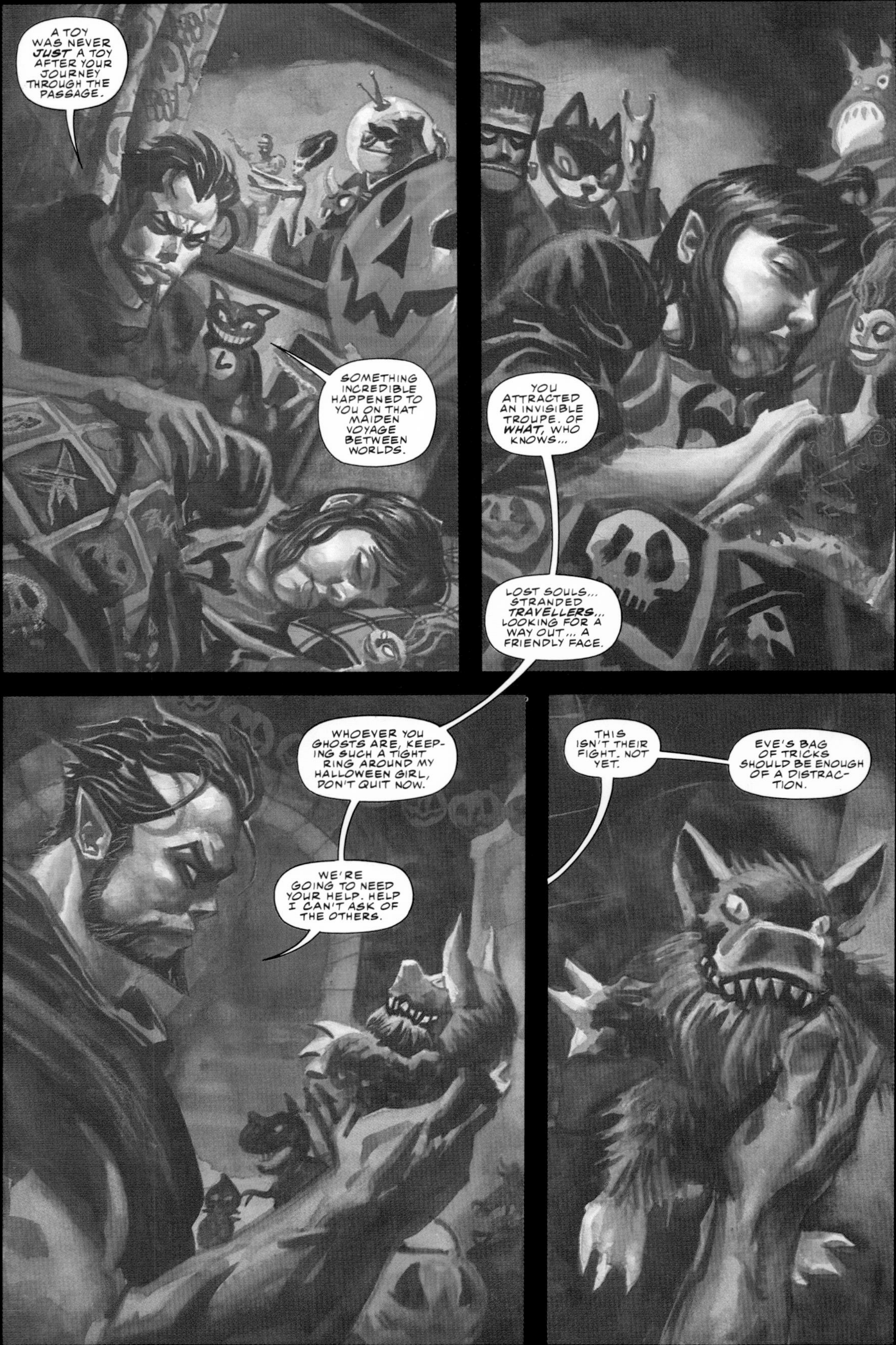
A TOY WAS NEVER JUST A TOY AFTER YOUR JOURNEY THROUGH THE PASSAGE.
SOMETHING INCREDIBLE HAPPENED TO YOU ON THAT MAIDEN VOYAGE BETWEEN WORLDS.
YOU ATTRACTED AN INVISIBLE TROUPE. OF WHAT, WHO KNOWS...
LOST SOULS... STRANDED TRAVELLERS... LOOKING FOR A WAY OUT... A FRIENDLY FACE.
WHOEVER YOU GHOSTS ARE, KEEPING SUCH A TIGHT RING AROUND MY HALLOWEEN GIRL, DON'T QUIT NOW.
WE'RE GOING TO NEED YOUR HELP. HELP I CAN'T ASK OF THE OTHERS.
THIS ISN'T THEIR FIGHT. NOT YET.
EVE'S BAG OF TRICKS SHOULD BE ENOUGH OF A DISTRACTION.

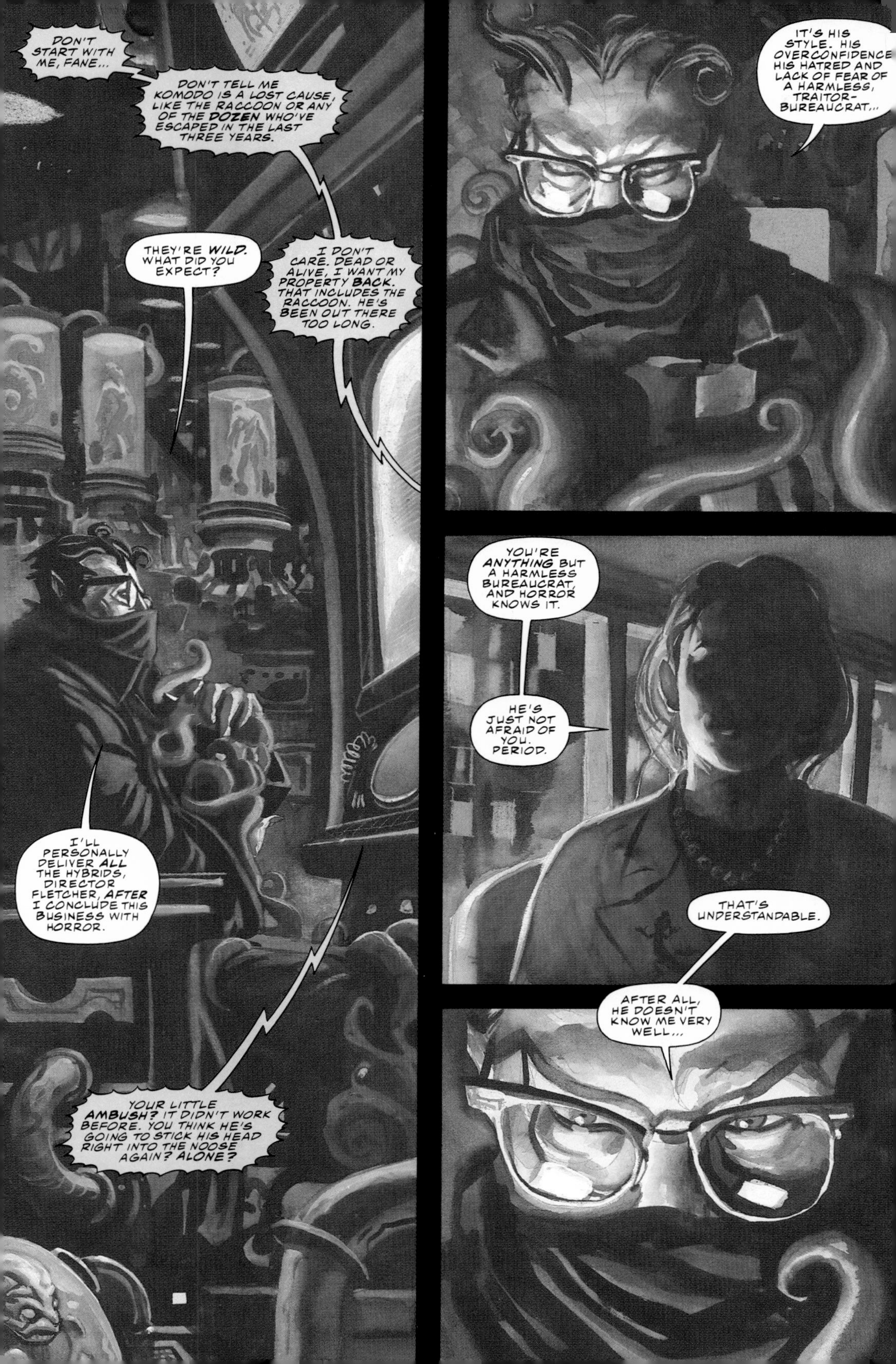

DON'T START WITH ME, FANE...
DON'T TELL ME KOMODO IS A LOST CAUSE, LIKE THE RACCOON OR ANY OF THE DOZEN WHO'VE ESCAPED IN THE LAST THREE YEARS.
THEY'RE WILD. WHAT DID YOU EXPECT?
I DON'T CARE. DEAD OR ALIVE, I WANT MY PROPERTY BACK. THAT INCLUDES THE RACCOON. HE'S BEEN OUT THERE TOO LONG.
I'LL PERSONALLY DELIVER ALL THE HYBRIDS, DIRECTOR FLETCHER, AFTER I CONCLUDE THIS BUSINESS WITH HORROR.
YOUR LITTLE AMBUSH? IT DIDN'T WORK BEFORE. YOU THINK HE'S GOING TO STICK HIS HEAD RIGHT INTO THE NOOSE AGAIN? ALONE?
IT'S HIS STYLE. HIS OVERCONFIDENCE HIS HATRED AND LACK OF FEAR OF A HARMLESS, TRAITOR-BUREAUCRAT...
YOU'RE ANYTHING BUT A HARMLESS BUREAUCRAT, AND HORROR KNOWS IT.
HE'S JUST NOT AFRAID OF YOU. PERIOD.
THAT'S UNDERSTANDABLE.
AFTER ALL, HE DOESN'T KNOW ME VERY WELL...

ZAMPA FAMILY HOME... 11 PM.
IT'S GOING TO RAIN TONIGHT.
I KNOW. I CAN'T WAIT.
YOUR TOYS TELL YOU THAT?
NO, DAD. I CAN SMELL IT.
BRERETON

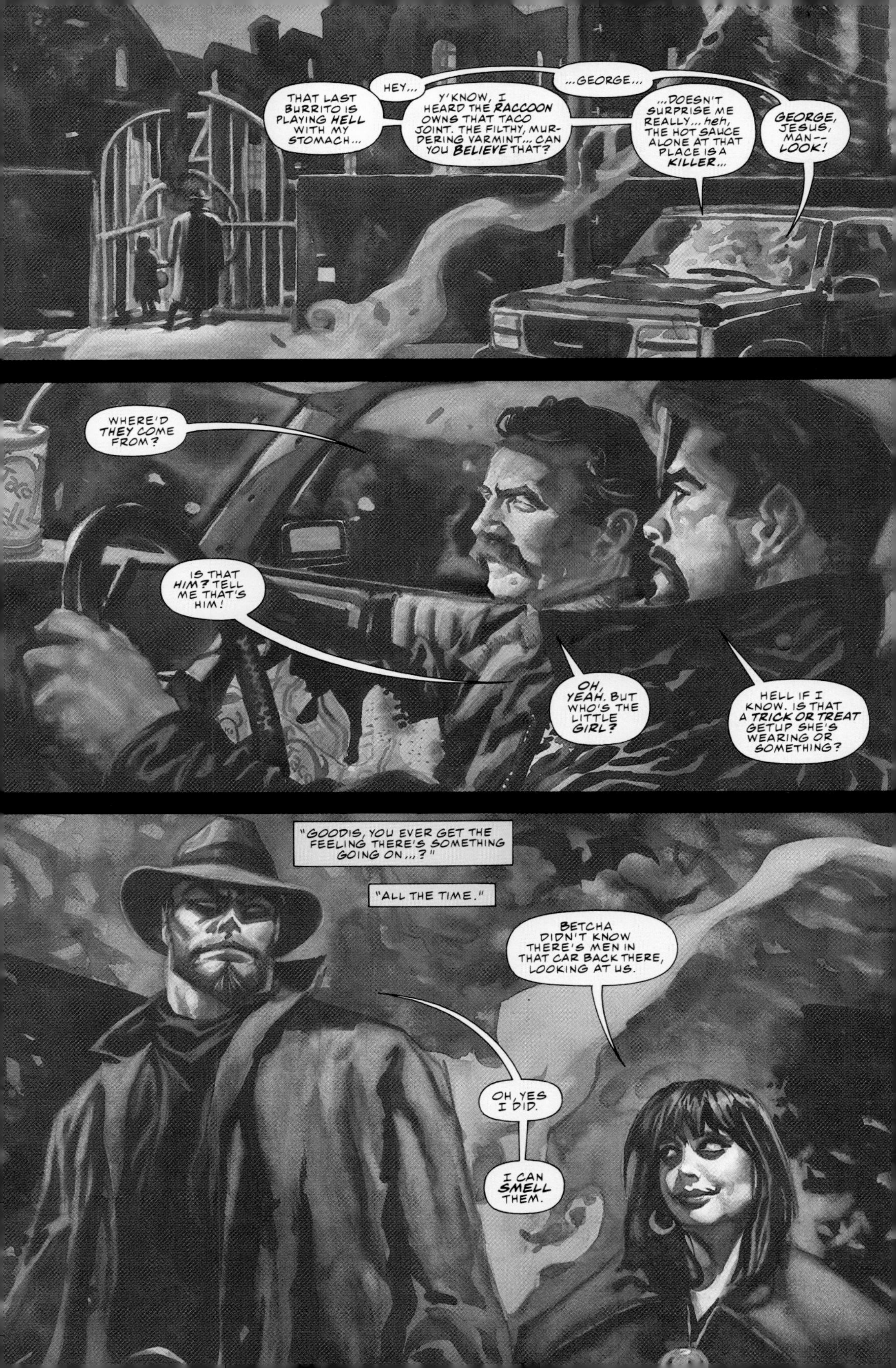
THAT LAST BURRITO IS PLAYING **HELL** WITH MY STOMACH...
HEY...
Y'KNOW, I HEARD THE **RACCOON** OWNS THAT TACO JOINT. THE FILTHY, MURDERING VARMINT... CAN YOU **BELIEVE** THAT?
...GEORGE...
...DOESN'T SURPRISE ME REALLY... heh, THE HOT SAUCE ALONE AT THAT PLACE IS A **KILLER**...
GEORGE, JESUS, MAN-- LOOK!
WHERE'D **THEY** COME FROM?
IS THAT **HIM?** TELL ME THAT'S HIM!
OH, YEAH. BUT WHO'S THE LITTLE **GIRL?**
HELL IF I KNOW. IS THAT A **TRICK OR TREAT** GETUP SHE'S WEARING OR SOMETHING?
"GOODIS, YOU EVER GET THE FEELING THERE'S SOMETHING GOING ON...?"
"ALL THE TIME."
BETCHA DIDN'T KNOW THERE'S MEN IN THAT CAR BACK THERE, LOOKING AT US.
OH, YES I DID.
I CAN **SMELL** THEM.

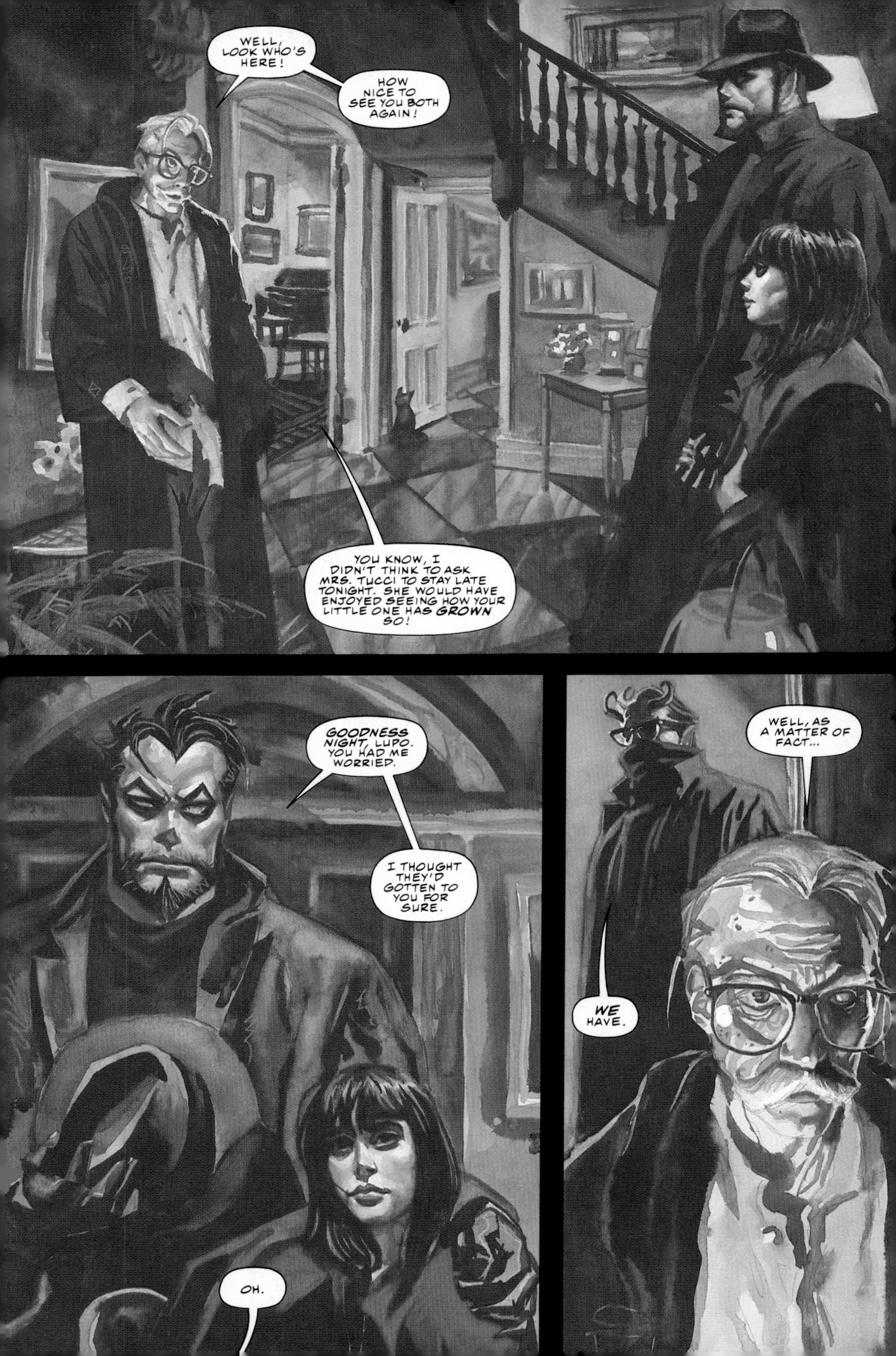
WELL, LOOK WHO'S HERE!
HOW NICE TO SEE YOU BOTH AGAIN!
YOU KNOW, I DIDN'T THINK TO ASK MRS. TUCCI TO STAY LATE TONIGHT. SHE WOULD HAVE ENJOYED SEEING HOW YOUR LITTLE ONE HAS **GROWN** SO!
GOODNESS NIGHT, LUPO. YOU HAD ME WORRIED.
I THOUGHT THEY'D GOTTEN TO YOU FOR SURE.
OH.
WELL, AS A MATTER OF FACT...
WE HAVE.

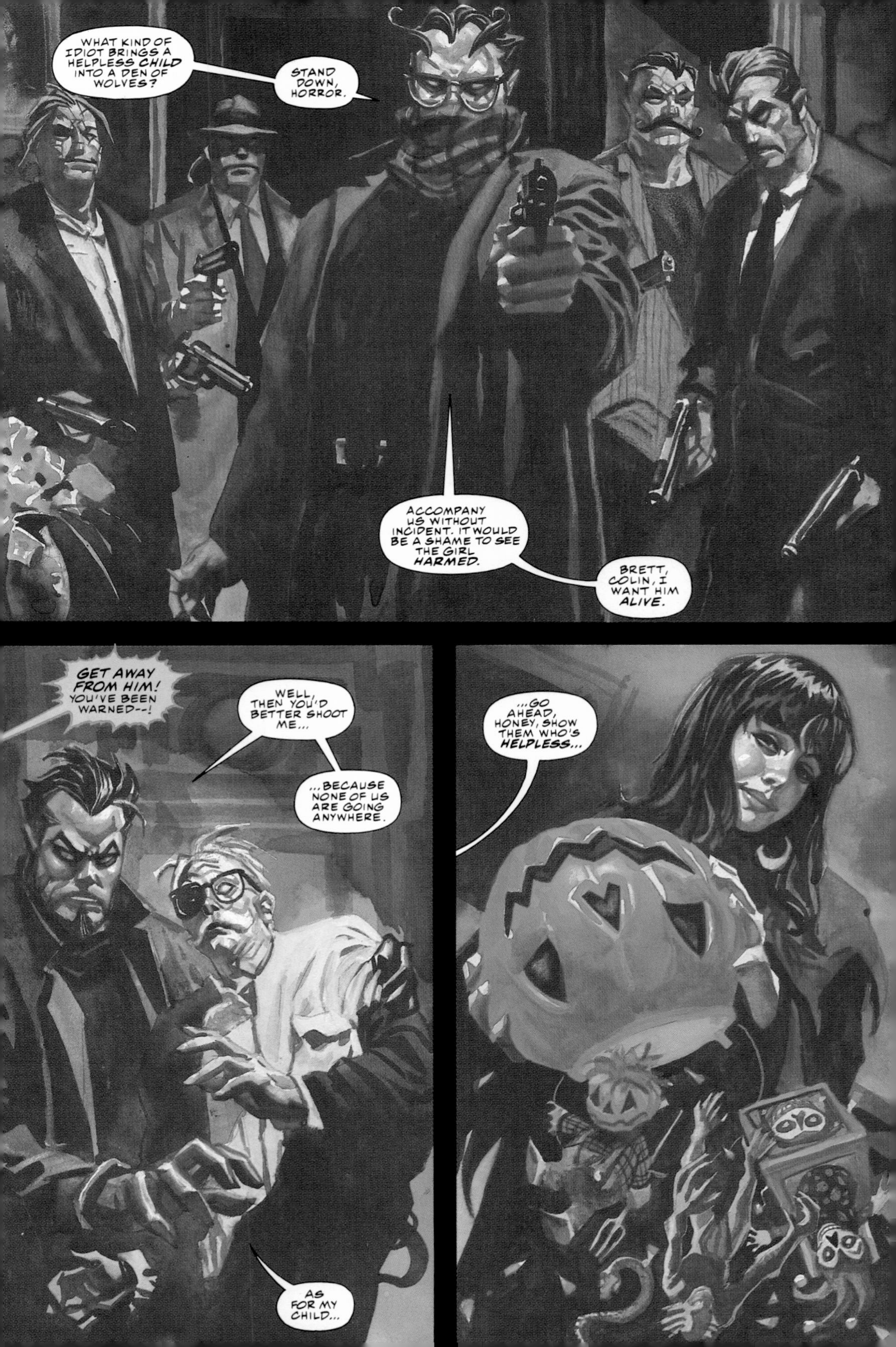
WHAT KIND OF IDIOT BRINGS A HELPLESS CHILD INTO A DEN OF WOLVES?
STAND DOWN, HORROR.
ACCOMPANY US WITHOUT INCIDENT. IT WOULD BE A SHAME TO SEE THE GIRL HARMED.
BRETT, COLIN, I WANT HIM ALIVE.
GET AWAY FROM HIM! YOU'VE BEEN WARNED--!
WELL, THEN YOU'D BETTER SHOOT ME...
...BECAUSE NONE OF US ARE GOING ANYWHERE.
AS FOR MY CHILD...
...GO AHEAD, HONEY, SHOW THEM WHO'S HELPLESS...

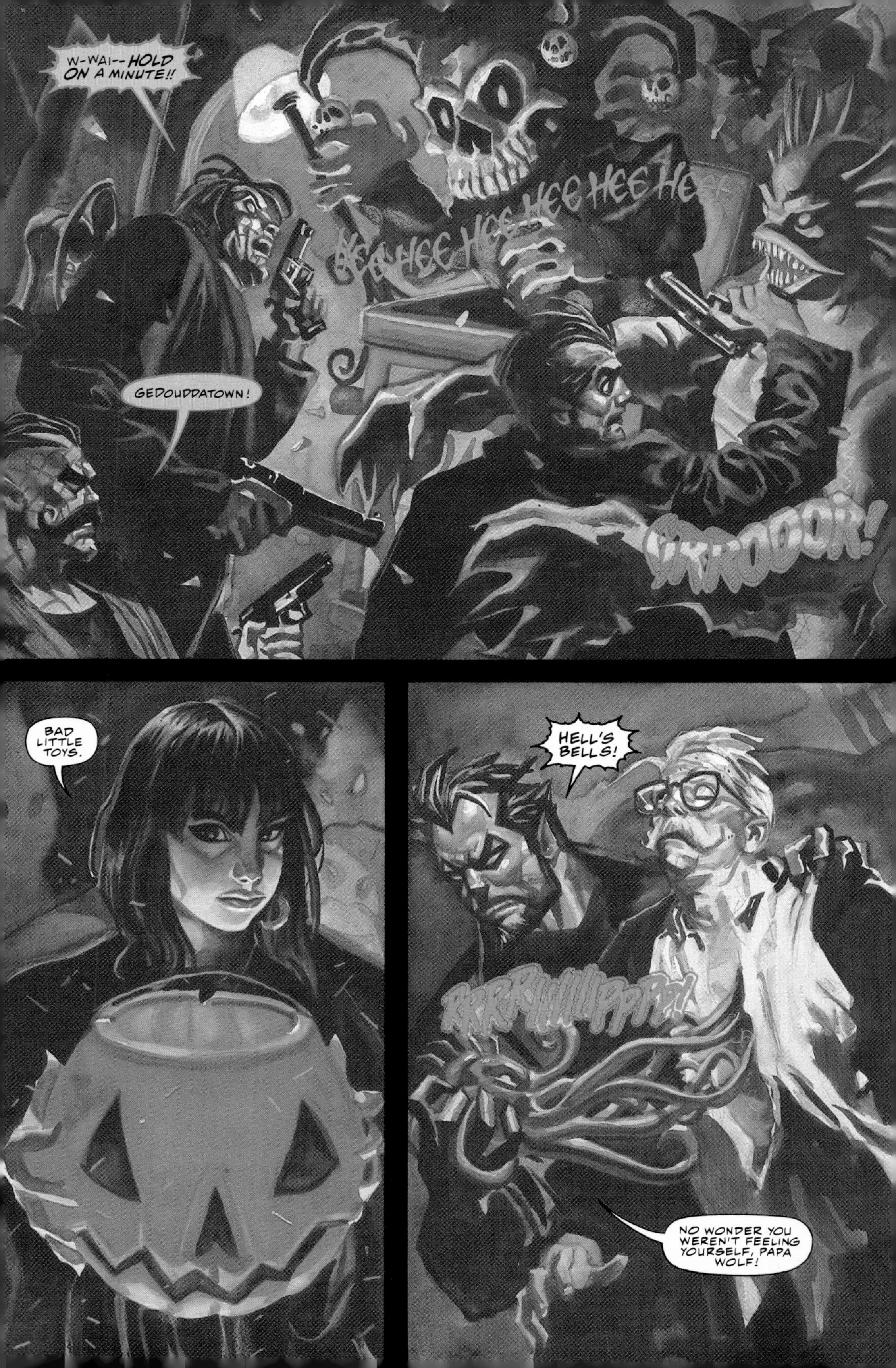

W-WAI-- HOLD ON A MINUTE!!
HEE HEE HEE HEE HEE HEE
GEDOUDDATOWN!
BAD LITTLE TOYS.
HELL'S BELLS!
NO WONDER YOU WEREN'T FEELING YOURSELF, PAPA WOLF!

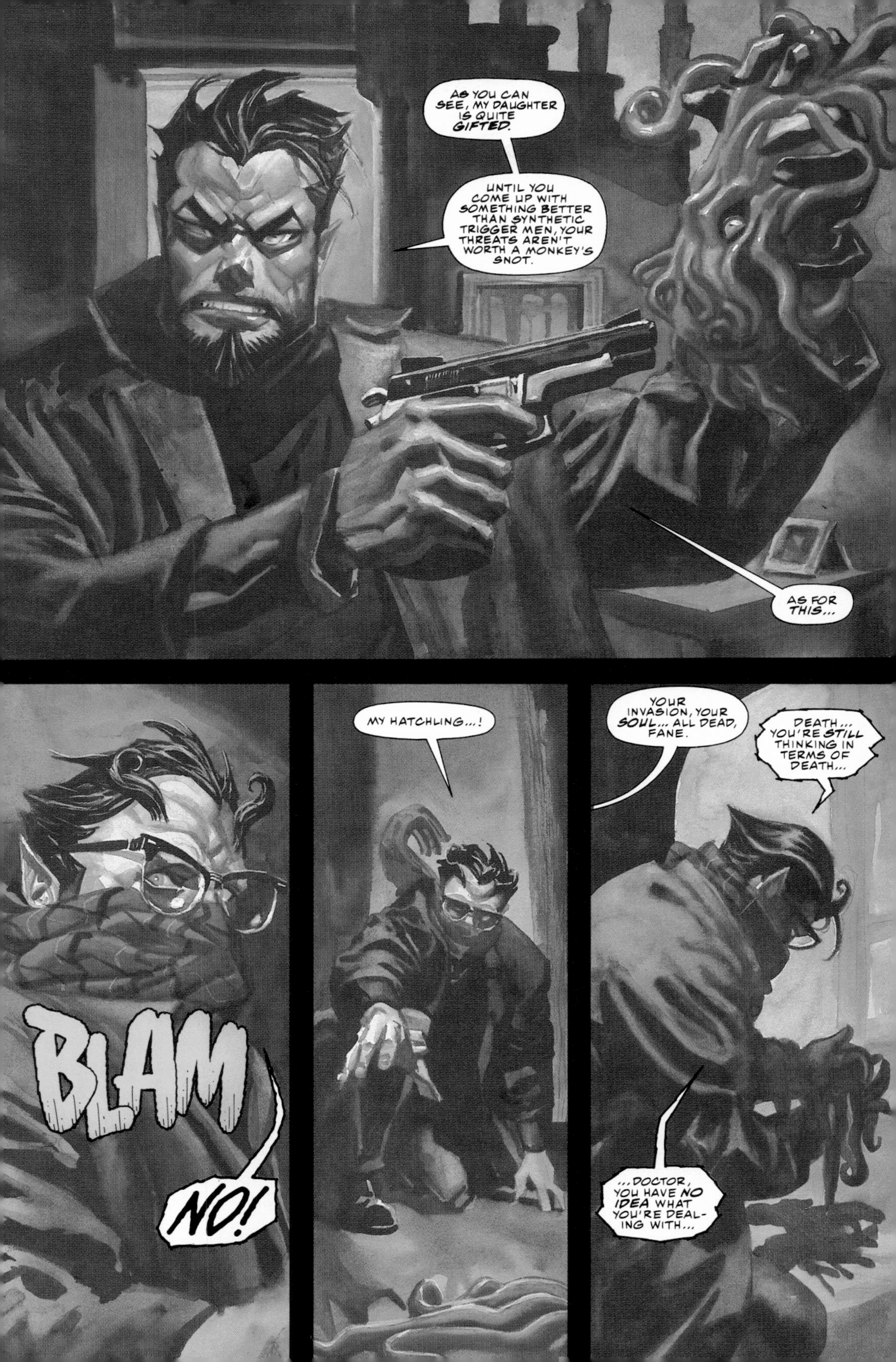

AS YOU CAN SEE, MY DAUGHTER IS QUITE GIFTED.
UNTIL YOU COME UP WITH SOMETHING BETTER THAN SYNTHETIC TRIGGER MEN, YOUR THREATS AREN'T WORTH A MONKEY'S SNOT.
AS FOR THIS...
BLAM
NO!
MY HATCHLING...!
YOUR INVASION, YOUR SOUL... ALL DEAD, FANE.
DEATH... YOU'RE STILL THINKING IN TERMS OF DEATH...
...DOCTOR, YOU HAVE NO IDEA WHAT YOU'RE DEALING WITH...

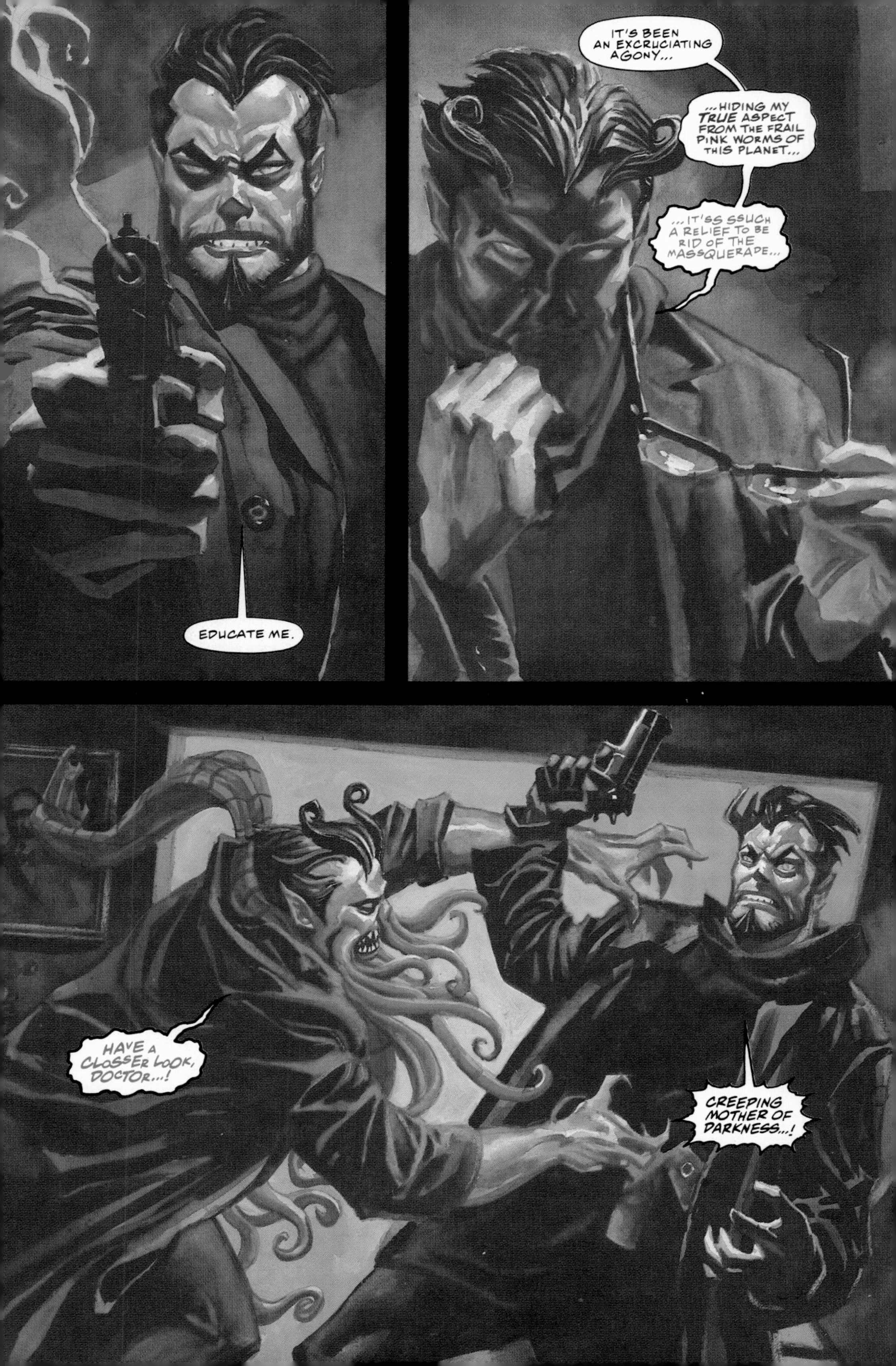
EDUCATE ME.
IT'S BEEN AN EXCRUCIATING AGONY...
...HIDING MY TRUE ASPECT FROM THE FRAIL PINK WORMS OF THIS PLANET...
...IT'SS SSUCH A RELIEF TO BE RID OF THE MASSQUERADE...
HAVE A CLOSSER LOOK, DOCTOR...!
CREEPING MOTHER OF DARKNESS...!

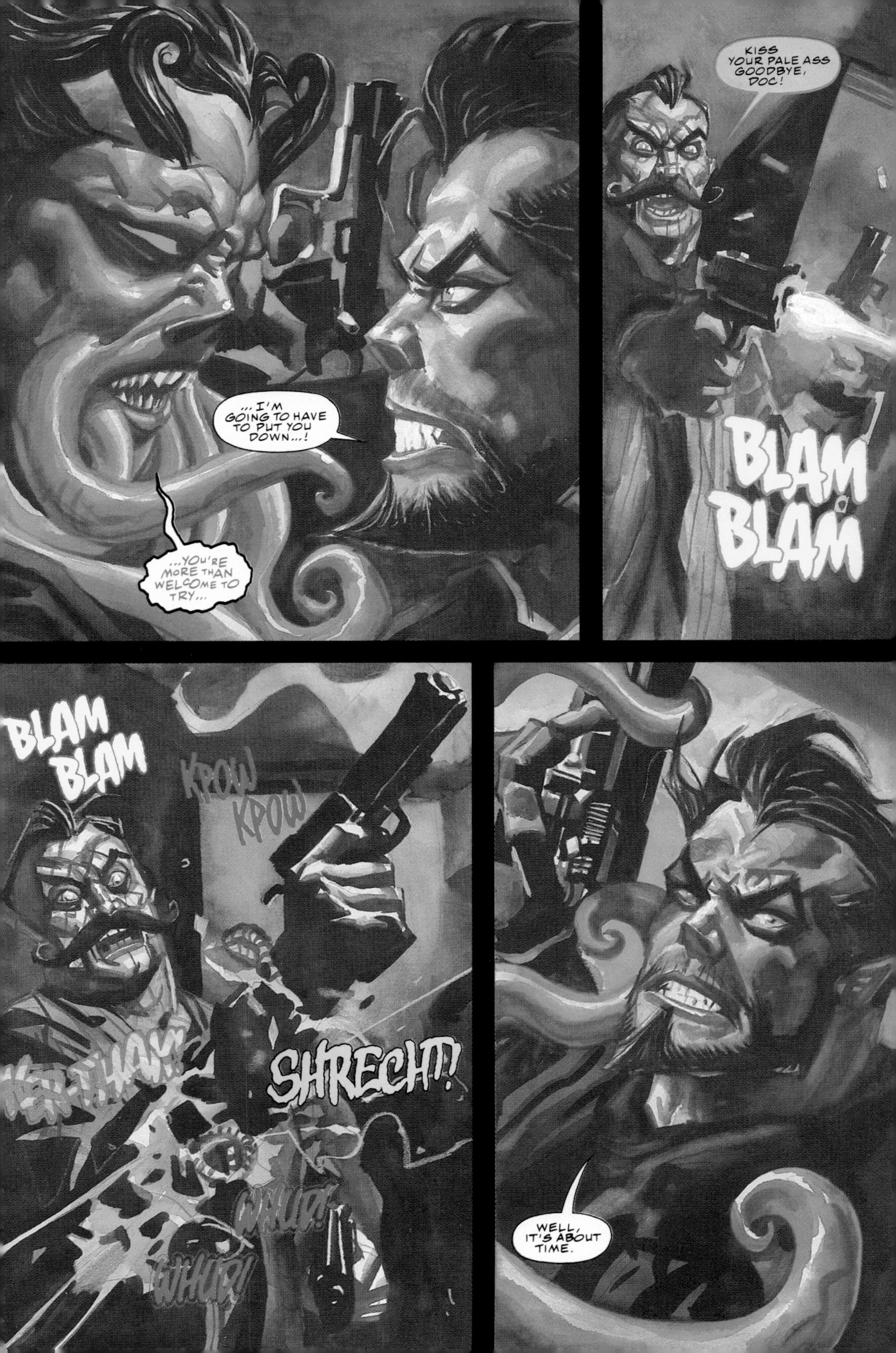
...I'M GOING TO HAVE TO PUT YOU DOWN...!
...YOU'RE MORE THAN WELCOME TO TRY...
KISS YOUR PALE ASS GOODBYE, DOC!
BLAM BLAM
BLAM BLAM
KPOW KPOW
SHRECHT!
WHUD!
WHUD!
WELL, IT'S ABOUT TIME.

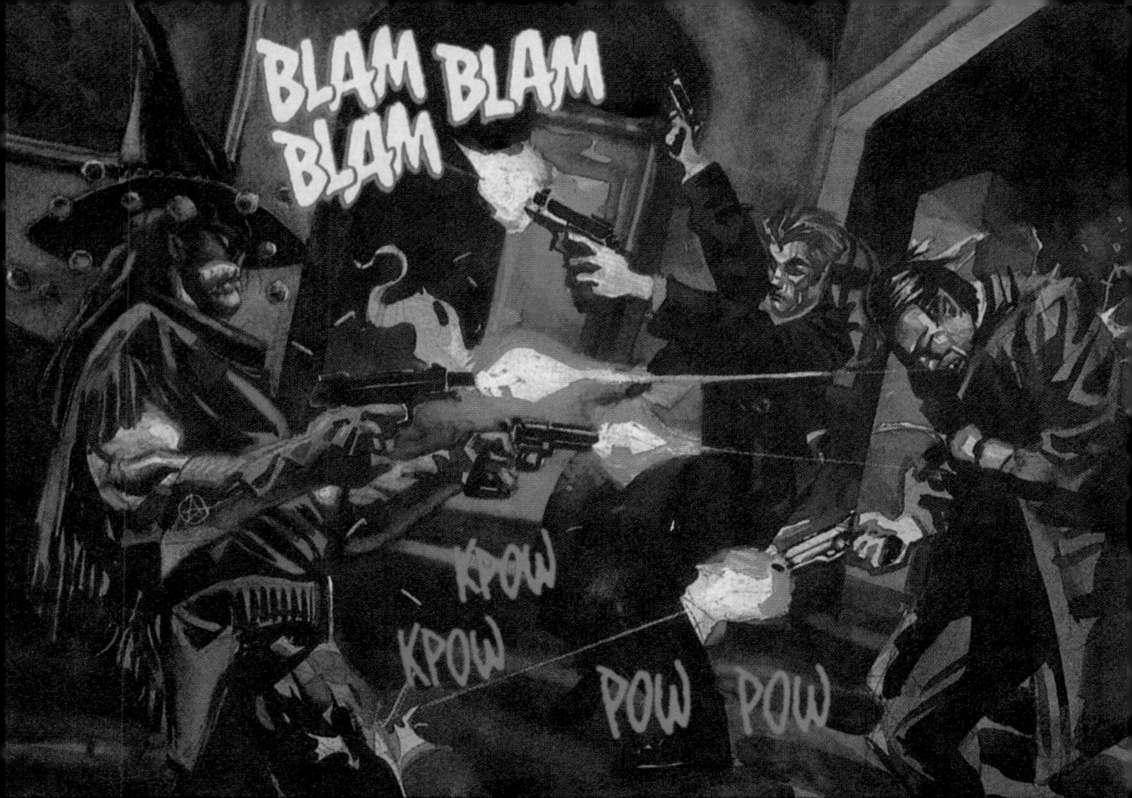
BLAM BLAM
BLAM
KPOW
KPOW
POW POW

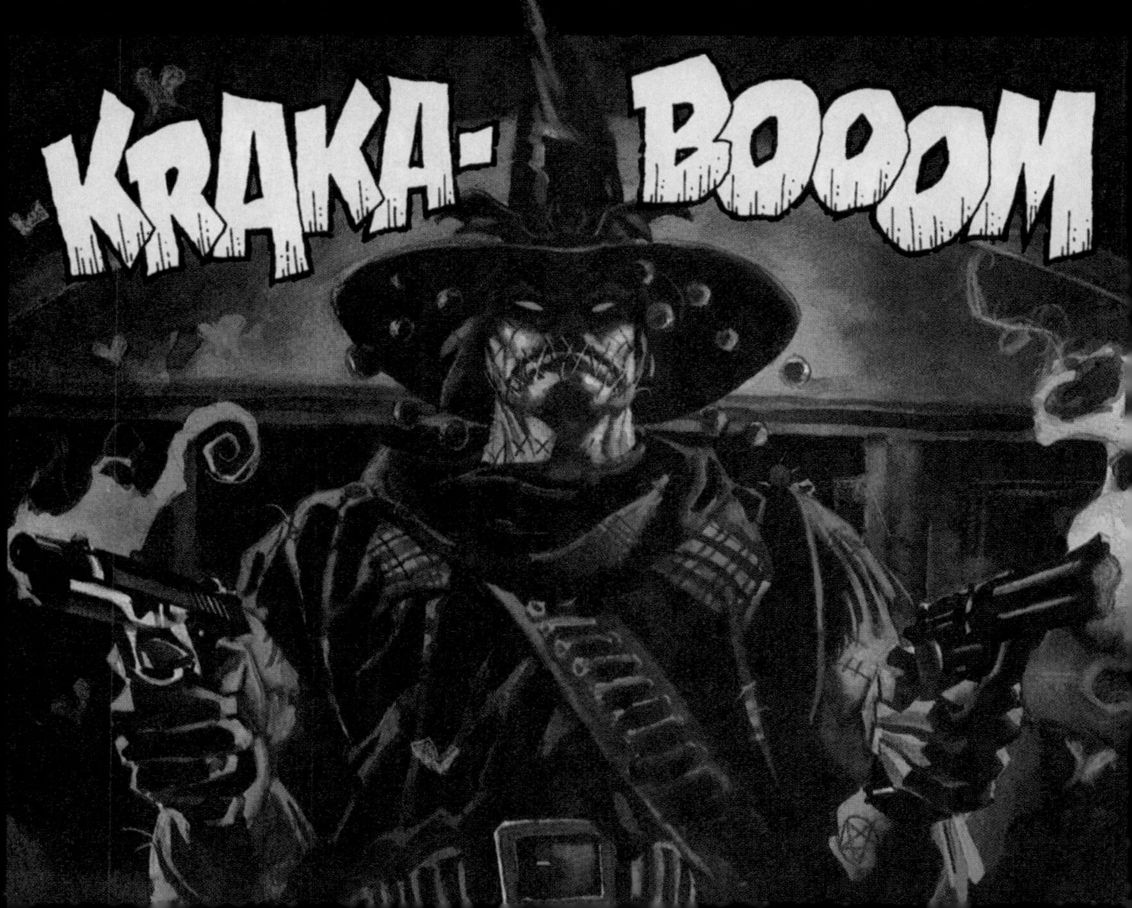
KRAKA- BOOOM

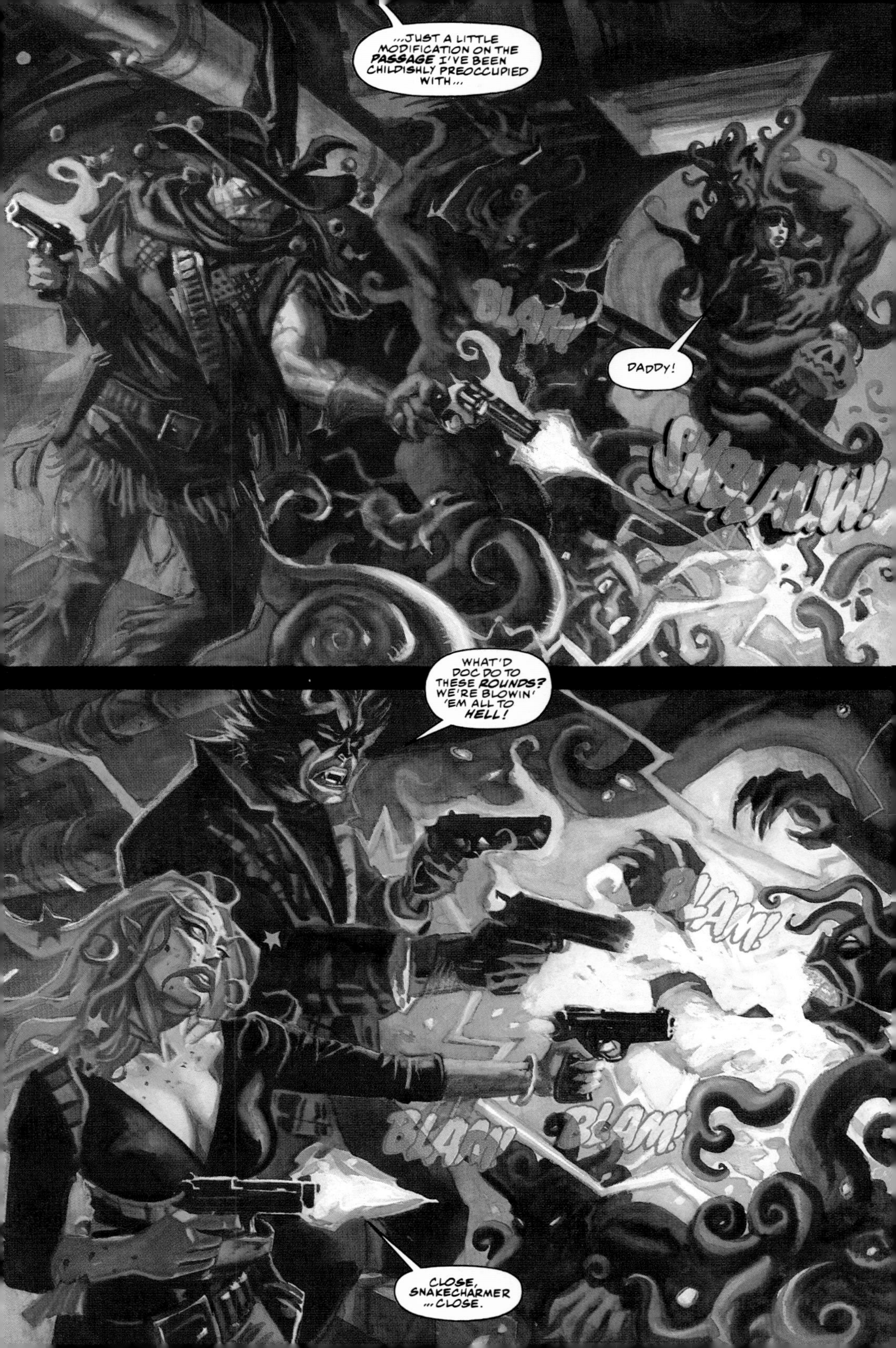
...JUST A LITTLE MODIFICATION ON THE **PASSAGE** I'VE BEEN CHILDISHLY PREOCCUPIED WITH...
BLAM!
DADDY!
WHAT'D DOC DO TO THESE **ROUNDS?** WE'RE BLOWIN' 'EM ALL TO **HELL!**
BLAM!
BLAM!
BLAM!
CLOSE, SNAKECHARMER ...CLOSE.

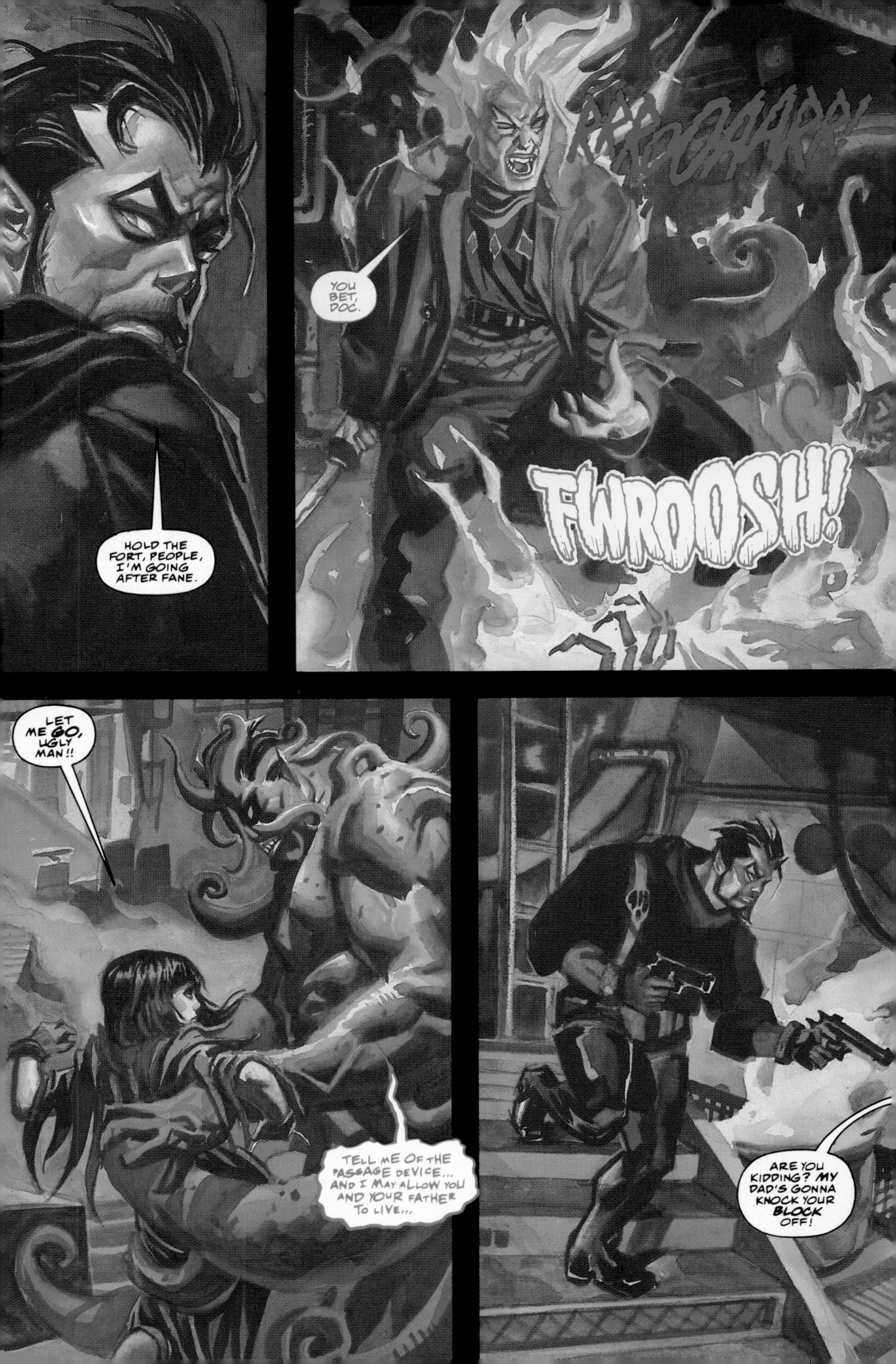
HOLD THE FORT, PEOPLE, I'M GOING AFTER FANE.
YOU BET, DOC.
RRROOAARR!
FWROOSH!
LET ME GO, UGLY MAN!!
TELL ME OF THE PASSAGE DEVICE... AND I MAY ALLOW YOU AND YOUR FATHER TO LIVE...
ARE YOU KIDDING? MY DAD'S GONNA KNOCK YOUR BLOCK OFF!

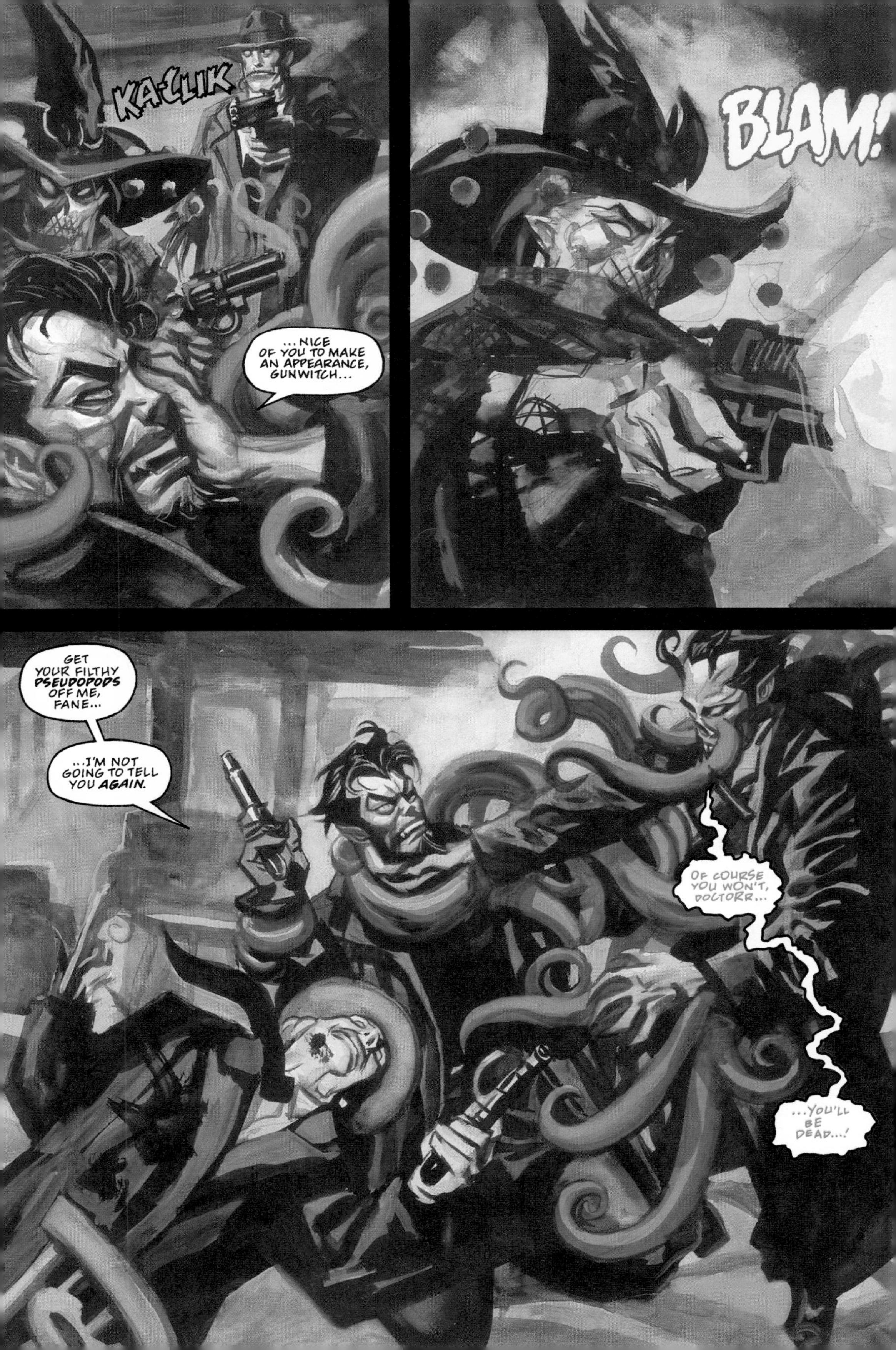
KA-CLIK
...NICE OF YOU TO MAKE AN APPEARANCE, GUNWITCH...
BLAM!
GET YOUR FILTHY PSEUDOPODS OFF ME, FANE...
...I'M NOT GOING TO TELL YOU AGAIN.
OF COURSE YOU WON'T, DOCTORR...
...YOU'LL BE DEAD...!

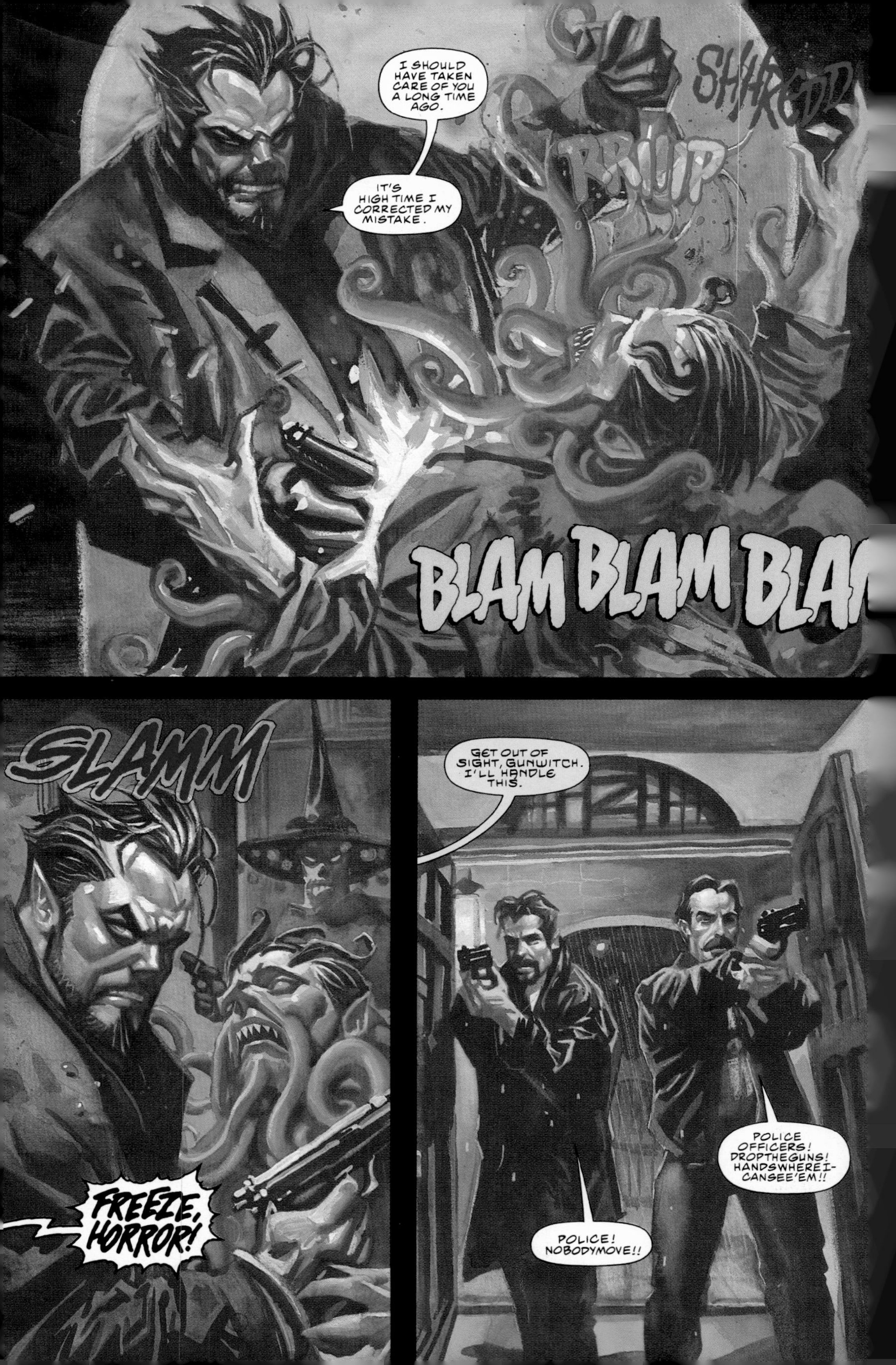
I SHOULD HAVE TAKEN CARE OF YOU A LONG TIME AGO.
IT'S HIGH TIME I CORRECTED MY MISTAKE.
SHHREDD!
RRIIP
BLAM BLAM BLAM
SLAMM
FREEZE, HORROR!
GET OUT OF SIGHT, GUNWITCH. I'LL HANDLE THIS.
POLICE! NOBODYMOVE!!
POLICE OFFICERS! DROPTHEGUNS! HANDSWHEREI-CANSEE'EM!!

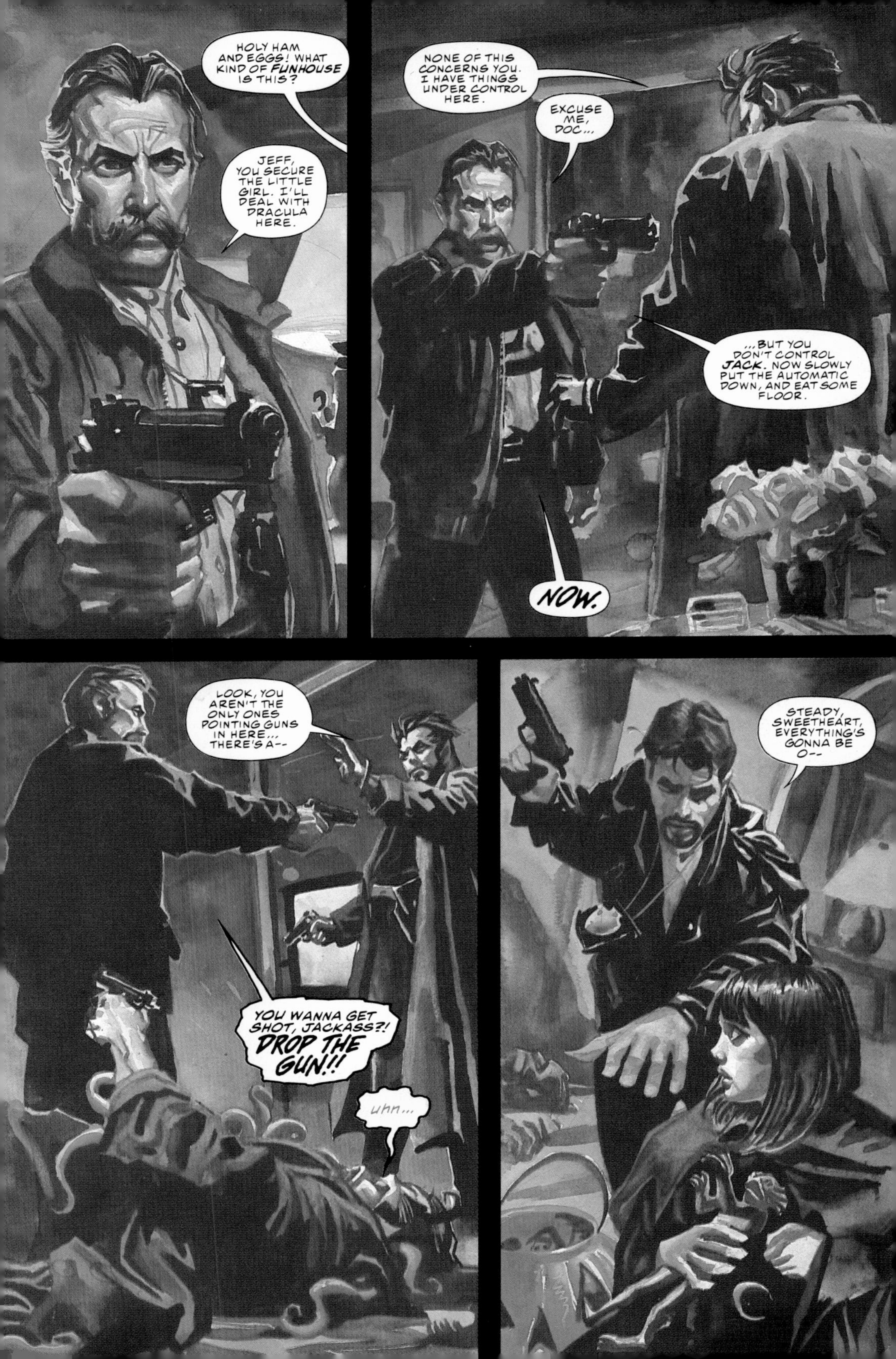
HOLY HAM AND EGGS! WHAT KIND OF FUNHOUSE IS THIS?
JEFF, YOU SECURE THE LITTLE GIRL. I'LL DEAL WITH DRACULA HERE.
NONE OF THIS CONCERNS YOU. I HAVE THINGS UNDER CONTROL HERE.
EXCUSE ME, DOC...
...BUT YOU DON'T CONTROL JACK. NOW SLOWLY PUT THE AUTOMATIC DOWN, AND EAT SOME FLOOR.
NOW.
LOOK, YOU AREN'T THE ONLY ONES POINTING GUNS IN HERE... THERE'S A--
YOU WANNA GET SHOT, JACKASS?! DROP THE GUN!!
uhn...
STEADY, SWEETHEART, EVERYTHING'S GONNA BE O--

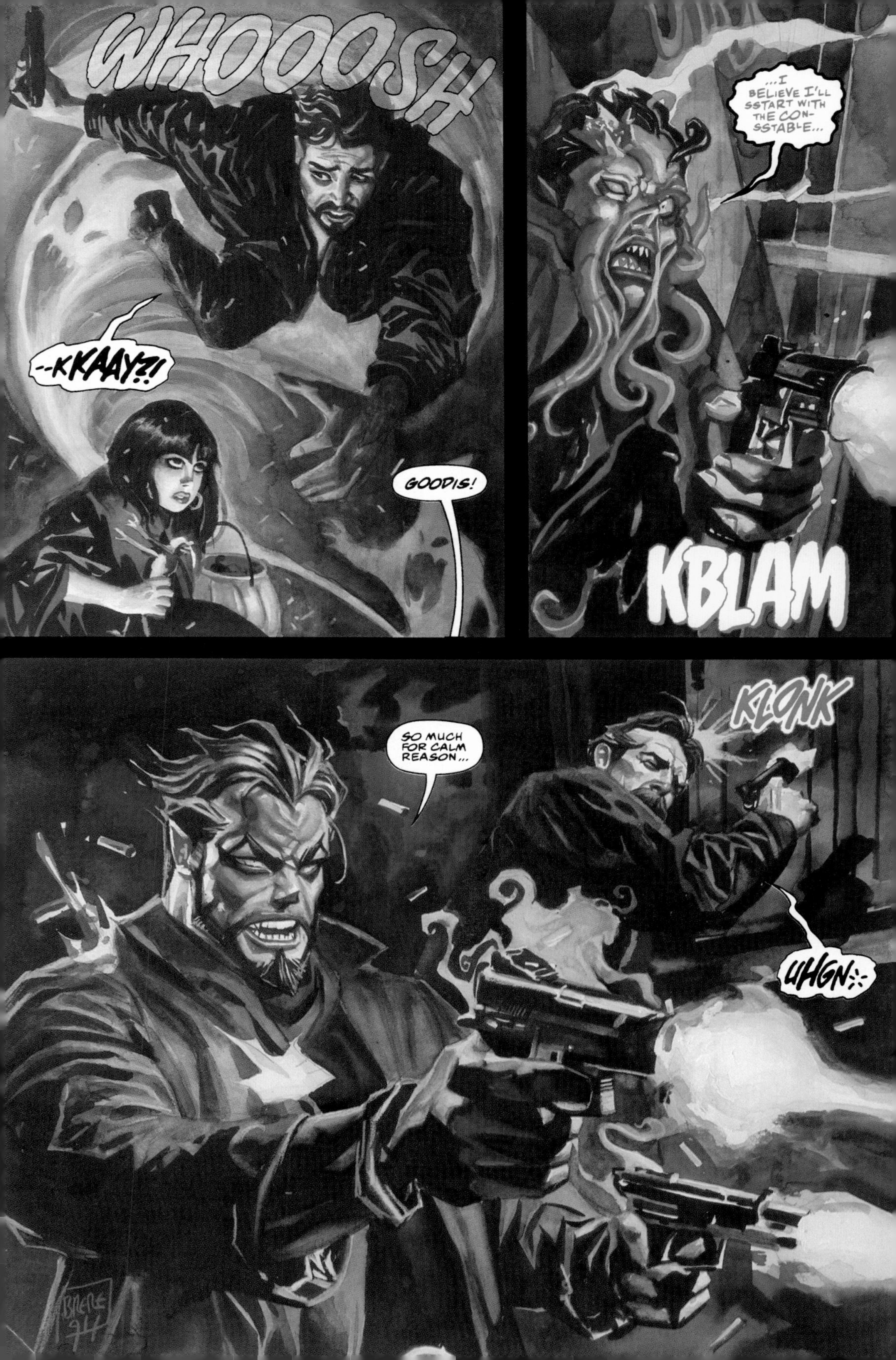
WHOOOSH
--KKAAY?!
GOODIS!
...I BELIEVE I'LL SSTART WITH THE CON-SSTABLE...
KBLAM
KLONK
SO MUCH FOR CALM REASON...
UHGN

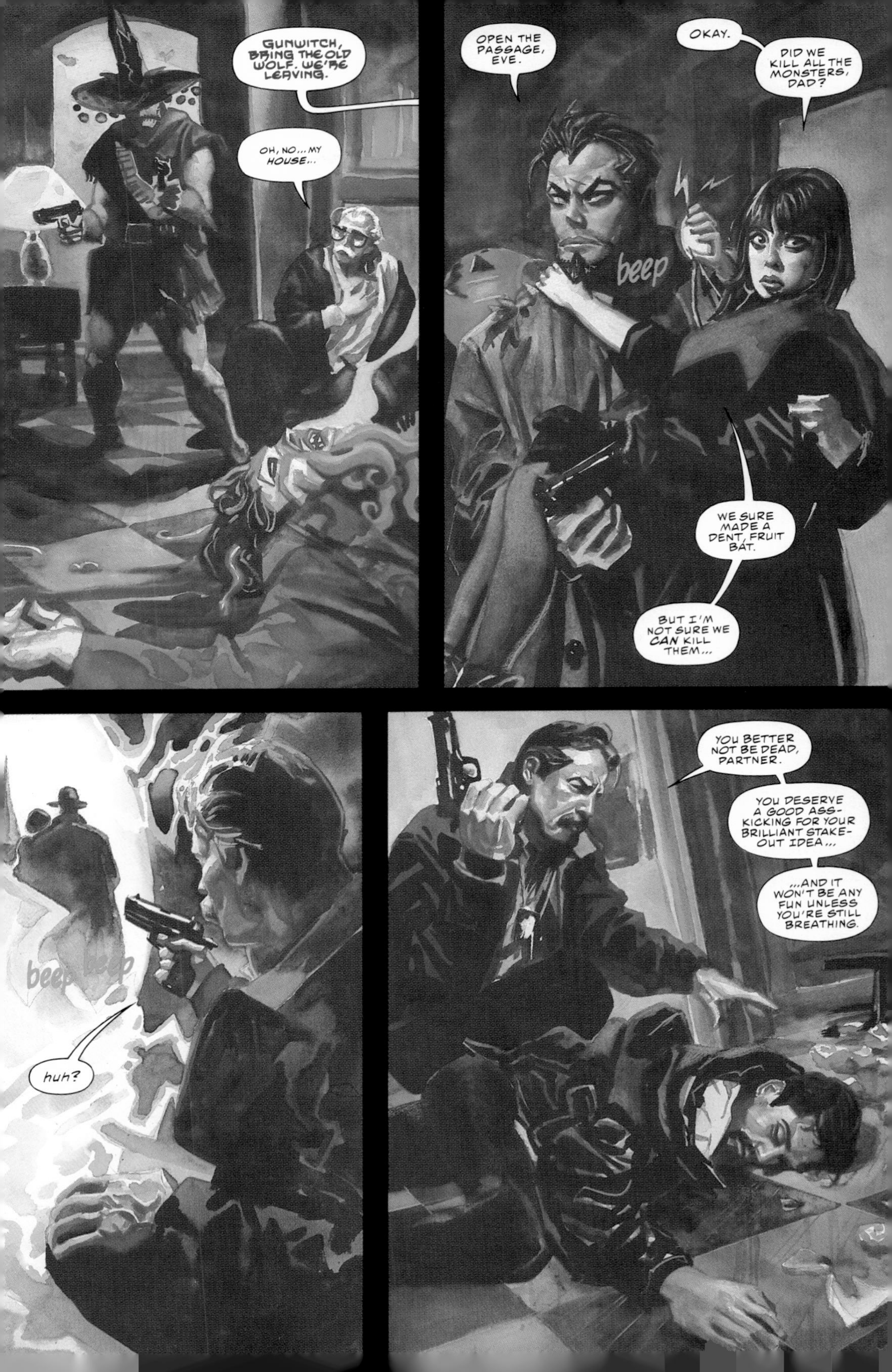

GUNWITCH, BRING THE OLD WOLF. WE'RE LEAVING.
OH, NO... MY HOUSE...
OPEN THE PASSAGE, EVE.
OKAY.
DID WE KILL ALL THE MONSTERS, DAD?
beep
WE SURE MADE A DENT, FRUIT BAT.
BUT I'M NOT SURE WE CAN KILL THEM...
beep beep
huh?
YOU BETTER NOT BE DEAD, PARTNER.
YOU DESERVE A GOOD ASS-KICKING FOR YOUR BRILLIANT STAKE-OUT IDEA...
...AND IT WON'T BE ANY FUN UNLESS YOU'RE STILL BREATHING.

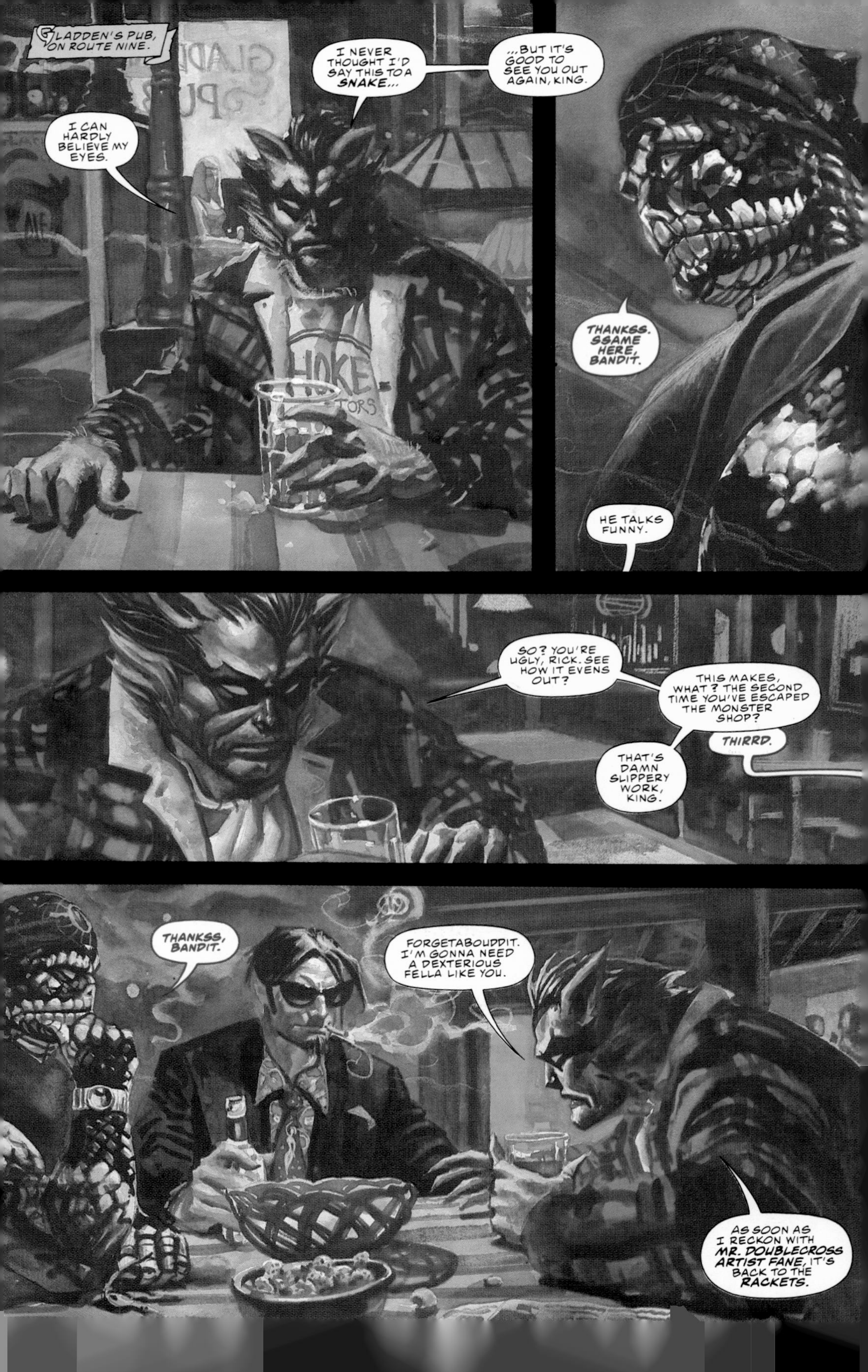

GLADDEN'S PUB, ON ROUTE NINE.
I CAN HARDLY BELIEVE MY EYES.
I NEVER THOUGHT I'D SAY THIS TO A SNAKE...
...BUT IT'S GOOD TO SEE YOU OUT AGAIN, KING.
THANKSS. SSAME HERE, BANDIT.
HE TALKS FUNNY.
SO? YOU'RE UGLY, RICK. SEE HOW IT EVENS OUT?
THIS MAKES, WHAT? THE SECOND TIME YOU'VE ESCAPED THE MONSTER SHOP?
THIRRD.
THAT'S DAMN SLIPPERY WORK, KING.
THANKSS, BANDIT.
FORGETABOUDDIT. I'M GONNA NEED A DEXTERIOUS FELLA LIKE YOU.
AS SOON AS I RECKON WITH MR. DOUBLECROSS ARTIST FANE, IT'S BACK TO THE RACKETS.

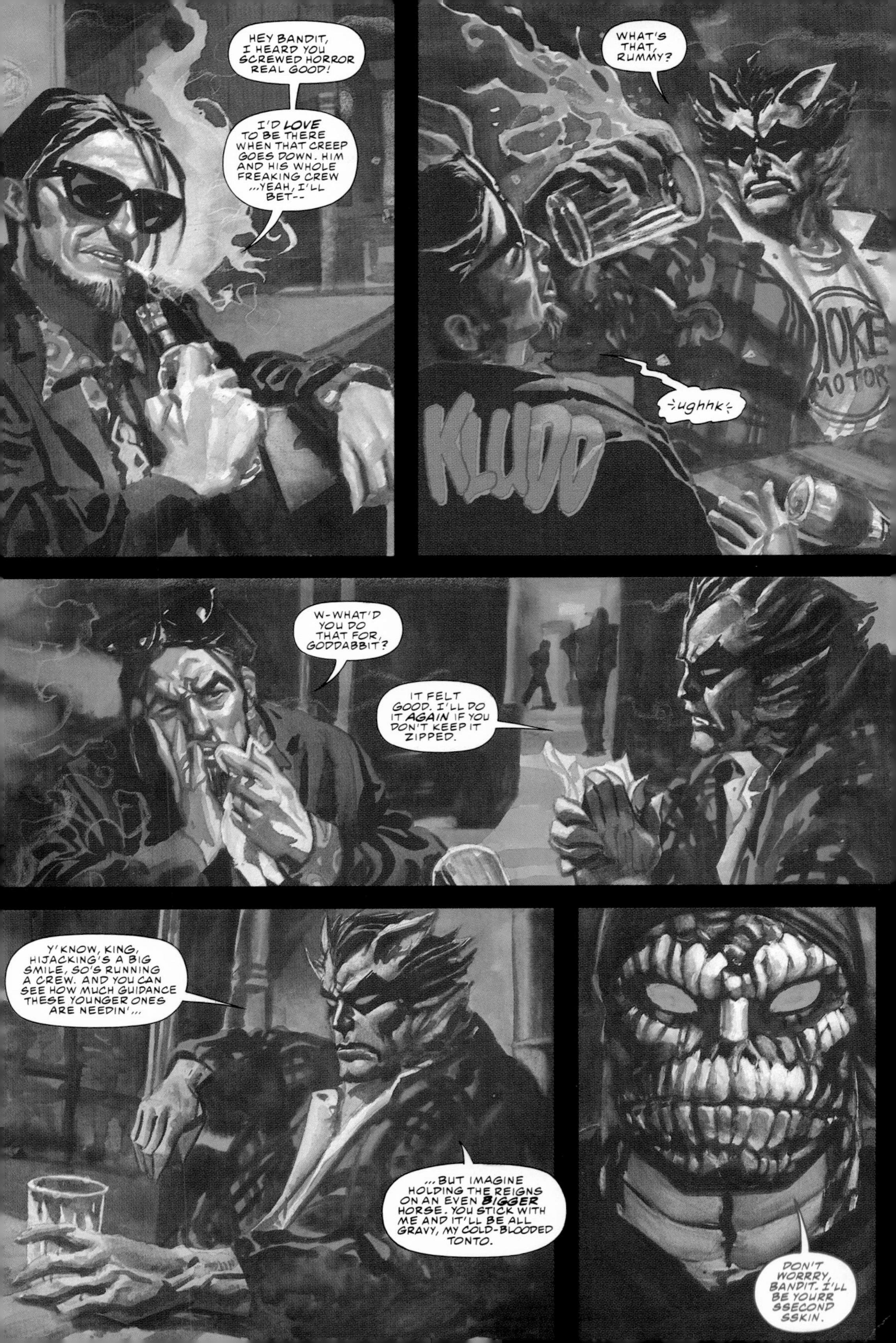

HEY BANDIT, I HEARD YOU SCREWED HORROR REAL GOOD!
I'D LOVE TO BE THERE WHEN THAT CREEP GOES DOWN. HIM AND HIS WHOLE FREAKING CREW ...YEAH, I'LL BET--
WHAT'S THAT, RUMMY?
KLUDD
-ughhk-
W-WHAT'D YOU DO THAT FOR, GODDABBIT?
IT FELT GOOD. I'LL DO IT AGAIN IF YOU DON'T KEEP IT ZIPPED.
Y'KNOW, KING, HIJACKING'S A BIG SMILE, SO'S RUNNING A CREW. AND YOU CAN SEE HOW MUCH GUIDANCE THESE YOUNGER ONES ARE NEEDIN'...
...BUT IMAGINE HOLDING THE REIGNS ON AN EVEN BIGGER HORSE. YOU STICK WITH ME AND IT'LL BE ALL GRAVY, MY COLD-BLOODED TONTO.
DON'T WORRRY, BANDIT. I'LL BE YOURR SSECOND SSKIN.

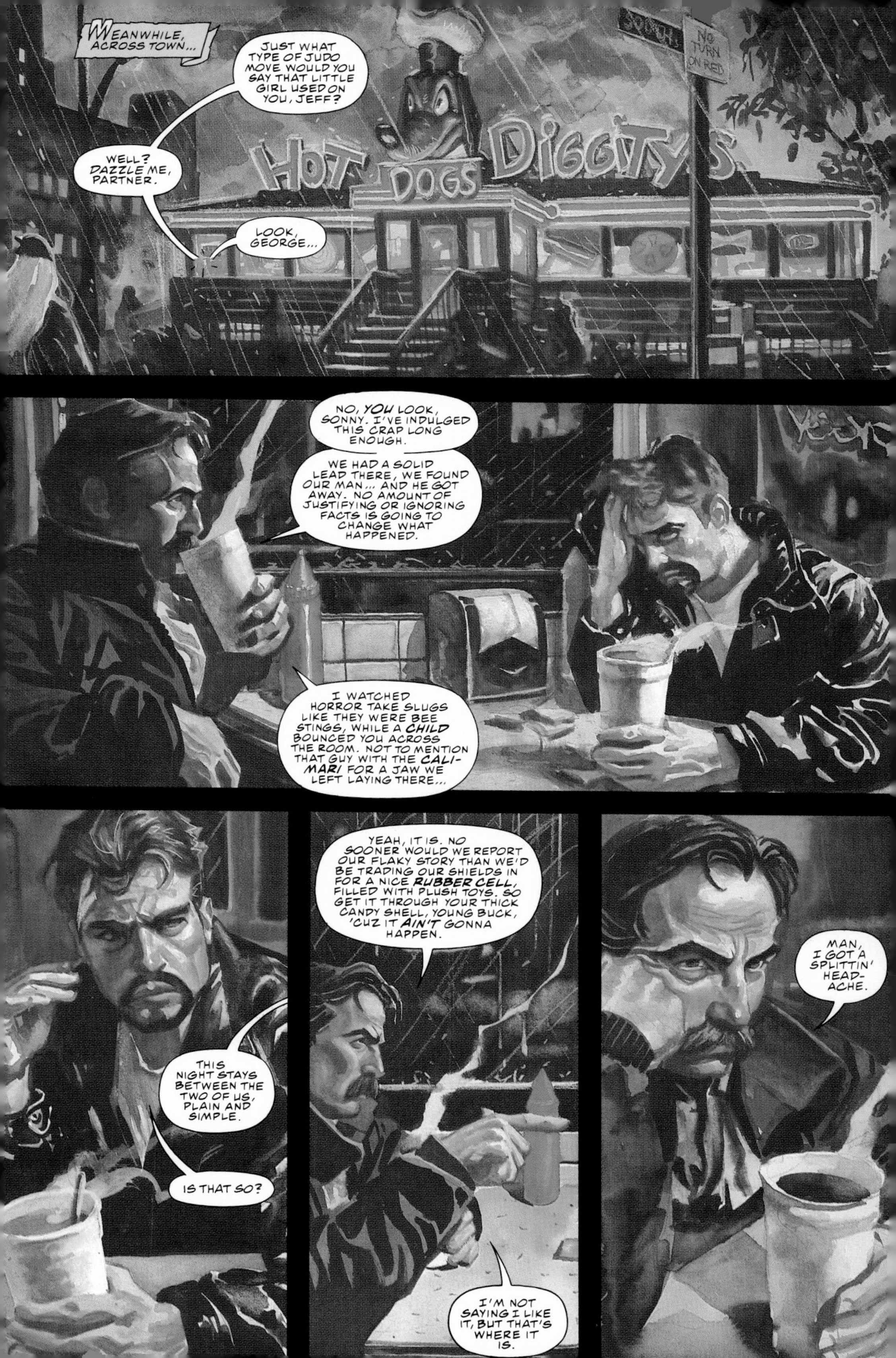
MEANWHILE, ACROSS TOWN...
JUST WHAT TYPE OF JUDO MOVE WOULD YOU SAY THAT LITTLE GIRL USED ON YOU, JEFF?
WELL? DAZZLE ME, PARTNER.
LOOK, GEORGE...
HOT DOGS DIGGITY'S
NO TURN ON RED
NO, YOU LOOK, SONNY. I'VE INDULGED THIS CRAP LONG ENOUGH.
WE HAD A SOLID LEAD THERE, WE FOUND OUR MAN... AND HE GOT AWAY. NO AMOUNT OF JUSTIFYING OR IGNORING FACTS IS GOING TO CHANGE WHAT HAPPENED.
I WATCHED HORROR TAKE SLUGS LIKE THEY WERE BEE STINGS, WHILE A CHILD BOUNCED YOU ACROSS THE ROOM. NOT TO MENTION THAT GUY WITH THE CALI-MARI FOR A JAW WE LEFT LAYING THERE...
THIS NIGHT STAYS BETWEEN THE TWO OF US, PLAIN AND SIMPLE.
IS THAT SO?
YEAH, IT IS. NO SOONER WOULD WE REPORT OUR FLAKY STORY THAN WE'D BE TRADING OUR SHIELDS IN FOR A NICE RUBBER CELL, FILLED WITH PLUSH TOYS. SO GET IT THROUGH YOUR THICK CANDY SHELL, YOUNG BUCK, 'CUZ IT AIN'T GONNA HAPPEN.
I'M NOT SAYING I LIKE IT, BUT THAT'S WHERE IT IS.
MAN, I GOT A SPLITTIN' HEAD-ACHE.

YEAH, WELL, MINE FEELS REAL GROOVY, TOO... YOU FINISHED NOW?
HELL, NO. I SAID THIS WAS BETWEEN US. WE'RE STILL ON A MANHUNT. NOBODY GETS OVER ON ME LIKE THAT. WE'RE GONNA BAG THAT BASTARD...
EXCUSE ME... IT'S REALLY COLD AND WET OUT...
THAT'S WHY THE CITY PROVIDES SHELTERS, BUDDY. TRY THE ONE ON 47TH, BY THE OLD LIBRARY.

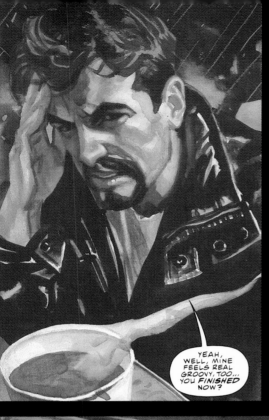

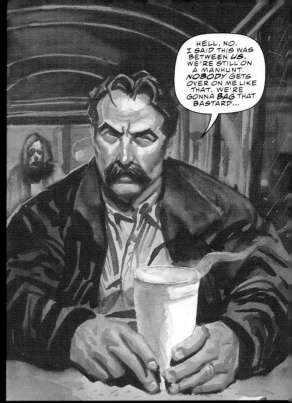

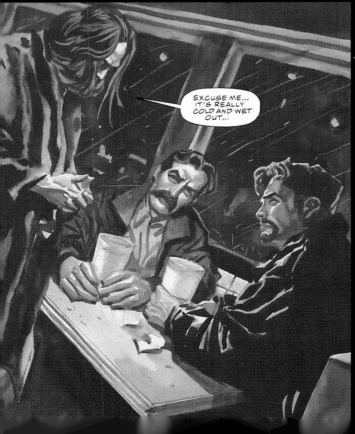

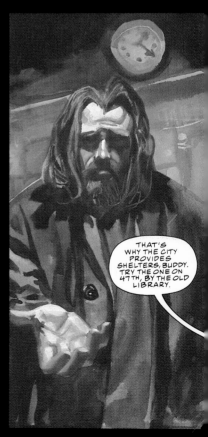

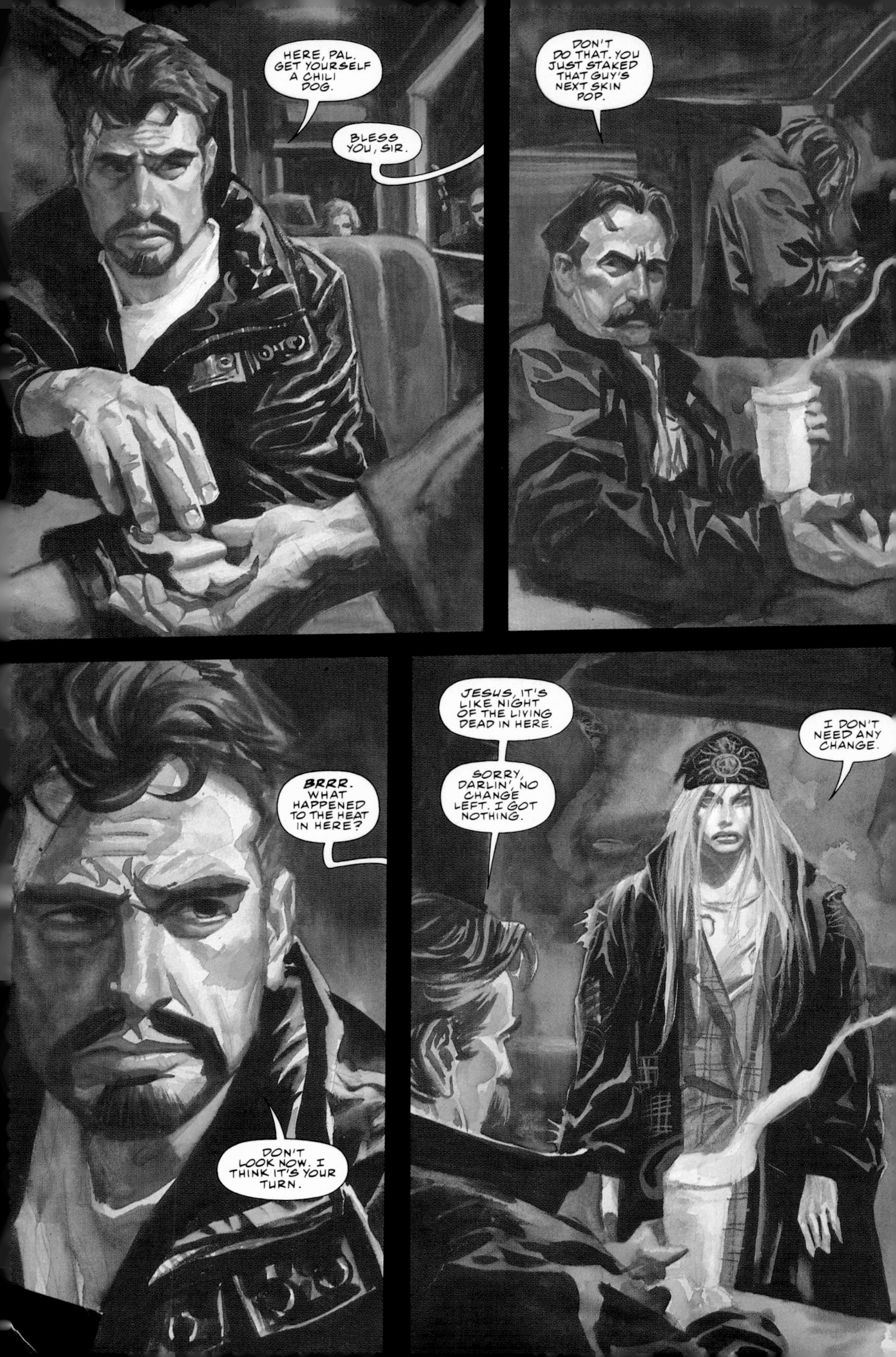
HERE, PAL. GET YOURSELF A CHILI DOG.
BLESS YOU, SIR.
DON'T DO THAT. YOU JUST STAKED THAT GUY'S NEXT SKIN POP.
BRRR. WHAT HAPPENED TO THE HEAT IN HERE?
DON'T LOOK NOW. I THINK IT'S YOUR TURN.
JESUS, IT'S LIKE NIGHT OF THE LIVING DEAD IN HERE.
SORRY, DARLIN', NO CHANGE LEFT. I GOT NOTHING.
I DON'T NEED ANY CHANGE.

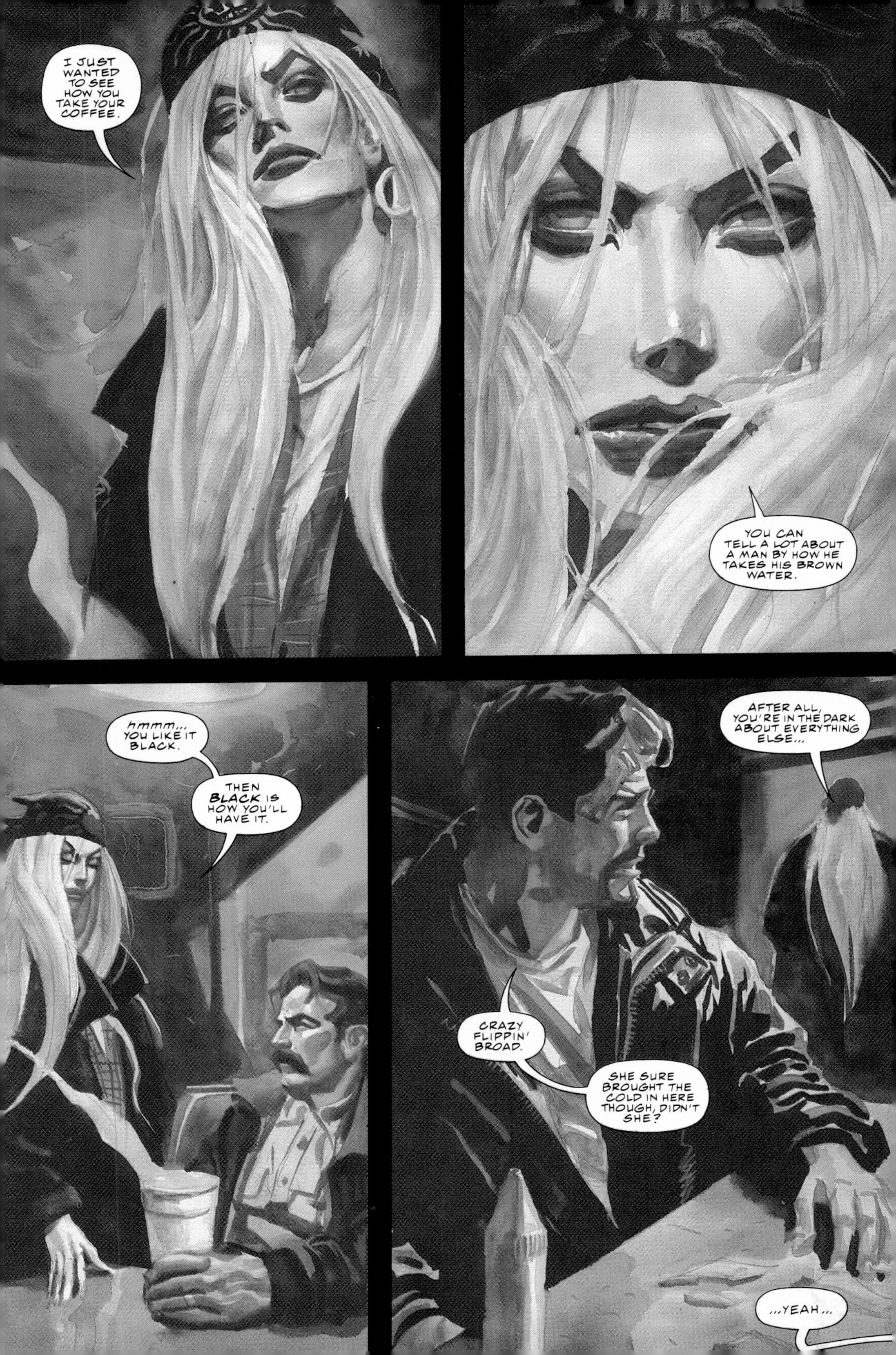
I JUST WANTED TO SEE HOW YOU TAKE YOUR COFFEE.
YOU CAN TELL A LOT ABOUT A MAN BY HOW HE TAKES HIS BROWN WATER.
hmmm... YOU LIKE IT BLACK.
THEN **BLACK** IS HOW YOU'LL HAVE IT.
AFTER ALL, YOU'RE IN THE DARK ABOUT EVERYTHING ELSE...
CRAZY FLIPPIN' BROAD.
SHE SURE BROUGHT THE COLD IN HERE THOUGH, DIDN'T SHE?
...YEAH...

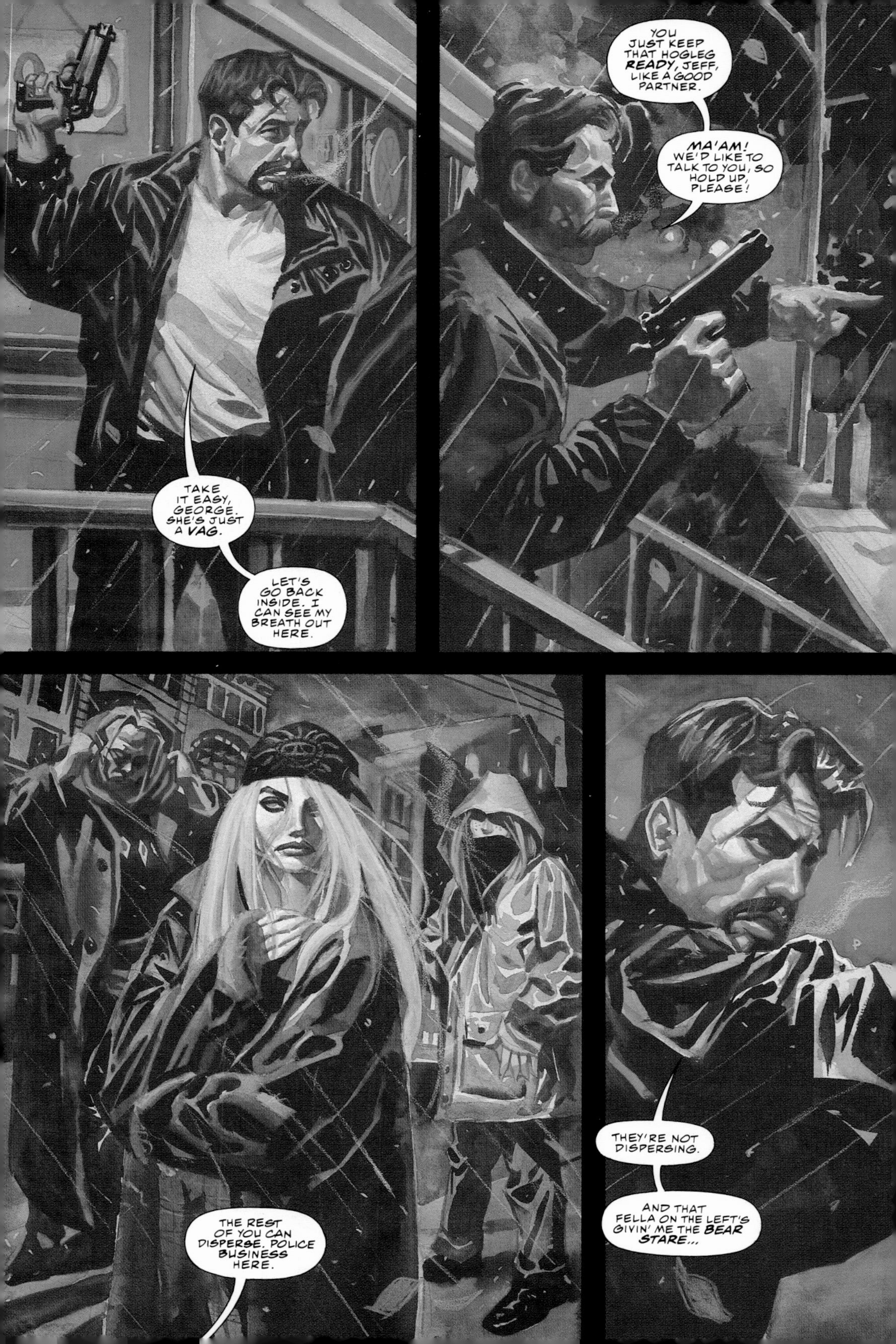
TAKE IT EASY, GEORGE. SHE'S JUST A VAG.
LET'S GO BACK INSIDE. I CAN SEE MY BREATH OUT HERE.
YOU JUST KEEP THAT HOGLEG READY, JEFF, LIKE A GOOD PARTNER.
MA'AM! WE'D LIKE TO TALK TO YOU, SO HOLD UP, PLEASE!
THE REST OF YOU CAN DISPERSE. POLICE BUSINESS HERE.
THEY'RE NOT DISPERSING.
AND THAT FELLA ON THE LEFT'S GIVIN' ME THE BEAR STARE...

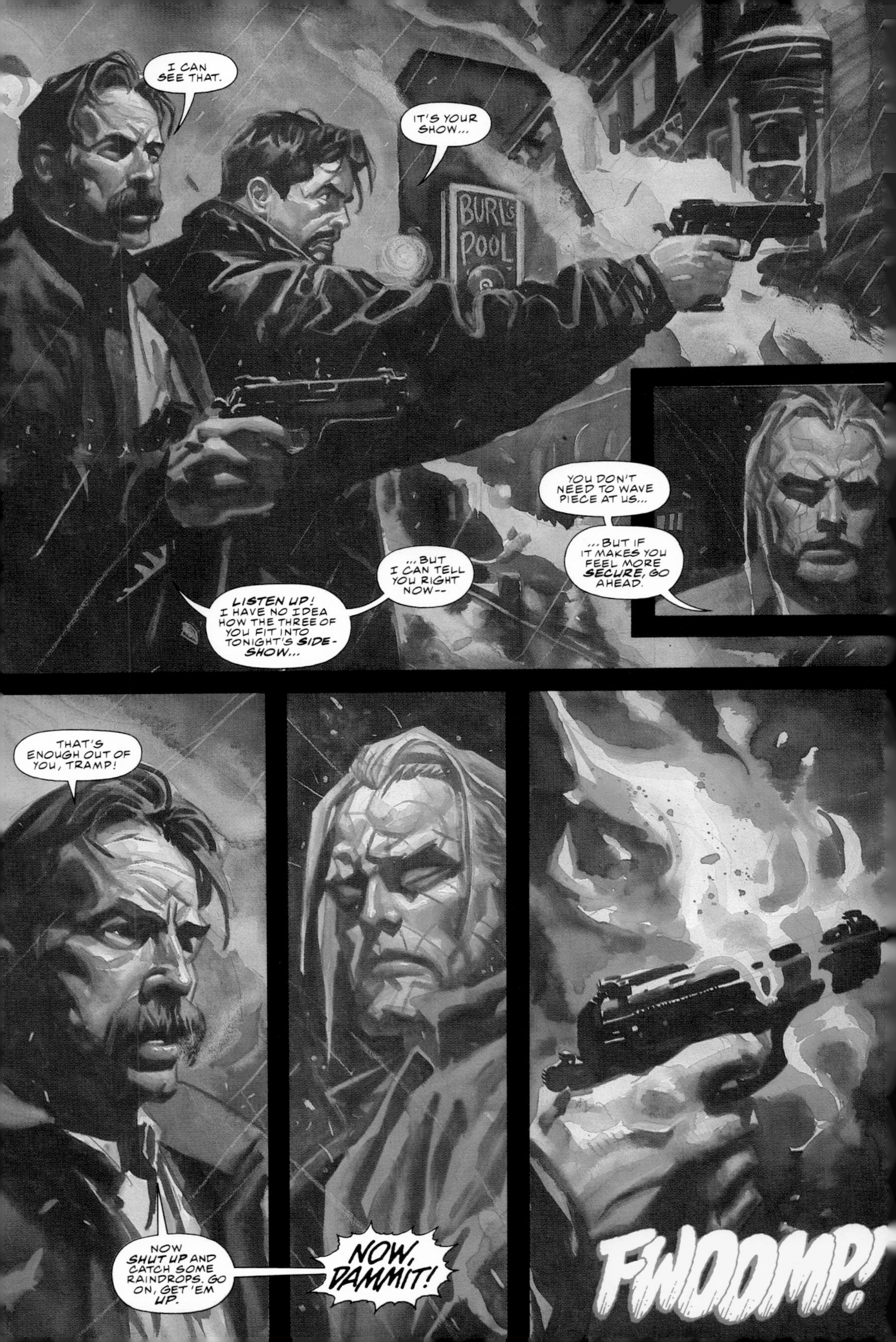

I CAN SEE THAT.
IT'S YOUR SHOW...
BURL'S POOL
LISTEN UP! I HAVE NO IDEA HOW THE THREE OF YOU FIT INTO TONIGHT'S SIDE-SHOW...
...BUT I CAN TELL YOU RIGHT NOW--
YOU DON'T NEED TO WAVE PIECE AT US...
...BUT IF IT MAKES YOU FEEL MORE SECURE, GO AHEAD.
THAT'S ENOUGH OUT OF YOU, TRAMP!
NOW SHUT UP AND CATCH SOME RAINDROPS. GO ON, GET 'EM UP.
NOW, DAMMIT!
FWOOMP!

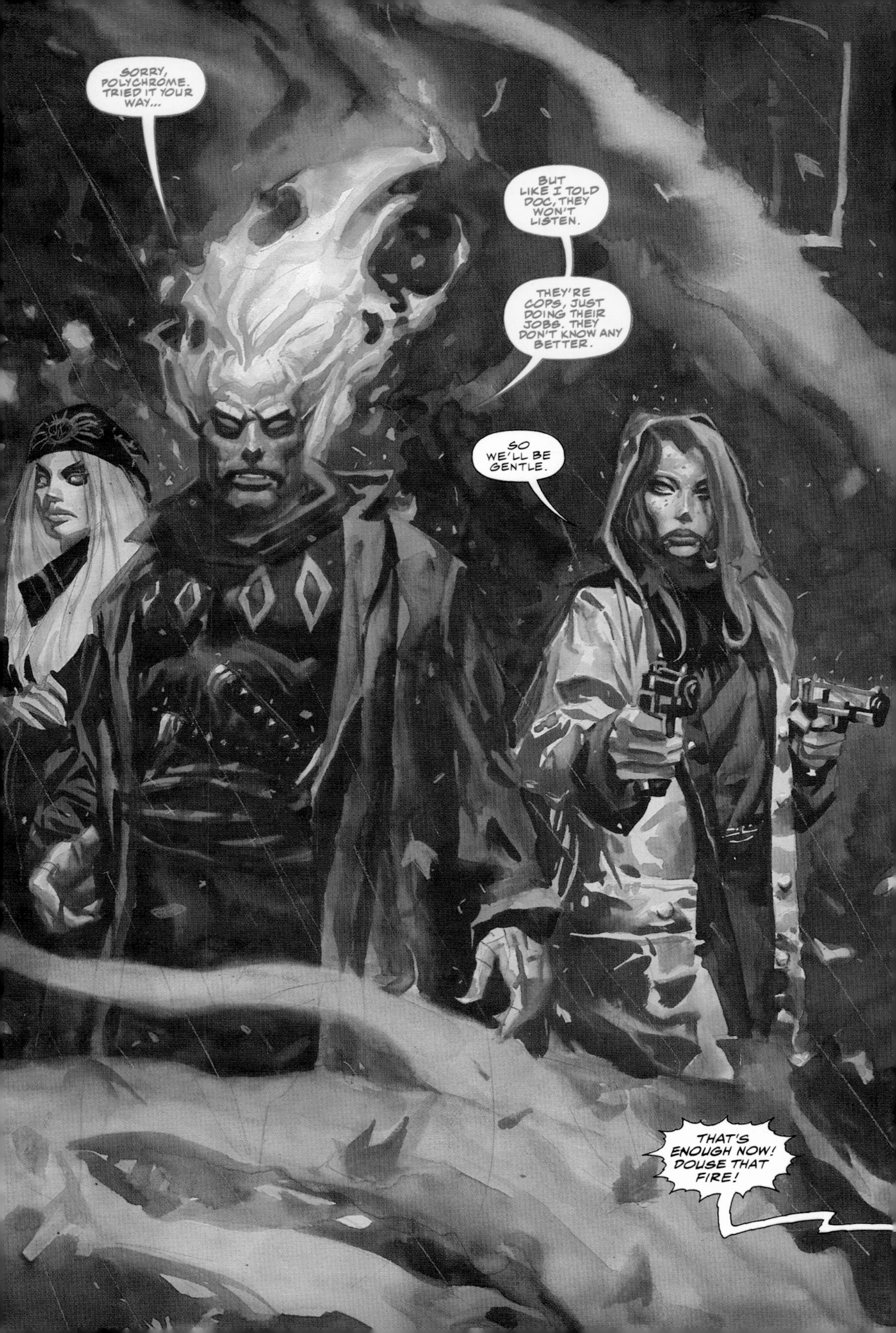
SORRY, POLYCHROME. TRIED IT YOUR WAY...
BUT LIKE I TOLD DOC, THEY WON'T LISTEN.
THEY'RE COPS, JUST DOING THEIR JOBS. THEY DON'T KNOW ANY BETTER.
SO WE'LL BE GENTLE.
THAT'S ENOUGH NOW! DOUSE THAT FIRE!

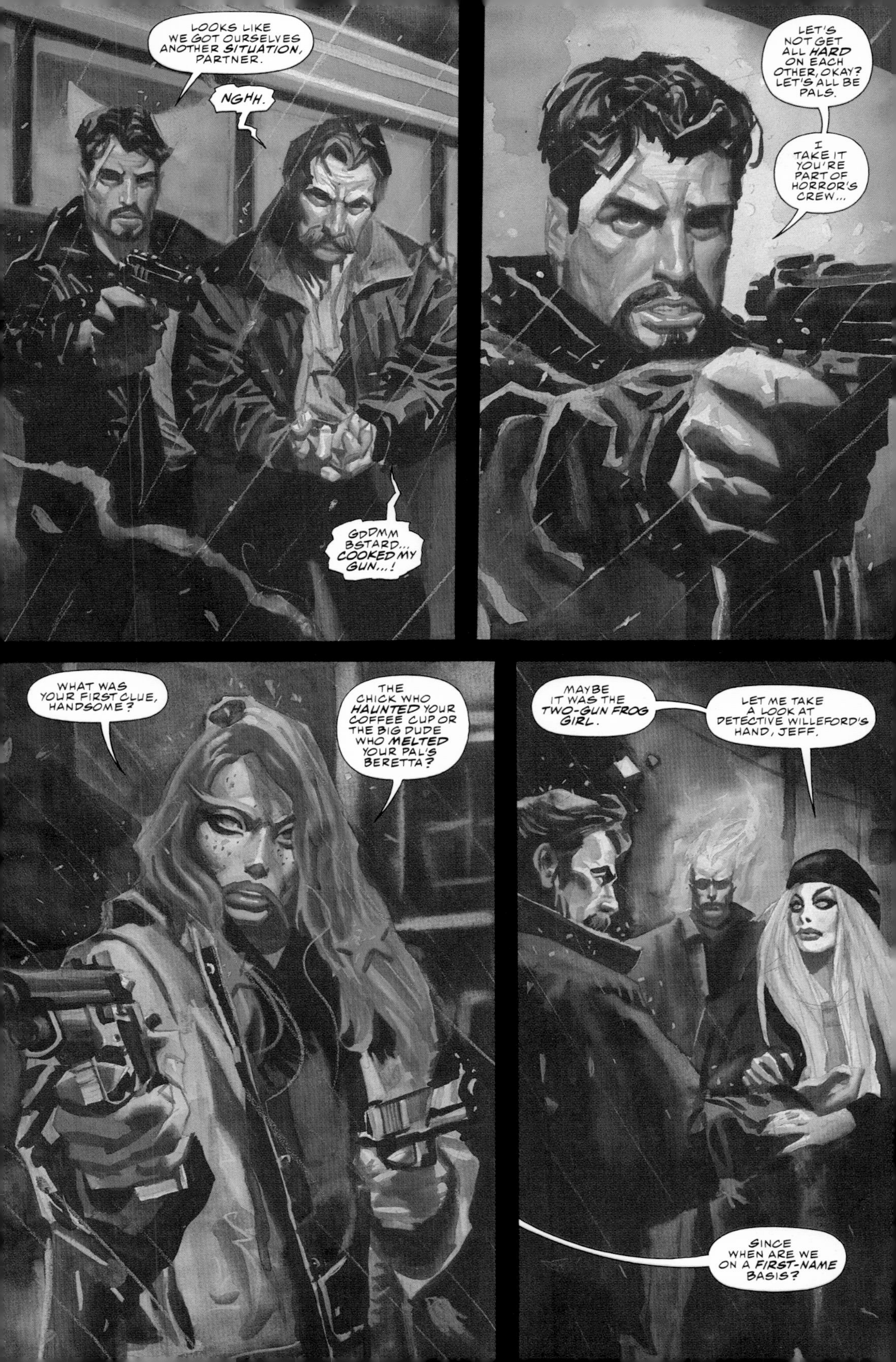
LOOKS LIKE WE GOT OURSELVES ANOTHER SITUATION, PARTNER.
NGHH.
GDDMM BSTARD... COOKED MY GUN...!
LET'S NOT GET ALL HARD ON EACH OTHER, OKAY? LET'S ALL BE PALS.
I TAKE IT YOU'RE PART OF HORROR'S CREW...
WHAT WAS YOUR FIRST CLUE, HANDSOME?
THE CHICK WHO HAUNTED YOUR COFFEE CUP OR THE BIG DUDE WHO MELTED YOUR PAL'S BERETTA?
MAYBE IT WAS THE TWO-GUN FROG GIRL.
LET ME TAKE A LOOK AT DETECTIVE WILLEFORD'S HAND, JEFF.
SINCE WHEN ARE WE ON A FIRST-NAME BASIS?

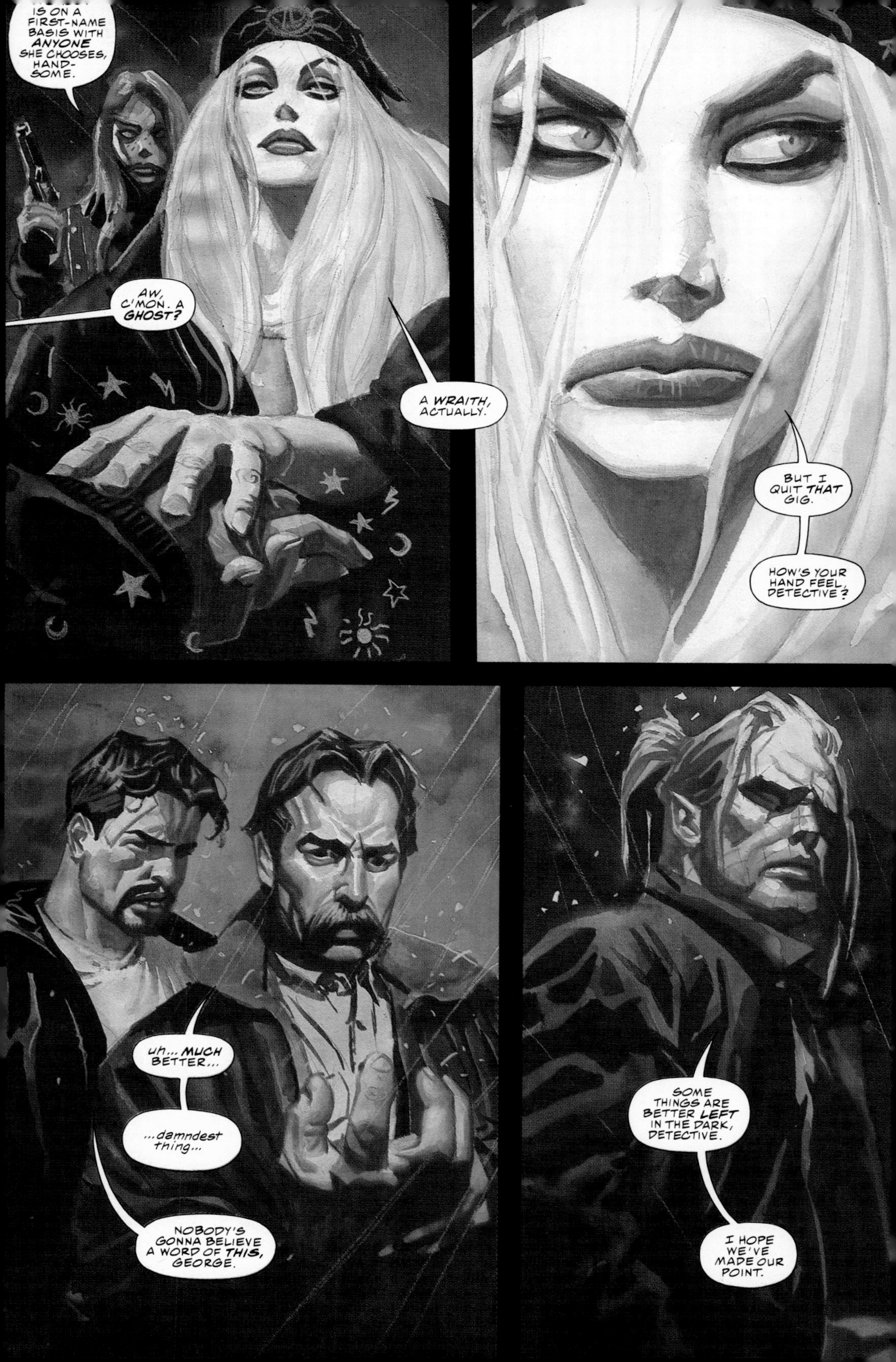

IS ON A FIRST-NAME BASIS WITH **ANYONE** SHE CHOOSES, HAND-SOME.
AW, C'MON. A **GHOST?**
A **WRAITH,** ACTUALLY.
BUT I QUIT **THAT** GIG.
HOW'S YOUR HAND FEEL, DETECTIVE?
uh... **MUCH** better...
...damndest thing...
NOBODY'S GONNA BELIEVE A WORD OF **THIS,** GEORGE.
SOME THINGS ARE BETTER **LEFT** IN THE DARK, DETECTIVE.
I HOPE WE'VE MADE OUR POINT.

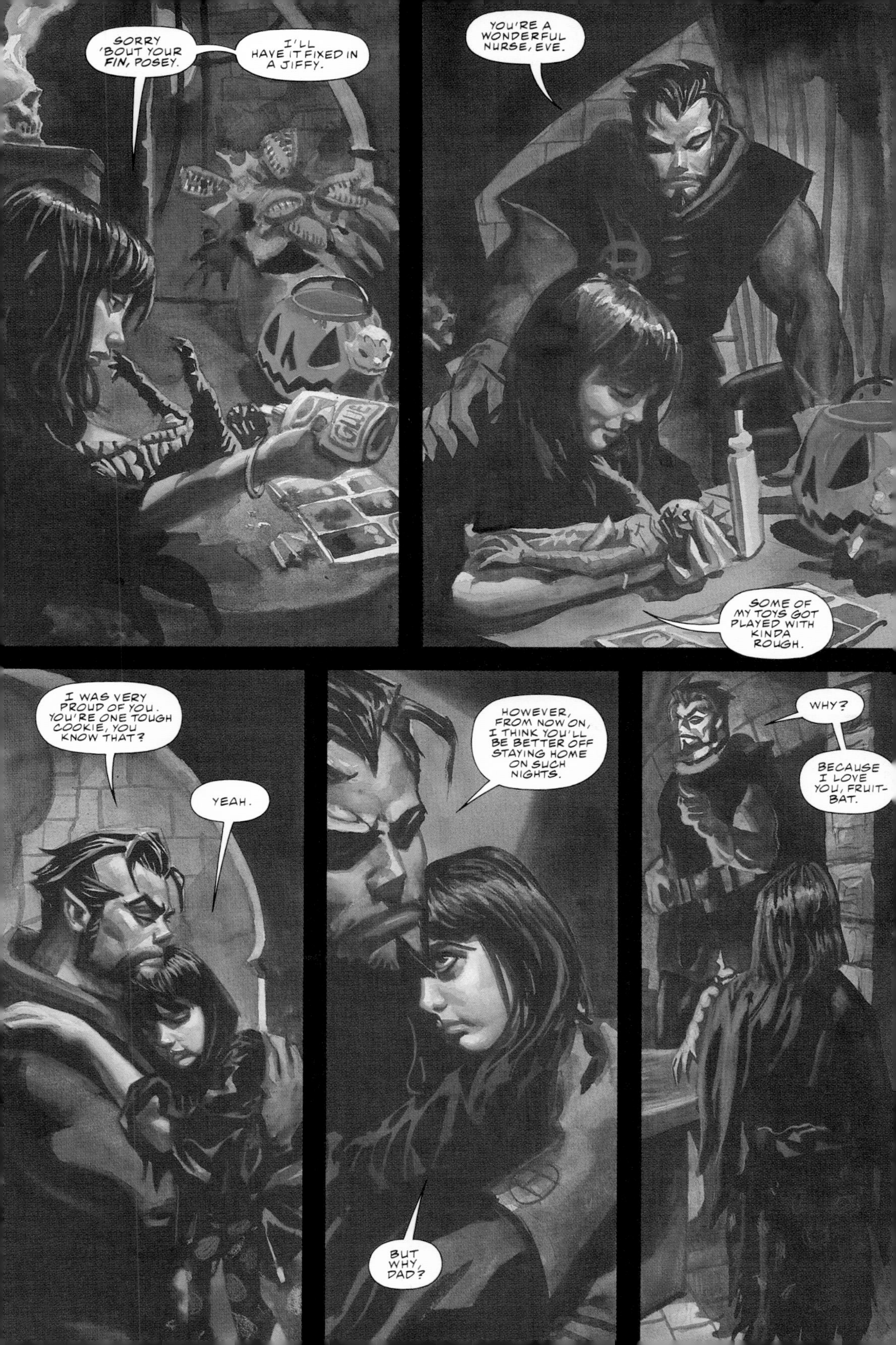
SORRY 'BOUT YOUR FIN, POSEY.
I'LL HAVE IT FIXED IN A JIFFY.
YOU'RE A WONDERFUL NURSE, EVE.
SOME OF MY TOYS GOT PLAYED WITH KINDA ROUGH.
I WAS VERY PROUD OF YOU. YOU'RE ONE TOUGH COOKIE, YOU KNOW THAT?
YEAH.
HOWEVER, FROM NOW ON, I THINK YOU'LL BE BETTER OFF STAYING HOME ON SUCH NIGHTS.
BUT WHY, DAD?
WHY?
BECAUSE I LOVE YOU, FRUIT-BAT.

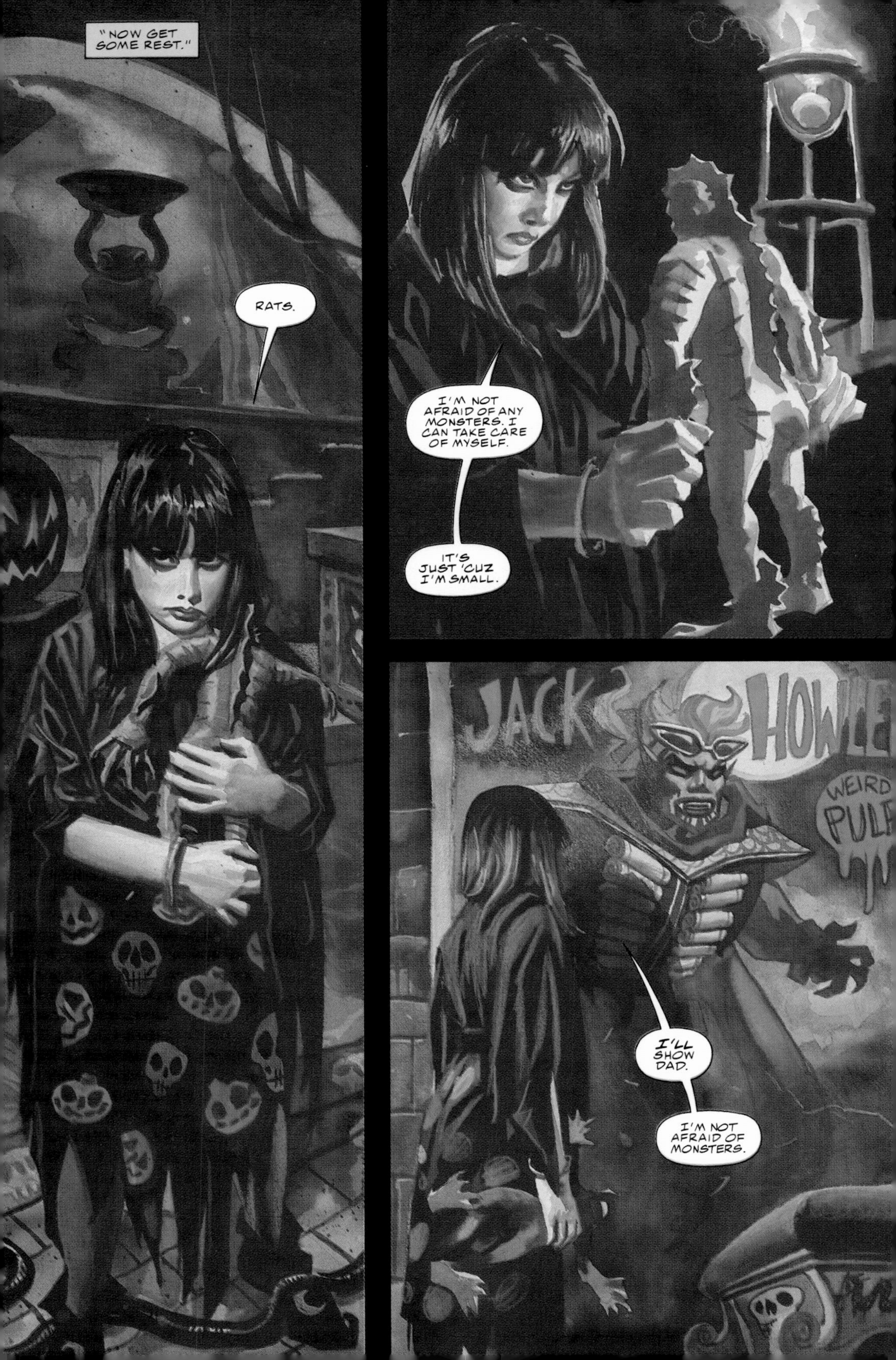
"NOW GET SOME REST."
RATS.
I'M NOT AFRAID OF ANY MONSTERS. I CAN TAKE CARE OF MYSELF.
IT'S JUST 'CUZ I'M SMALL.
JACK
WEIRD
I'LL SHOW DAD.
I'M NOT AFRAID OF MONSTERS.

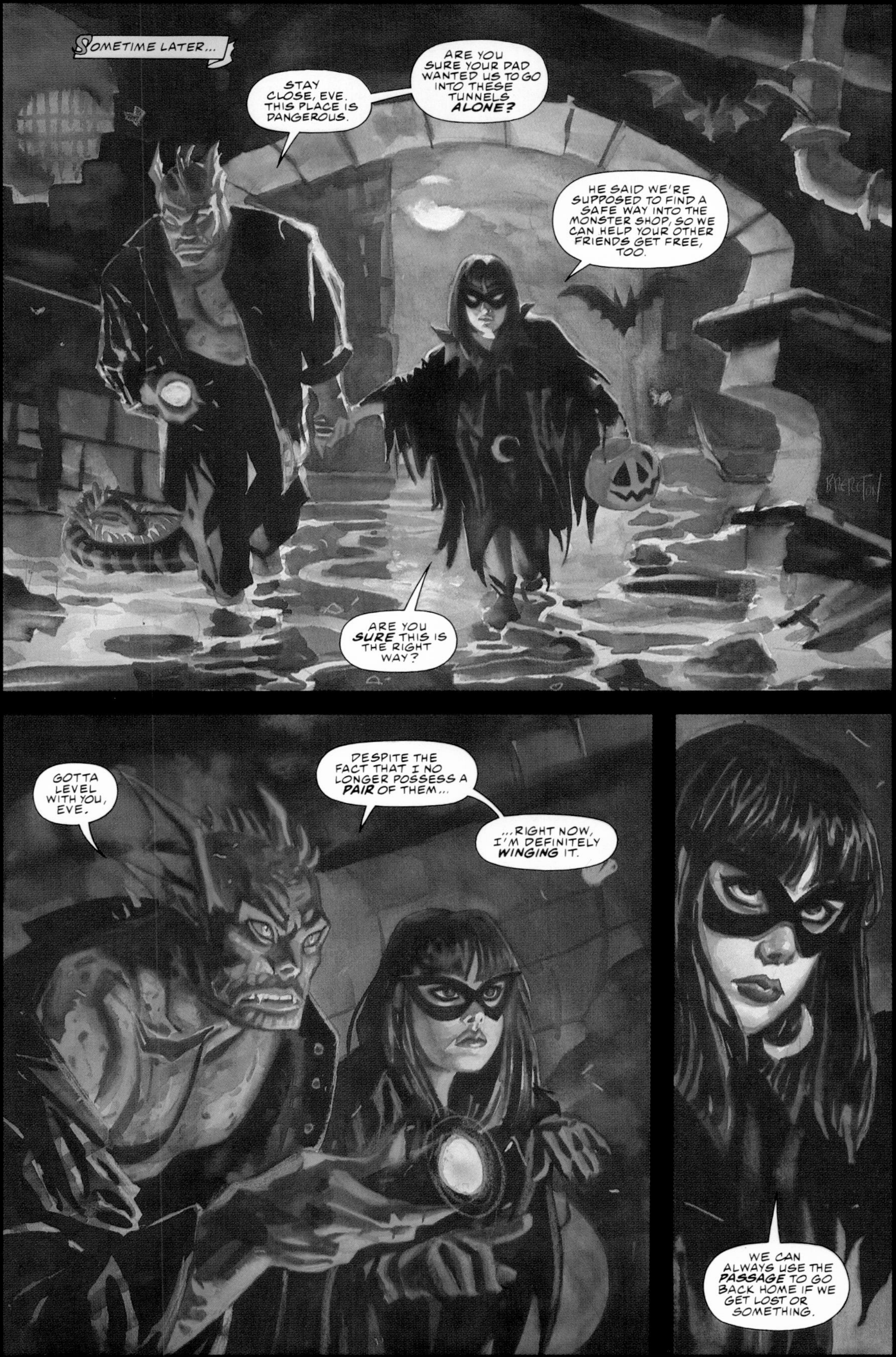

SOMETIME LATER...
STAY CLOSE, EVE. THIS PLACE IS DANGEROUS.
ARE YOU SURE YOUR DAD WANTED US TO GO INTO THESE TUNNELS ALONE?
HE SAID WE'RE SUPPOSED TO FIND A SAFE WAY INTO THE MONSTER SHOP, SO WE CAN HELP YOUR OTHER FRIENDS GET FREE, TOO.
ARE YOU SURE THIS IS THE RIGHT WAY?
GOTTA LEVEL WITH YOU, EVE.
DESPITE THE FACT THAT I NO LONGER POSSESS A PAIR OF THEM...
...RIGHT NOW, I'M DEFINITELY WINGING IT.
WE CAN ALWAYS USE THE PASSAGE TO GO BACK HOME IF WE GET LOST OR SOMETHING.

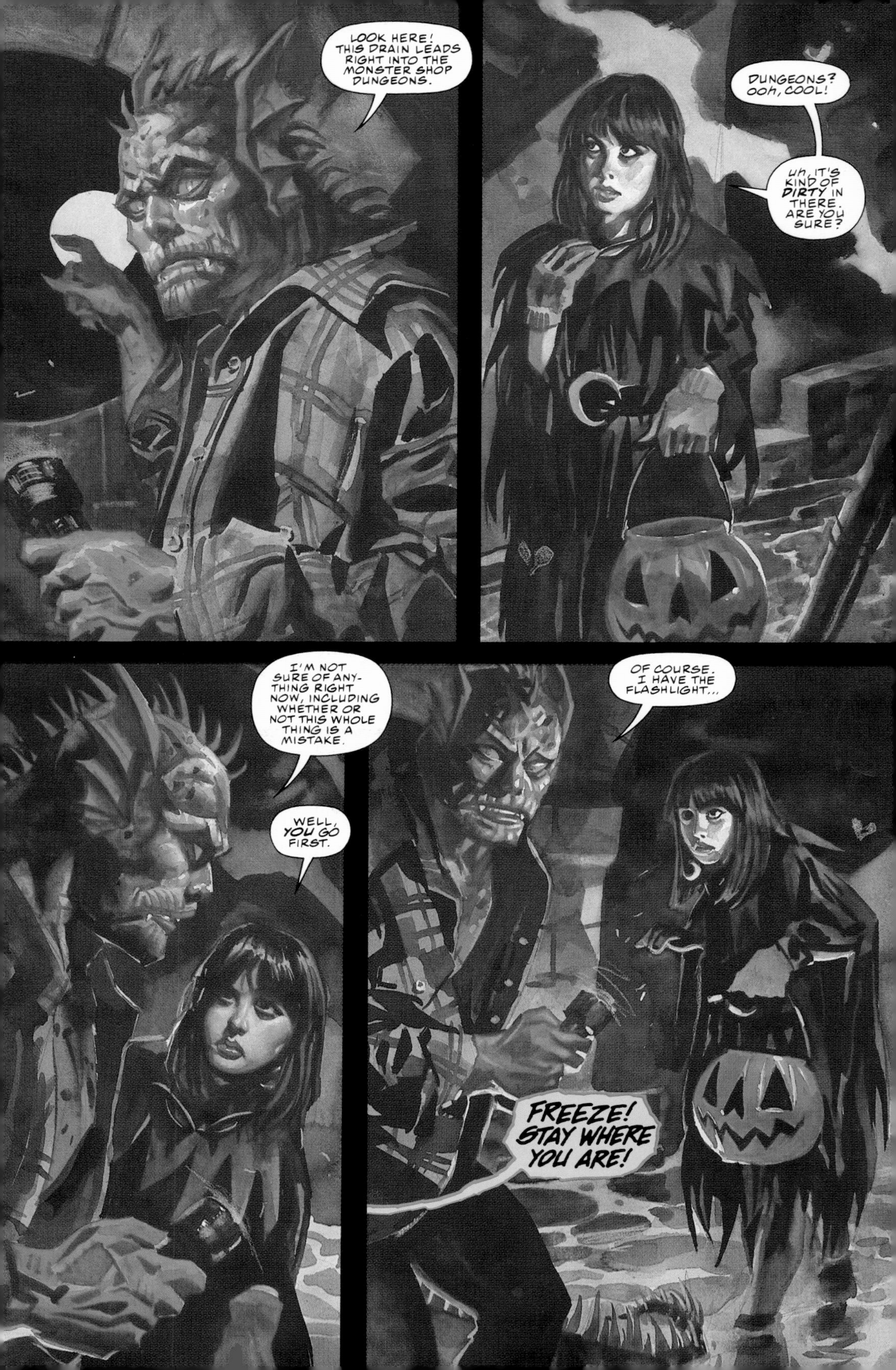
LOOK HERE! THIS DRAIN LEADS RIGHT INTO THE MONSTER SHOP DUNGEONS.
DUNGEONS? ooh, COOL!
uh, IT'S KIND OF DIRTY IN THERE. ARE YOU SURE?
I'M NOT SURE OF ANYTHING RIGHT NOW, INCLUDING WHETHER OR NOT THIS WHOLE THING IS A MISTAKE.
WELL, YOU GO FIRST.
OF COURSE. I HAVE THE FLASHLIGHT...
FREEZE! STAY WHERE YOU ARE!

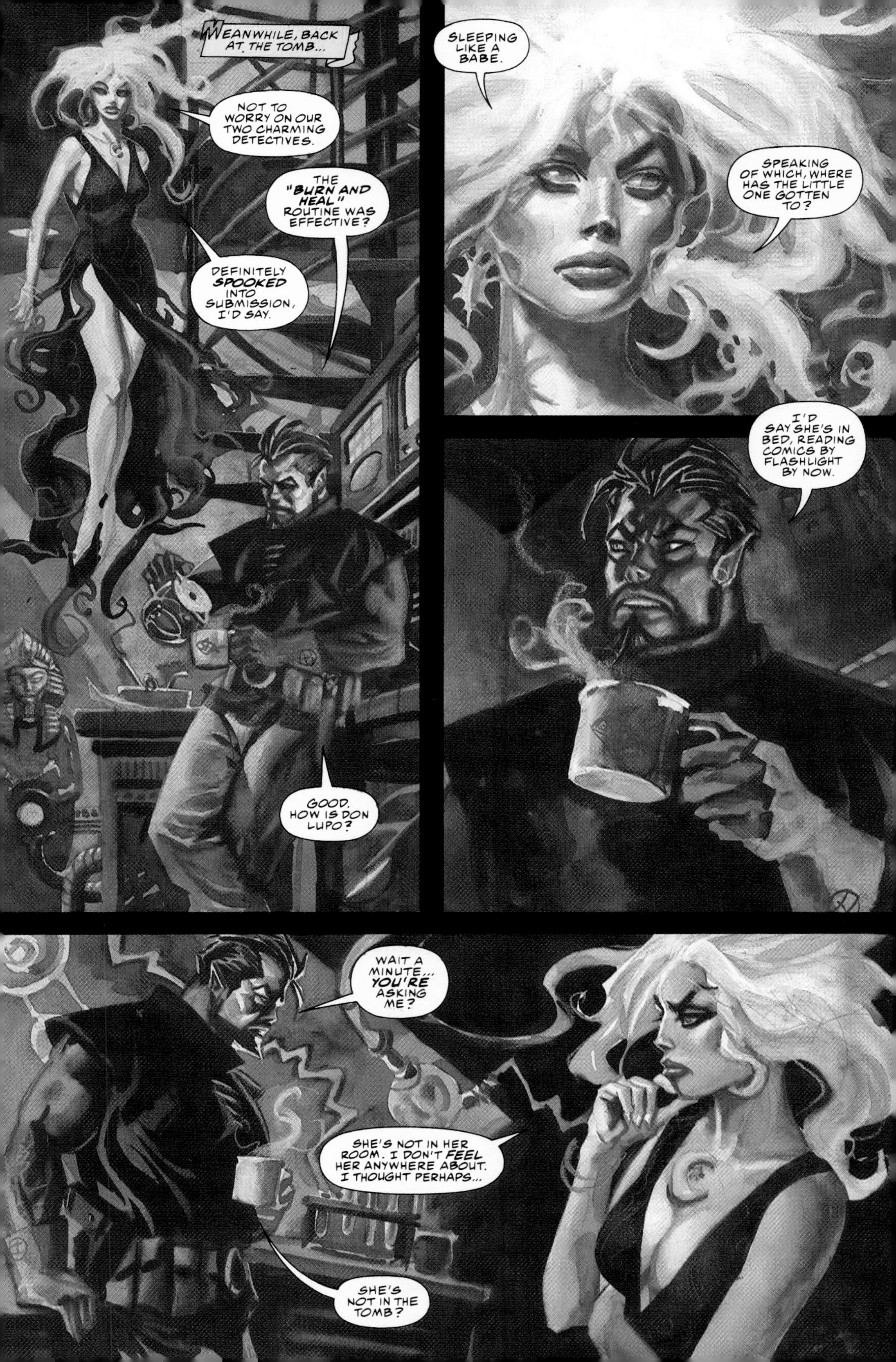
MEANWHILE, BACK AT THE TOMB...
NOT TO WORRY ON OUR TWO CHARMING DETECTIVES.
DEFINITELY **SPOOKED** INTO SUBMISSION, I'D SAY.
THE **"BURN AND HEAL"** ROUTINE WAS EFFECTIVE?
GOOD. HOW IS DON LUPO?
SLEEPING LIKE A BABE.
SPEAKING OF WHICH, WHERE HAS THE LITTLE ONE GOTTEN TO?
I'D SAY SHE'S IN BED, READING COMICS BY FLASHLIGHT BY NOW.
WAIT A MINUTE... **YOU'RE** ASKING ME?
SHE'S NOT IN HER ROOM. I DON'T **FEEL** HER ANYWHERE ABOUT. I THOUGHT PERHAPS...
SHE'S NOT IN THE TOMB?

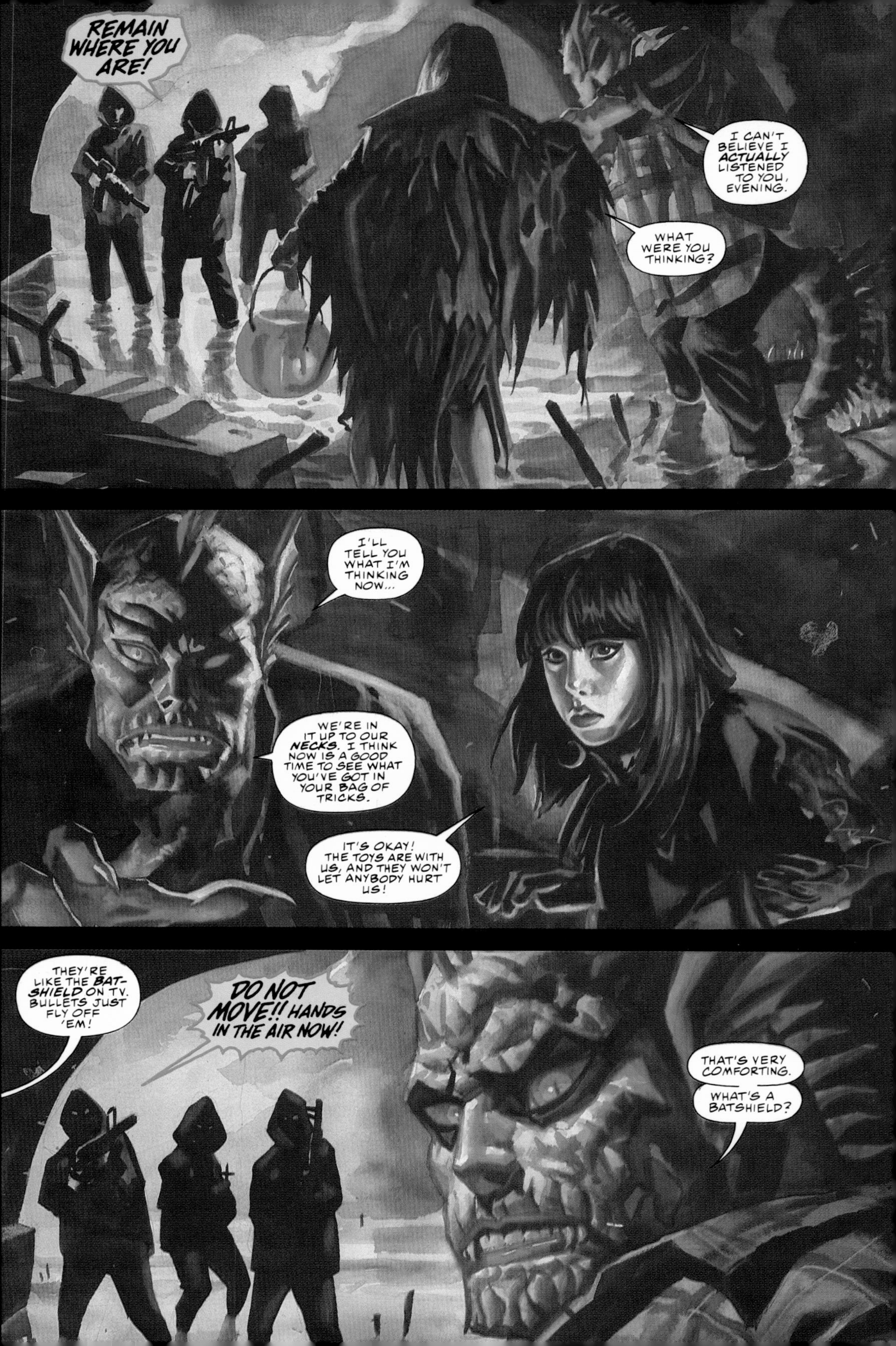
REMAIN WHERE YOU ARE!
I CAN'T BELIEVE I ACTUALLY LISTENED TO YOU, EVENING.
WHAT WERE YOU THINKING?
I'LL TELL YOU WHAT I'M THINKING NOW...
WE'RE IN IT UP TO OUR NECKS. I THINK NOW IS A GOOD TIME TO SEE WHAT YOU'VE GOT IN YOUR BAG OF TRICKS.
IT'S OKAY! THE TOYS ARE WITH US, AND THEY WON'T LET ANYBODY HURT US!
THEY'RE LIKE THE BAT-SHIELD ON TV. BULLETS JUST FLY OFF 'EM!
DO NOT MOVE!! HANDS IN THE AIR NOW!
THAT'S VERY COMFORTING.
WHAT'S A BATSHIELD?

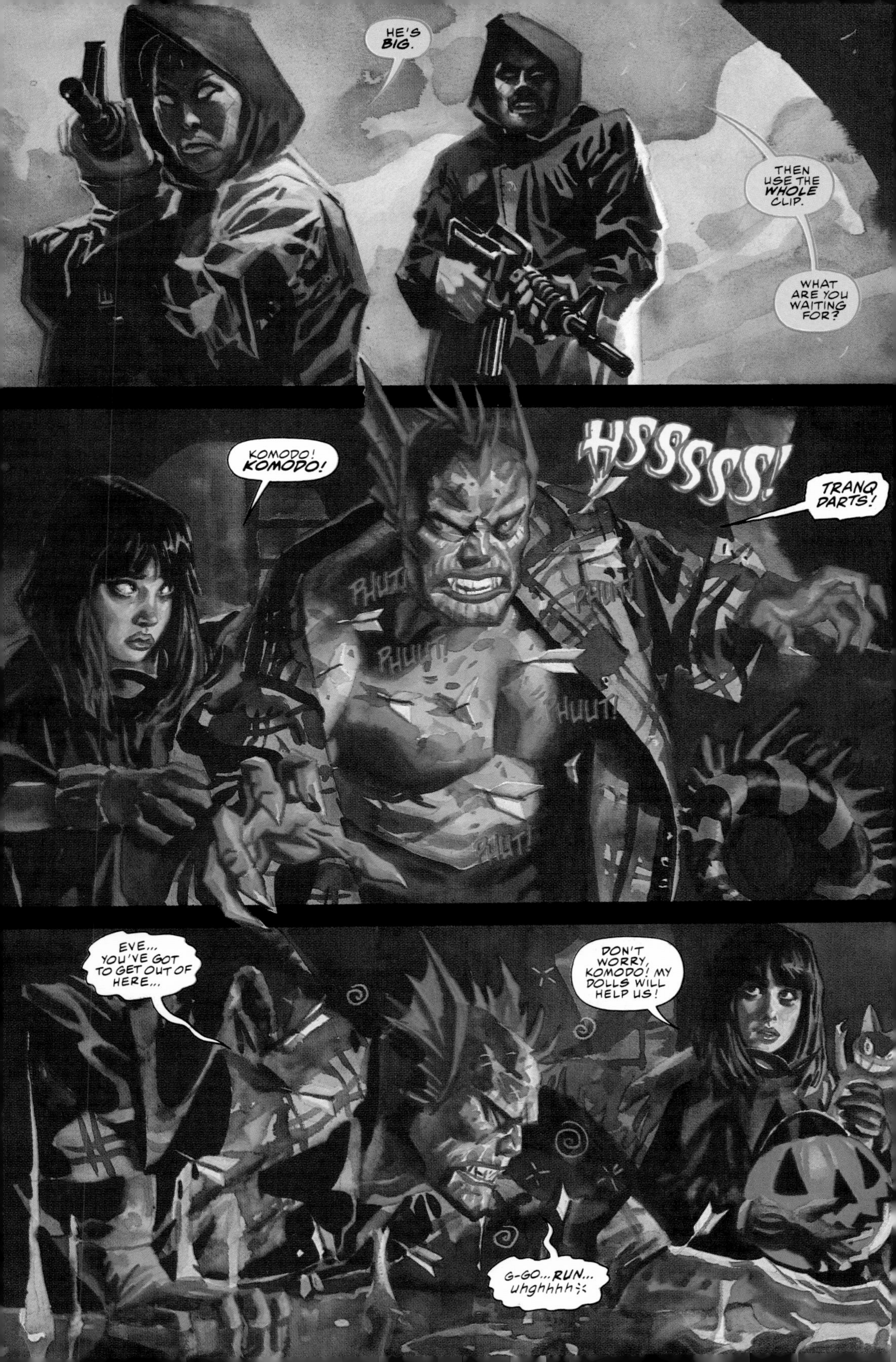
HE'S BIG.
THEN USE THE WHOLE CLIP.
WHAT ARE YOU WAITING FOR?
KOMODO! KOMODO!
HSSSSSS!
TRANQ DARTS!
PHUUT!
PHUUT!
PHUUT!
PHUUT!
PHUUT!
EVE... YOU'VE GOT TO GET OUT OF HERE...
DON'T WORRY, KOMODO! MY DOLLS WILL HELP US!
G-GO... RUN... uhghhhh

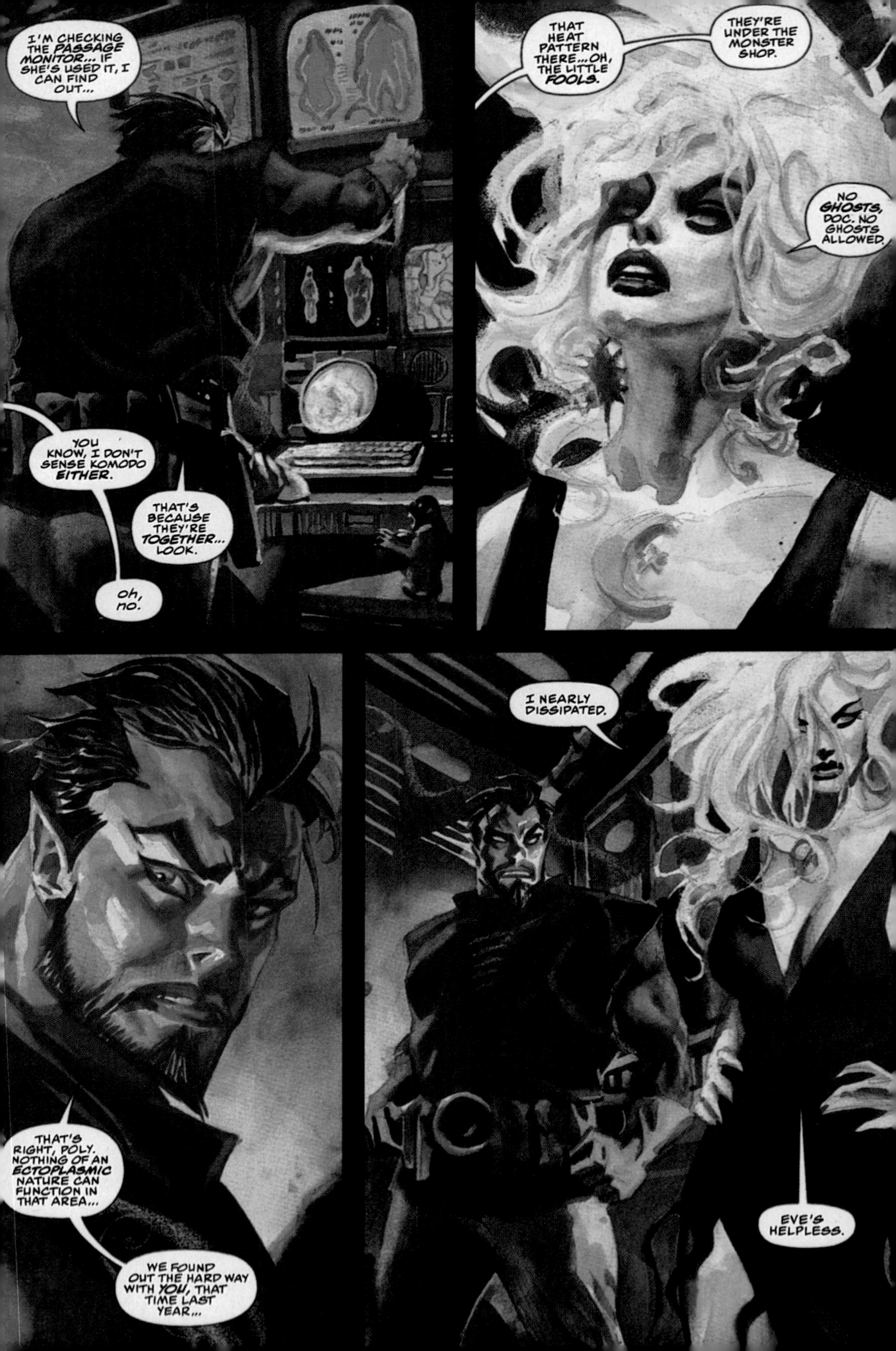
I'M CHECKING THE PASSAGE MONITOR... IF SHE'S USED IT, I CAN FIND OUT...
YOU KNOW, I DON'T SENSE KOMODO EITHER.
THAT'S BECAUSE THEY'RE TOGETHER... LOOK.
Oh, no.
THAT HEAT PATTERN THERE... OH, THE LITTLE FOOLS.
THEY'RE UNDER THE MONSTER SHOP.
NO GHOSTS, DOC. NO GHOSTS ALLOWED.
THAT'S RIGHT, POLY. NOTHING OF AN ECTOPLASMIC NATURE CAN FUNCTION IN THAT AREA...
WE FOUND OUT THE HARD WAY WITH YOU, THAT TIME LAST YEAR...
I NEARLY DISSIPATED.
EVE'S HELPLESS.

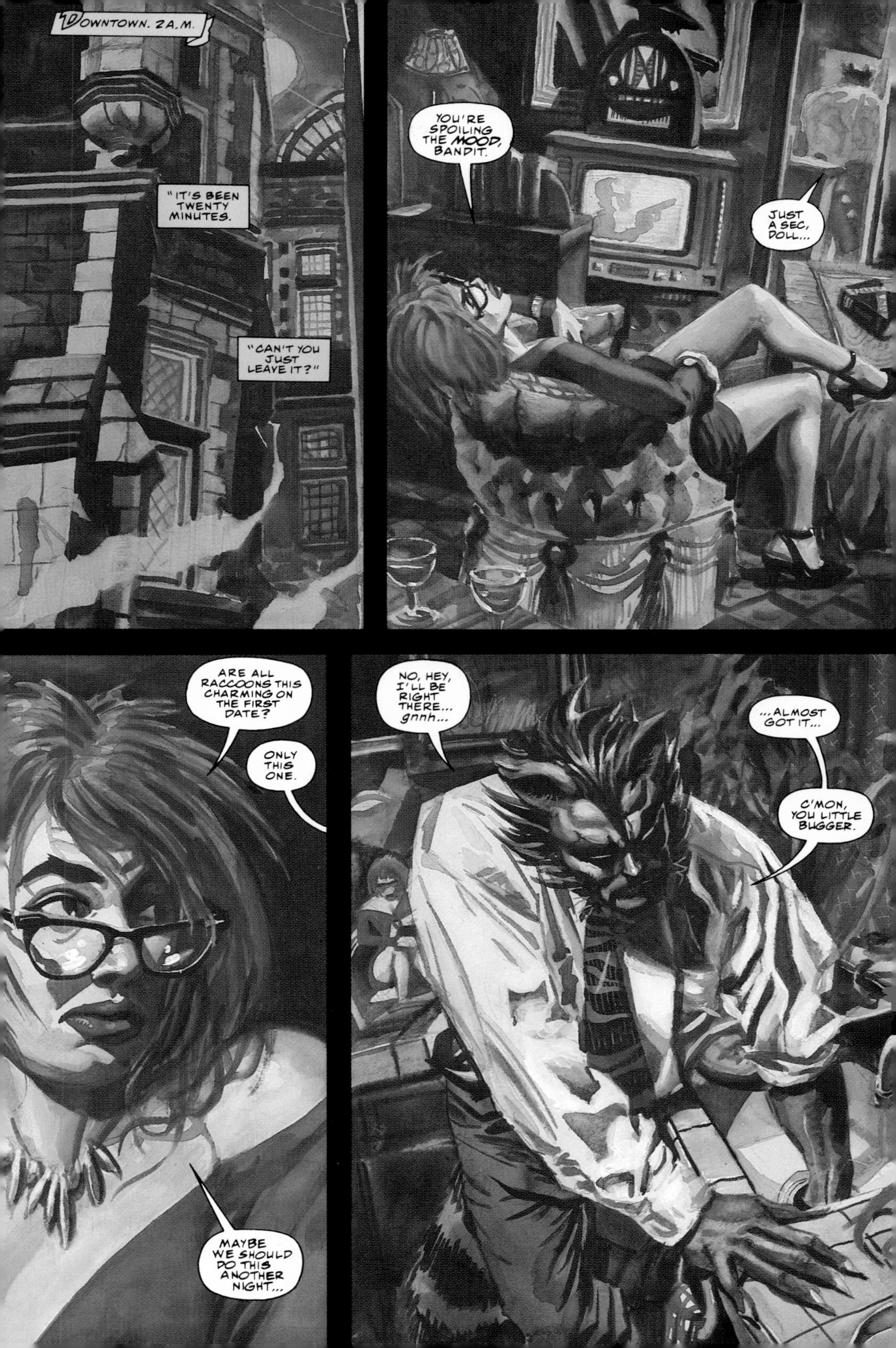
DOWNTOWN. 2A.M.
"IT'S BEEN TWENTY MINUTES.
"CAN'T YOU JUST LEAVE IT?"
YOU'RE SPOILING THE MOOD, BANDIT.
JUST A SEC, DOLL...
ARE ALL RACCOONS THIS CHARMING ON THE FIRST DATE?
ONLY THIS ONE.
MAYBE WE SHOULD DO THIS ANOTHER NIGHT...
NO, HEY, I'LL BE RIGHT THERE... gnnh...
...ALMOST GOT IT...
C'MON, YOU LITTLE BUGGER.

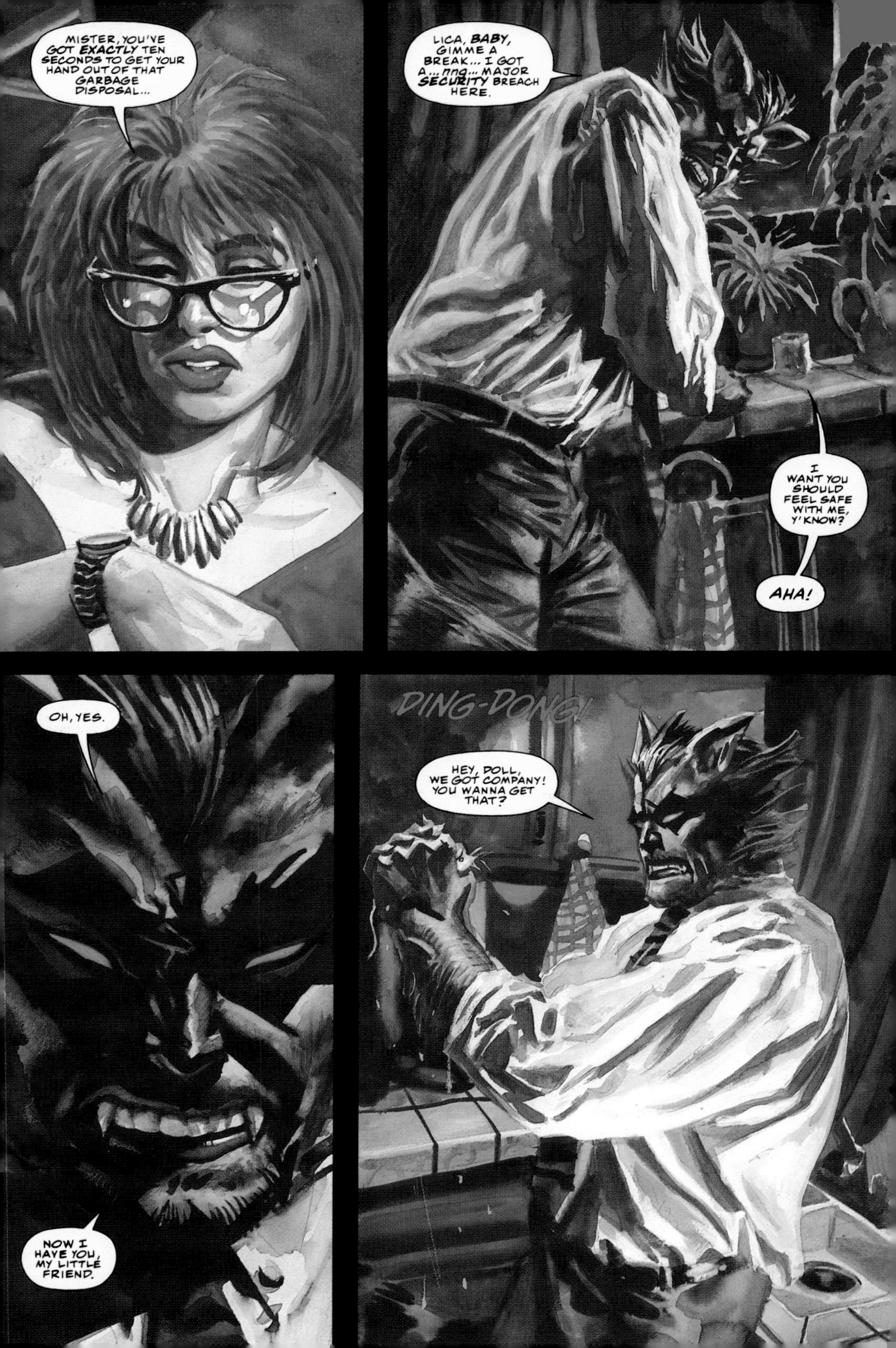
MISTER, YOU'VE GOT EXACTLY TEN SECONDS TO GET YOUR HAND OUT OF THAT GARBAGE DISPOSAL...
LICA, BABY, GIMME A BREAK... I GOT A... nng... MAJOR SECURITY BREACH HERE.
I WANT YOU SHOULD FEEL SAFE WITH ME, Y'KNOW?
AHA!
OH, YES.
NOW I HAVE YOU, MY LITTLE FRIEND.
DING-DONG!
HEY, DOLL, WE GOT COMPANY! YOU WANNA GET THAT?

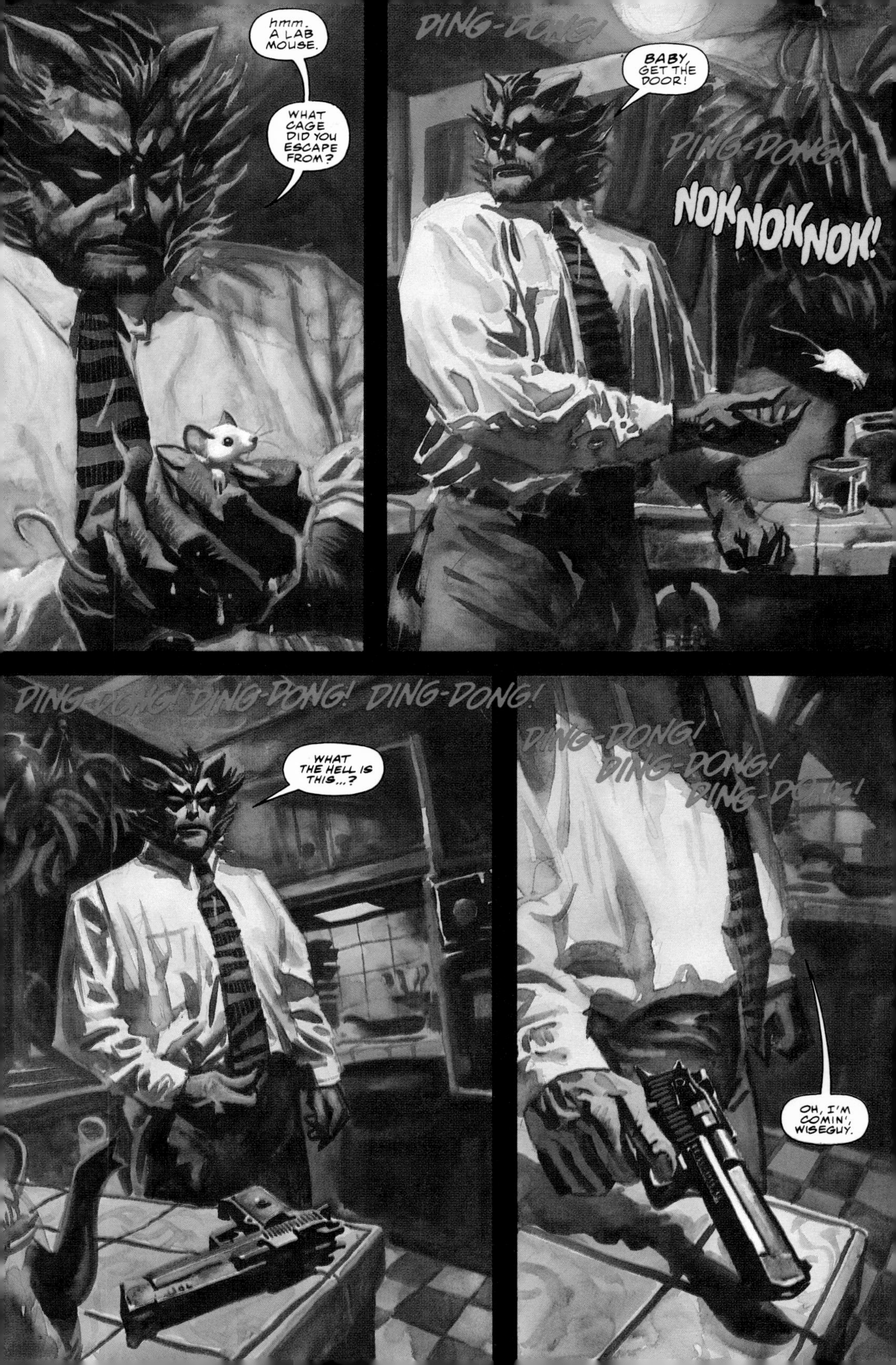
hmm. A LAB MOUSE.
WHAT CAGE DID YOU ESCAPE FROM?
DING-DONG!
BABY, GET THE DOOR!
DING-DONG!
NOK NOK NOK!
DING-DONG! DING-DONG! DING-DONG!
WHAT THE HELL IS THIS...?
DING-DONG! DING-DONG! DING-DONG!
OH, I'M COMIN', WISEGUY.

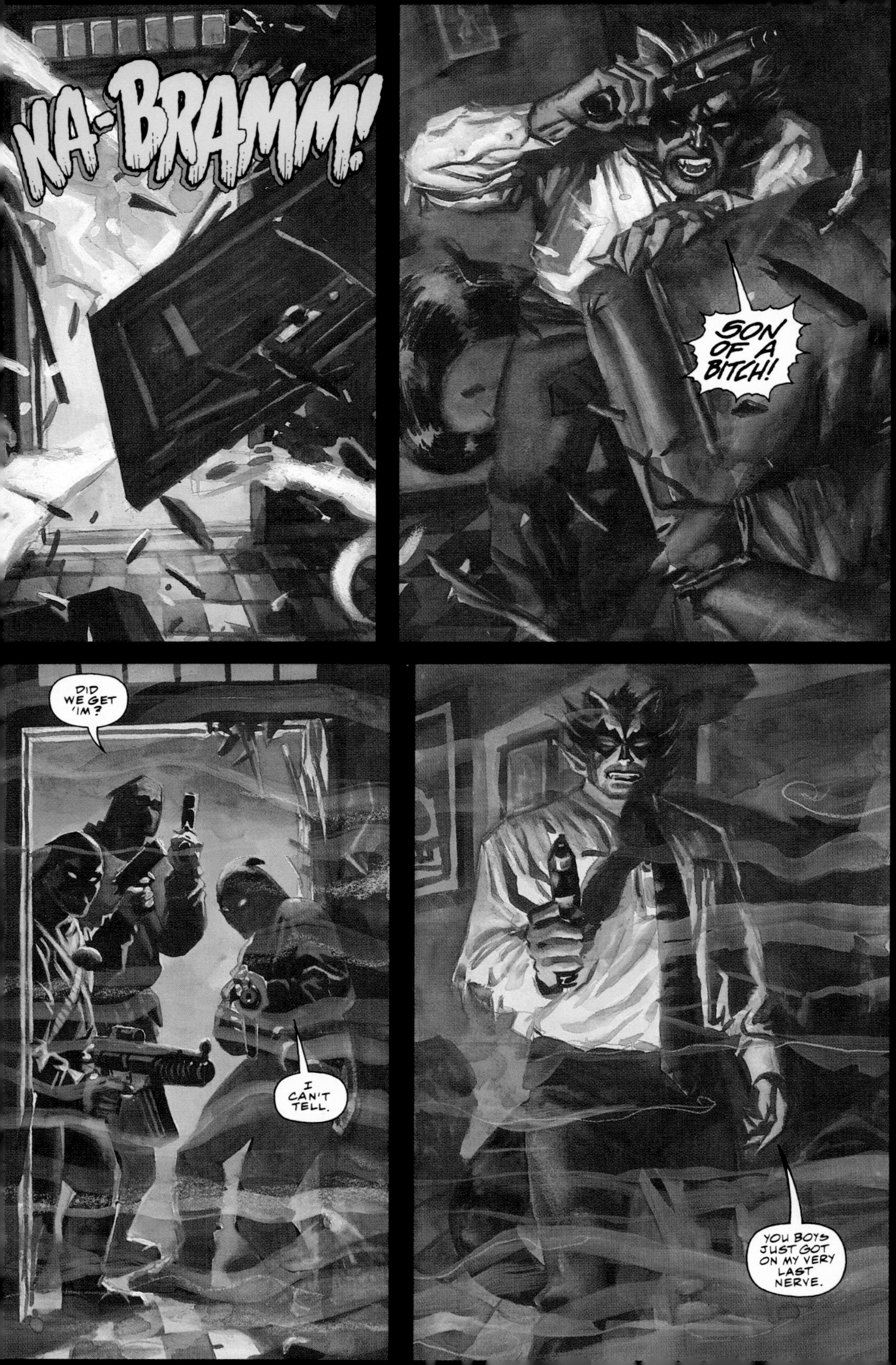
KA-BRAMM!
SON OF A BITCH!
DID WE GET 'IM?
I CAN'T TELL.
YOU BOYS JUST GOT ON MY VERY LAST NERVE.

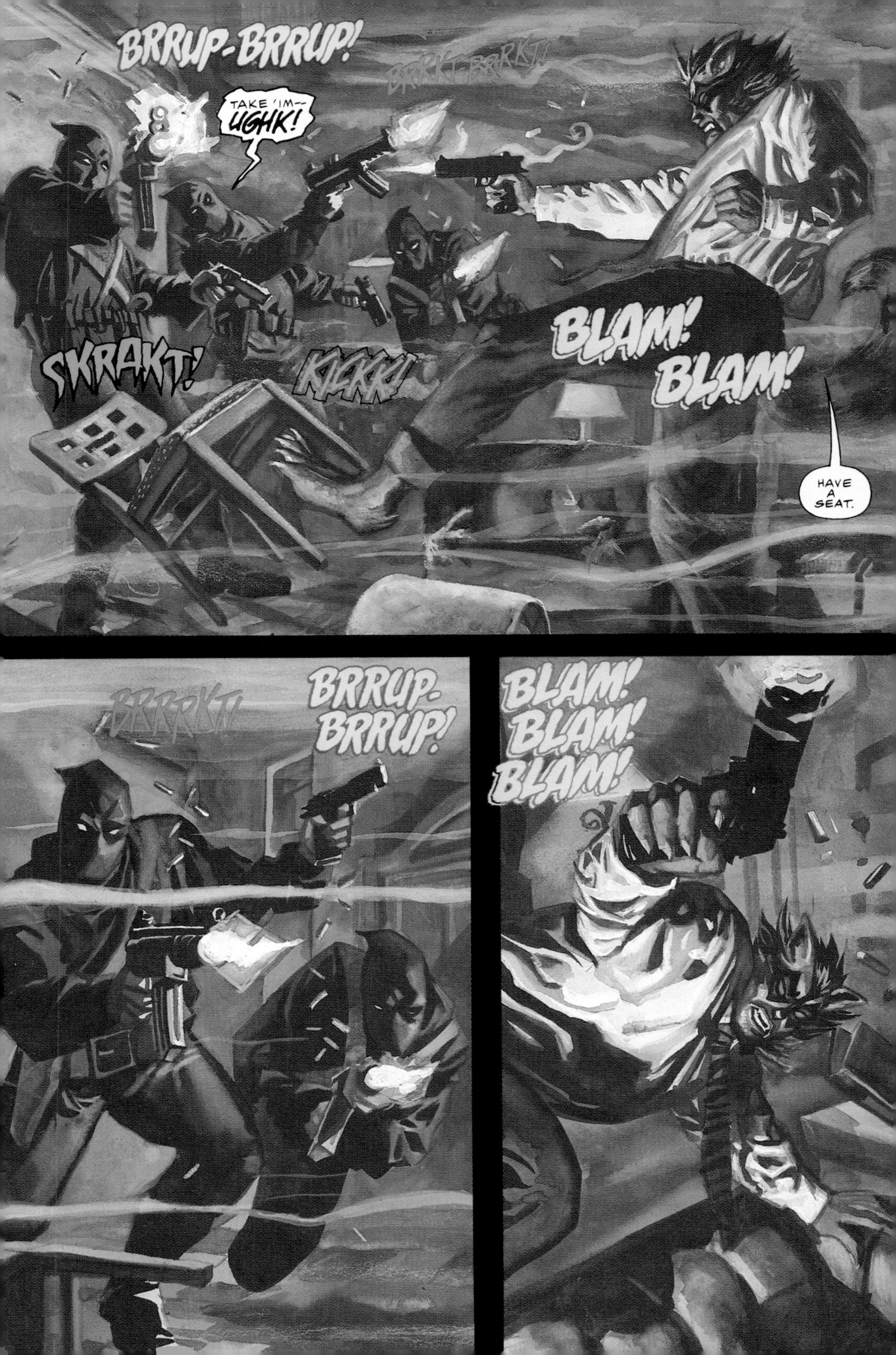
BRRUP-BRRUP!
BRRKT-BRRKT!
TAKE 'IM-- UGHK!
SKRAKT!
BLAM! BLAM!
HAVE A SEAT.
BRRRKT!
BRRUP- BRRUP!
BLAM! BLAM! BLAM!

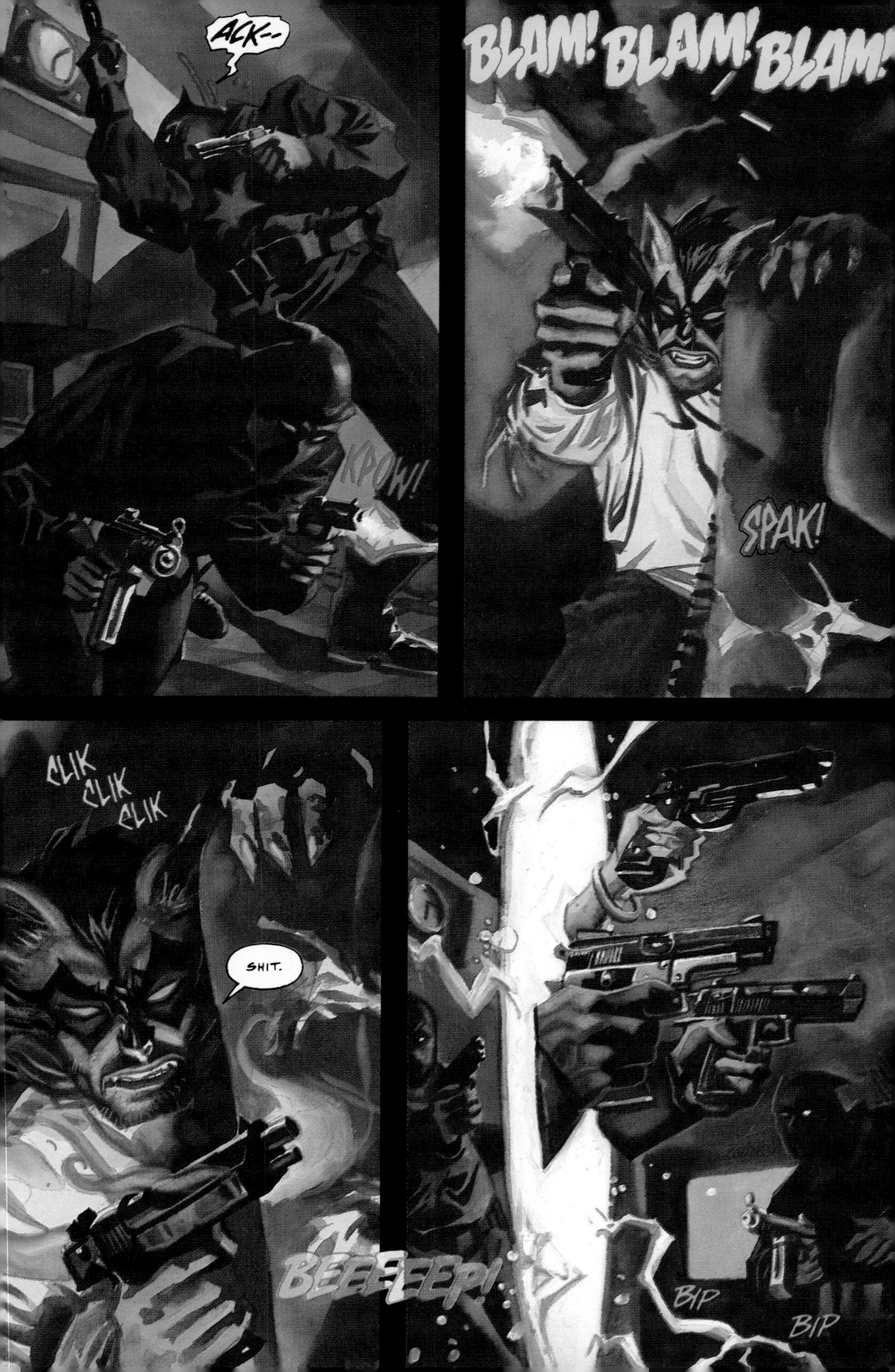
ACK--
KPOW!
BLAM! BLAM! BLAM!
SPAK!
CLIK
CLIK
CLIK
SHIT.
BEEEEEEP!
BIP
BIP

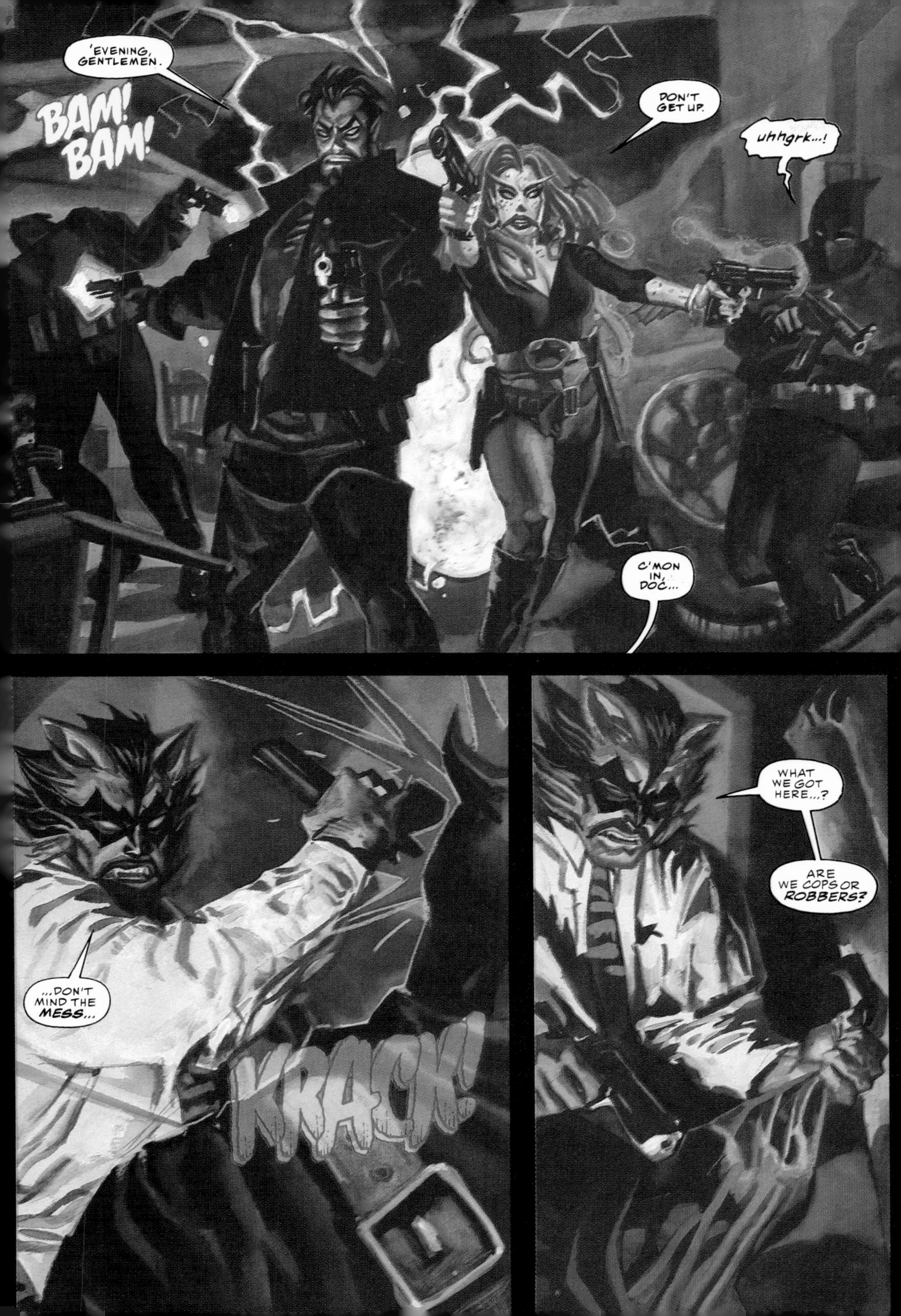

'EVENING, GENTLEMEN.
BAM! BAM!
DON'T GET UP.
uhhgrk...!
C'MON IN, DOC...
...DON'T MIND THE MESS...
KRACK!
WHAT WE GOT HERE...?
ARE WE COPS OR ROBBERS?

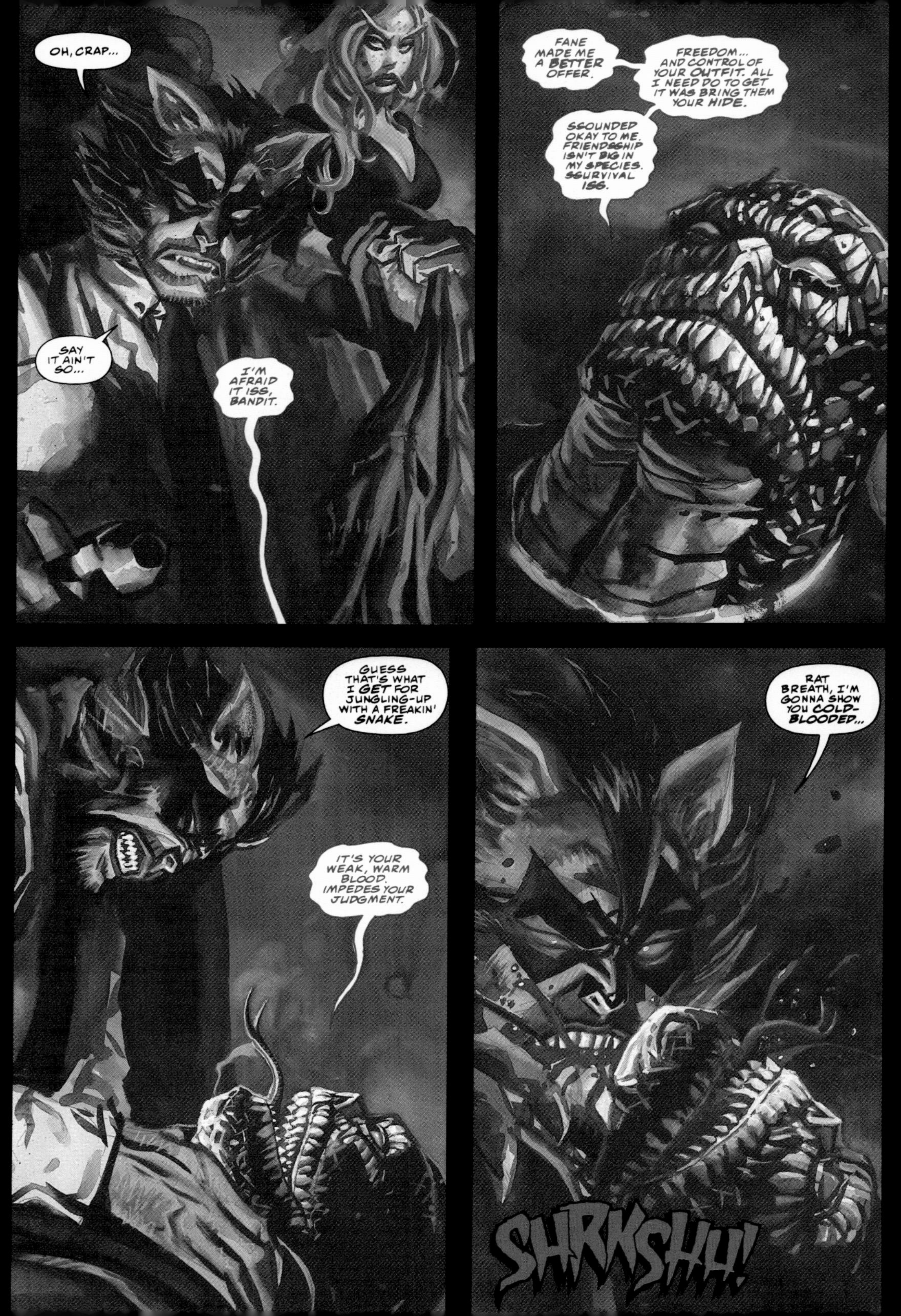
OH, CRAP...
SAY IT AIN'T SO...
I'M AFRAID IT ISS, BANDIT.
FANE MADE ME A BETTER OFFER.
FREEDOM... AND CONTROL OF YOUR OUTFIT. ALL I NEED DO TO GET IT WAS BRING THEM YOUR HIDE.
SSOUNDED OKAY TO ME. FRIENDSSHIP ISN'T BIG IN MY SPECIES. SSURVIVAL ISS.
GUESS THAT'S WHAT I GET FOR JUNGLING-UP WITH A FREAKIN' SNAKE.
IT'S YOUR WEAK, WARM BLOOD. IMPEDES YOUR JUDGMENT.
RAT BREATH, I'M GONNA SHOW YOU COLD-BLOODED...
SHRKSHU!

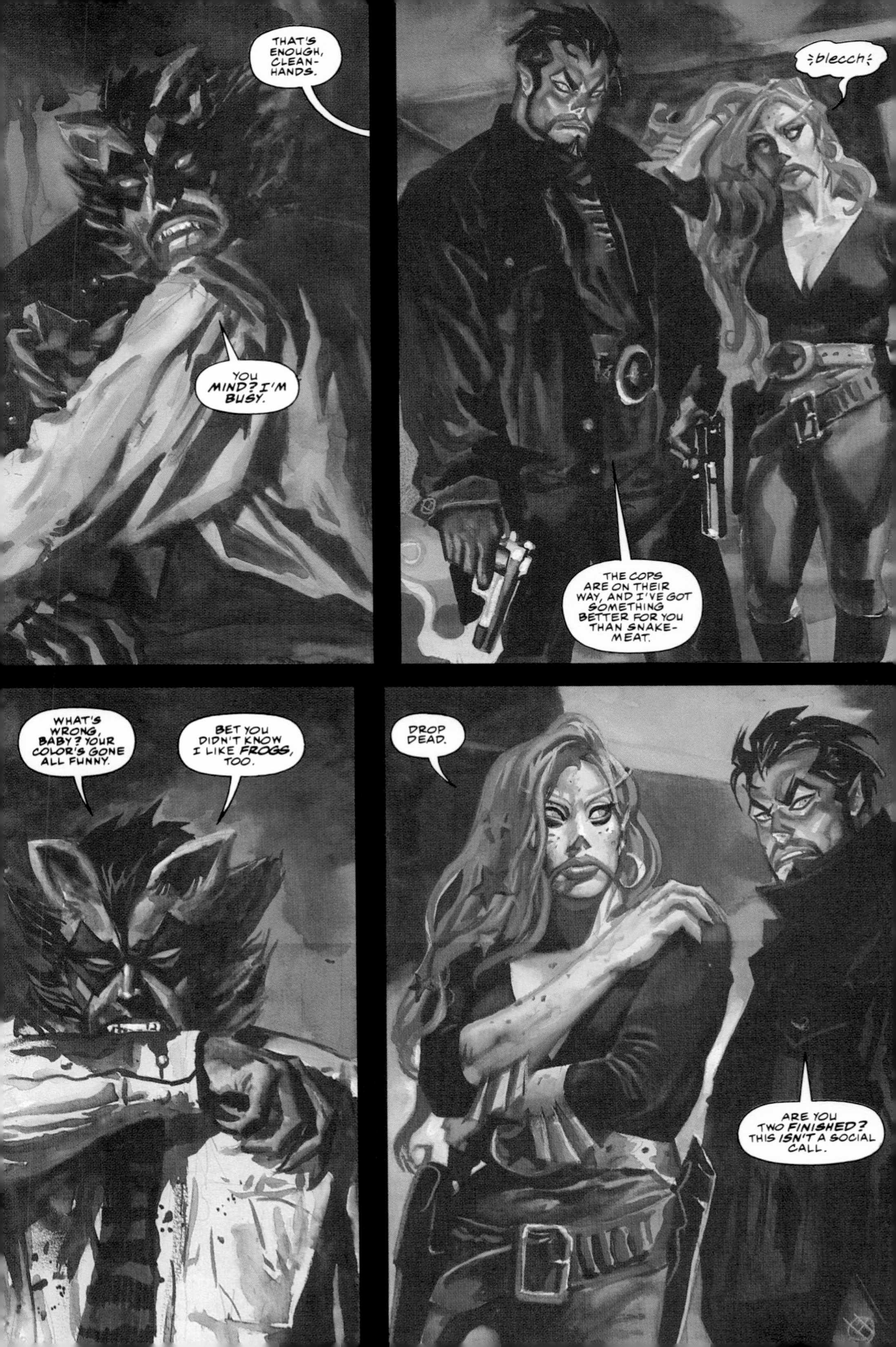
THAT'S ENOUGH, CLEAN-HANDS.
YOU MIND? I'M BUSY.
blecch
THE COPS ARE ON THEIR WAY, AND I'VE GOT SOMETHING BETTER FOR YOU THAN SNAKE-MEAT.
WHAT'S WRONG, BABY? YOUR COLOR'S GONE ALL FUNNY.
BET YOU DIDN'T KNOW I LIKE FROGS, TOO.
DROP DEAD.
ARE YOU TWO FINISHED? THIS ISN'T A SOCIAL CALL.

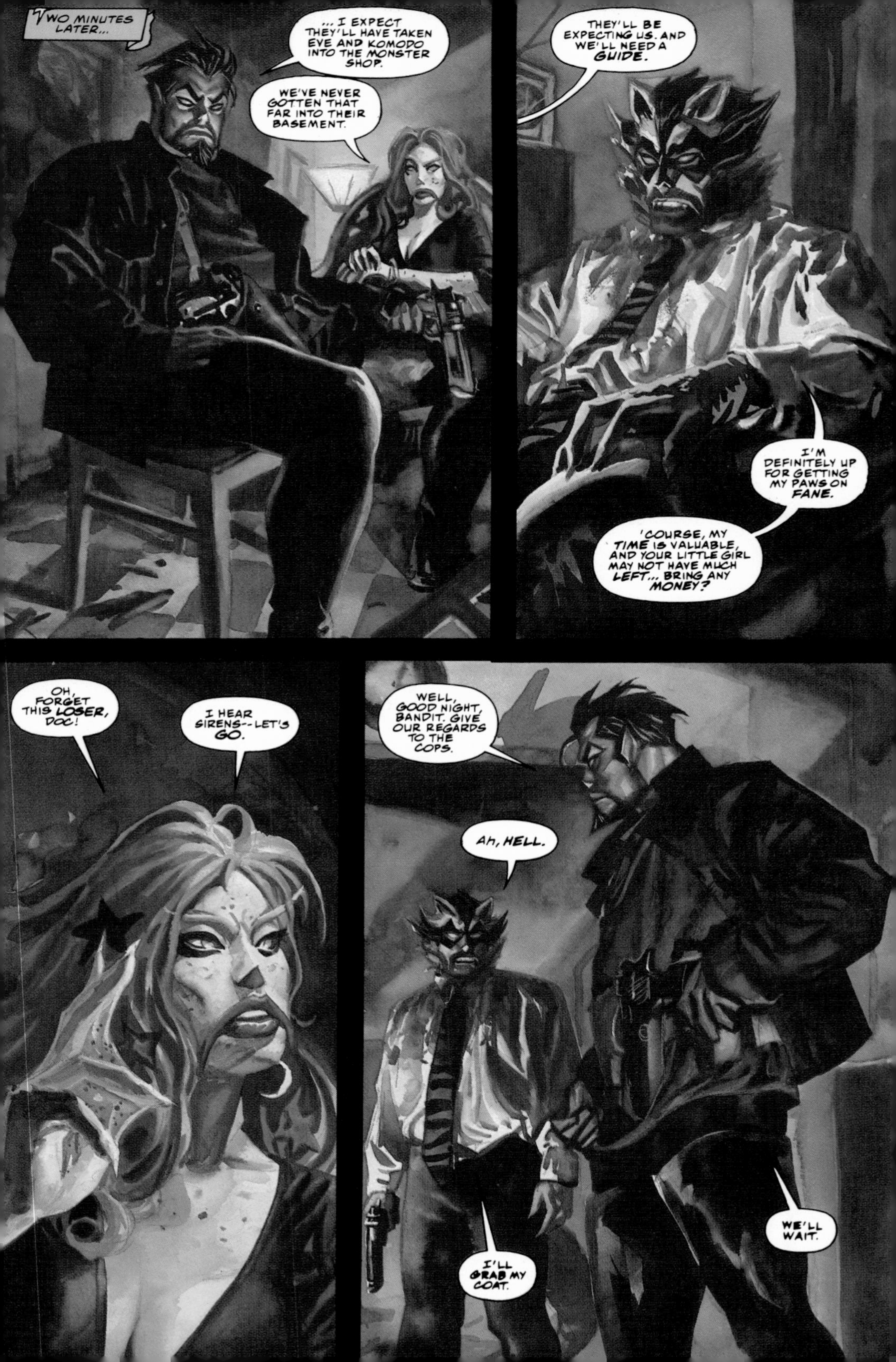
TWO MINUTES LATER...
...I EXPECT THEY'LL HAVE TAKEN EYE AND KOMODO INTO THE MONSTER SHOP.
WE'VE NEVER GOTTEN THAT FAR INTO THEIR BASEMENT.
THEY'LL BE EXPECTING US. AND WE'LL NEED A GUIDE.
I'M DEFINITELY UP FOR GETTING MY PAWS ON FANE.
'COURSE, MY TIME IS VALUABLE, AND YOUR LITTLE GIRL MAY NOT HAVE MUCH LEFT... BRING ANY MONEY?
OH, FORGET THIS LOSER, DOC!
I HEAR SIRENS--LET'S GO.
WELL, GOOD NIGHT, BANDIT. GIVE OUR REGARDS TO THE COPS.
Ah, HELL.
I'LL GRAB MY COAT.
WE'LL WAIT.

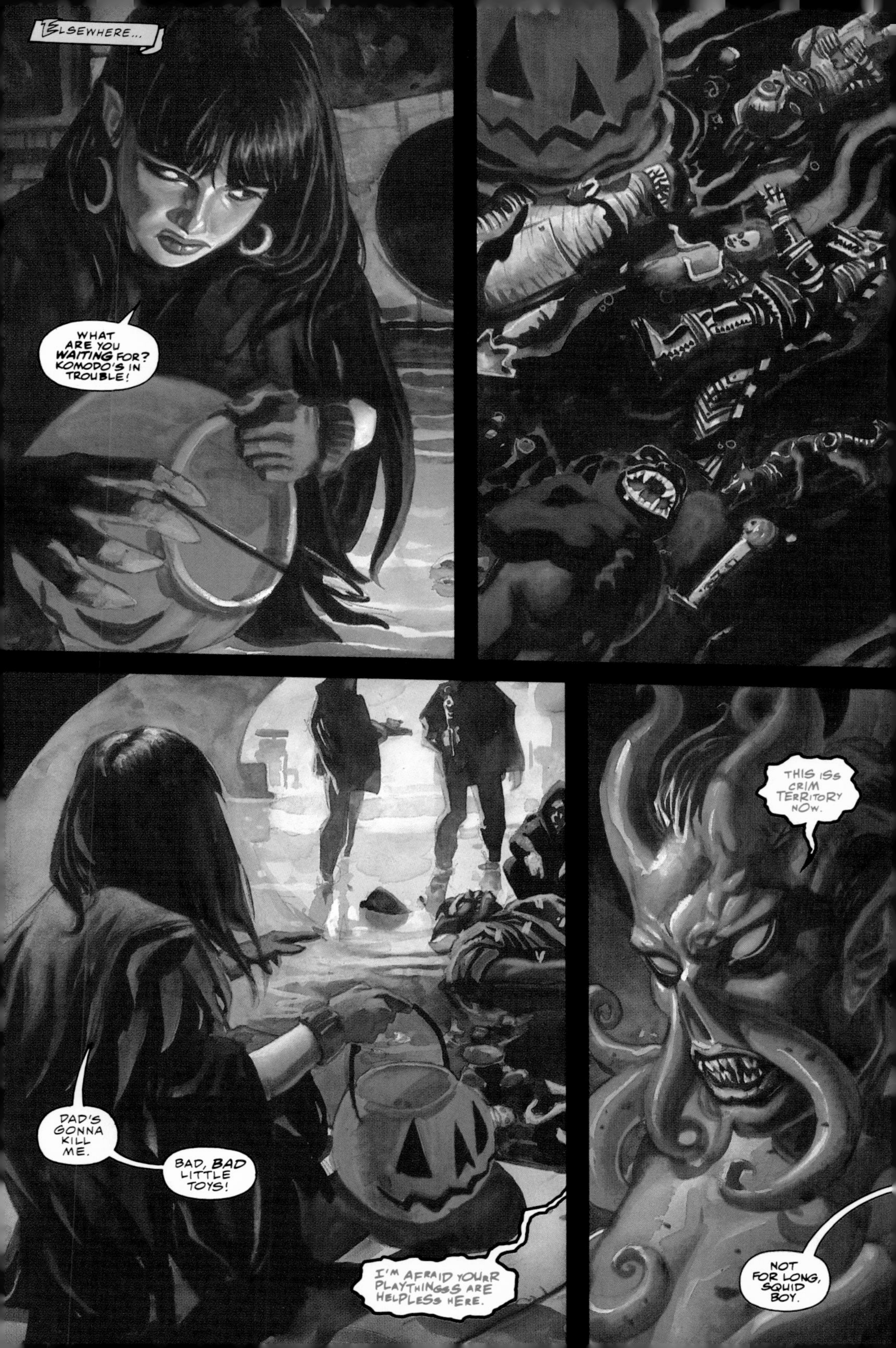
ELSEWHERE...
WHAT ARE YOU WAITING FOR? KOMODO'S IN TROUBLE!
DAD'S GONNA KILL ME.
BAD, BAD LITTLE TOYS!
I'M AFRAID YOURR PLAYTHINGSS ARE HELPLESS HERE.
THIS ISs CRIM TERRITORY NOW.
NOT FOR LONG, SQUID BOY.

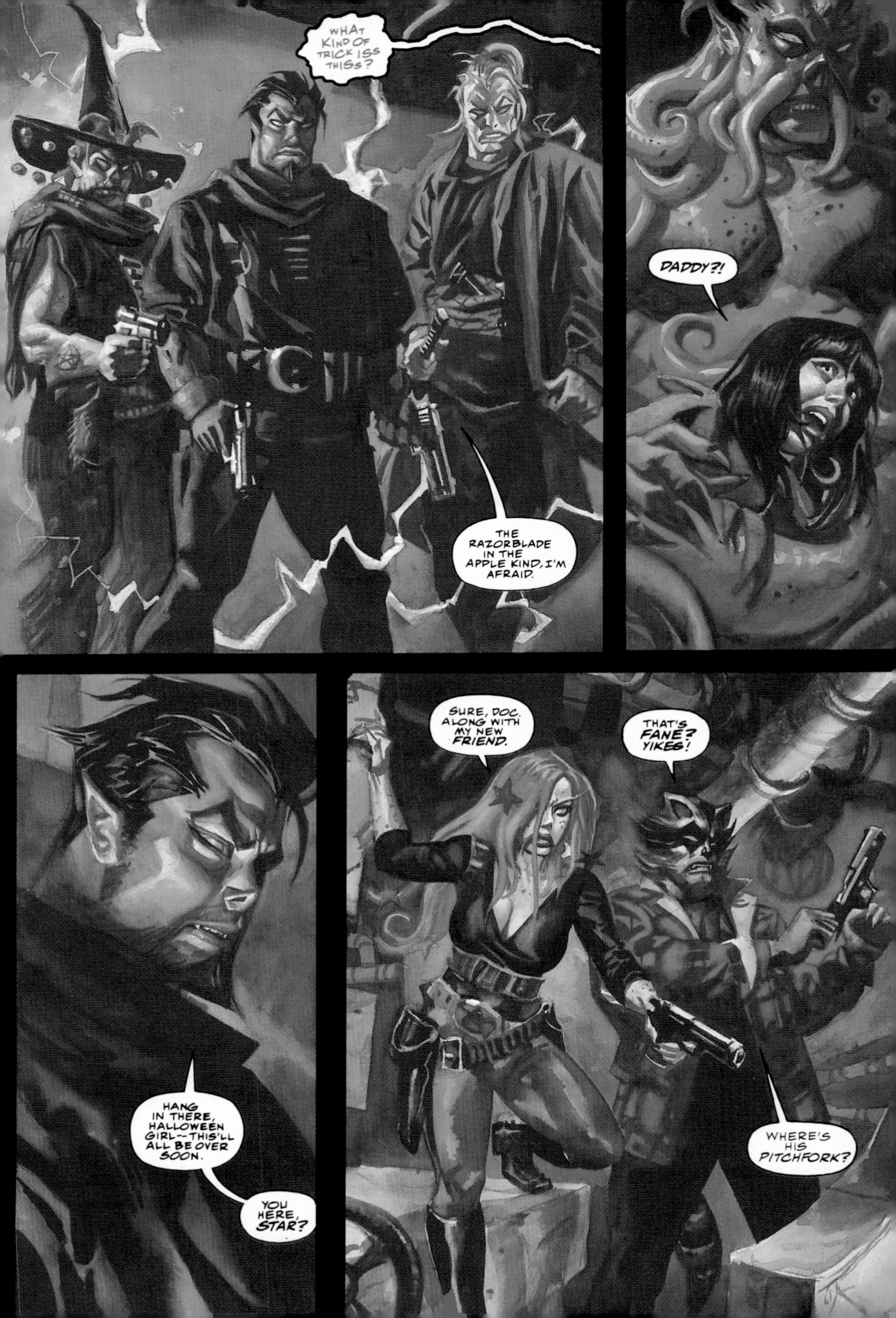
WHAT KIND OF TRICK ISS THISS?
THE RAZORBLADE IN THE APPLE KIND, I'M AFRAID.
DADDY?!
HANG IN THERE, HALLOWEEN GIRL--THIS'LL ALL BE OVER SOON.
YOU HERE, STAR?
SURE, DOC, ALONG WITH MY NEW FRIEND.
THAT'S FANE? YIKES!
WHERE'S HIS PITCHFORK?

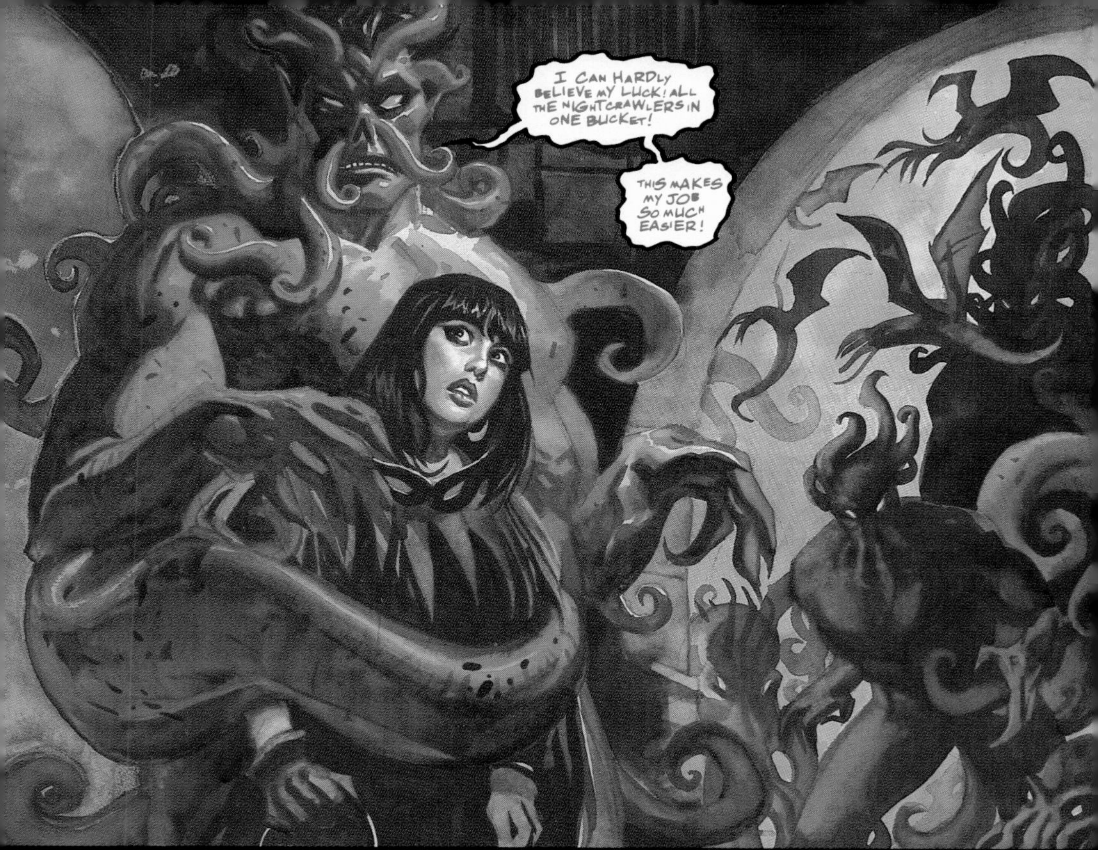
I CAN HARDLY BELIEVE MY LUCK! ALL THE NIGHTCRAWLERS IN ONE BUCKET!
THIS MAKES MY JOB SO MUCH EASIER!

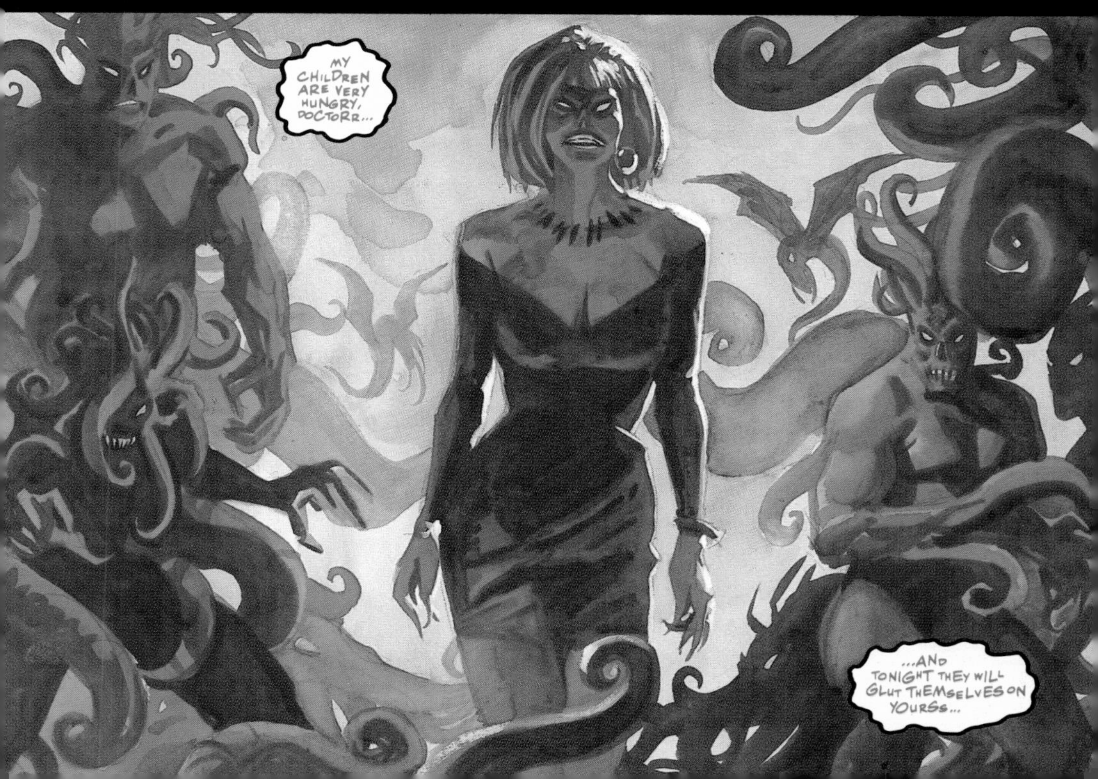
MY CHILDREN ARE VERY HUNGRY, DOCTORR...
...AND TONIGHT THEY WILL GLUT THEMSELVES ON YOURSS...

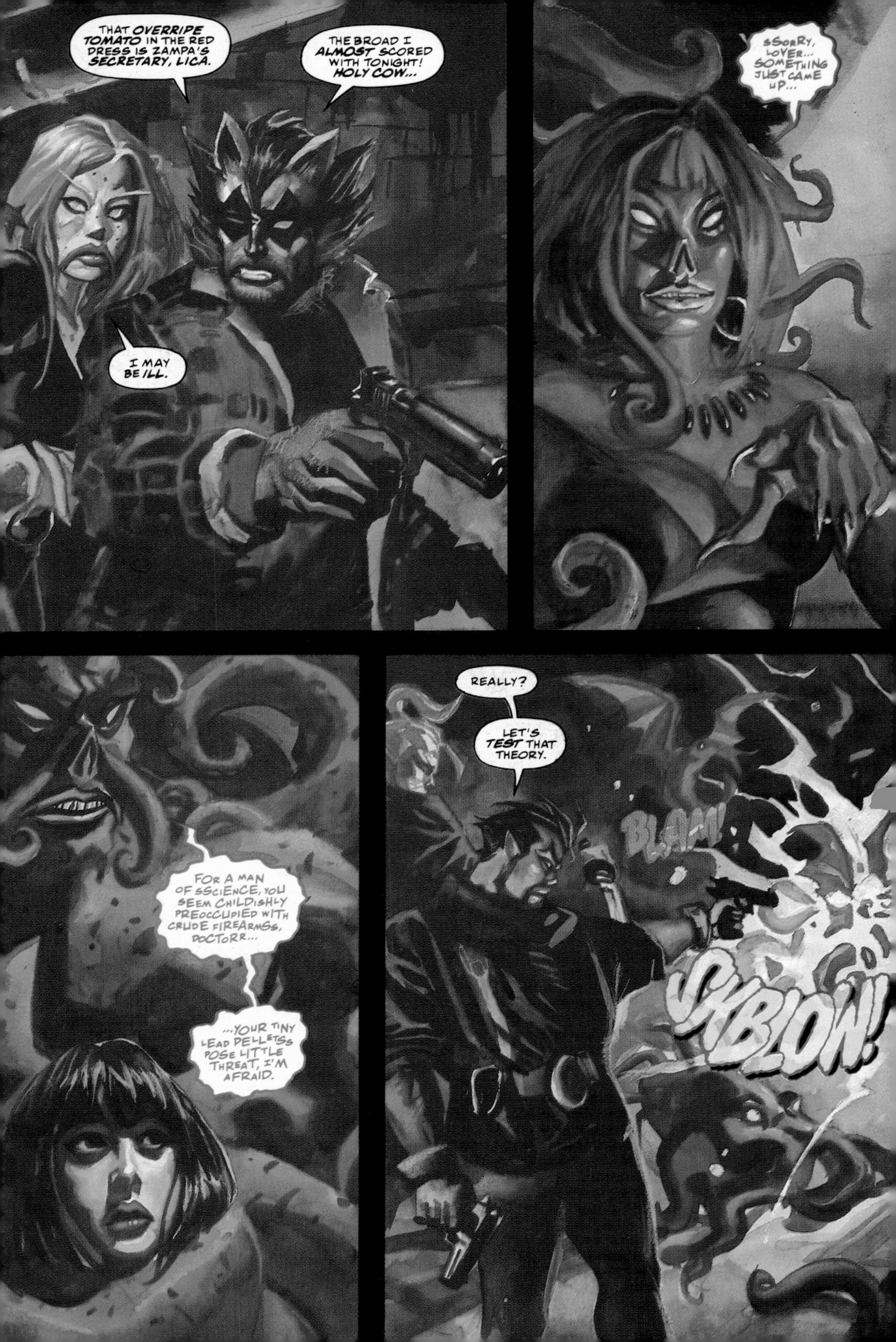
THAT OVERRIPE TOMATO IN THE RED DRESS IS ZAMPA'S SECRETARY, LICA.
THE BROAD I ALMOST SCORED WITH TONIGHT! HOLY COW...
I MAY BE ILL.
SSORRY, LOVER... SOMETHING JUST CAME UP...
FOR A MAN OF SSCIENCE, YOU SEEM CHILDISHLY PREOCCUPIED WITH CRUDE FIREARMSS, DOCTORR...
...YOUR TINY LEAD PELLETSS POSE LITTLE THREAT, I'M AFRAID.
REALLY?
LET'S TEST THAT THEORY.
BLAM!
SKBLOW!

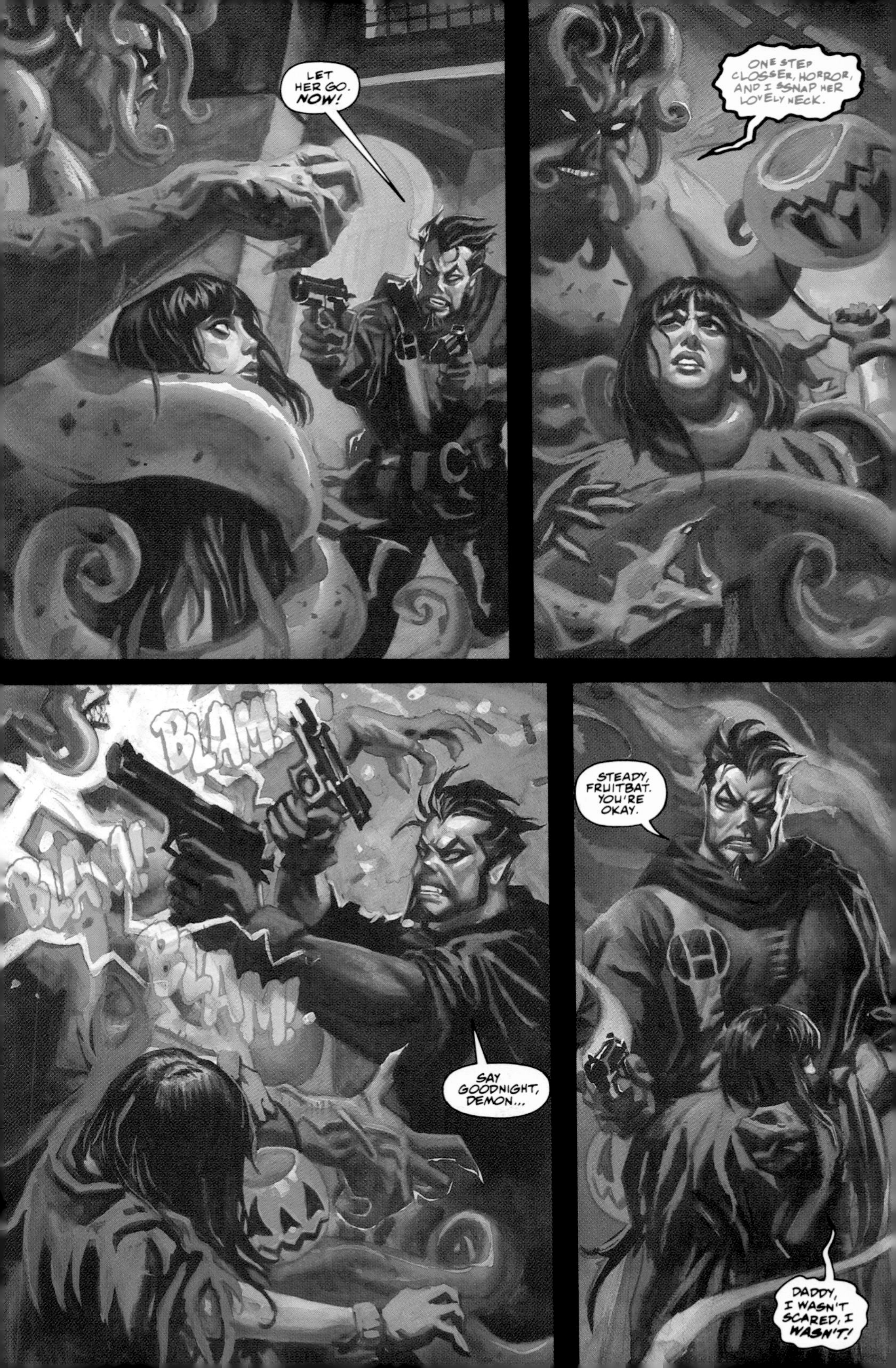

LET HER GO. **NOW!**
ONE STEP CLOSSER, HORROR, AND I SNAP HER LOVELY NECK.
BLAM!
BLAM!
BLAM!
SAY GOODNIGHT, DEMON...
STEADY, FRUITBAT. YOU'RE OKAY.
DADDY, I WASN'T SCARED, I **WASN'T!**

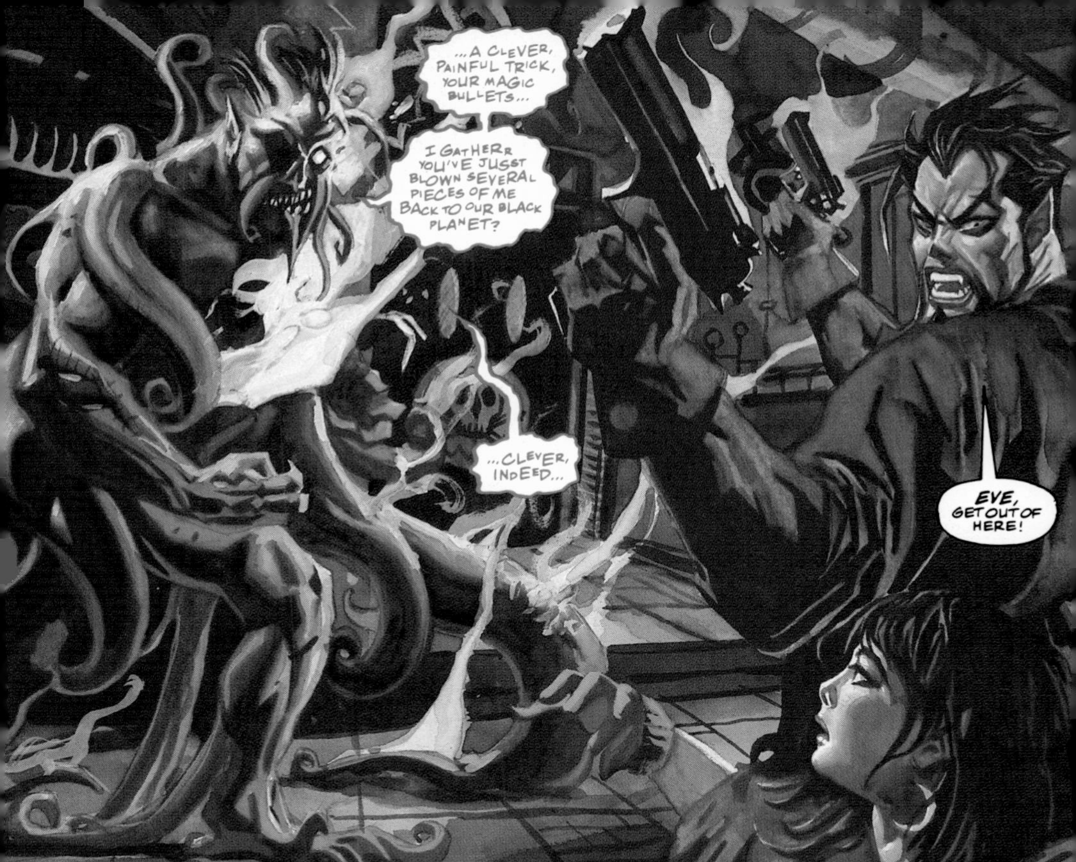
...A CLEVER, PAINFUL TRICK, YOUR MAGIC BULLETS...
I GATHERR YOU'VE JUSST BLOWN SEVERAL PIECES OF ME BACK TO OUR BLACK PLANET?
...CLEVER, INDEED...
EVE, GET OUT OF HERE!

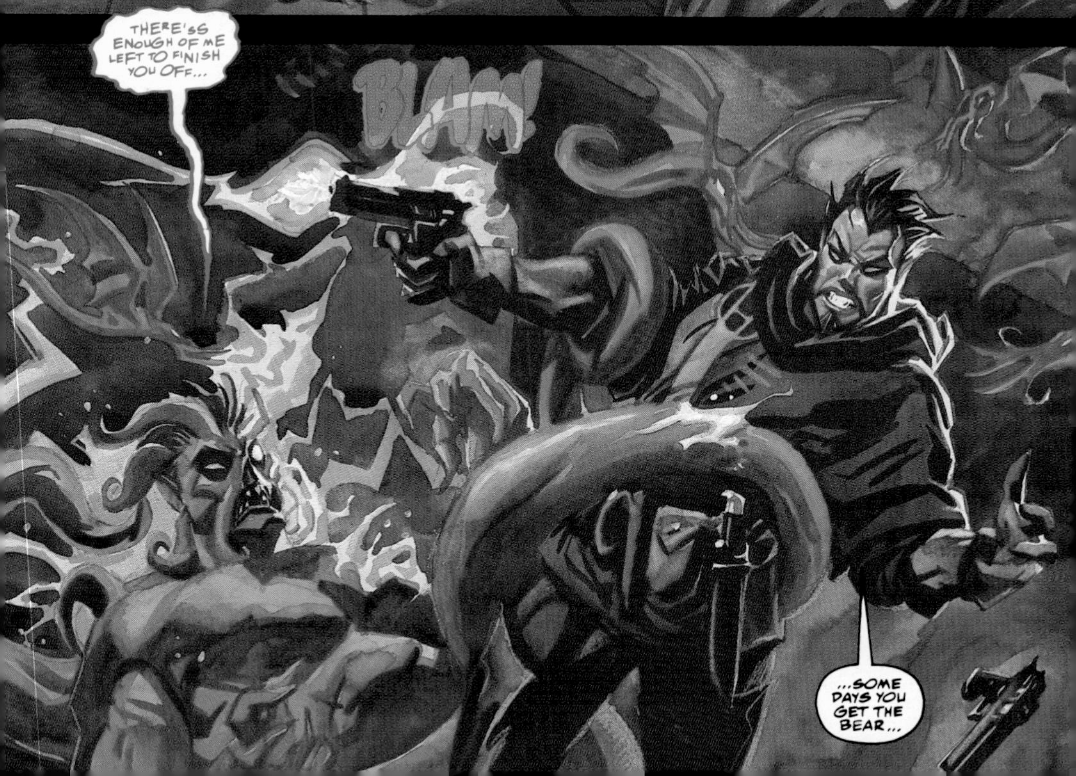
THERE'SS ENOUGH OF ME LEFT TO FINISH YOU OFF...
BLAM!
...SOME DAYS YOU GET THE BEAR...

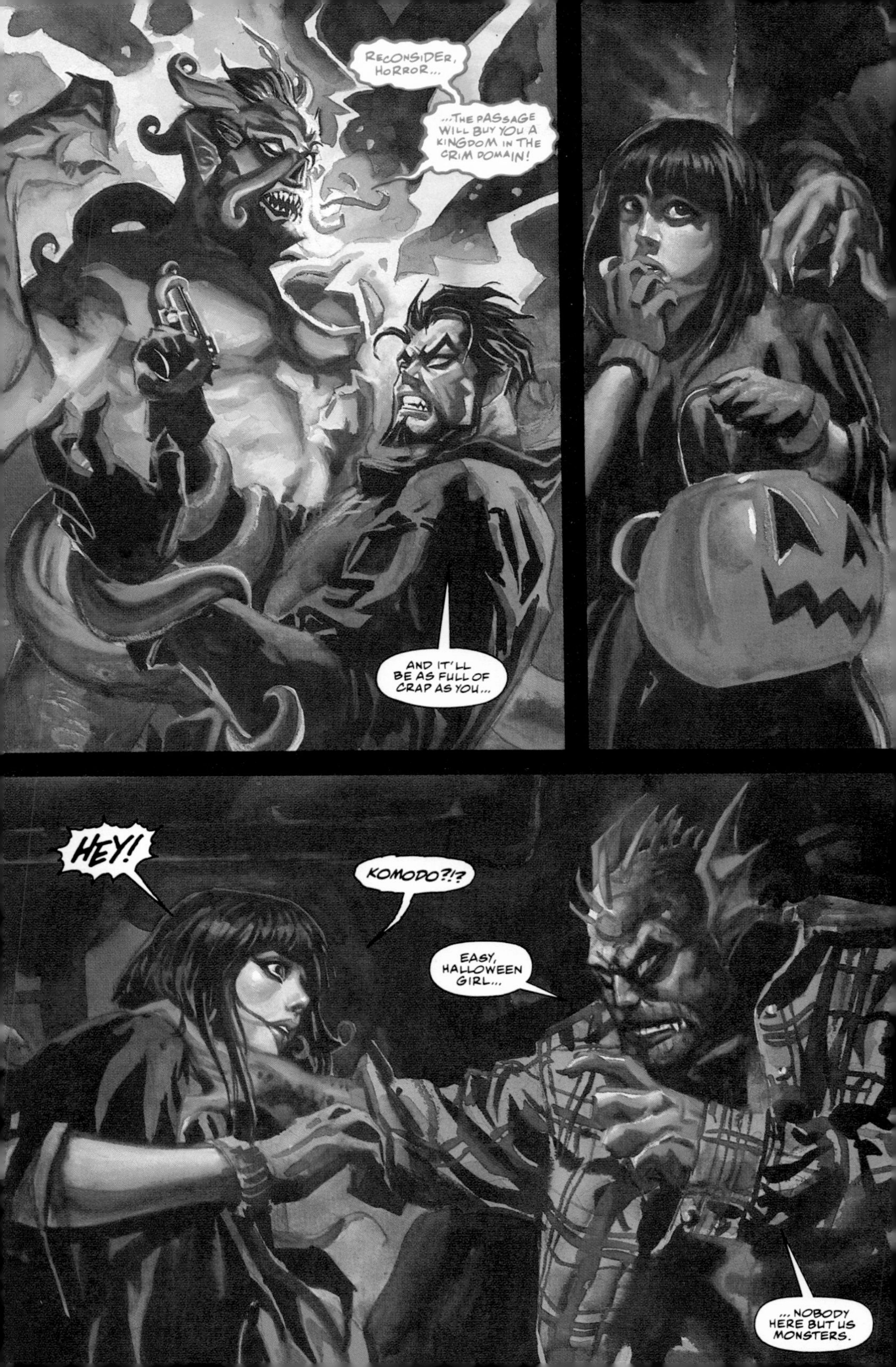
RECONSIDER, HORROR...
...THE PASSAGE WILL BUY YOU A KINGDOM IN THE GRIM DOMAIN!
AND IT'LL BE AS FULL OF CRAP AS YOU...
HEY!
KOMODO?!?
EASY, HALLOWEEN GIRL...
...NOBODY HERE BUT US MONSTERS.

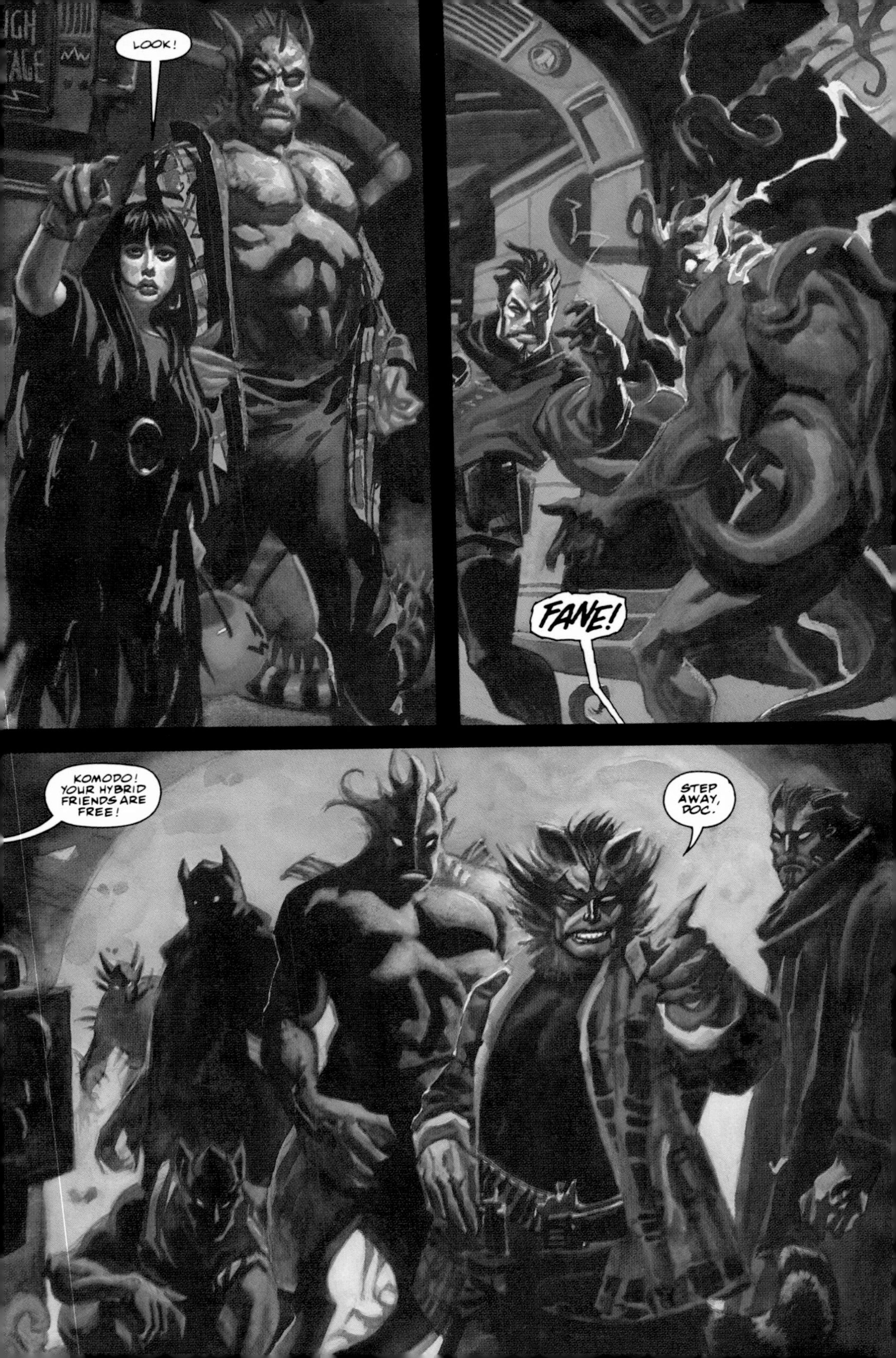
LOOK!
FANE!
KOMODO! YOUR HYBRID FRIENDS ARE FREE!
STEP AWAY, DOC.

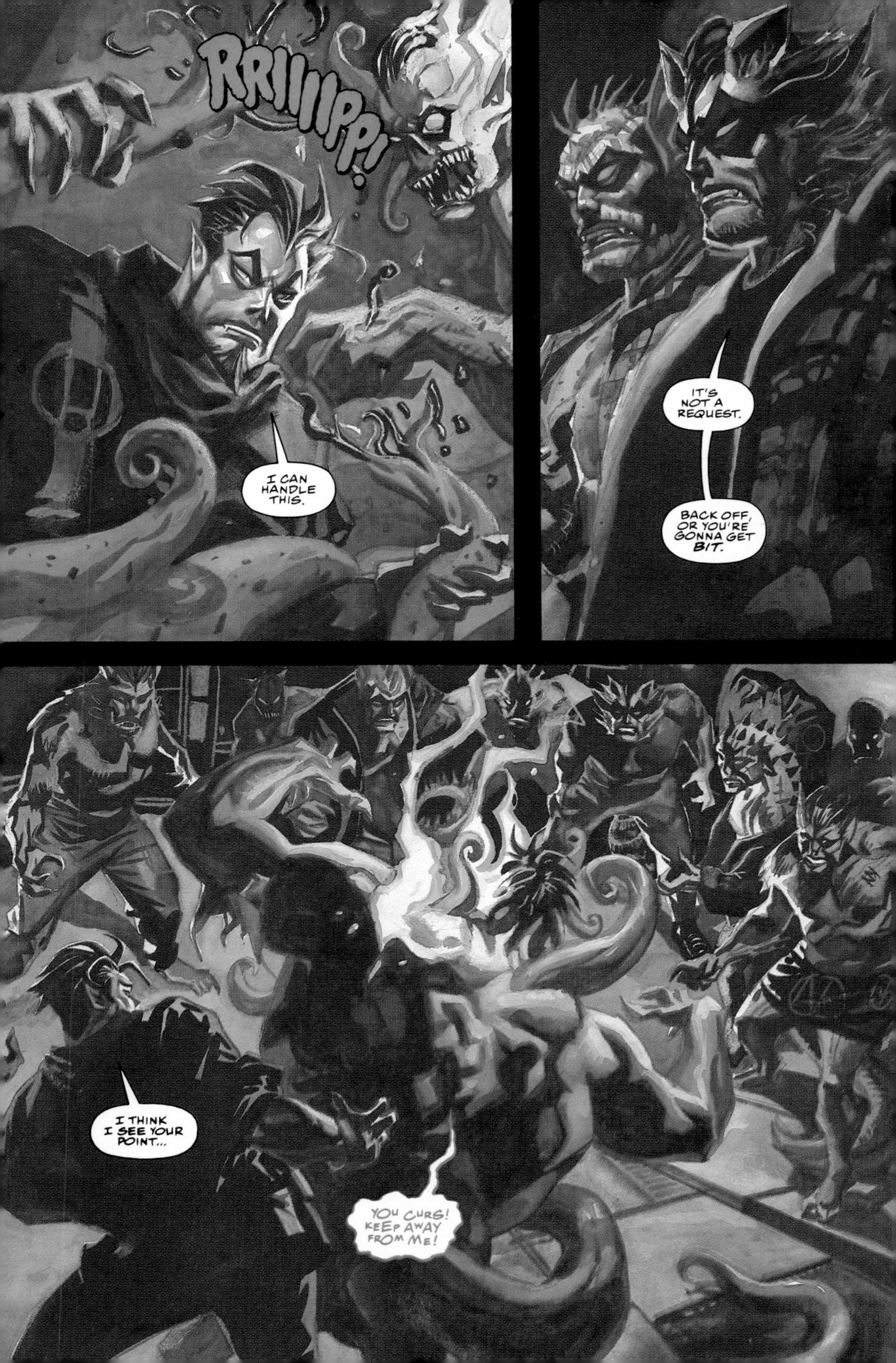
RRIIIIPP!
I CAN HANDLE THIS.
IT'S NOT A REQUEST.
BACK OFF, OR YOU'RE GONNA GET BIT.
I THINK I SEE YOUR POINT...
YOU CURS! KEEP AWAY FROM ME!

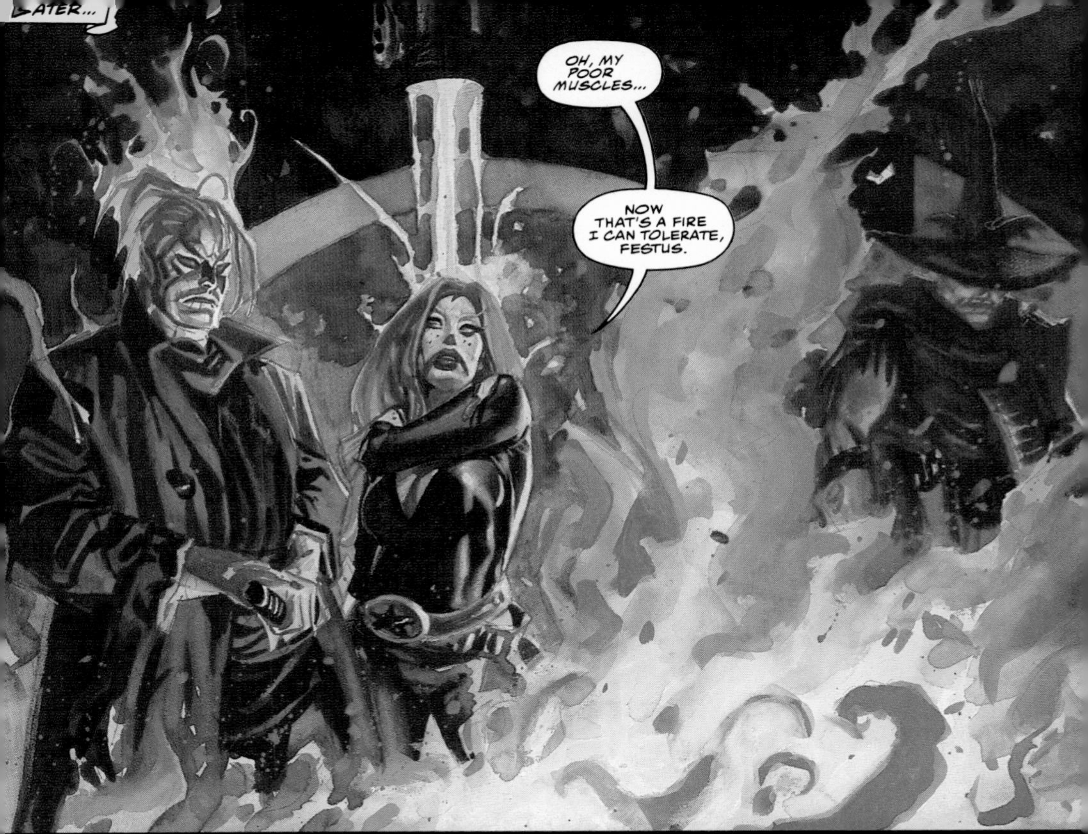
LATER...
OH, MY POOR MUSCLES...
NOW THAT'S A FIRE I CAN TOLERATE, FESTUS.

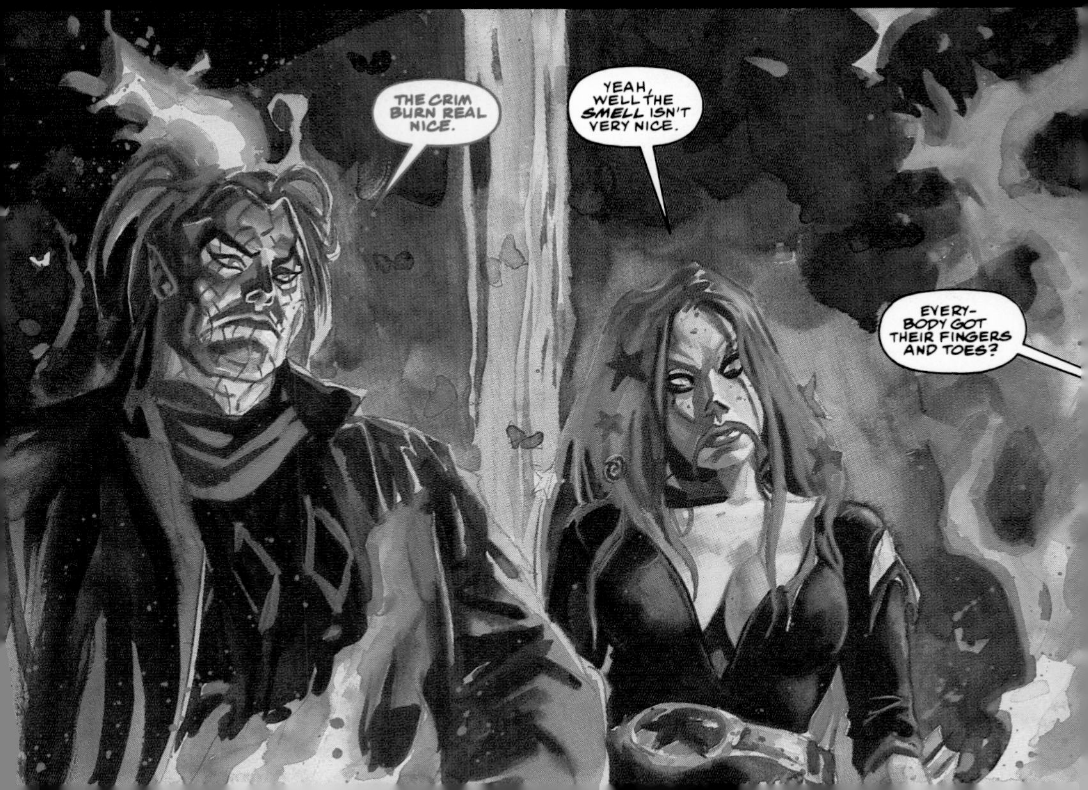
THE CRIM BURN REAL NICE.
YEAH, WELL THE SMELL ISN'T VERY NICE.
EVERY-BODY GOT THEIR FINGERS AND TOES?

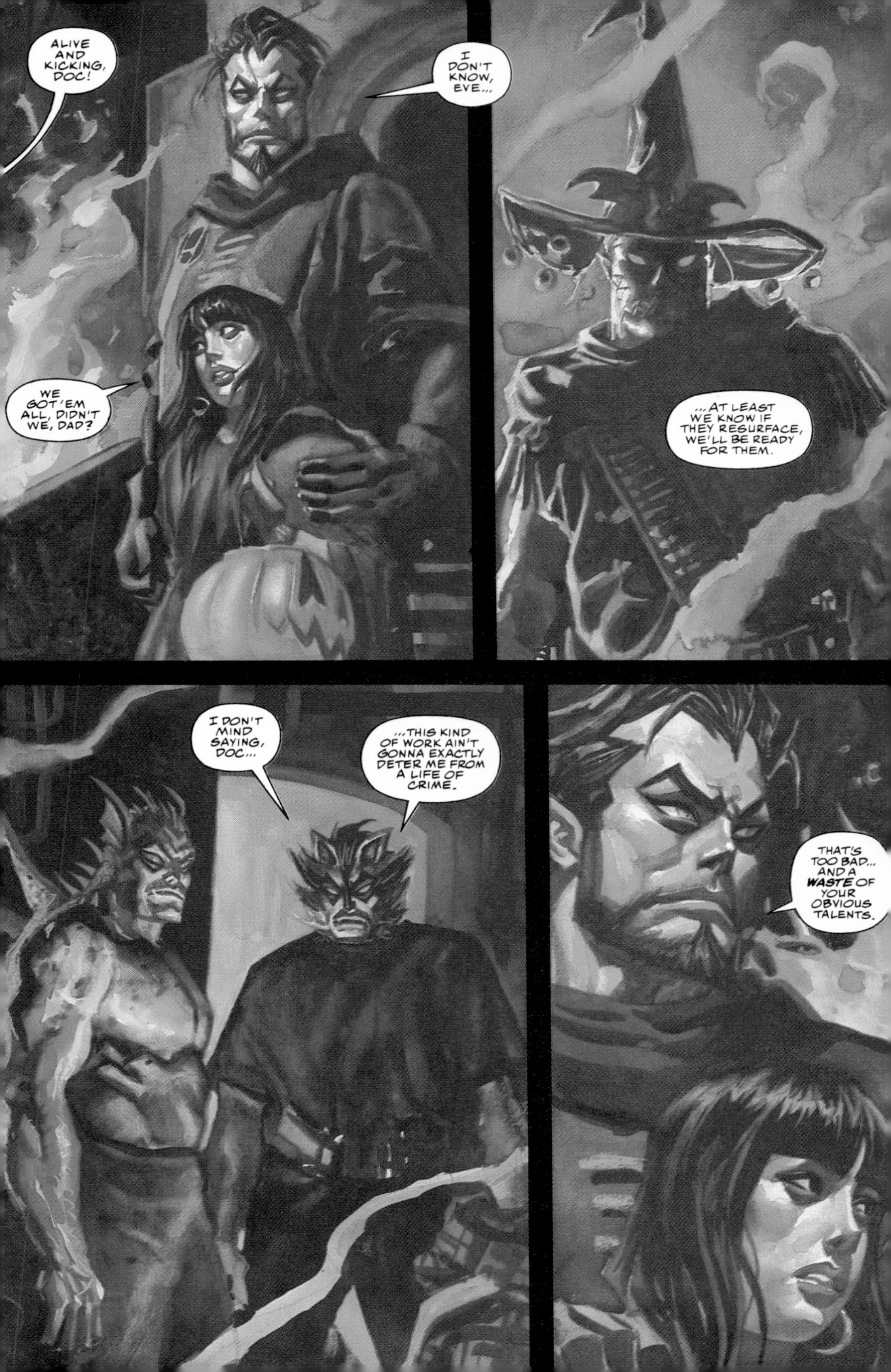
ALIVE AND KICKING, DOC!
I DON'T KNOW, EVE...
WE GOT'EM ALL, DIDN'T WE, DAD?
...AT LEAST WE KNOW IF THEY RESURFACE, WE'LL BE READY FOR THEM.
I DON'T MIND SAYING, DOC...
...THIS KIND OF WORK AIN'T GONNA EXACTLY DETER ME FROM A LIFE OF CRIME.
THAT'S TOO BAD... AND A WASTE OF YOUR OBVIOUS TALENTS.

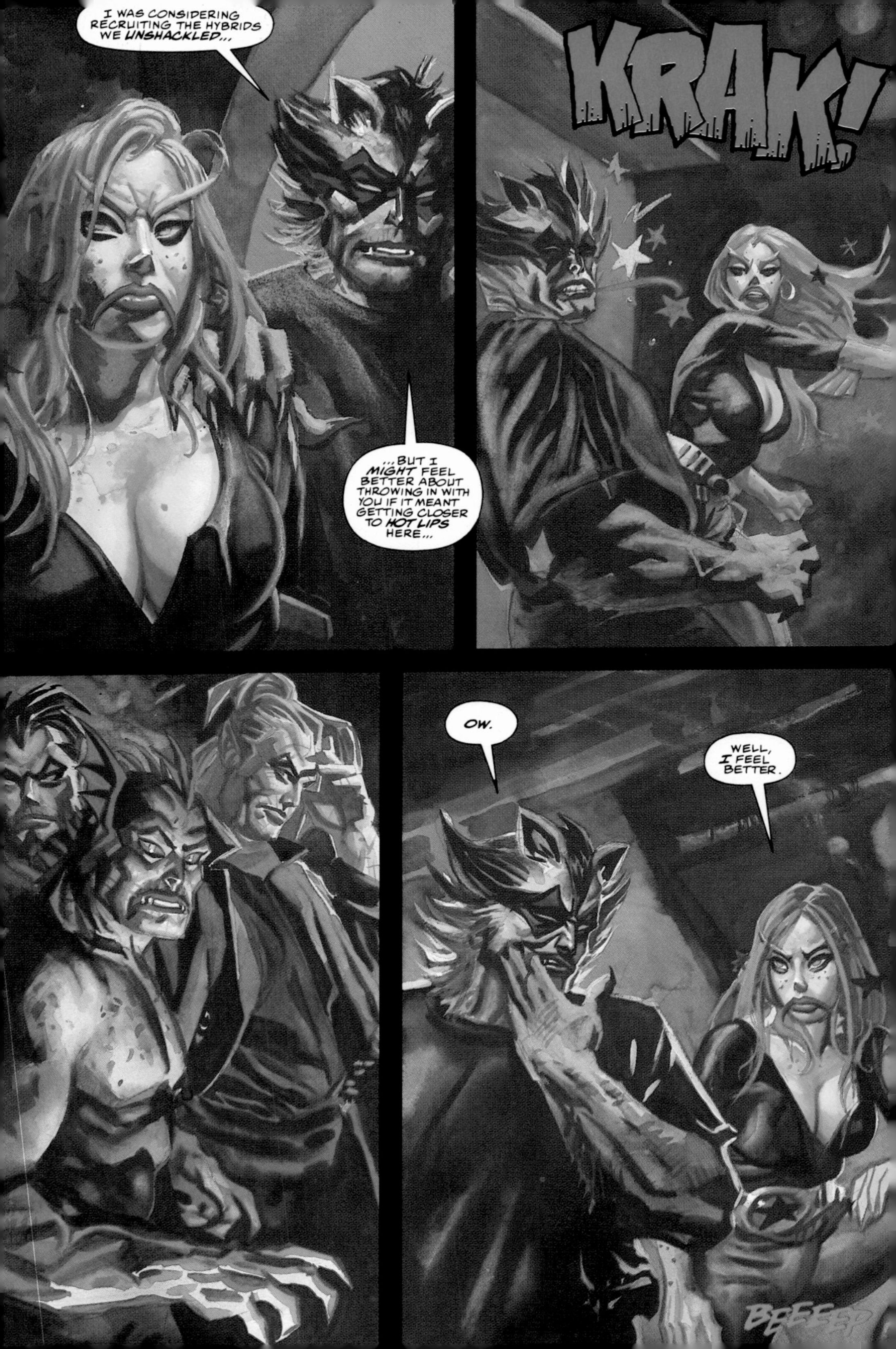
I WAS CONSIDERING RECRUITING THE HYBRIDS WE UNSHACKLED...
...BUT I MIGHT FEEL BETTER ABOUT THROWING IN WITH YOU IF IT MEANT GETTING CLOSER TO HOT LIPS HERE...
KRAK!
OW.
WELL, I FEEL BETTER.

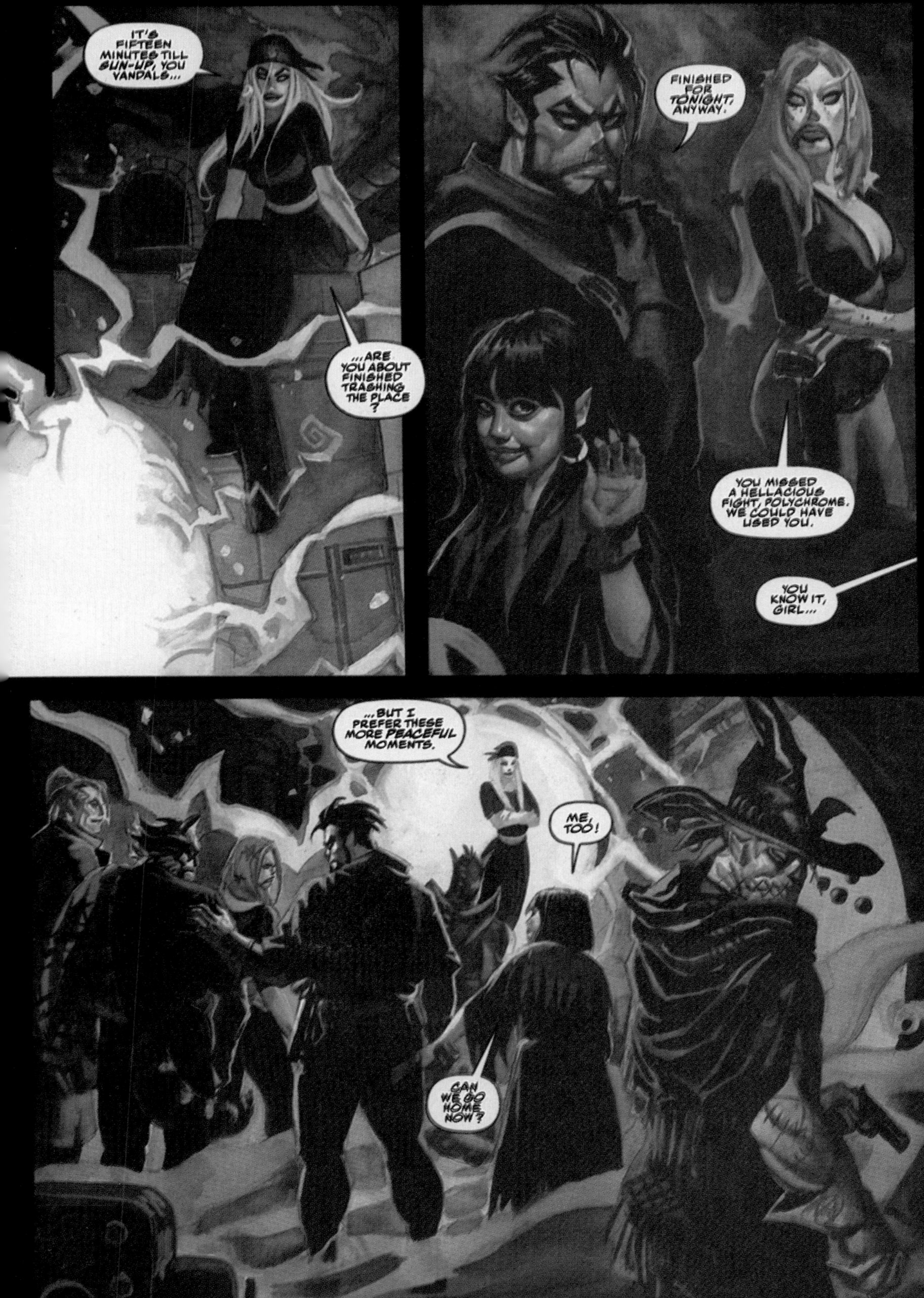
IT'S FIFTEEN MINUTES TILL SUN-UP, YOU VANDALS...
...ARE YOU ABOUT FINISHED TRASHING THE PLACE?
FINISHED FOR TONIGHT, ANYWAY.
YOU MISSED A HELLACIOUS FIGHT, POLYCHROME. WE COULD HAVE USED YOU.
YOU KNOW IT, GIRL...
...BUT I PREFER THESE MORE PEACEFUL MOMENTS.
ME, TOO!
CAN WE GO HOME, NOW?

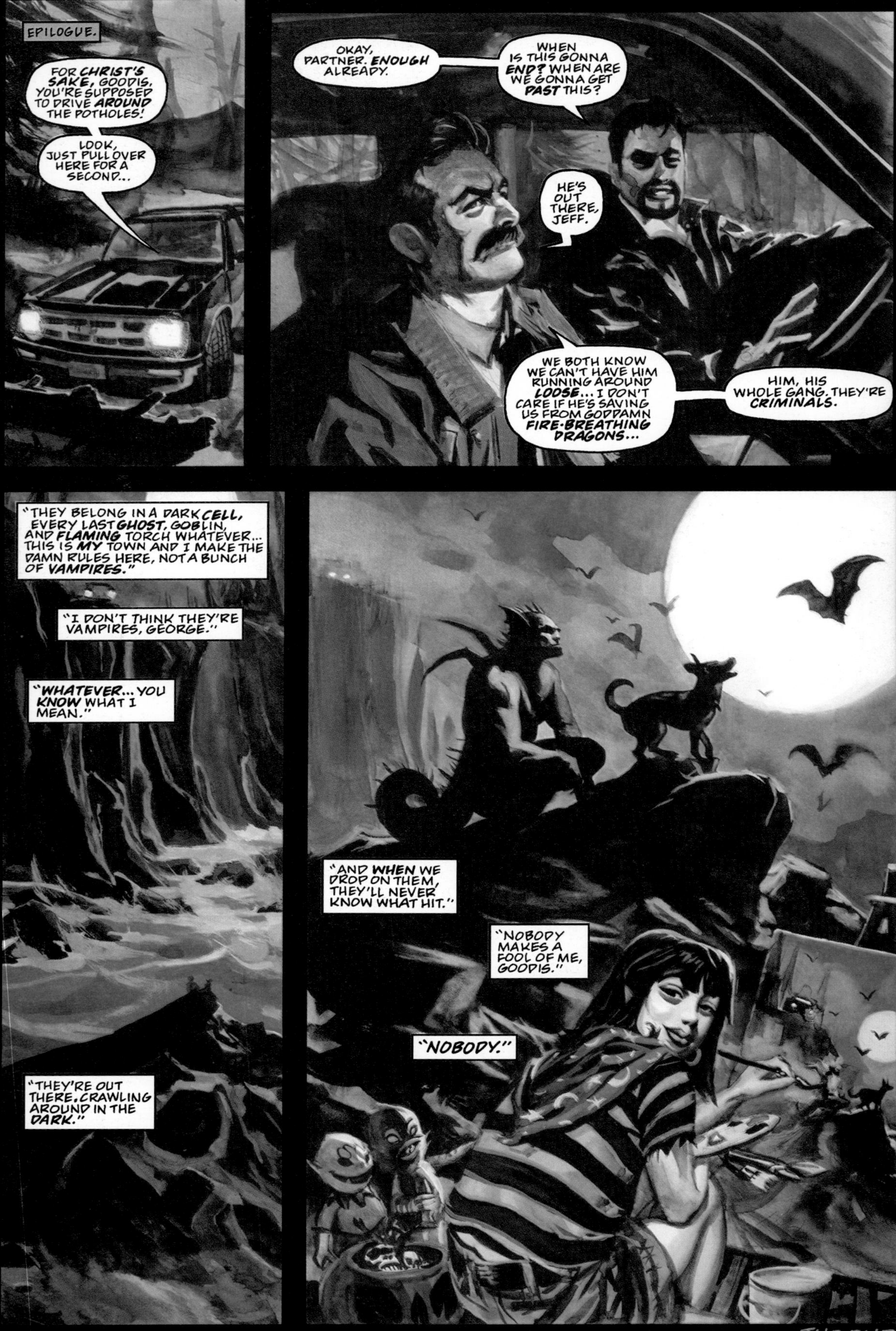
EPILOGUE.
FOR CHRIST'S SAKE, GOODIS, YOU'RE SUPPOSED TO DRIVE AROUND THE POTHOLES!
LOOK, JUST PULL OVER HERE FOR A SECOND...
OKAY, PARTNER. ENOUGH ALREADY.
WHEN IS THIS GONNA END? WHEN ARE WE GONNA GET PAST THIS?
HE'S OUT THERE, JEFF.
WE BOTH KNOW WE CAN'T HAVE HIM RUNNING AROUND LOOSE... I DON'T CARE IF HE'S SAVING US FROM GODDAMN FIRE-BREATHING DRAGONS...
HIM, HIS WHOLE GANG. THEY'RE CRIMINALS.
"THEY BELONG IN A DARK CELL, EVERY LAST GHOST, GOBLIN, AND FLAMING TORCH WHATEVER... THIS IS MY TOWN AND I MAKE THE DAMN RULES HERE, NOT A BUNCH OF VAMPIRES."
"I DON'T THINK THEY'RE VAMPIRES, GEORGE."
"WHATEVER... YOU KNOW WHAT I MEAN."
"THEY'RE OUT THERE. CRAWLING AROUND IN THE DARK."
"AND WHEN WE DROP ON THEM, THEY'LL NEVER KNOW WHAT HIT."
"NOBODY MAKES A FOOL OF ME, GOODIS."
"NOBODY."

THE END

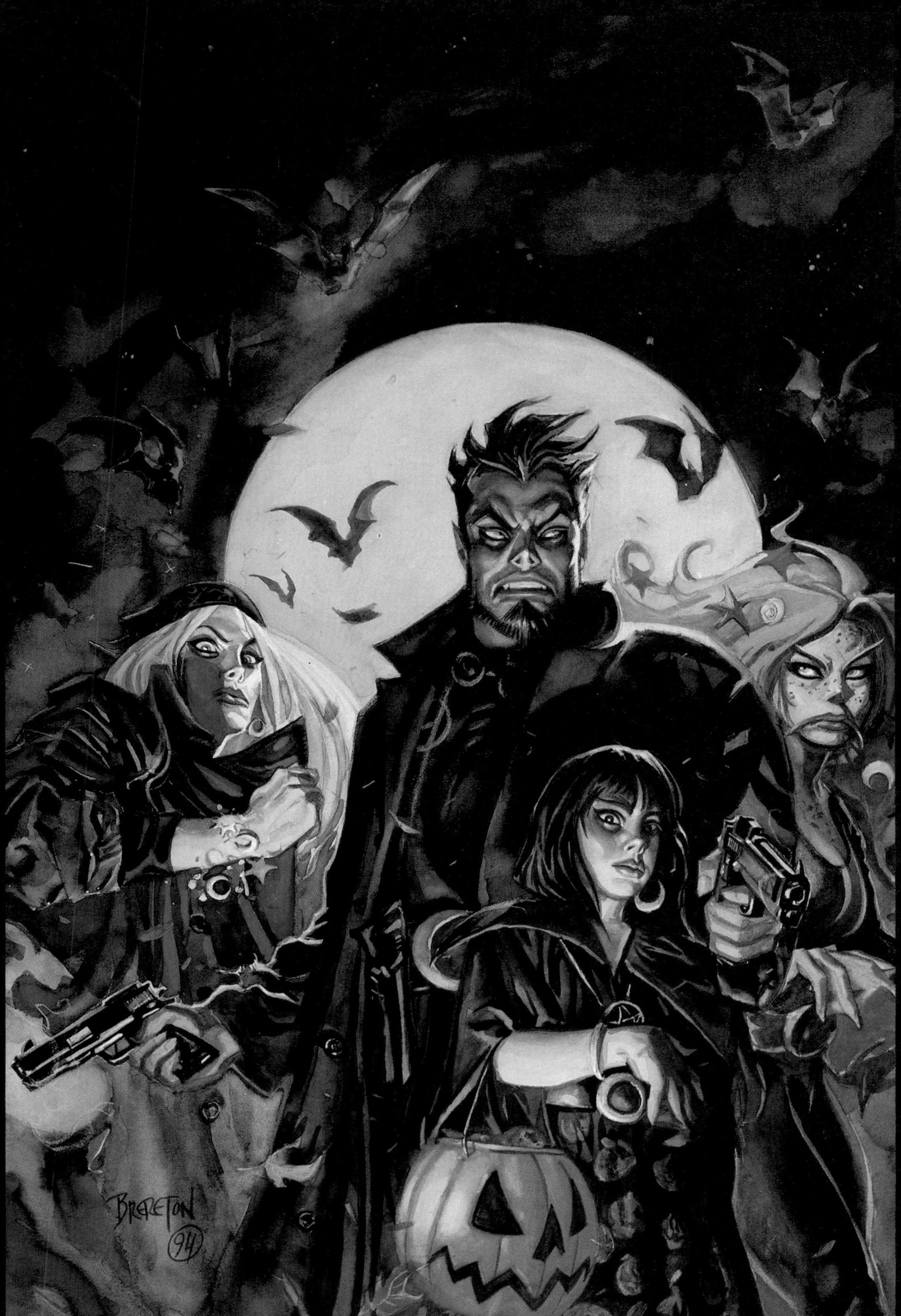
BRERETON
94

NOCTURNALS: BLACK PLANET 1 JANUARY 1995

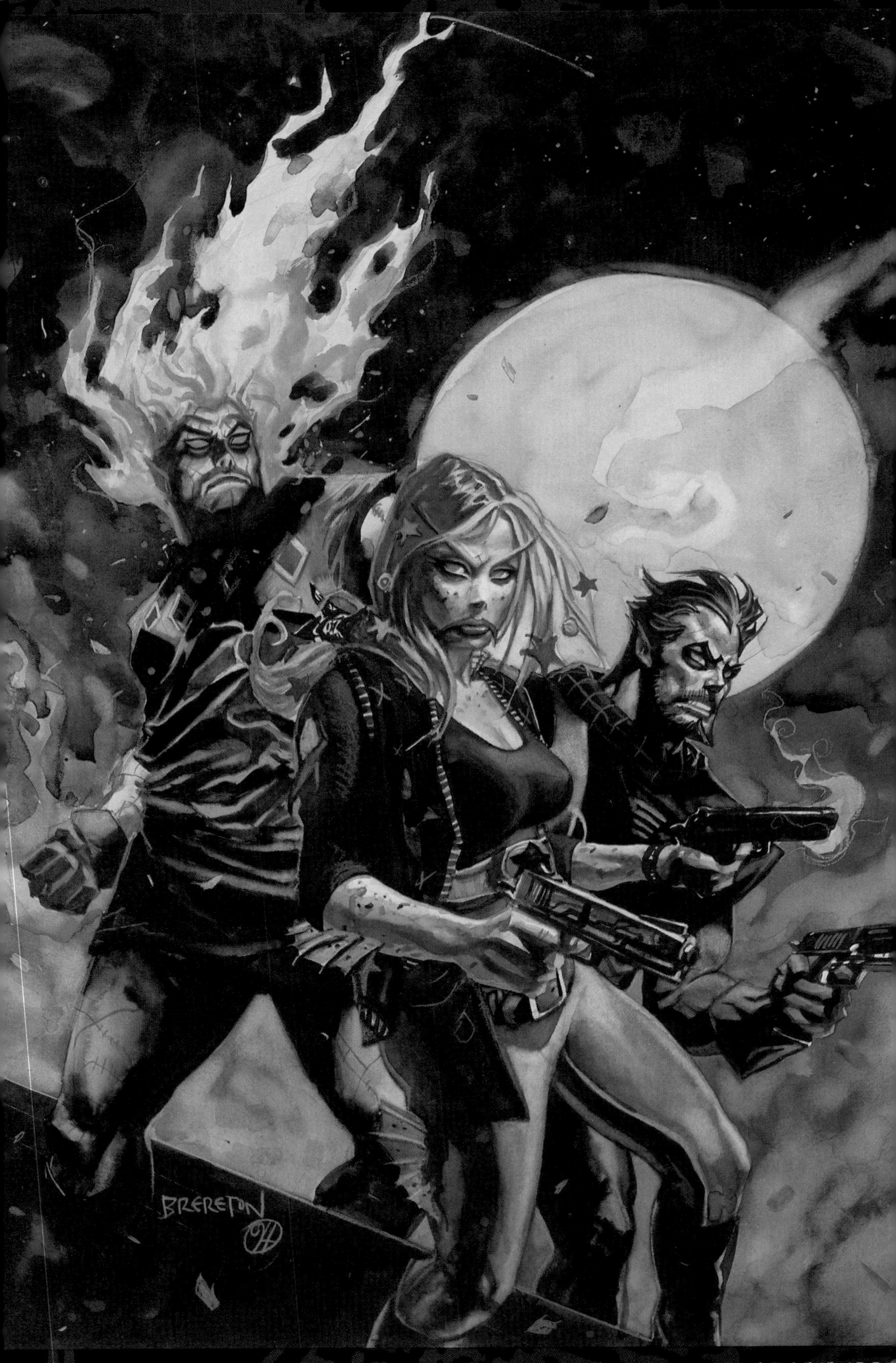
BRERETON
OH

NOCTURNALS: BLACK PLANET 2 FEBRUARY 199

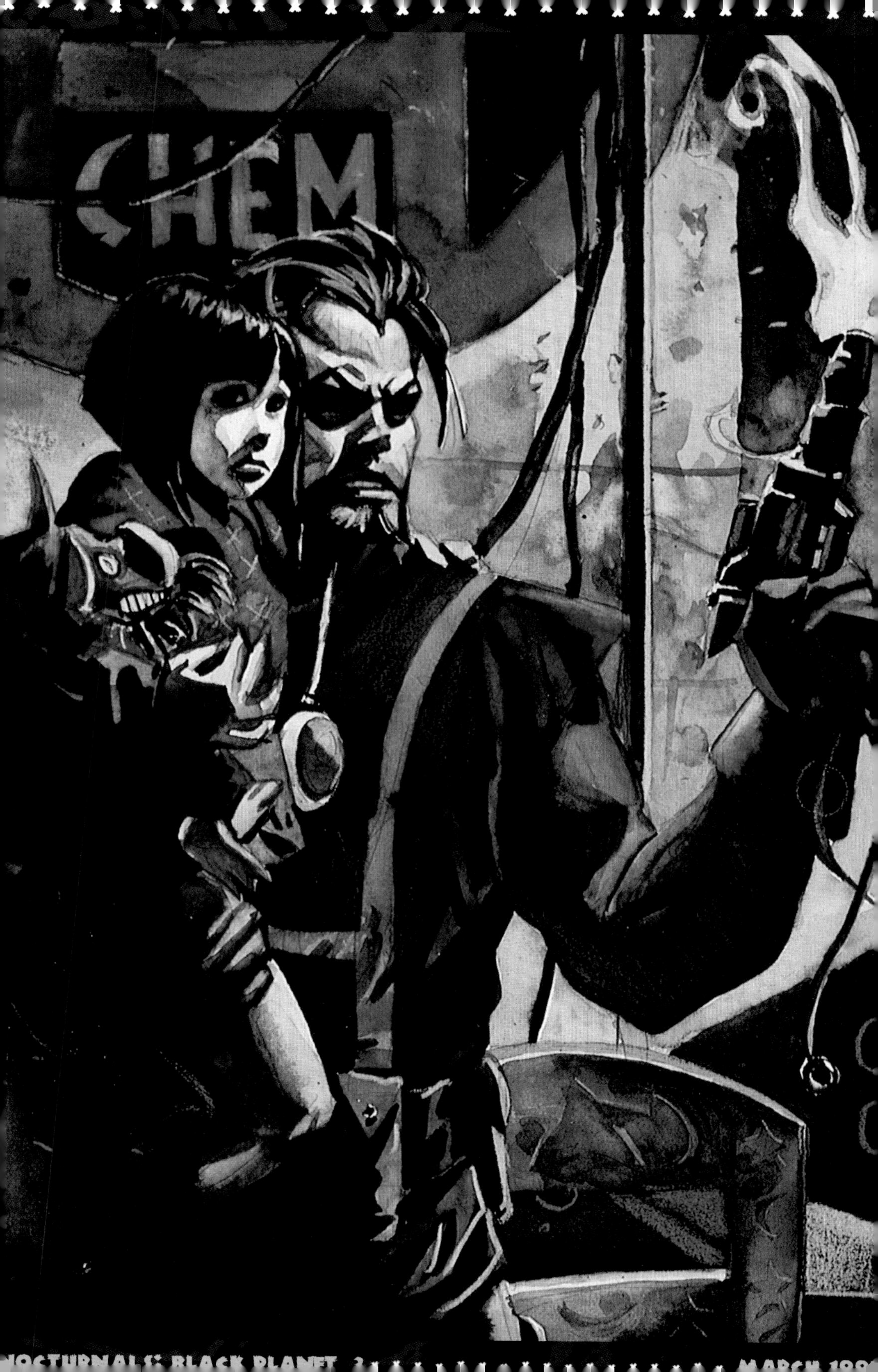
CHEM
NOCTURNALS: BLACK PLANET
MARCH

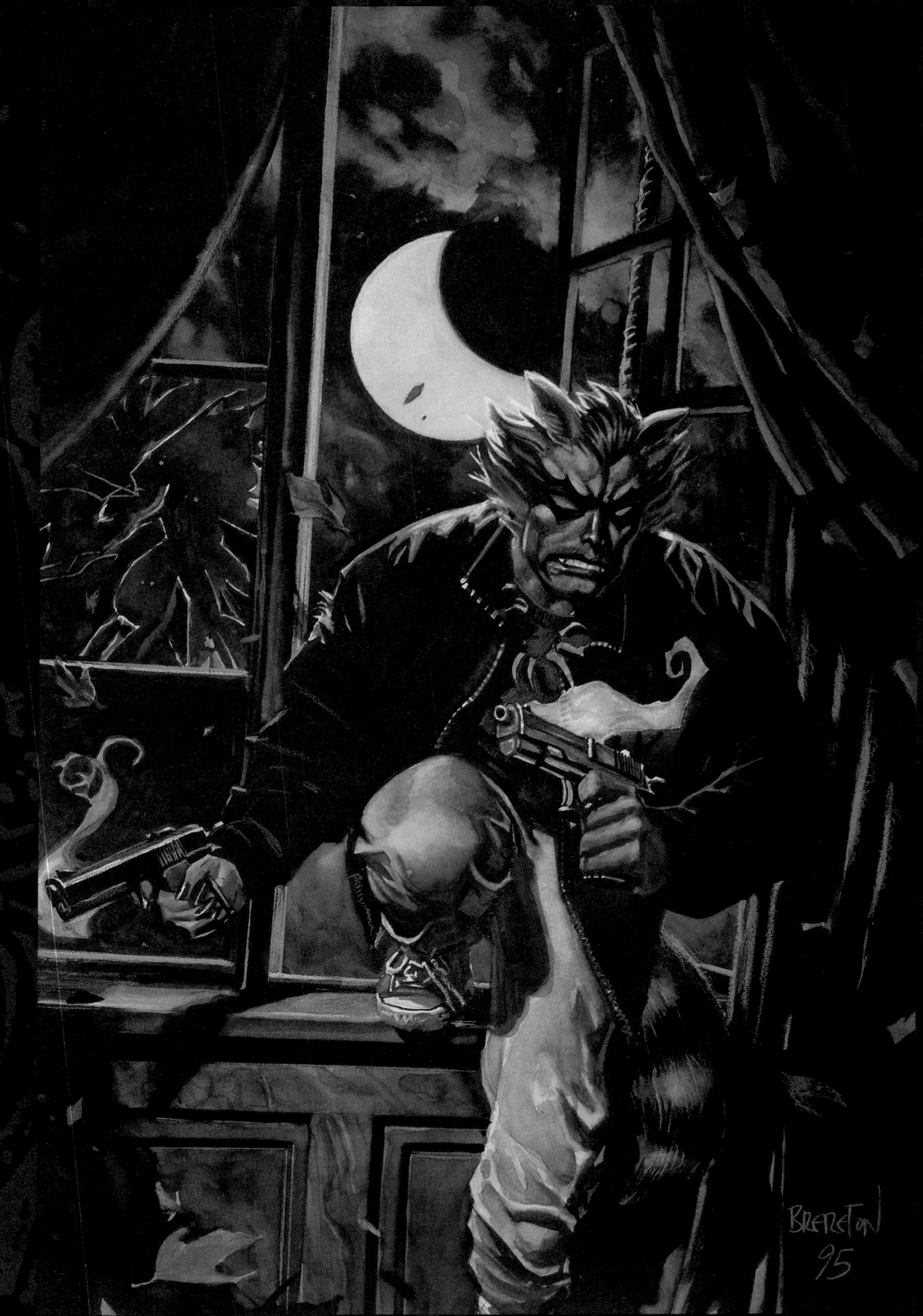
BRERETON
95

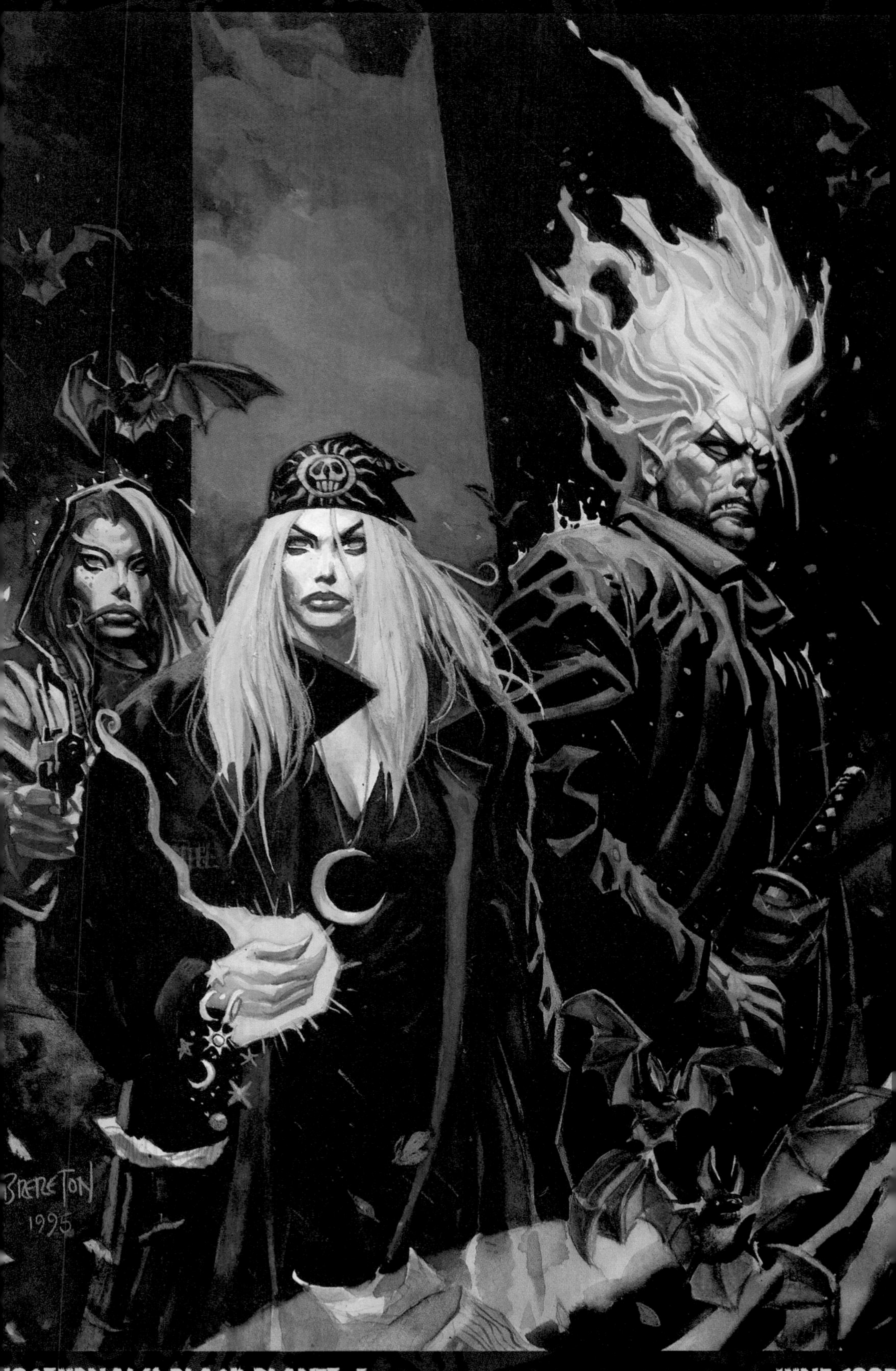
BRERETON
1995

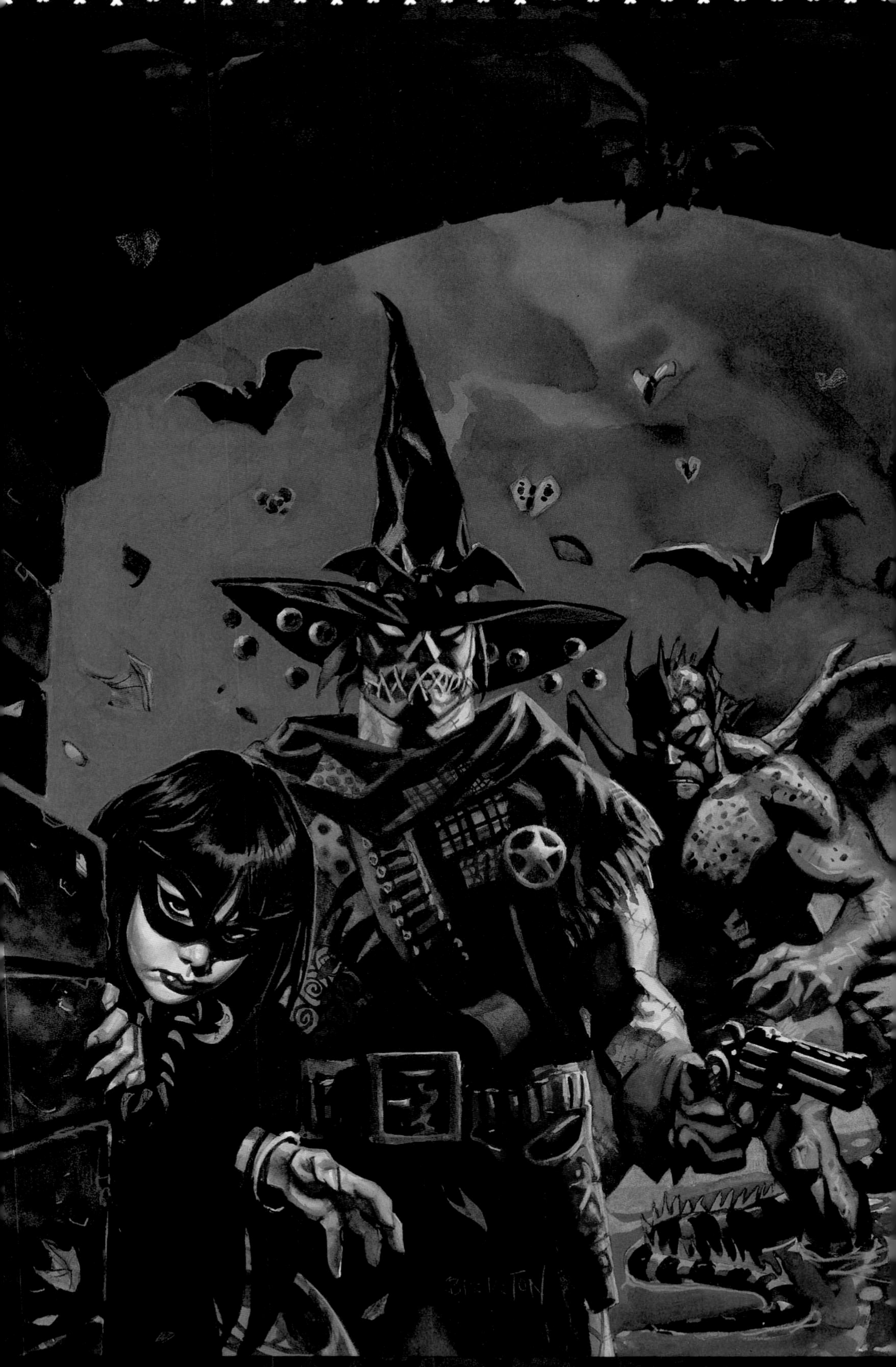

NOCTURNALS: BLACK PLANET 6 AUGUST 1995

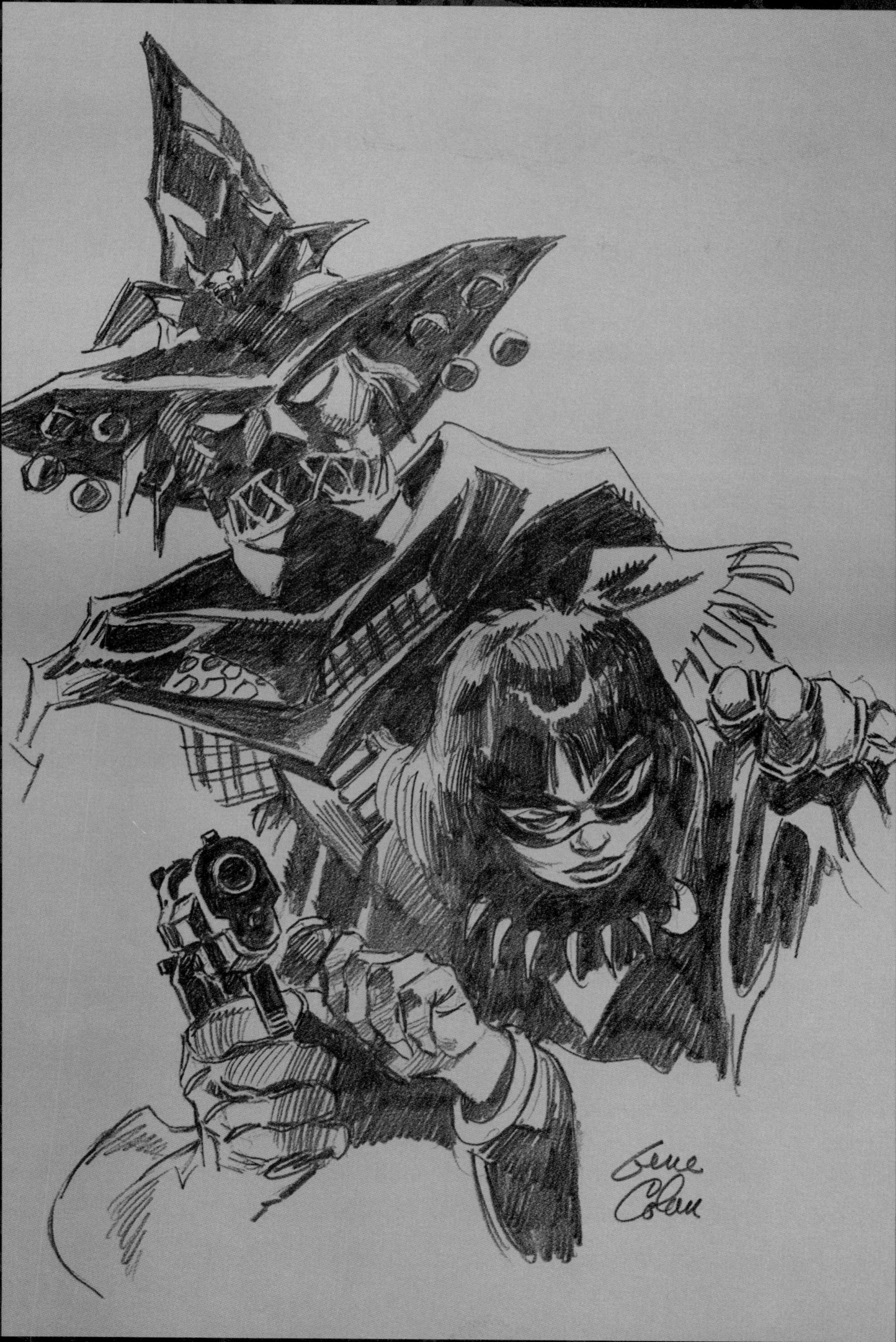
Gene Colan

GENE COLAN

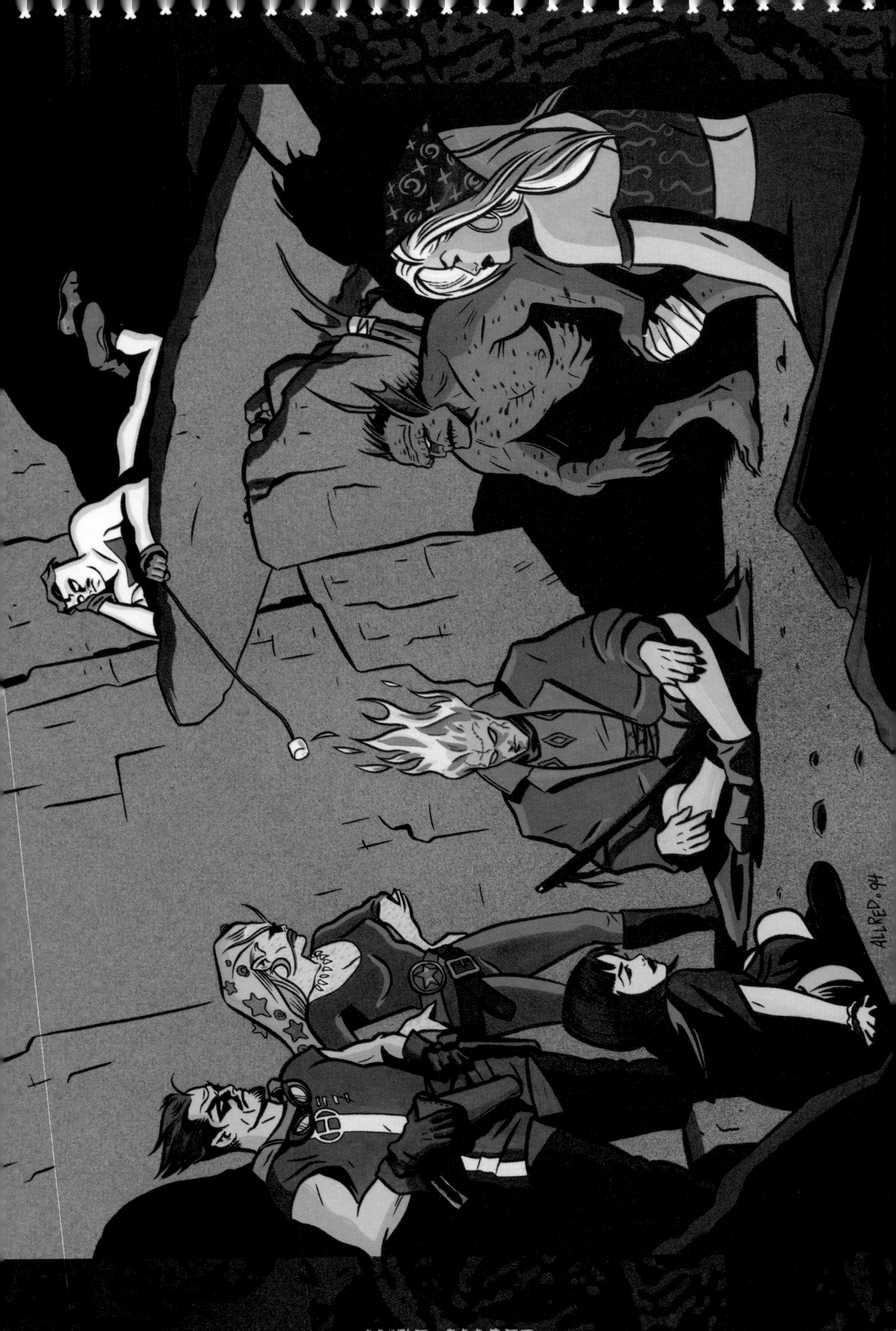
ALLRED.94

MIKE ALLRED

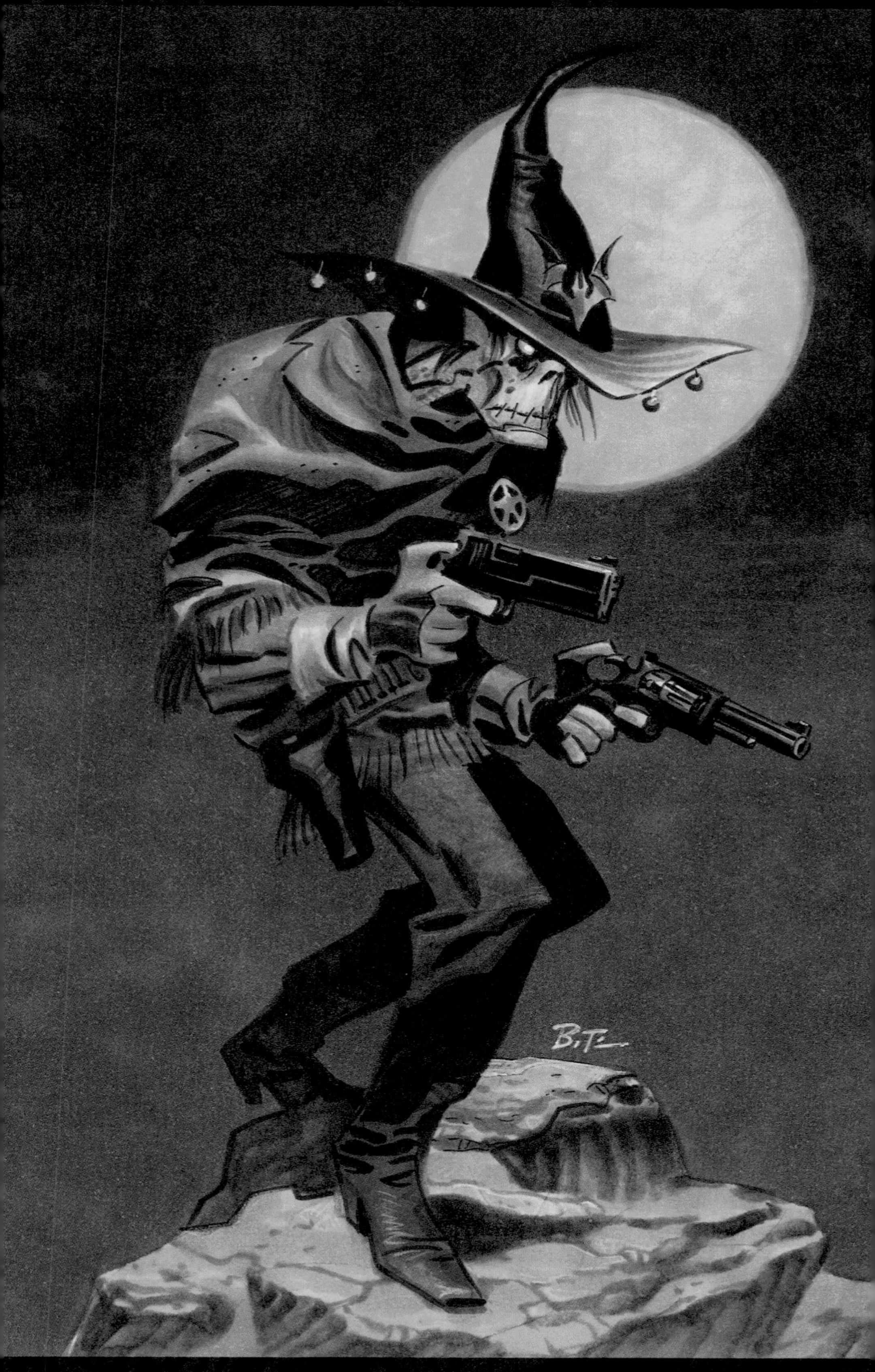

BRUCE TIMM

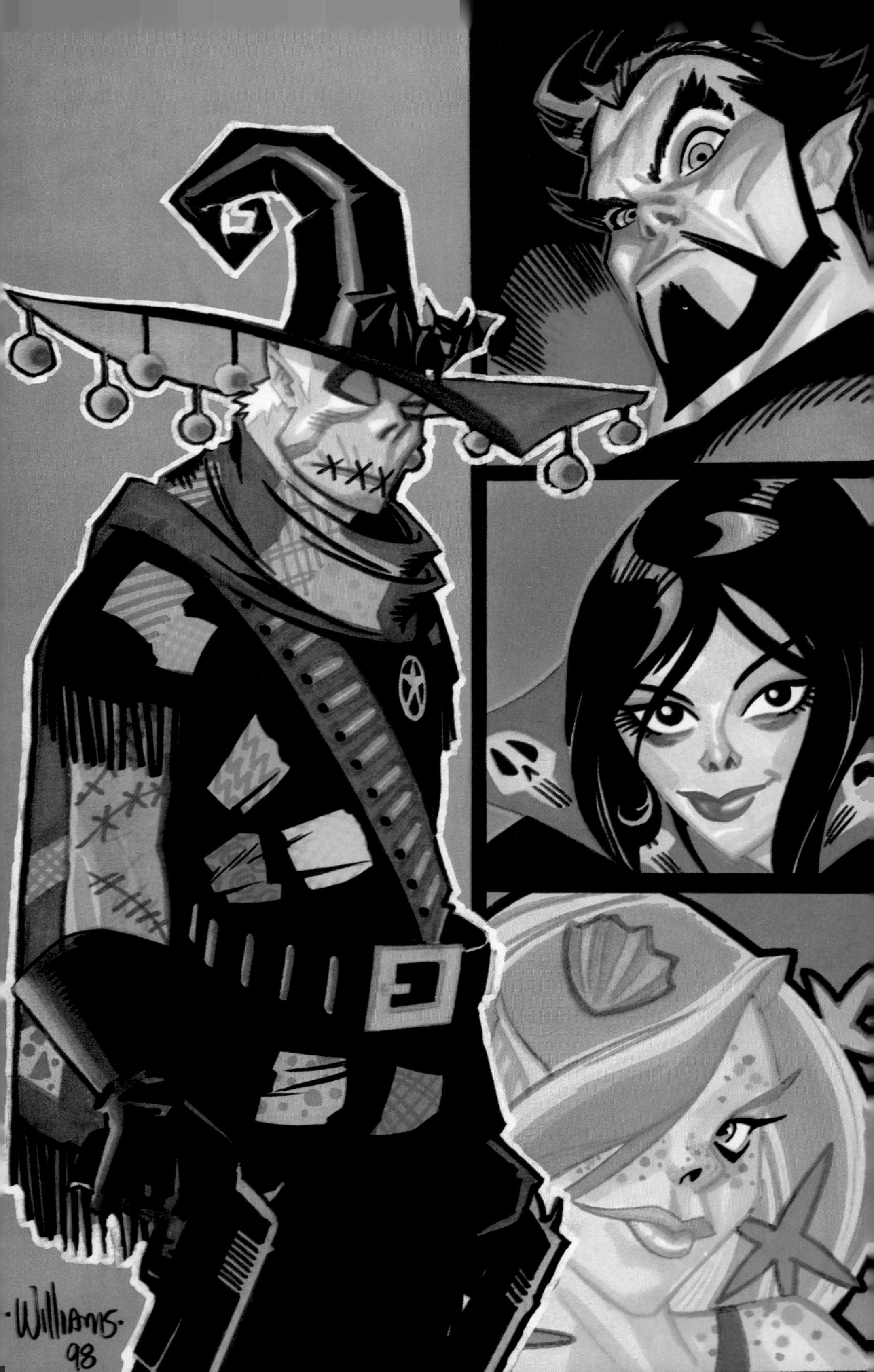
Williams
98

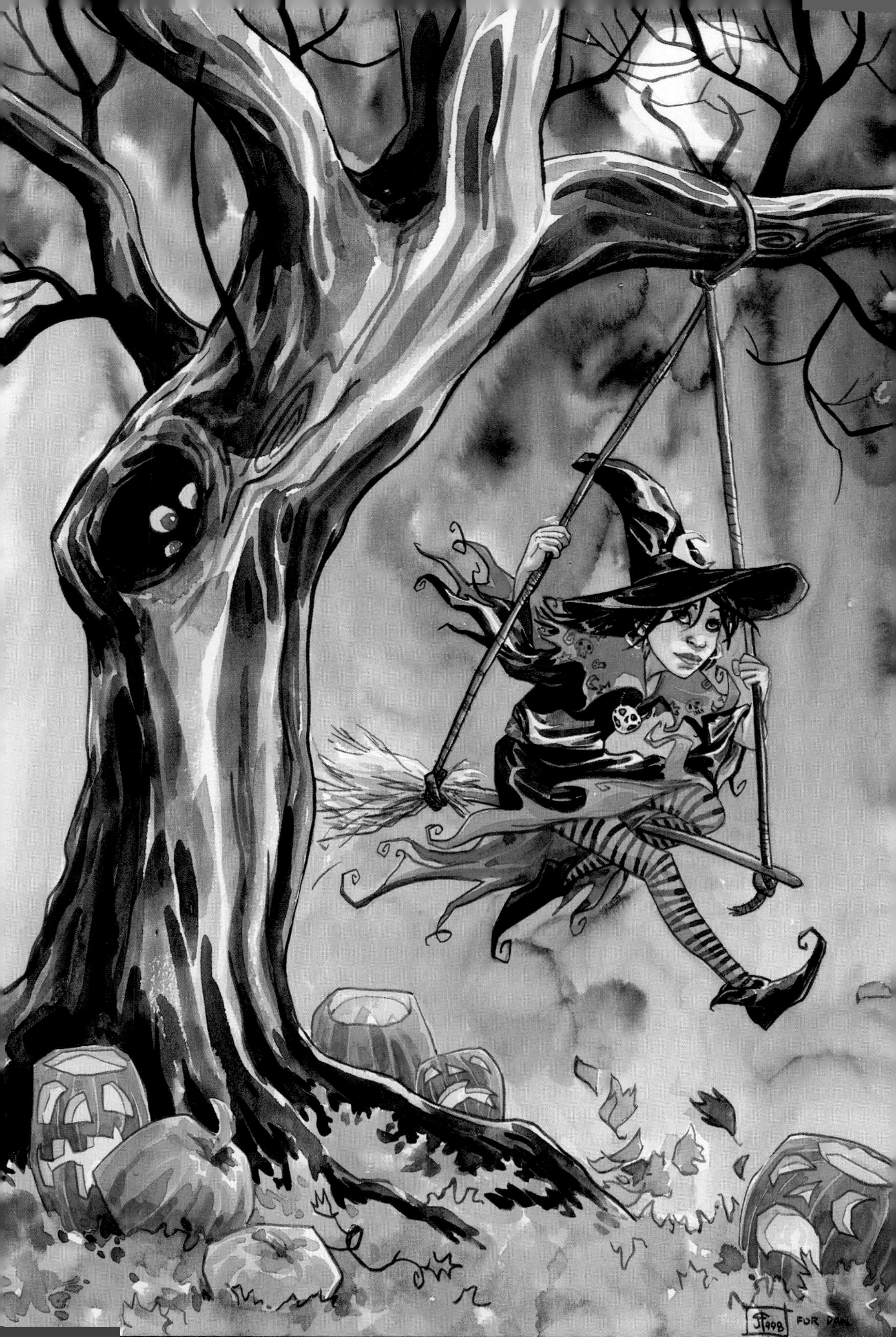
FOR

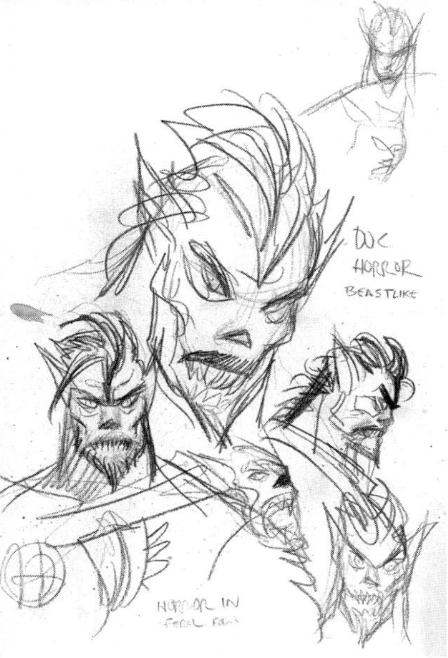
DOC
HORROR
BEASTLIKE
HORROR IN
FERAL

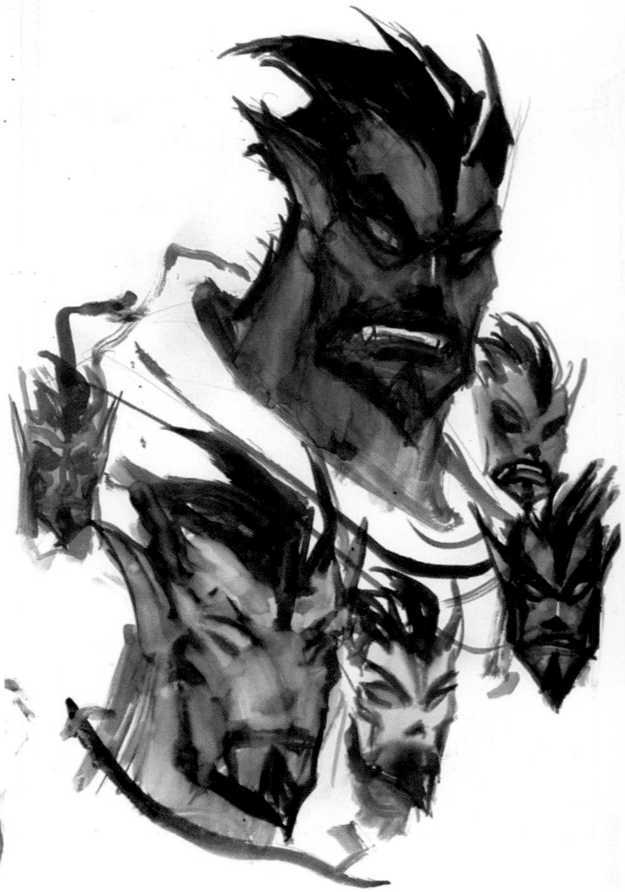

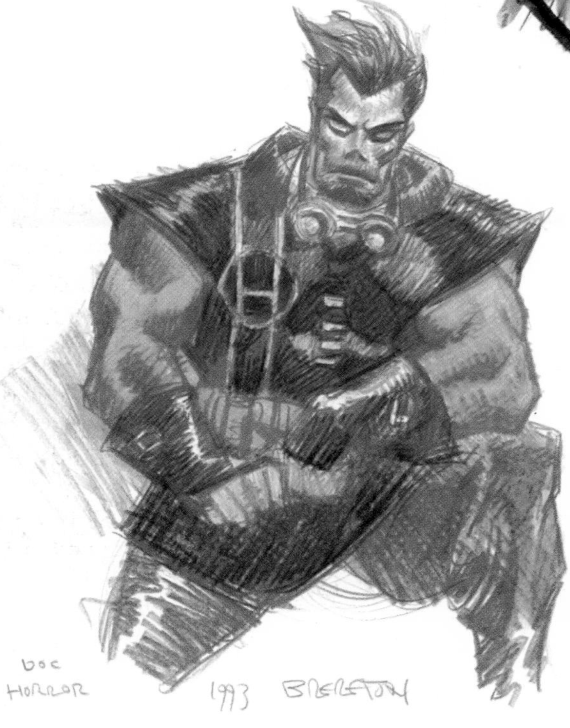
DOC
HORROR
1993 BRERETON

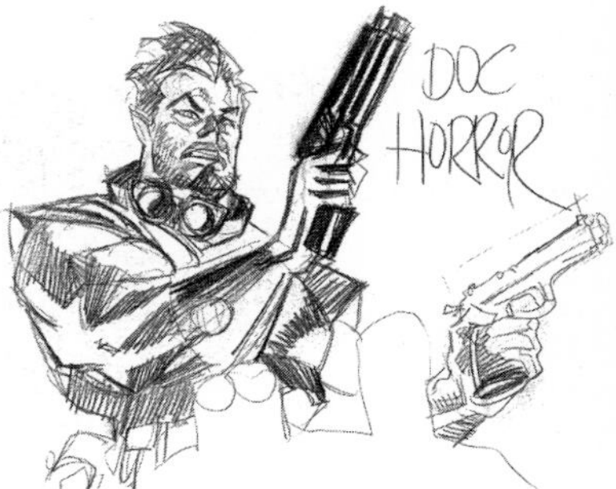
DOC
HORROR

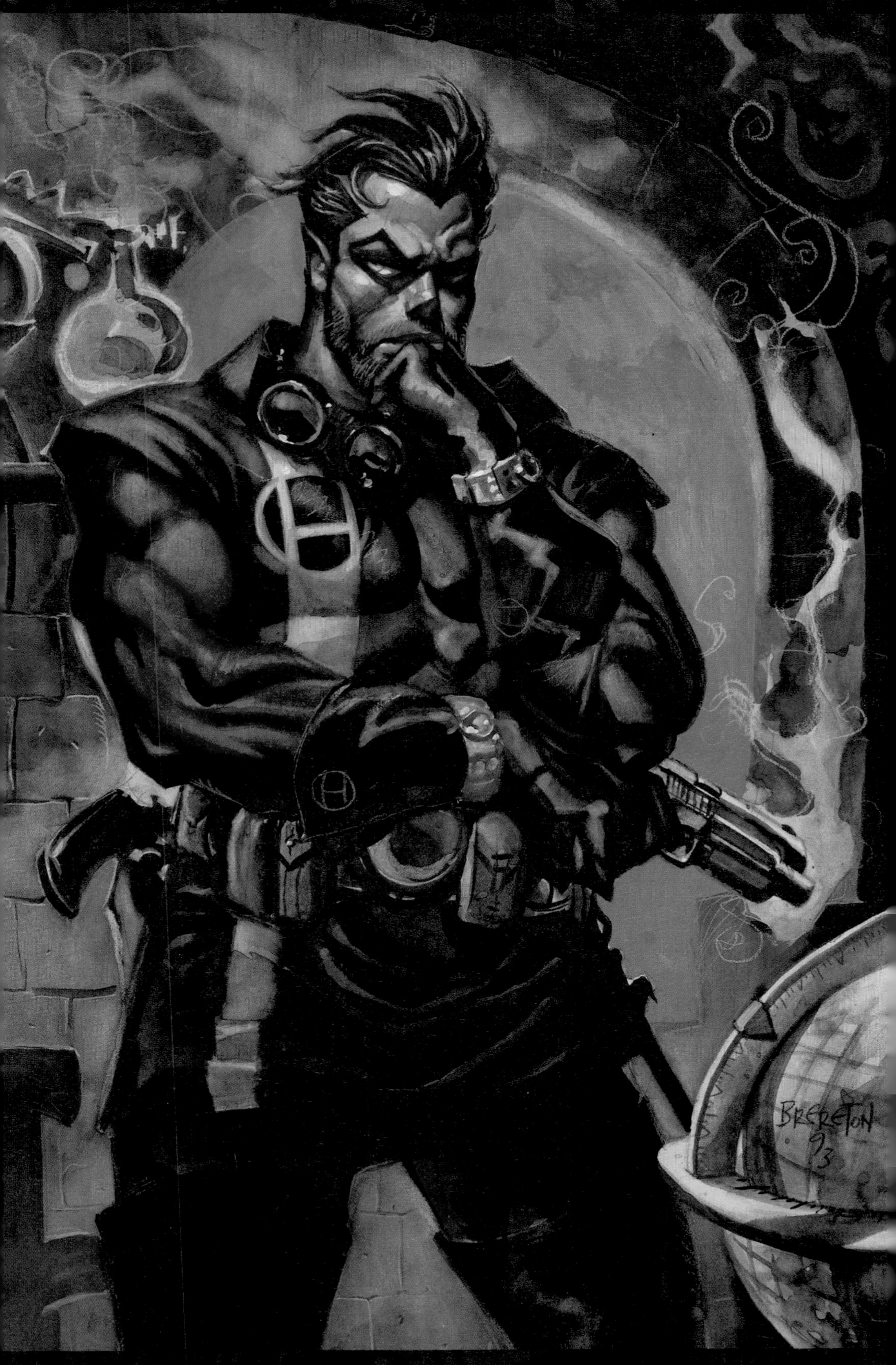
BRERETON
93

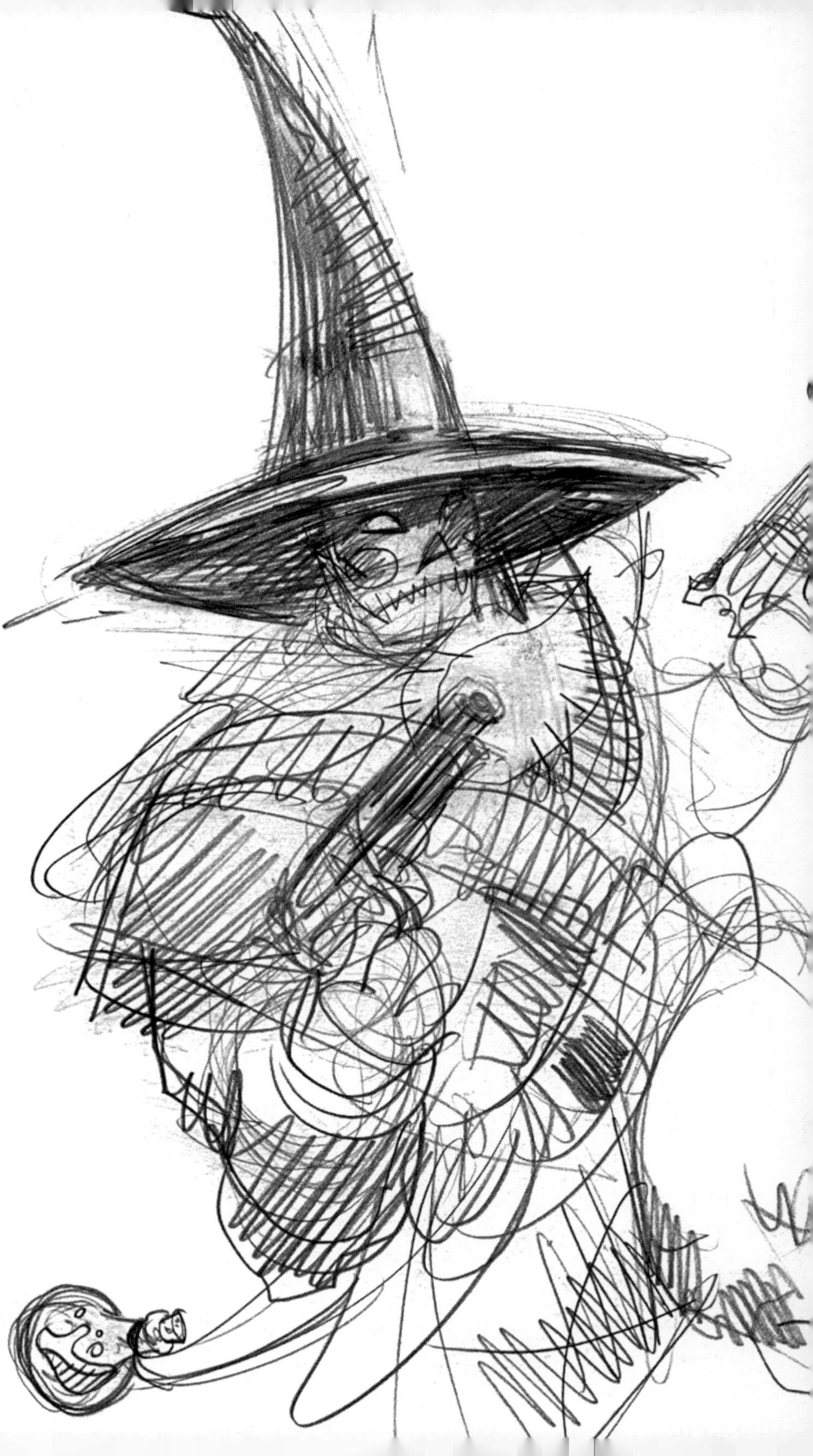

BRERETON
'93

THE GUNWITCH

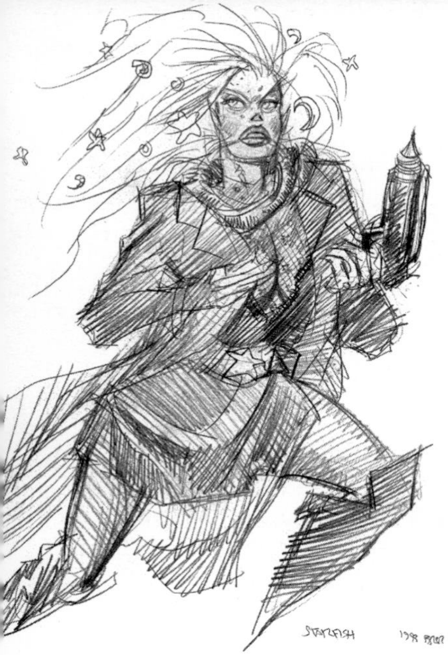
STARFISH
1998

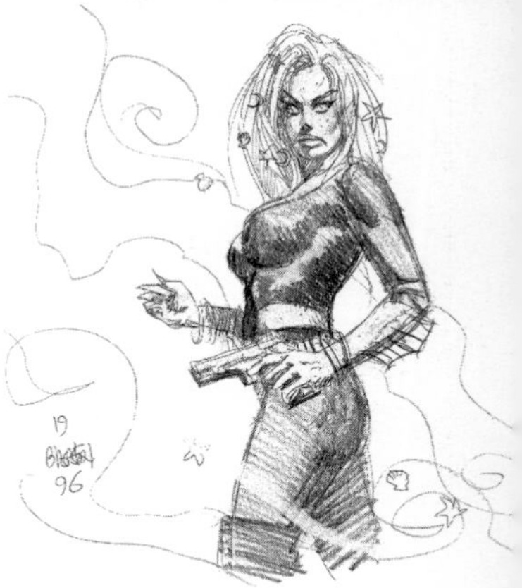

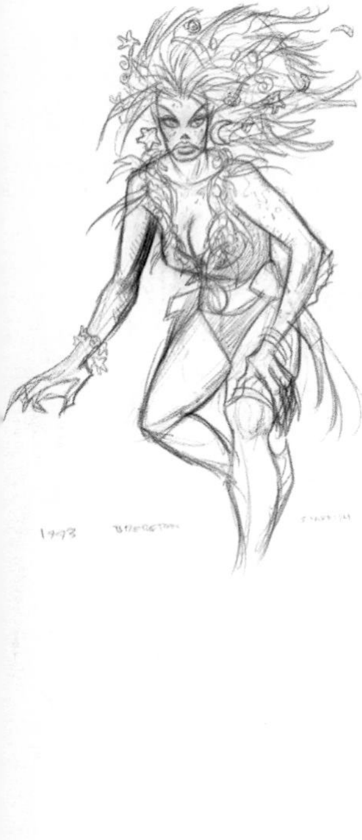
1993

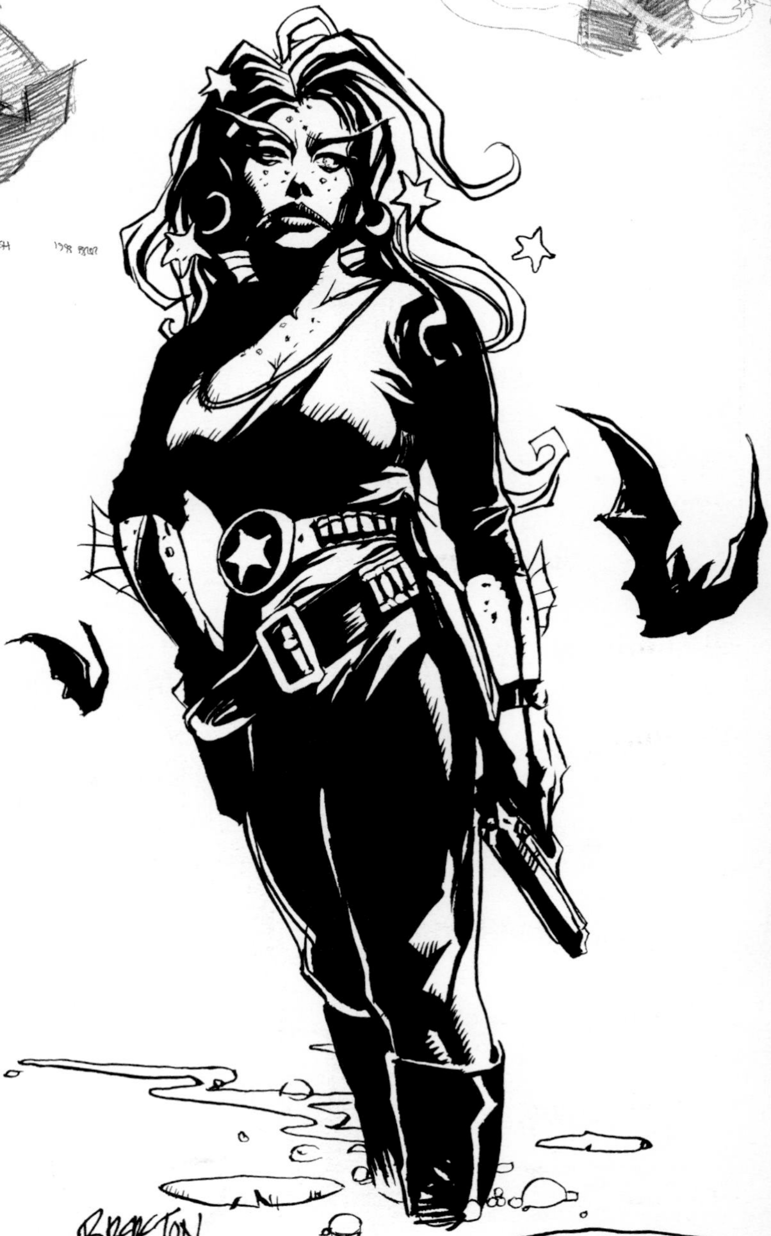
BRERETON

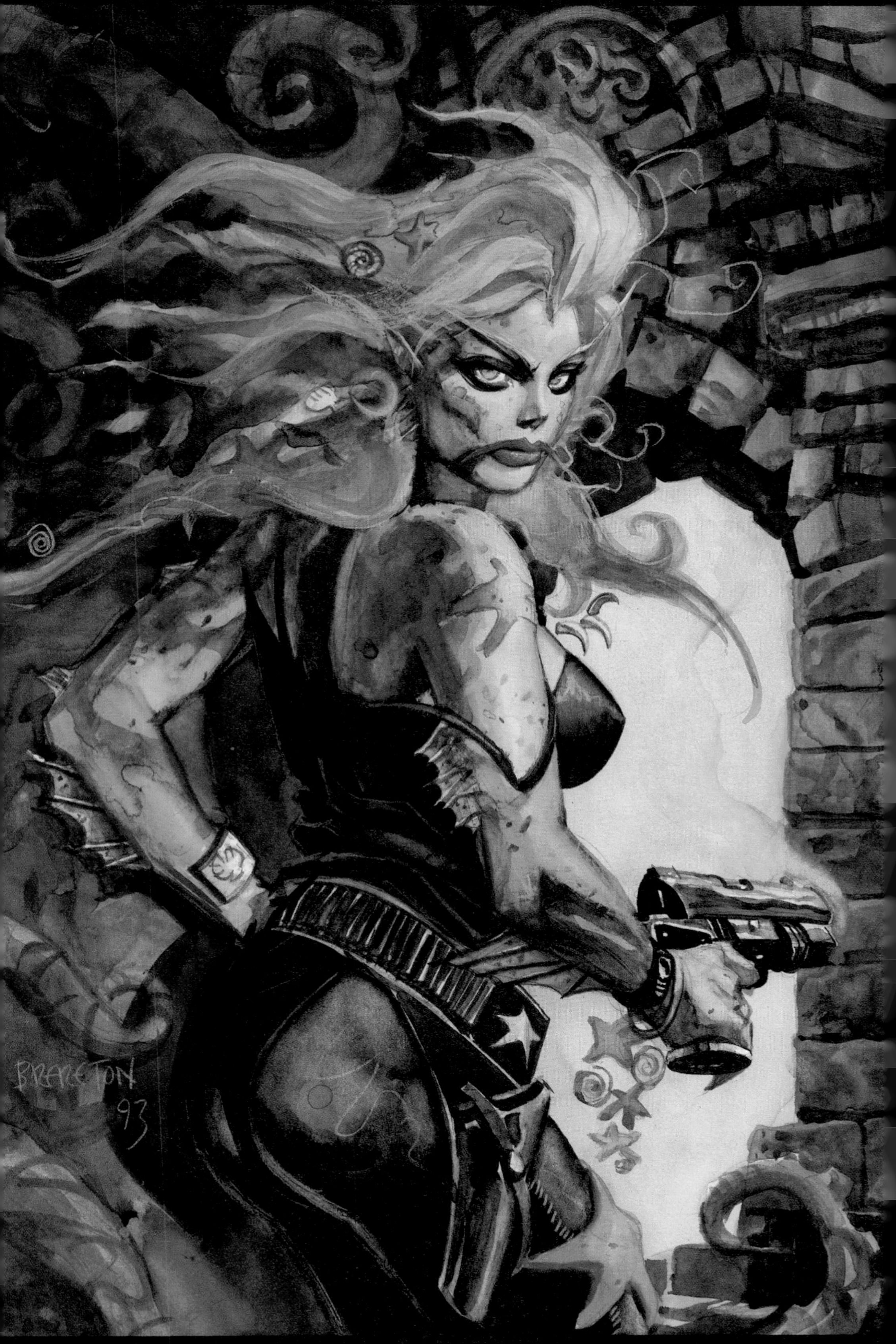
BRERETON
93

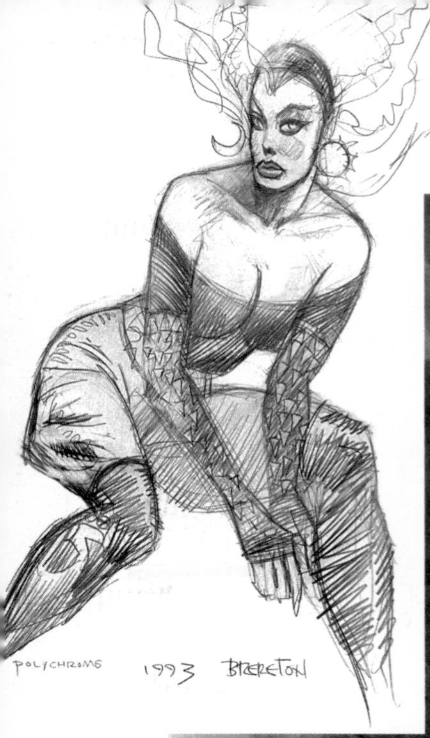
POLYCHROME 1993 BRERETON

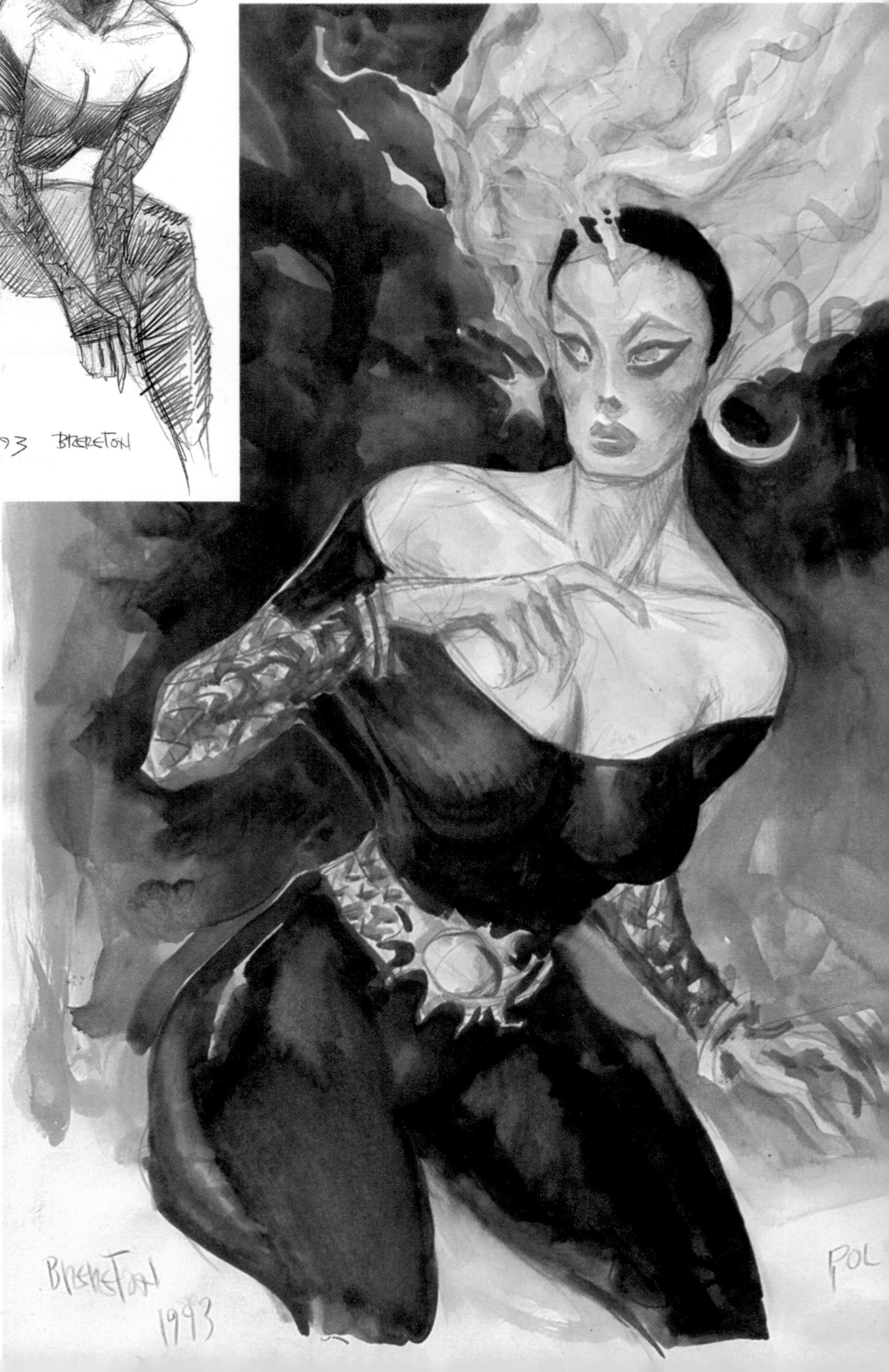
Brereton
1993
POL

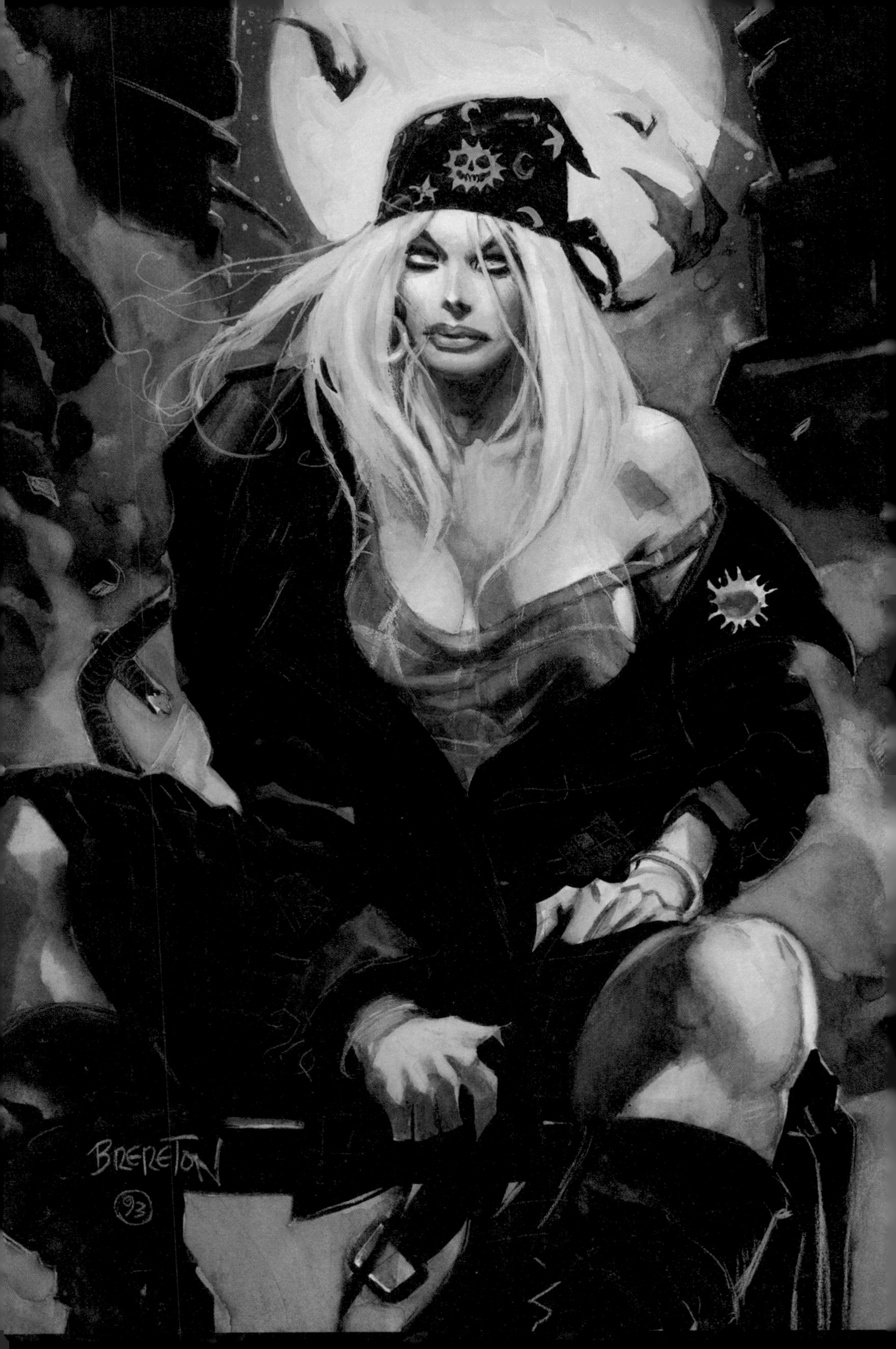
BRERETON
93

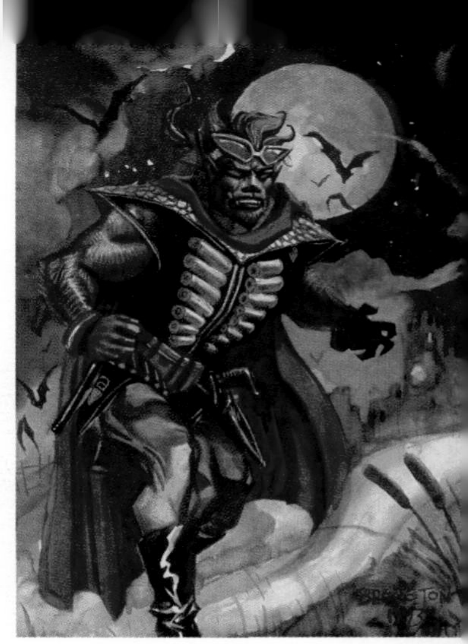

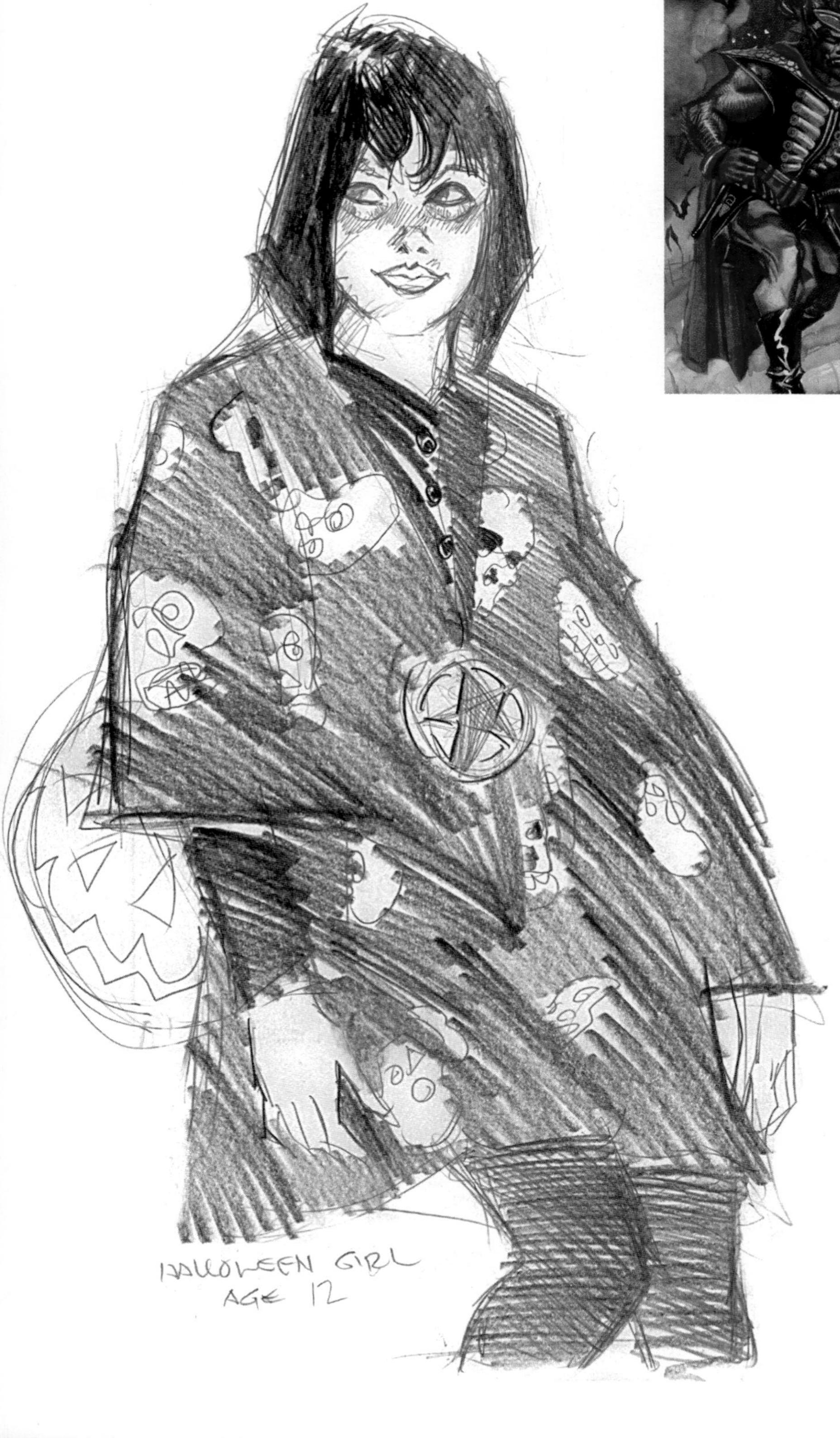
HALLOWEEN GIRL
AGE 12

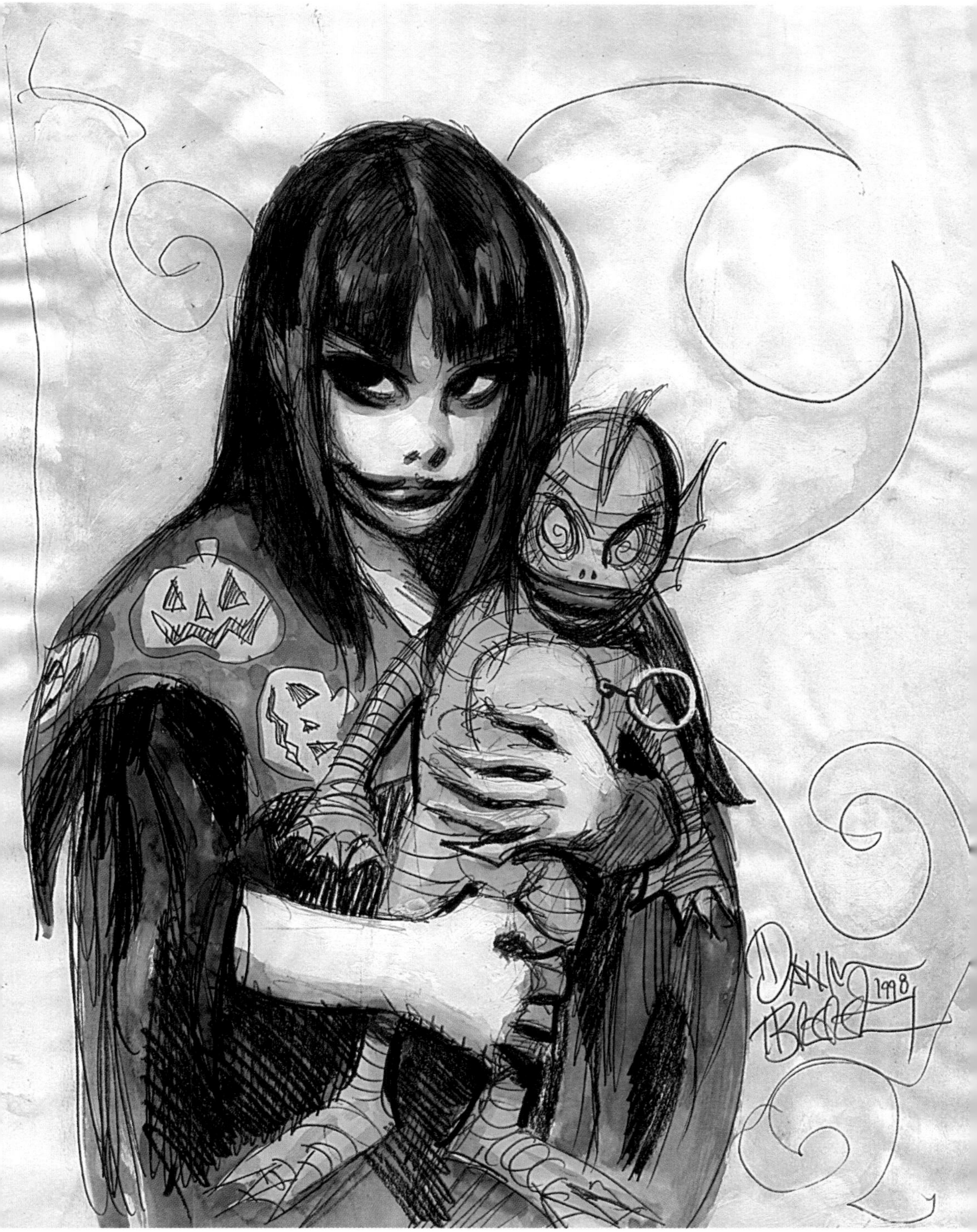
1998

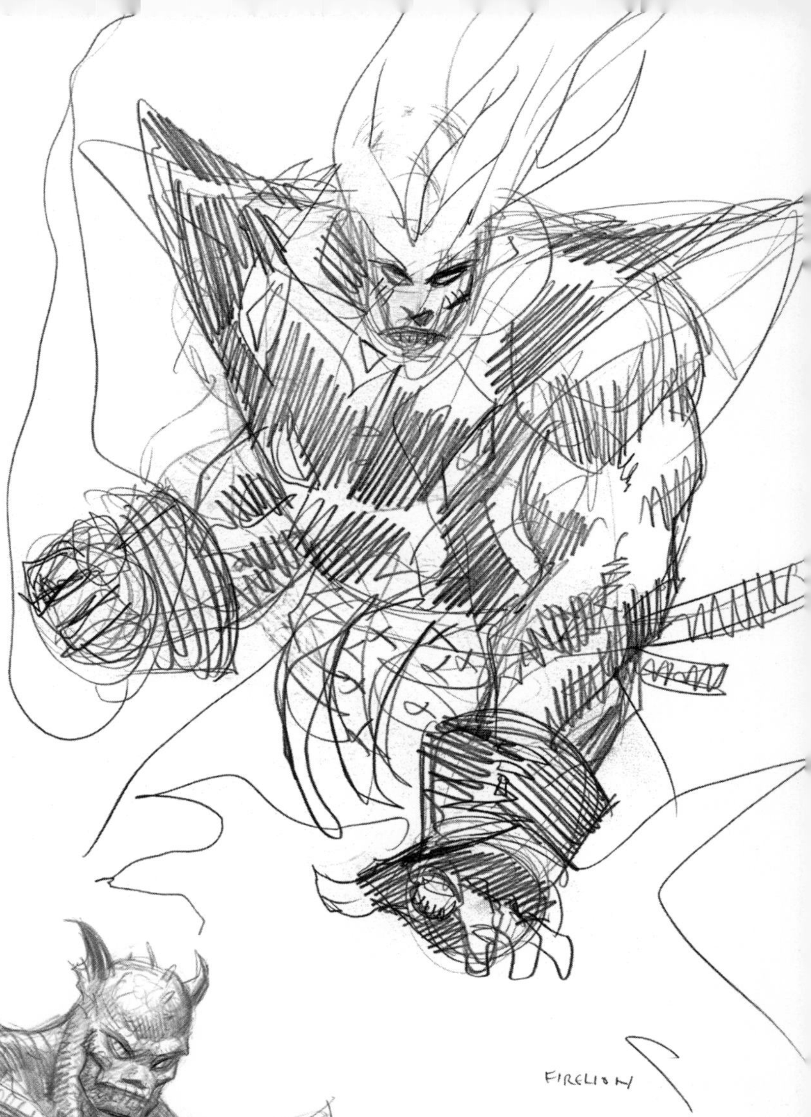
FIRELION

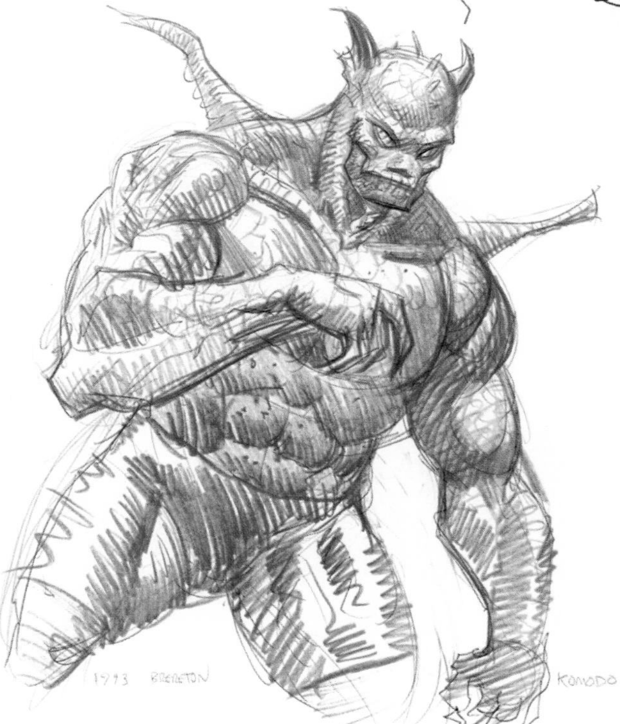
1993 BRERETON
KOMODO

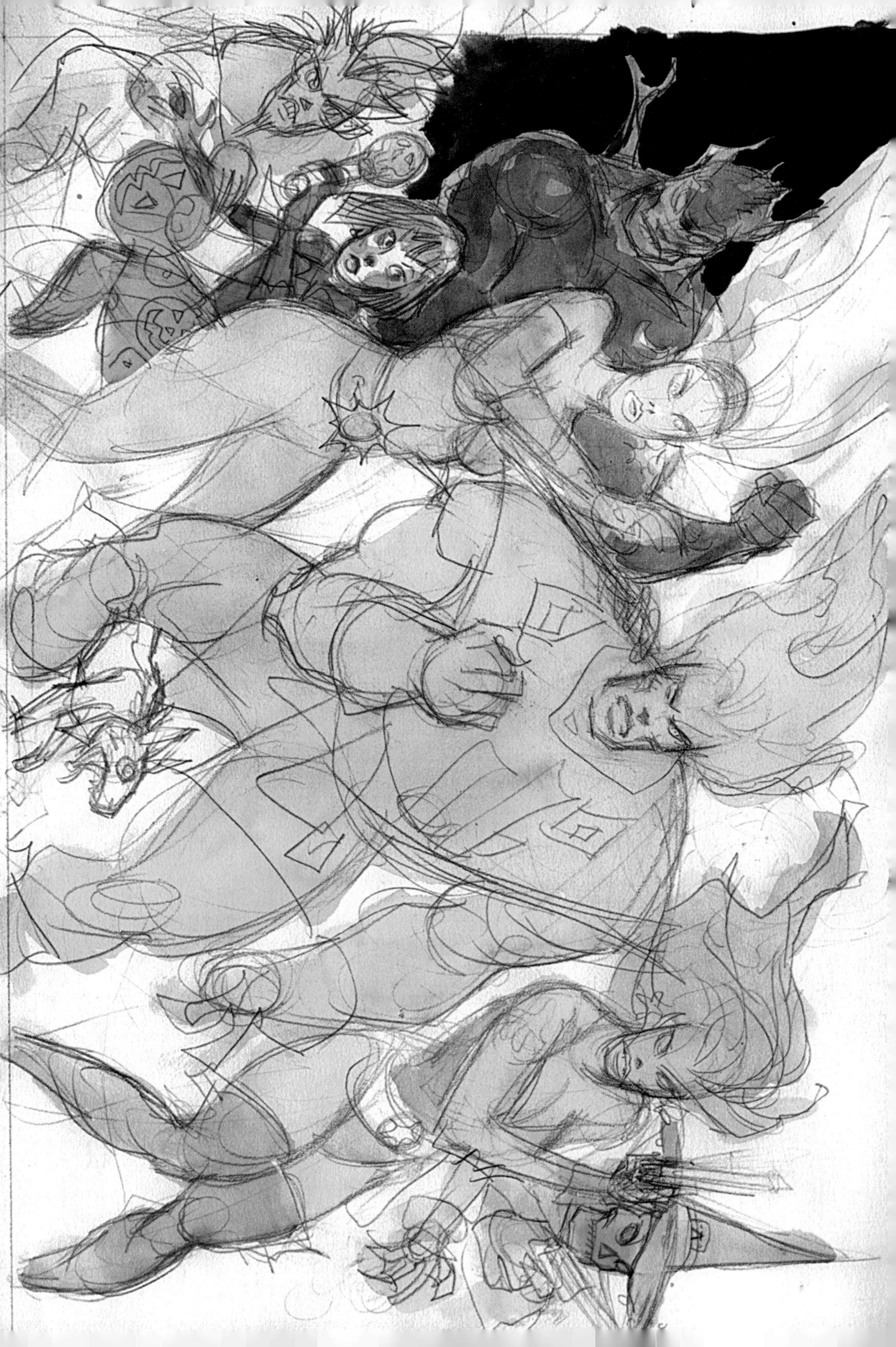

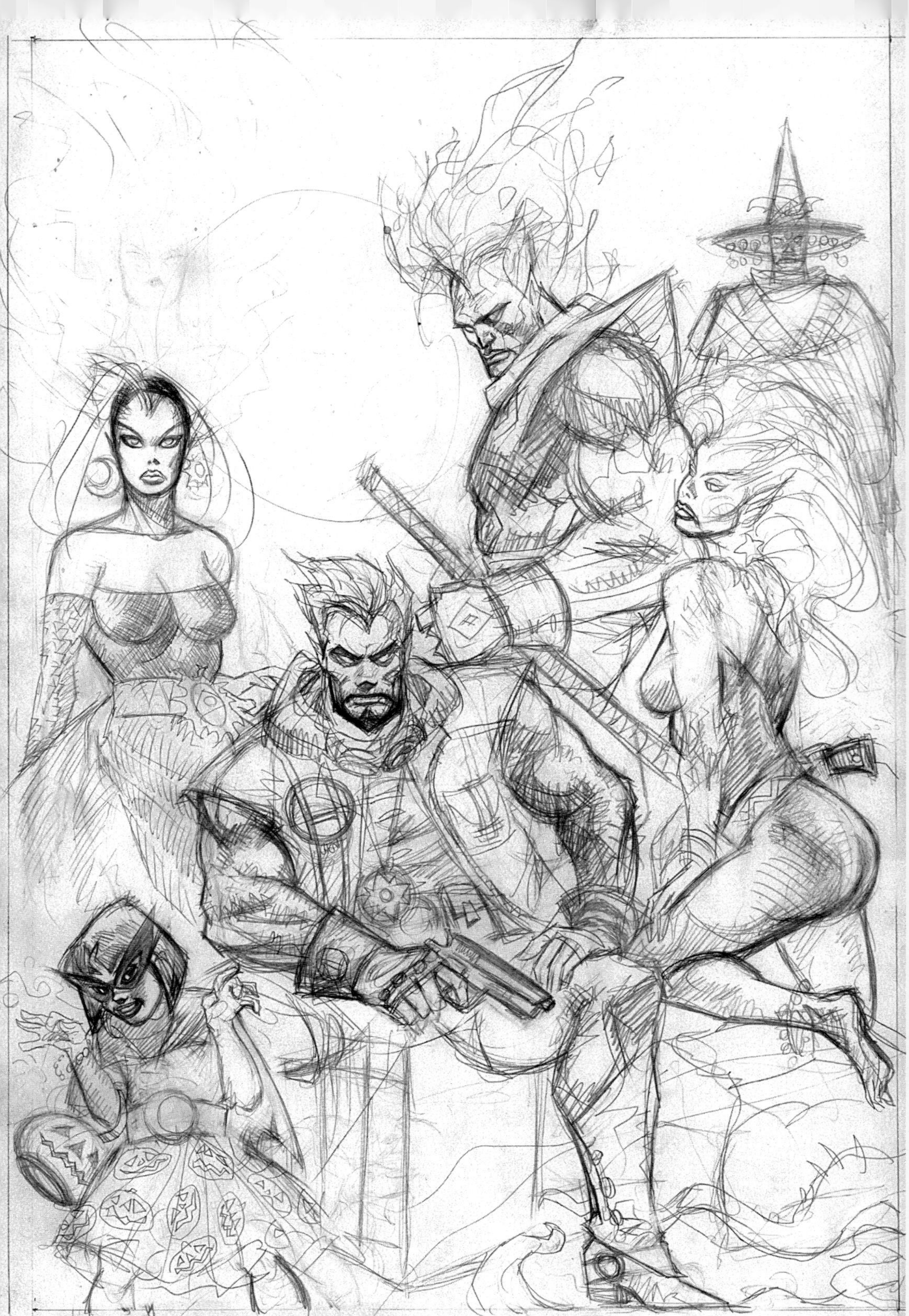
FOR THEM, EVERY NIGHT IS HALLOWEEN.

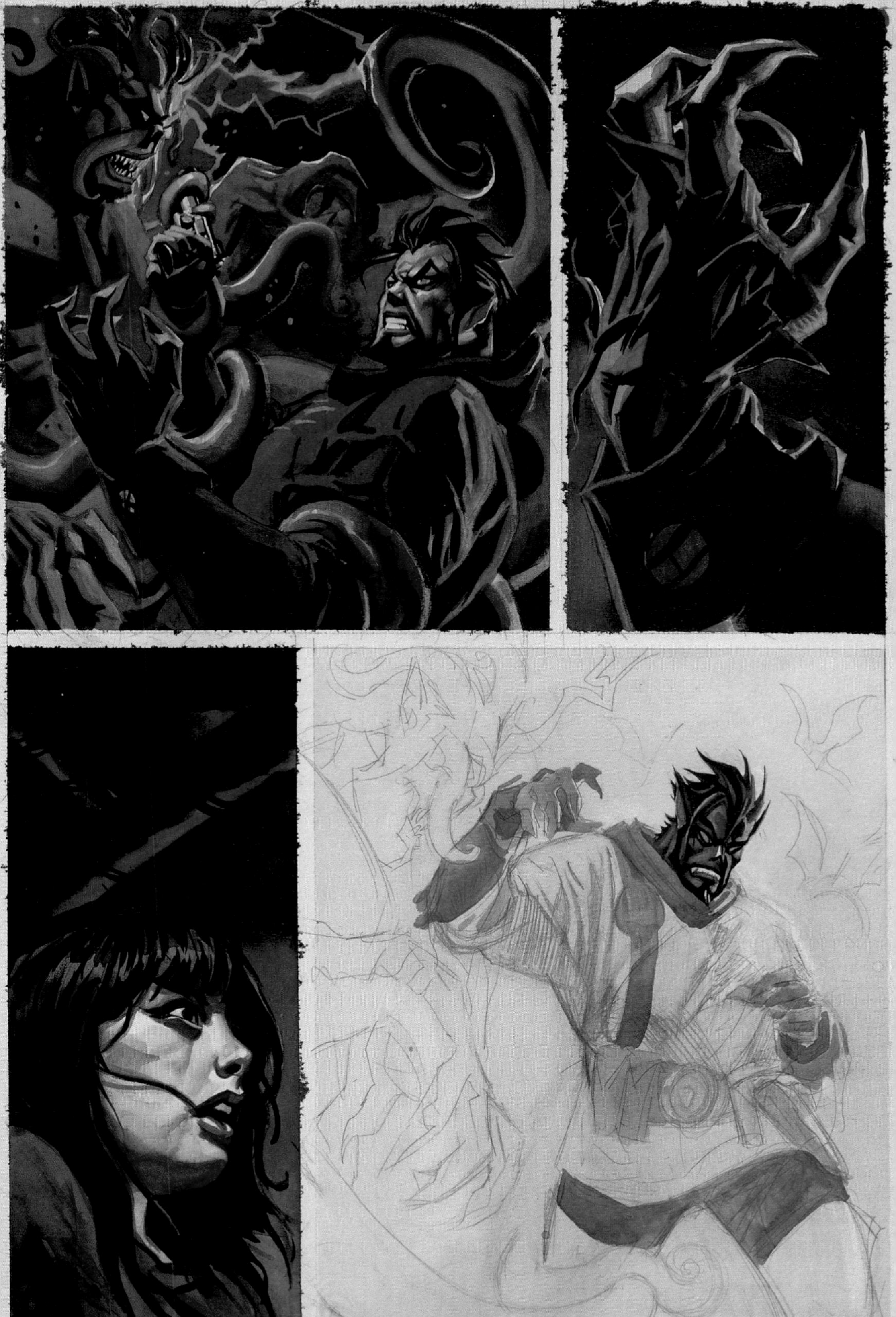

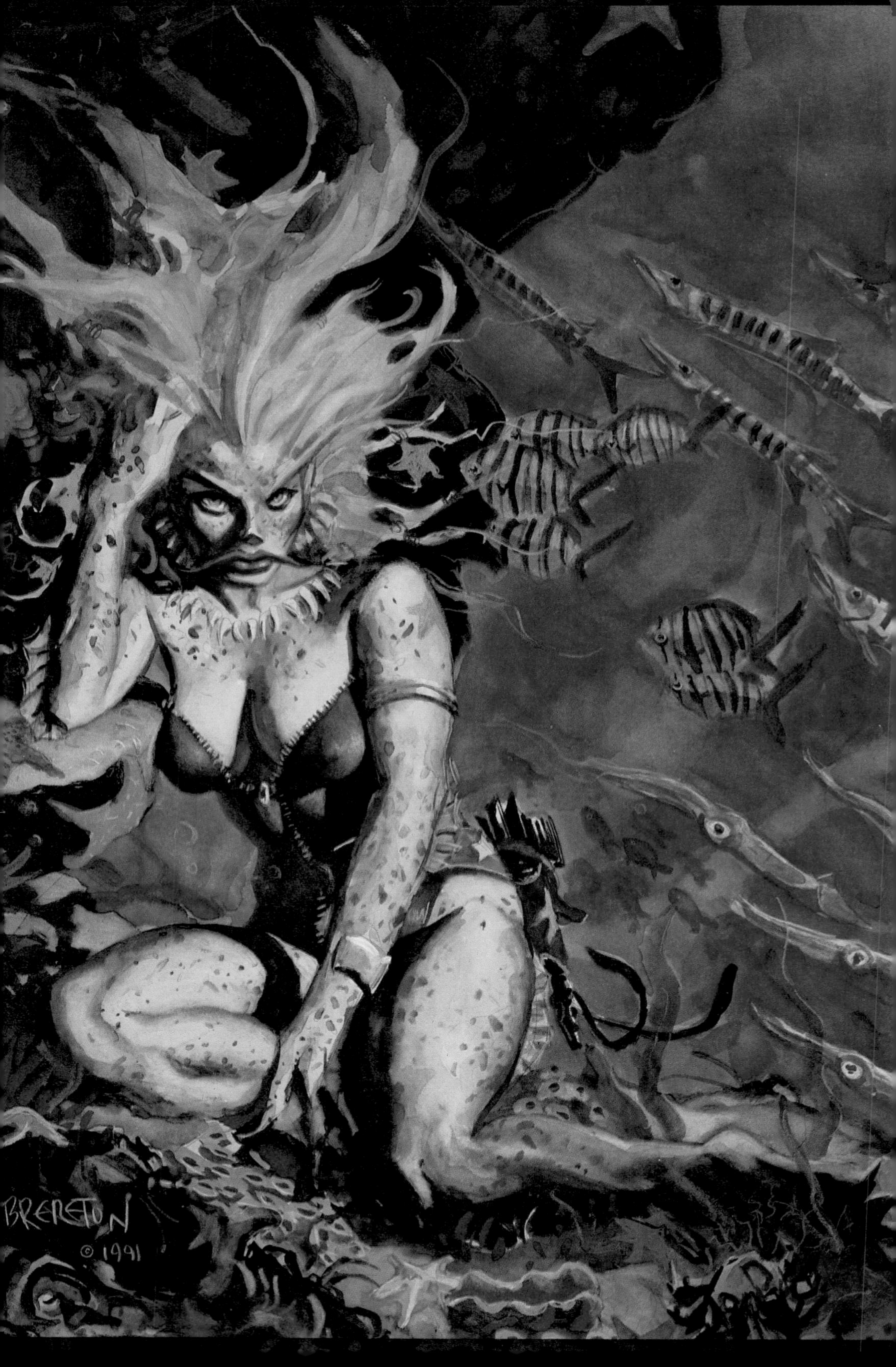
BRERETON
© 1991

DEDICATIONS

This book is dedicated to Gene Colan.

I'd like to thank my parents for constantly being there for me.
Big squeezes to my kids, and to my brother and sister.

Many thanks as well to Nancy Ogami, Shawna Ervin-Gore, and Chris Golden; to the men of Oni: Bob, Shannon, Joe, and Jamie; and to fellow Bravura brothers Howard Chaykin, Steven Grant, Walter Simonson, Jim Starlin, Gil Kane, and Harris Miller.

Much love and fat props to Gene, Bruce, Jill, Mike and Laura, and David for their stunning illustrations in this book. You all make it look so damn easy....

Special thanks to the series original editors, Kara Lamb and Larry Reynosa, and to Dave Olbrich.

Keep your eyes peeled, folks! The Nocturnals will return!

Dan Brereton

x x x x x x x x x x x x x x x x x x x x x x x x x x x x x x

NOCTURNALS: WITCHING HOUR

an all-new 48-page special written and illustrated by Dan Brereton.

Featuring exclusive pin-ups by Mike Mignola, Art Adams, Jay Stephens, Eric Pigors, Brian O'Connell & Derek Thompson, Jay Geldhof, Andi Watson, and Paul Smith, as well as an intro-duction and art by Rob Zombie.

Published by Dark Horse Comics.

For a comic book store near you, call 1-888-COMIC-BOOK.

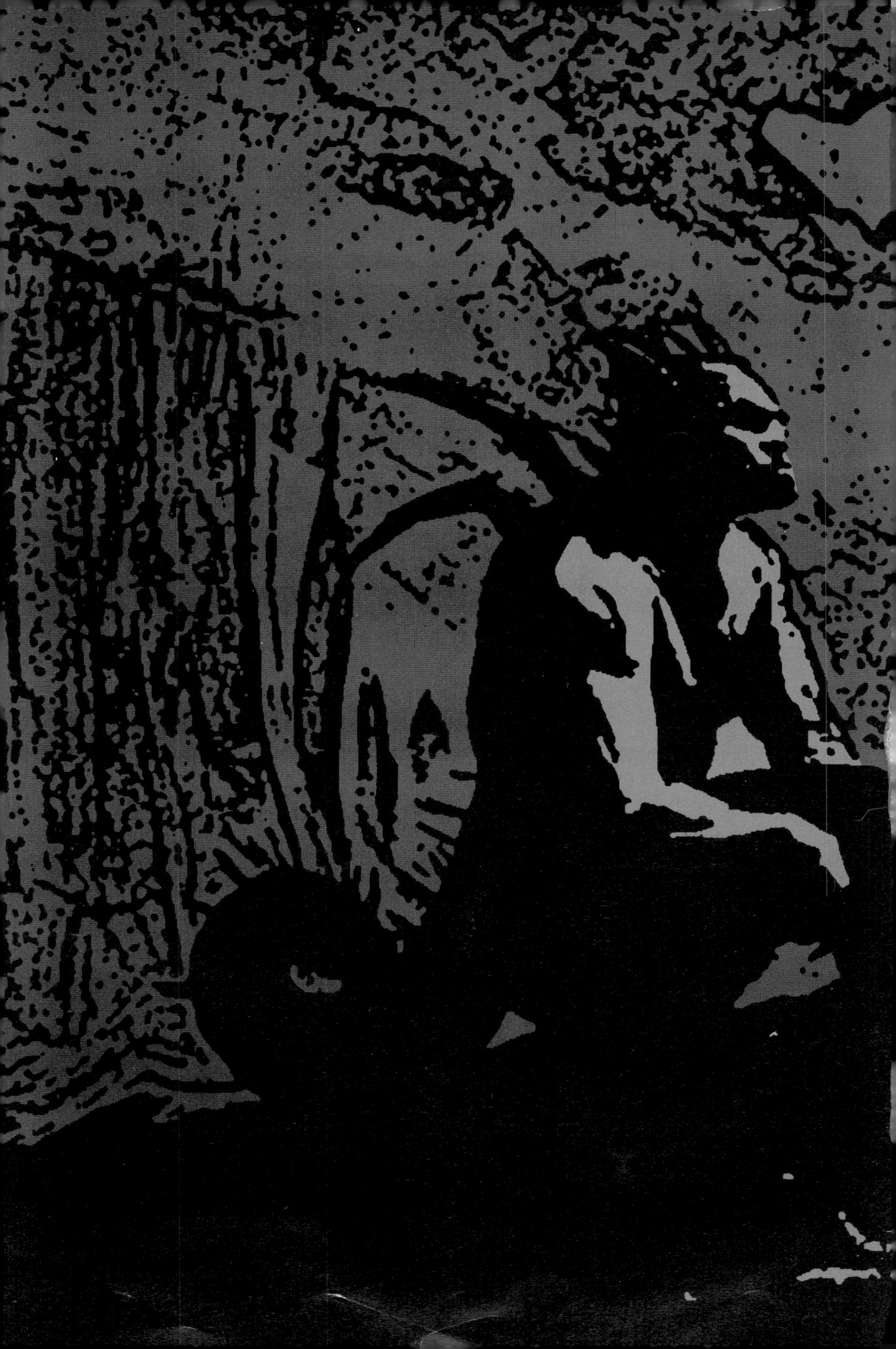